THE EMERGENCE
OF GLOBALISM

THE EMERGENCE
OF GLOBALISM

VISIONS OF WORLD ORDER IN BRITAIN AND
THE UNITED STATES, 1939–1950

Or Rosenboim

PRINCETON UNIVERSITY PRESS
PRINCETON AND OXFORD

Copyright © 2017 by Or Rosenboim

Requests for permission to reproduce material from this work should be sent to Permissions, Princeton University Press

Published by Princeton University Press, 41 William Street, Princeton, New Jersey 08540

In the United Kingdom: Princeton University Press, 6 Oxford Street, Woodstock, Oxfordshire OX20 1TR

press.princeton.edu

Jacket image: MacDonald Gill, *Cable & Wireless Great Circle Map*, 1945

All Rights Reserved

ISBN 978-0-691-16872-2

Library of Congress Control Number: 2016952027

British Library Cataloging-in-Publication Data is available

This book has been composed in Charis

Printed on acid-free paper. ∞

Printed in the United States of America

1 3 5 7 9 10 8 6 4 2

Contents

Maps

CHAPTER 1

Introduction

A New Global Order

ON 21 FEBRUARY 1939, a few months after British Prime Minister Neville Chamberlain travelled to Munich in an attempt to appease Adolf Hitler, the Royal Institute of International Affairs in London held a panel discussion about world order. The main speaker, Lionel Curtis, argued that interdependency was the main characteristic of the modern world: 'What one small country, a Serbia or a Czechoslovakia, does or leaves undone instantly affects the whole of human society'. He added that in spite of the fact that 'socially and economically human society is now one closely integrated unit', the political order reflected fragmentation rather than unity. His conclusion was clearly stated: 'I am now convinced that a world commonwealth embracing all nations and kindreds [*sic*] and tongues is the goal at which we must aim before we can hope to move to a higher plane of civilisation. Indeed, I will now go so far as to say that unless we conceive that goal in time, and take steps to approach it, our present stage of civilisation is doomed to collapse'.[1] Curtis's address was followed by a lively debate about the merits of his suggestions, which reassured him of the public interest in the problem of 'world order' and led him to convene a Chatham House study group on the topic.

Curtis was not the only one to find the problem of world order particularly timely and intriguing. In January 1940, H. G. Wells published his own global vision, under the title *The New World Order. Whether It Is Attainable, How It Can Be Attained and What Sort of World a World at Peace Will Have to Be*.[2] By then, Europe was already at war. The National Peace Council in London organised a panel discussion about Wells's book, including the philosopher C. E. M. Joad and the Spanish diplomat Salvador de Madariaga, at which the author was confronted with proponents of alternative

---

[1] Lionel Curtis, 'World Order', *International Affairs* 18 (1939): 301–320. Curtis was one of the founders of the Royal Institute of International Affairs (Chatham House).

[2] H. G. Wells, *The New World Order. Whether It Is Attainable, How It Can Be Attained and What Sort of World a World at Peace Will Have to Be* (London: Secker and Warburg, 1940).

visions of post-war world order.[3] In the United States, the sinologist and geopolitical thinker Owen Lattimore published in 1942 an article on 'Asia in a New World Order', while his friend, US Vice President Henry Wallace, gave an address at Ohio Wesleyan University on the Christian foundations of a new world order.[4] Luigi Sturzo, Hans Kuhn, E. H. Carr, Robert M. Hutchins, and Quincy Wright were just some of many commentators and intellectuals who wrote books and delivered speeches under the title of 'world order'.[5]

Google Ngram analysis of twentieth-century English-language publications registers a significant rise of interest in 'world order' in the 1940s, with its frequency peaking in 1945. But the concern with the problem of order extended beyond references to the specific expression 'world order'. The fundamental problem of ordering and reordering the world after a devastating conflict seemed a worthy preoccupation for many public intellectuals in Britain and the United States. The destabilising war was perceived not only as a menacing prospect of doom, but also as an opportunity to question and redefine the fundamental categories of politics. These reconsiderations were often motivated by the perception of a growing tendency towards technological, economic, cultural, and political interconnectedness, which for many mid-century thinkers gave rise to a new political concept, the global.

The Emergence of Globalism is an intellectual history of the complex and nonlinear genealogy of globalism in mid-century visions of world order. Ever since the outbreak of the war, American, British, and émigré intellectuals had diagnosed the emergence of globalism as the defining condition of the post-war era. Their proposals for ordering the post-war world envisaged competing schemes of global orders motivated by concerns for the future of democracy, the prospects of liberty and diversity, and the decline of the imperial system. In this book, I explore the languages employed to outline the meaning of the 'global' as a political idea to shed light on the configurations of 'world order' as a normative foundation for geopolitical, economic, and legal structures.

Mid-century commentators, as well as later historians, have often invoked the term 'world order' when writing about international politics. The statistical data match the textual evidence in revealing that ever since

[3] National Peace Council, *On the New World Order* (London: National Peace Council, 1940).

[4] Owen Lattimore, 'Asia in a New World Order', *Foreign Policy Reports* 28 (1942): 150–163; Henry A. Wallace et al., *Christian Bases of World Order* (New York: Abingdon-Cokesbury Press, 1943).

[5] The University of Denver organised a series of lectures on world order by Robert Maynard Hutchins, E. H. Carr, Robert Oppenheimer, W. E. Rappard, and E. M. Earle, later published in E. L. Woodward, ed., *Foundations of World Order* (Denver: University of Denver, 1949); Quincy Wright, *Human Rights and the World Order* (New York: Commission to Study the Organization of Peace, 1943); Luigi Sturzo, *Italy and the New World Order* (New York: Macdonald, 1944); Hans Kohn, *World Order in Historical Perspective* (Cambridge, MA: Harvard University Press, 1942).

the beginning of the war, public intellectuals in Britain and the United States have sought to imagine the shape of the world to come. The idea of order embodied their attempt to make sense and reorganise the belligerent and disordered post-war world.[6] They hoped to overcome the political chaos that was seen as the tragic consequence of the international disorder, economic strife, and social unrest of the interwar years. The idea of order did not necessarily imply a rigid, unifying, or homogeneous system. Rather, many conceptions of world order revolved around the aspiration to accommodate change and flexibility as valuable and desirable aspects of human life. The tension between order and instability remained a central aspect of mid-century political commentary.

The political debates about world order explored in this study exhibited a growing sensitivity to a particular dimension of politics that I define as 'global'. One of my main objectives is, therefore, to outline the competing meanings of the global as a political space in mid-century thought. If we examine the statistical analysis of published texts in English language provided by Google, we can see that the term 'global' started to gain ground just after the outbreak of the war. It was at that moment that the new political space of the global was generated as a response to the total and all-encompassing nature of the war, facilitated by technological innovations. If the war was global, an adequately global plan for peacetime order was necessary. Thinking about the global sphere did not signify the abandonment of all other constituent elements of politics; states, empires, federations, non-state communities, and supranational organisations were reimagined and redefined—but not necessarily abolished—before they could acquire a new place in the modern, global world. In this book, I use the term 'global' in the widest, most inclusive sense, as a perspective on politics, a sometimes abstract space that was modified, redefined, and challenged in lively transnational conversations.

The 'global' was invoked to outline a different political order than the international, transnational, and cosmopolitan spaces of politics. In the writings of mid-century public intellectuals, all four categories make their appearance in content if not by name. As a political category, the international attributes importance to the nation, or the state, as a defining, order-creating

---

[6] For some references to 'world order' in the study of international relations, see, for example, Daniele Archibugi and David Held, *Cosmopolitan Democracy: An Agenda for a New World Order* (Cambridge: Polity, 1995); Sebastian Conrad and Dominic Sachsenmaier, *Competing Visions of World Order: Global Moments and Movements, 1880s–1930s* (New York: Palgrave Macmillan, 2007); Patrick J. Hearden, *Architects of Globalism: Building a New World Order during World War II* (Fayetteville: University of Arkansas Press, 2002); Christopher D. O'Sullivan, *Sumner Welles, Post-war Planning, and the Quest for a New World Order, 1937–1943* (New York: Columbia University Press, 2008); Benn Steil, *The Battle of Bretton Woods: John Maynard Keynes, Harry Dexter White, and the Making of a New World Order* (Princeton, NJ: Princeton University Press, 2013).

unit, and explores the relations between nations as sovereign entities.[7] The transnational space stretches beyond national boundaries to explore interconnections across borders, without undermining the significance of national communities and states.[8] Cosmopolitanism, by contrast, typ- ically assumes that all human beings are part of a world community, and should orient their political and moral allegiances accordingly.[9] Globalism emerged from an awareness of the political significance of the globe as a unitary whole made of interconnected, diverse political units. The rec- ognition of the world's 'oneness' did not always mean political monism. Globalism often implied a renewed awareness of diversity, and an attempt to envisage a world order to preserve it. The tension between diversity and unity is, therefore, a central aspect of the idea of globalism.

The assumption that the post-war order should reflect the spatial unity of the globe often relied on technological innovations like flights and tele- phone communications, which contributed, for mid-century commenta- tors, to the world's interconnectedness. One of the best-selling books advo- cating this view was *One World*, the account of the 1942 world tour of the American Republican politician Wendell Willkie.[10] Two years after his de- feat in the presidential race to Franklin D. Roosevelt, Willkie embarked on a private airplane for a goodwill tour of Egypt, Palestine, Turkey, Russia, Siberia, and China, meeting with leading politicians and local residents. His book provides colourful and enthusiastic commentary on disparate topics: from the beauty of Mongolia and Mount Scopus seen from the air to Charles de Gaulle's Beirut home, where 'every corner, every wall, held busts, statues, and pictures of Napoleon', to an enthusiastic analysis of the Chinese economy. The general message was that there were no more dis- tant or uncovered places in the world; one could easily travel to any re- mote spot, meet its inhabitants, and discover their lifestyle and opinions. In consequence, for Willkie, the post-war world order should be drafted ac- cording to the interests of the world as a whole, not only of powerful states or empires. Political and economic freedom in China or the Middle East

---

[7] Akira Iriye, *Global and Transnational History: The Past, Present, and Future* (Basingstoke: Palgrave, 2013), 10–12.

[8] C. A. Bayly et al., 'AHR Conversation: On Transnational History', *American Historical Review* 111 (2006): 1441–1464.

[9] There are many possible definitions of cosmopolitanism in current literature. One definition for Kantian cosmopolitanism is 'an attitude taken up in acting: an attitude of recognition, respect, openness, interest, beneficence and concern toward other human individuals, cultures, and peoples as members of one global community'. See Pauline Kleingeld, *Kant and Cosmopolitanism: The Philosophical Ideal of World Citizenship* (Cambridge: Cambridge University Press, 2011), 1. For recent intellectual histories of interna- tionalism and cosmopolitanism, see, for example, Glenda Sluga, *Internationalism in the Age of Nationalism* (Philadelphia: University of Pennsylvania Press, 2013); Luca Scuccimarra, *I confini del mondo: Storia del cosmopolitismo dall'antichità al settecento* (Bologna: Il Mulino, 2006).

[10] Wendell L. Willkie, *One World* (New York: Simon & Schuster, 1943).

was no less important than American freedom. The increasing availability of air power rendered, for him, the space of politics more interconnected, closed, and therefore 'global'.

Thinking about the global as a material and conceptual political space emphasises the complexity of this idea. The 'spatial turn' in historical research highlighted the importance of space, place, location, and spatiality as categories for understanding and analysing historical knowledge.[11] The study of international thought is concerned, explicitly and implicitly, with the category of space. Geographic space, its perceptions and representations, provides a fundamental and intriguing conceptual framework for understanding and analysing world politics. Put differently, political space is the theoretical conceptualisation of the geographic materiality of politics. Yet, as Harvey Starr suggests, scholars of International Relations usually ignore the notion of 'space', misinterpret it as deterministic, or dismiss it as irrelevant to their analysis.[12] Starr's proposal to take the concept of 'space' more seriously applies also for historians of international thought. In this study, I argue that the category of political space offers a useful perspective on political thought, which is particularly appropriate to delineate and locate the meanings of world order and globalism. I employ this category to reflect on the mid-century perceptions of the physical geographic conditions of the world and their impact on political and social order.[13] The notion of political space suggests that the interpretation of the relationship between politics and geography depends on perception: the global was not a mere objective description of the actual spherical geographic conditions of planet Earth. The political space created by the globalist ideology was anchored in observations about geography but shaped by a range of other philosophical, sociological, and political assumptions. This is not a unilinear relationship, but a mutual one: politics can influence the geographical conditions of the world, as well as be influenced by them.

The idea of political space provides a helpful connection between the concrete geopolitics of international relations and the abstract notion of order. It clarifies how various public intellectuals perceived the actual organisation and interaction of different political units in the world. My goal in using this concept is not to impose a rigid theory of political space on past thinkers, but rather to investigate how they characterised and theorised political space in their own writings. Examining the theoretical and

---

[11] Charles W. J. Withers, 'Place and the "Spatial Turn" in Geography and in History', *Journal of the History of Ideas* 70 (2009): 637–658.

[12] Harvey Starr, 'On Geopolitics: Spaces and Places', *International Studies Quarterly* 57 (2013): 433–439.

[13] Carlo Galli, *Political Spaces and Global War*, trans. Elisabeth Fay, ed. Adam Sitze (Minneapolis: University of Minnesota Press, 2010), 4; Leif Jerram, 'Space: A Useless Category for Historical Analysis?', *History and Theory* 52 (2013): 400–419.

material spatial dimension of political structures helps understand their internal functions and dispositions towards other units and towards the global space.

DRAWING THE CONTOURS
OF GLOBALISM

Globalism meant different things to different people. The book explores aspects of the 1940s discourse of globalism through seven mid-century conversations about world order. Political commentators drew on various fields of knowledge to conceptualise the rise of the global space in world politics. Economics, philosophy of science, sociology, law, geopolitics, theology, political thought—each provided a distinct set of tools for shaping the global order. The multifaceted, flexible character of the idea of the global enhanced its appeal but also highlighted its weakness. There was no one 'global' ideology, no single definition of the 'global' political sphere. Yet three main themes can be discerned from mid-century attempts to conceptualise globalism.

First, globalism offered an alternative to empire. The global order embodied a growing acceptance of the decline of the imperial world order established by the European powers: France, Britain, and to a lesser extent the Netherlands.[14] By 1945, the new empires *in potentia*, Germany, Italy, and Japan, were effectively defeated. After the war, some feared the rise of the United States and Soviet Russia as powerful empires controlling vast territories around the world. While the political experience of empire could not be expunged from the international public sphere, and indeed had significant ideological and structural influence on the institutions of liberal internationalism, the League of Nations, and the United Nations, mid-century thinkers sought to fashion the global space as an alternative to imperial relations.[15] Some, like Owen Lattimore and Barbara Wootton, expressed a clear hostility to the very idea of empire. Arguably, as Ian Hall suggests, many British liberal international thinkers felt the urge to reformulate their theories of world order in view of the decline in Britain's

---

[14] On the end of empire, see, for example, John Darwin, *The End of the British Empire: The Historical Debate* (Oxford: Blackwell, 1991); Piers Brendon, *The Decline and Fall of the British Empire, 1781–1997* (London: Vintage, 2008); Jacques Frémeaux, *Les empires coloniaux dans le processus de mondialisation* (Paris: Maisonneuve et Larose, 2002).

[15] For example, see Mark Mazower, *No Enchanted Palace: The End of Empire and the Ideological Origins of the United Nations* (Princeton, NJ: Princeton University Press, 2009); Susan Pedersen, *The Guardians: The League of Nations and the Crisis of Empire* (Oxford: Oxford University Press, 2015); Patricia Clavin, *Securing the World Economy: The Reinvention of the League of Nations, 1920–1946* (Oxford: Oxford University Press, 2013).

global supremacy and the dissolution of its empire.[16] Yet, as I will show, the rejection of empire emerged not only from observations of imperial political and military decay but also from a growing ambivalence about the cultural and political legacy of empire. Thus, the globalist ideology sought to elaborate an alternative defining principle of world order, against the exploitative, unequal political space of empire.

Writing about the foundations of international thought, David Armitage has suggested that historians should explore the international transition from a system of empires to the current system of states.[17] This transition, I argue, was not linear or neat: mid-century thinkers developed competing and sometimes incompatible visions to accommodate not only states and empires in the world system, but also federations, regional unions, transnational communities, and international organisations. The space between empires and states was complex, multilayered, and at times incoherent. Political thinkers have long been engaged in assessing the political legacy of empire, and questioning the place of liberty therein.[18] In the interwar years, both imperial and anti-imperial dynamics inspired British thinkers to imagine a new international order.[19] As Jeanne Morefield has shown, by relying on the imperial experience to construct a new world order, interwar liberal internationalists failed to overcome the repressive and exclusive aspects of the imperial mind-set.[20] By the 1940s, however, many

[16] Ian Hall, *Dilemmas of Decline: British Intellectuals and World Politics, 1945–1975* (Berkeley: University of California Press, 2012).

[17] David Armitage, *Foundations of Modern International Thought* (Cambridge: Cambridge University Press, 2013), 12–20.

[18] On the relations between international order and imperialism, see, for example, Jennifer Pitts, *A Turn to Empire: The Rise of Imperial Liberalism in Britain and France* (Princeton, NJ: Princeton University Press, 2005); Uday Singh Mehta, *Liberalism and Empire: A Study in Nineteenth-Century British Liberal Thought* (Chicago: University of Chicago Press, 1999); Sankar Muhtu, 'Adam Smith's Critique of International Trading Companies: Theorizing "Globalization" in the Age of Enlightenment', *Political Theory* 36 (2008): 185–212; Karuna Mantena, *Alibis of Empire: Henry Maine and the Ends of Liberal Imperialism* (Princeton, NJ: Princeton University Press, 2010); Duncan Bell, *The Idea of Greater Britain: Empire and the Future of World Order, 1860–1900* (Princeton, NJ: Princeton University Press, 2007); Duncan Bell, ed., *Victorian Visions of Global Order: Empire and International Relations in Nineteenth-Century Political Thought* (Cambridge: Cambridge University Press, 2007).

[19] On the rise of interwar liberal internationalism, see, for example, Daniel Laqua, ed., *Internationalism Reconfigured: Transnational Ideas and Movements between the World Wars* (London: I.B. Tauris, 2011); Daniel Gorman, *The Emergence of International Society in the 1920s* (Cambridge: Cambridge University Press, 2012); Michael Pugh, *Liberal Internationalism: The Interwar Movement for Peace in Britain* (Basingstoke: Palgrave, 2012); Louis Bisceglia, *Norman Angell and Liberal Internationalism in Britain, 1931–1935* (New York: Garland, 1982); Inderjeet Parmar, 'Anglo-American Elites in the Interwar Years: Idealism and Power in the Intellectual Roots of Chatham House and the Council on Foreign Relations', *International Relations* 16 (2002): 53–75; Cornelia Navari, *Internationalism and the State in the Twentieth Century* (London: Routledge, 2000).

[20] Jeanne Morefield, *Covenants without Swords: Idealist Liberalism and the Spirit of Empire* (Princeton, NJ: Princeton University Press, 2005). For other accounts of interwar critiques of empire, see David Long, *Towards a New Liberal Internationalism: The International Theory of J. A. Hobson* (Cambridge: Cambridge University Press, 1996); Bernard Porter, *Critics of Empire* (London: Macmillan, 1968); Nicholas Owen, *The British Left and India: Metropolitan Anti-imperialism, 1885–1947* (Oxford: Oxford University Press, 2007).

argued that the damages created by the imperial order outnumbered its benefits.

The second constitutive element of the global ideologies was a concern for the future of democracy. During and after the war, it was difficult to predict the long-term survival of democracy as a political system; domestic and international threats loomed large.[21] The global perspective on the future of democracy relied on regional, transnational, federal, or global institutions, rather than on the basic unit of the territorial state. For some mid-century commentators, democracy could not function well if limited to the domestic realm: a new conception of global democratic order that transcended the boundaries of the state was necessary. This required reconceptualising the basic values commonly associated with democracy: equality, inclusion in the political community, political participation, and—the greatest challenge for the ideologues of globalism—a new global political subject.[22]

Democracy was central to American and British efforts of post-war planning and reconstruction, which configured the world order discourse in institutional and private political debate.[23] Wartime Chatham House–based committees on world order and reconstruction united prominent British thinkers on international relations to discuss a post-war internationalist and democratic order.[24] After the war against totalitarianism was won, deliberations in the United Nations aimed at refashioning democracy for the post-war era.[25] While many shared the conviction that democracy was the best political system to foster liberty and prosperity, efforts were made to reinforce its stability and enhance its flexibility to adapt to diverse social and economic conditions. No one model of democracy was deemed fit for all. The challenge of creating a pluralist yet coherent global democratic order, of globalising its political culture and institutions, required a new conception of modernity. For some mid-century thinkers, the solution would be to draw on a wider range of sources that represented the unify-

---

[21] On the crisis of democracy after the war, see David Runciman, *The Confidence Trap* (Princeton, NJ: Princeton University Press, 2013), chap. 3; Edward A. Purcell, Jr., *The Crisis of Democratic Theory: Scientific Naturalism and the Problem of Value* (Lexington: University Press of Kentucky, 1973).

[22] Jan-Werner Müller explored the multifaceted democratic discourse in twentieth-century European history, without dedicating attention to the place of democracy in the globalist discourse. See *Contesting Democracy: Political Ideas in Twentieth-Century Europe* (New Haven, CT: Yale University Press, 2011).

[23] On American post-war planning, see Hearden, *Architects of Globalism*; Stephen A. Wertheim, 'Tomorrow, the World: The Birth of U.S. Global Supremacy in World War II' (PhD dissertation, Columbia University, 2015). On American post-war planning regarding Britain and the dominions, see Andrew Baker, *Constructing a Post-war Order: The Rise of US Hegemony and the Origins of the Cold War* (London: I.B. Tauris, 2011).

[24] On the American and British post-war planners and the role of Chatham House, see Andrew J. Williams, *Failed Imagination? New World Orders of the Twentieth Century* (Manchester: Manchester University Press, 1998), 126–140.

[25] Sluga, *Internationalism in the Age of Nationalism*, 79–80.

ing elements of humanity. The conceptual toolbox of modern global democracy included not only rationality and scientific progress but also morality, faith, myth, and religion, which attained an increasingly greater importance for mid-century planners of world order.

The attempts to come up with new interpretations of democracy for the global age were later castigated by historians as 'a failure' since most ideas received no practical application.[26] However, anachronistic and hindsight judgments run the risk of obscuring the issues that past commentators were concerned with. My main aim, therefore, is not to investigate if and how these global schemes were actualised, but to uncover the political terms and conceptual vocabulary employed to promote certain ideas about politics in historical context. The approach I adopt focuses on examining the aims behind international theories to discern their meaning at the time and their implications for later conceptions of world order. Thus, I argue that mid-century interpretations of democracy beyond the state can provide insights on the intellectual origins of the globalist discourse even if the concrete political visions they proposed—such as a world democratic federation or a regional union—were not realised.

Third, globalism was anchored, for mid-century thinkers, in a pluralistic conception of world order.[27] Many of the intellectuals I discuss here argued that the post-war global order should reflect the political, cultural, and social pluralism that they had diagnosed in their world. The existing condition of political and moral diversity should, they suggested, acquire a normative expression in the new global order. Inspired by the British pluralists, especially Harold Laski and Lord Acton, these thinkers explored the potential implications of pluralism on political order in the global, rather than domestic sphere.[28]

Arguably, there is more than one way to define and interpret pluralism in the history of political thought. For Avigail Eisenberg, pluralism goes beyond mere freedom of association: 'Political pluralism are theories that seek to organize and conceptualize political phenomena on the basis of the plurality of groups to which individuals belong and by which individuals

---

[26] On visions of global order as (at least partially) a failure, see, for example, Wesley T. Wooley, *Alternatives to Anarchy: American Supranationalism since World War II* (Bloomington: Indiana University Press, 1988) 40–65; Williams, *Failed Imagination?*; Mark Mazower, *Governing the World: The History of an Idea* (London: Allen Lane, 2012), 284–290; Jo-Anne Pemberton, *Global Metaphors: Modernity and the Quest for One World* (London: Pluto Press, 2001), 115–166.

[27] On Anglo-American pluralism in the twentieth century, see Mark Bevir, ed., *Modern Pluralism: Anglo-American Debates since 1880* (Cambridge: Cambridge University Press, 2012); Marc Stears, *Progressives, Pluralists, and the Problems of the State: Ideologies of Reform in the United States and Britain, 1909–1926* (Oxford: Oxford University Press, 2002).

[28] For the history of pluralism as a political idea in the context of the state, see David Runciman, *Pluralism and the Personality of the State* (Cambridge: Cambridge University Press, 1997); David Nicholls, *The Pluralist State: The Political Ideas of J. N. Figgis and His Contemporaries* (New York: St. Martin's Press, 1975).

seek to advance, and more importantly, to develop, their interests'.[29] In this book, I adopt an inclusive definition of pluralism to propose that mid-century political commentators and public intellectuals employed this term to suggest that states could not claim sole authority over individuals. Other associations, groups, and organisations provided individuals—and 'persons'—with important opportunities to interact and construct political spaces to advance their political, social, and cultural interests. Pluralism was not a source of political and social chaos, but a form of global order. Nonetheless, these thinkers did not always distinguish clearly between value pluralism and political pluralism, between pluralism of acceptable moral views and pluralism of political institutions governing the community. The opacity of the term 'pluralism' contributed to its rhetorical efficacy, but undermined its analytical power in the globalist discourse.

The attention to pluralism as a key factor in the globalist agenda does not imply making a case for the inclusion of all these figures in the pluralist tradition of political thought. However, in view of recent interest in the political theory of pluralism, I suggest that looking back at the 1940s attempts to deploy the vocabulary of pluralism within the globalist discourse can reveal the limits of conceptualising a pluralist world order.[30] There were evident tensions between the pluralistic approach and the support for democracy as the preferable form of government. It was difficult to valorise non-Western forms of political order and insist that the Western interpretation of humanity embodied a universal truth.[31] By consequence, the proponents of the globalist discourse struggled to reconcile the universalising and the pluralistic aspects of their visions of world order, which thus collapsed sometimes into a defence of Western moral and political values.

THE MID-CENTURY DISCOURSE OF GLOBALISM

The time frame of this study is the decade between the outbreaks of two wars: World War II and the Korean War. It is a recurrent claim that 'we still live in the shadow of the most dramatic and decisive decade of the

---

[29] Avigail I. Eisenberg, *Reconstructing Political Pluralism* (New York: State University of New York Press, 1995), 2.

[30] For recent analytical accounts of pluralism as a philosophical position, see Victor Muñiz-Fraticelli, *The Structure of Pluralism* (Oxford: Oxford University Press, 2014); William A. Galston, *Liberal Pluralism: The Implications of Value Pluralism for Political Theory and Practice* (Cambridge: Cambridge University Press, 2002).

[31] Jacob T. Levy identified a similar tension between pluralism and rationalistic universalism in the history of liberal thought. See Levy, *Rationalism, Pluralism, and Freedom* (Oxford: Oxford University Press, 2014).

twentieth century'.[32] Over the course of the decade, the European powers were starting to lose grip on their empires, while new voices in the American public debate called for greater intervention in world politics.[33] The war years and their immediate aftermath represent a significant moment of world crisis, understood in terms of change and transition, if not decisive innovation. Allied political leaders established governmental think tanks to envisage the post-war settlement and reconstruction on domestic and global scales.[34] After the war, the Truman Doctrine and Marshall Aid led to a stronger American presence in Europe. The redefined spatiality of the Atlantic region was sanctified in legal agreements through the Atlantic Charter of 1941 and the North Atlantic Treaty of 1949, which established a closer American-British cooperation, highlighting the shift from the old to the new imperial power.[35]

New experiments in international organisations brought about the Charter of the United Nations (1945) and the Universal Declaration of Human Rights (1948), both influential efforts to redefine international and transnational relations on a global scale.[36] In 1945, delegates of fifty states gathered in San Francisco to agree upon the Charter of the United Nations. The document was finalised in April and subsequently signed on 26 June 1945.[37] At the Dumbarton Oaks and Yalta conferences in 1944 and 1945, the Allied powers had already launched a series of discussions to create a long-term post-war settlement to guarantee international peace. The UN Charter built upon and expanded these earlier proposals and created a new international organisation, the United Nations, to 'reaffirm faith in fundamental human rights', establish a regime of justice based on international law, and 'promote social progress'.[38] The main aim of the new organisation was a peaceful settlement of international disputes by employing legal as

---

[32] David Reynolds, *From World War to Cold War: Churchill, Roosevelt, and the International History of the 1940s* (Oxford: Oxford University Press, 2006), 1.

[33] John A. Thompson, 'The Geopolitical Vision: The Myth of an Outmatched USA', in *Uncertain Empire: American History and the Idea of the Cold War*, ed. Joel Isaac and Duncan Bell (Oxford: Oxford University Press, 2012), 91–114. See also Pemberton, *Global Metaphors*, 115; Wm. Roger Louis, *Imperialism at Bay, 1941–1945: The United States and the Decolonization of the British Empire* (Oxford: Clarendon, 1977).

[34] On post-war reconstruction, see, for example, Reynolds, *From World War to Cold War*; David Reynolds, *One World Divisible: A Global History since 1945* (London: Allen Lane, 2000), 9–30; Mark Mazower, Jessica Reinisch, and David Feldman, eds., *Post-war Reconstruction in Europe: International Perspectives, 1945–1949* (Oxford: Oxford University Press, 2011); Alan S. Milward, *The Reconstruction of Western Europe 1945–51* (London: Methuen, 1984); István Deák, Jan Tomasz Gross, and Tony Judt, eds., *The Politics of Retribution in Europe: World War II and Its Aftermath* (Princeton, NJ: Princeton University Press, 2000).

[35] Louis, *Imperialism at Bay*; John Darwin, *After Tamerlane: The Global History of Empire since 1405* (London: Allen Lane, 2007), 470.

[36] Akira Iriye, *Global Community: The Role of International Organizations in the Making of the Contemporary World* (Berkeley: University of California Press, 2002).

[37] For a detailed history of the United Nations, see, for example, Evan Luard, *A History of the United Nations* (London: Macmillan, 1982); Alessandro Polsi, *Storia dell'ONU* (Rome: Laterza, 2006).

[38] UN Charter, Preamble, www.un.org/en/sections/un-charter/un-charter-full-text/index.html.

well as military means, and by encouraging the development of friendly and harmonious relations between its members. The charter outlined the various organs of the new organisation, including a General Assembly, a Security Council, an Economic and Social Council, a Trusteeship Council, an International Court of Justice, and a Secretariat.

The UN Charter outlined a world order based on the principle of the sovereign equality of its members; the constitutive unit of this world vision was the state as a self-governing, independent, and autonomous polity. Regional organisations, such as unions or federations, were permitted, but not required for the functioning of the new international system.

However, the institutional design of the United Nations suggested that, in practice, not all member states were equal. The Security Council, which held 'primary responsibility for the maintenance of international peace and security', included fifteen members, of which five were permanent. The permanent members of the council, China, France, the Soviet Union, the United Kingdom, and the United States, held a veto right that endowed them with a privileged position within the nascent international order. The apparent equality of states was, in fact, a deeply hierarchical order aimed at defending the interests of the victors.[39] The outsized role of a few states was not accepted without protest.[40] It led many, including the Chicago constitutionalists whom I discuss in chapter 6, to doubt that the new organisation could indeed set the foundation for a radically new world order, not infested with the faults of the League of Nations.

Chapter I of the charter reaffirmed the centrality of state sovereignty: 'Nothing contained in the present Charter shall authorize the United Nations to intervene in matters which are essentially within the domestic jurisdiction of any state or shall require the Members to submit such matters to settlement under the present Charter; but this principle shall not prejudice the application of enforcement measures under Chapter VII'. The emphasis on domestic sovereignty set a severe condition on the activities and jurisdiction of the new international organisation, in a way that many political commentators at the time found ineffective and counterproductive. The UN Charter announced the creation of a new, long-lasting international order; yet mid-century globalists found it unsatisfactory, and continued their quest for an alternative.

If the charter promoted the principle of state sovereignty, the Universal Declaration of Human Rights apparently embodied a commitment for universality and shared values. The declaration, proclaimed by the UN General Assembly in Paris on 10 December 1948, was a significant land-

---

[39] Mazower, *Governing the World*, 213.

[40] A. W. Brian Simpson, *Human Rights and the End of Empire: Britain and the Genesis of the European Convention* (Oxford: Oxford University Press, 2001), 264.

mark in mid-century debates on world order. Eleanor Roosevelt was a prominent member of the drafting committee, which included representatives from eight different countries.[41] Building on ideas and draft bills provided by a variety of civil organisations and governments, the committee sought to form a universally consensual vision of human rights and their implementation in the post-war order. As I demonstrate, the declaration was one of many attempts to come to terms with the need to define the basic qualities of humanity that embodied entitlements to be respected and defended. Catholic scholars, global constitutionalists, and European federalists each had their own interpretation of the universal rights of humanity. The feeling of urgency that surrounded the drafting of the declaration reflected the wider mid-century concern with the idea of human rights and their potential role in the new world order. Yet, as Samuel Moyn argued, the declaration 'was less the annunciation of a new age than a funeral wreath laid on the grave of wartime hopes'.[42] The mid-century debate on order and rights was truncated by the Cold War.

The decisive geopolitical changes in the early 1950s set the temporal limits for this study. The rise of the Cold War mentality in the United States undermined the support for new schemes of global order, and rendered many of these visions impractical.[43] In American public debate, and to a lesser extent in Britain, the idea of globalism was overpowered by the idea of bipolarism. By the outbreak of the Korean War, imagining a new global order of the world seemed futile, and sometimes dangerously naïve.

Setting a precise time frame for an intellectual history embodies the risk of obfuscating important continuities and imposing anachronistic temporal divides. The spotlight on one decade should not become a rigid artificial constraint. On the one hand, this study constructs the 1940s as a coherent historical period, rather than as two half decades, divided by the world-changing detonation of the atomic bomb in August 1945.[44] On the other hand, it recognises evident overlaps and continuities with earlier and later modes of thinking about world politics, especially along the 'transwar' period, stretching from 1930 to 1950.[45]

After 1950, the central themes of the globalist ideology of the previous decade did not completely disappear from political debate. Instead, the 'global' space was marginalised, until its return to centre stage after 1989.

---

[41] On Eleanor Roosevelt and the declaration, see Mary Ann Glendon, *A World Made New: Eleanor Roosevelt and the Universal Declaration of Human Rights* (New York: Random House, 2002).

[42] Samuel Moyn, *The Last Utopia: Human Rights in History* (Cambridge, MA: Belknap, 2010), 2.

[43] Campbell Craig, 'The Resurgent Idea of World Government', *Ethics & International Affairs* 22 (2008): 133–142.

[44] William Graebner, *The Age of Doubt: American Thought and Culture in the 1940s* (Boston: Twayne, 1993), 1.

[45] Philip Nord, *France's New Deal from the Thirties to the Postwar Era* (Princeton, NJ: Princeton University Press, 2010), 12–13.

Today, globalism and globalisation embody important patterns of thinking about the spatiality of political and economic order.[46] The processes of
European integration and globalisation and the development of international institutions including the United Nations and its agencies brought
to the fore many questions about the desirable and viable spaces of politics that had already been discussed in the 1940s.[47] Political philosophers
today face, to a certain extent, similar challenges to the ones that daunted
mid-century thinkers, and seek to apply the same political categories—
such as constitutionalism, federalism, and pluralism—to outline a solution.
In this context, *The Emergence of Globalism* presents an archaeological ex-
cavation of unrealised plans, an investigation of past attempts to translate
observations about the world into new forms of political order. The contemporary revival of the idea of the global provides another motivation for
looking more closely at the rendering of global ideas by mid-century public intellectuals.

The 1940s should be understood, I suggest, not only against an analysis
of historical events, but also against debates about globalism and world
order that proliferated in the British and American public sphere during
the decade. Scholarly literature on mid-century political thought has been
largely focused on the creation of international institutions and the human rights regime or on individual figures and political leaders of the
time.[48] However, as this book aims to show, without understanding the
development of the discourse of globalism and the intellectual history of
'world order', the history of twentieth-century Western political thought
remains incomplete.

In writings about world order during and immediately after the war,
many political commentators embraced a degree of dynamism and instability as inherent in the new globality of politics. Yet these mid-century
representations of the concept of order have been downplayed by International Relations scholars who have delineated the foundational moments
of their discipline.[49] The conceptual tools provided by conventional his-

[46] The relations between globalisation, history, and politics have been the subject of innumerable
studies in various disciplines, including, for example, Yale H. Ferguson and R. J. Barry Jones, eds., *Political Space: Frontiers of Change and Governance in a Globalizing World* (Albany: State University of New York
Press, 2002); John A. Agnew, *Globalization & Sovereignty* (Lanham, MD: Rowman & Littlefield, 2009).

[47] There are many intellectual histories of the European Union. See, for example, Fabrizio Sciacca,
ed., *La dimensione istituzionale europea: teoria, storia e filosofia Politica* (Florence: Le Lettere, 2009); Justine
Lacroix and Kalypso Nicolaïdis, eds., *European Stories: Intellectual Debates on Europe in National Contexts*
(Oxford: Oxford University Press, 2010).

[48] Recent publications include Mazower, *Governing the World*; Elizabeth Borgwardt, *A New Deal for the
World: America's Vision for Human Rights* (Cambridge, MA: Harvard University Press, 2005); Moyn, *Last
Utopia.* The UN Intellectual History Project similarly aims at expanding the historical scholarship about
this organisation (www.unhistory.org).

[49] A recent revisionist history of International Relations (IR) focuses on an earlier period; see Brian
C. Schmidt, *The Political Discourse of Anarchy: A Disciplinary History of International Relations* (Albany:

torical accounts of international thought, exemplified by the paradigm of the debate between realism and idealism, can do little to explain the emergence of globalism in mid-century thought, when concerns about power, order, morality, and democracy were closely intertwined.[50] In drawing on a wide range of intellectual sources, including science, law, religion, economics, geopolitics, and ideology, the 1940s discourse on globalism was not confined by disciplinary boundaries and rigid paradigms. To explore the intellectual development of the idea of the global, one needs to cast a wider net.

THE IDEOLOGUES OF GLOBALISM

Public intellectuals in the 1940s shared an awareness of the role of public debate in sustaining political change. If the war was fought for democracy, many thought that the post-war order should be decided democratically through open debate in the public sphere, and not exclusively through parliamentary deliberations and diplomatic conferences. Thus, debate on world politics attracted many keen commentators who hoped to contribute to shaping the post-war order by joining public conversations, if not by drafting concrete policy plans. Who were the participants in these conversations, and why did they highlight the importance of the global political sphere? These were not secluded scholars, writing comfortably from their academic ivory towers. Rather, most of the figures examined in this book can be defined as public intellectuals, academically trained experts who engaged in public debate in order to influence popular opinion and decision makers.[51]

State University of New York Press, 1998). Two recent accounts of the history of American IR explore mid-century international thought without reference to the idea of the 'global'; see Nicolas Guilhot, ed., *The Invention of International Relations Theory: Realism, the Rockefeller Foundation, and the 1954 Conference on Theory* (New York: Columbia University Press, 2011); Robert Vitalis, *White World Order, Black Power Politics: The Birth of American International Relations* (Ithaca, NY: Cornell University Press, 2015).

[50] The classic version of this argument is Edward H. Carr, *The Twenty Years' Crisis, 1919–1939: An Introduction to the Study of International Relations* (1939; repr., Basingstoke: Palgrave, 2001). For a revisionist history of the interwar discipline of IR, see Peter Wilson and David Long, eds., *Thinkers of the Twenty Years' Crisis: Inter-war Idealism Reassessed* (Oxford: Clarendon, 1995); Peter Wilson, 'The Myth of the "First Great Debate"', *Review of International Studies* 24 (1998): 1–16; Lucian M. Ashworth, 'Where Are the Idealists in Interwar International Relations?', *Review of International Studies* 32 (2006): 291–308. On the interplay between intellectual history and IR, see David Armitage, 'The Fifty Years Rift: Intellectual History and International Relations', *Modern Intellectual History* 1 (2004): 97–109; Duncan Bell, 'Writing the World: Disciplinary History and Beyond', *International Affairs* 85 (2009): 3–22.

[51] For definitions of the public role of intellectuals, see, for example, Cornelia Navari, *Public Intellectuals and International Affairs: Essays on Public Thinkers and Political Projects* (Dordrecht: Republic of Letters, 2012), 1–12; Julia Stapleton, *Political Intellectuals and Public Identities in Britain since 1850* (Manchester: Manchester University Press, 2001); Stefan Collini, *Public Moralists: Political Thought and Intellectual Life in Britain 1850–1930* (Oxford: Clarendon, 1991), 1–25.

The ideologues of globalism at the centre of this study were predominantly white male scholars who were privileged enough to be able to travel the world, lecture to educated audiences, and publish their ideas in widely read outlets. They invested considerable time and energy to generate public support for their ideas about world order.[52] Nonetheless, there was no one authoritative version of the 'global' ideology, but rather there were many competing visions striving to attain political purchase and public support. In this context, I refer to the global ideologies as 'clusters of ideas, beliefs, opinions, values and attitudes usually held by identifiable groups, that provided directives, even plans, of action for public policy-making in an endeavour to uphold, justify, change or criticise the social and political arrangements of a state or other political community'.[53] Without committing themselves to a direct involvement in politics, the promoters of the global ideologies considered their participation in public debate as a responsibility that came with their role as preeminent scholars in prestigious universities (although their main field of expertise was not always politics).

The elusiveness of the globalist agenda in the 1940s allowed a range of public intellectuals to participate in transnational debates on the desirable form and substance of the post-war world order. These individuals came from different disciplinary and national backgrounds. They were renowned scholarly experts in politics, sociology, law, economics, theology, philosophy of science, or geopolitics. While the conversations I explore in the book took place in Britain and the United States, some of the participants were émigrés who had escaped political and racial persecution in their native countries, including Italy, France, Hungary, Austria, Germany, and Romania. Others were frequent travellers with expert knowledge of various parts of the world. Thus, the protagonists of this study represent, to a certain extent, diverse cultural, political, and geographic realities, which, I suggest, contributed to their particular attention to the global aspects of politics.

The rhetoric employed by these intellectuals was an essential part of their global visions since, for them, actualisation depended on popular consent.[54] Their works aimed at a general audience that included but was

---

[52] Some of these authors may be considered 'public moralists', who, according to Stefan Collini, based their ideas on ethical arguments rather than expertise. Yet in the context of this study, I use the more flexible term 'public intellectuals' to describe individuals who engaged in public debate to promote both political and moral ends. Stefan Collini, *Absent Minds: Intellectuals in Britain* (Oxford: Oxford University Press, 2007).

[53] Michael Freeden, 'Ideology, Political Theory and Political Philosophy', in *Handbook of Political Theory*, ed. Gerald Gaus and Chandran Kukathas (London: Sage, 2004), 6.

[54] For general accounts of the cultural and political roles of the public intellectual in the twentieth century, see Helen Small, ed., *The Public Intellectual* (Oxford: Blackwell, 2002); Richard A. Posner, *Public Intellectuals: A Study of Decline* (Cambridge, MA: Harvard University Press, 2001).

not limited to politicians. Thus, political commentary meant engaging with the wider evils of their age rather than with specific problem solving. Many of these commentators saw their role in adapting generic theoretical categories to their political reality. Their public authority depended on the ability to communicate effectively with their audience, through a variety of media: radio broadcasts, public meetings, speeches, pamphlets, newspapers and magazines, books, and scholarly articles.

The intellectuals I discuss in the book construct a loose network united by a shared concern with world order. This transnational Republic of Letters includes Raymond Aron, Giuseppe Antonio Borgese, Lionel Curtis, Friedrich Hayek, Owen Lattimore, Jacques Maritain, Richard McKeon, Charles E. Merriam, David Mitrany, Lewis Mumford, Michael Polanyi, Lionel Robbins, Nicholas J. Spykman, Clarence Streit, Luigi Sturzo, H. G. Wells, and Barbara Wootton. This intellectual cohort is not a homogeneous group of thinkers adhering to a well-defined ideology. Their interest in the global dimension of politics forms a bond of unity in diversity without giving rise to a dominant or representative political stance. This study outlines their relations, fleshing out points of agreement and divergence, in order to suggest the intellectual force of the discourse on globalism was its capacity to attract individuals of diverging worldviews, thus transcending many of the traditional classifications of political thought: liberals, socialists, Catholics, radicals, conservatives, and atheists all found appeal in the promise of global order.

Some of the book's protagonists might be considered by historians as 'minor thinkers' who lacked the intellectual stamina to develop philosophically sophisticated accounts. My aim is not to argue in favour of the inclusion of these thinkers in any canon, nor to lament the neglect of some in standard treatments of the history of political thought. Other mid-century international figures are doubtlessly no less deserving of the historian's attention. I suggest, however, that the 'great' minds of political thought embody an exception rather than a representative example of the general trends of public debate. The intellectual sources for the emergence of globalism as a political category are not necessarily confined to the publications of outstanding philosophers and brilliant theorists. Instead, I focus on the writings of a diverse group of scholars and commentators who actively engaged in transnational debates on world order and sought to influence public opinion on international affairs.

This book reconstructs the globalist conversations by interrogating the writings of a transnational network of intellectuals through their publications, speeches, and newspapers articles. This study has no pretence to provide a comprehensive or final assessment of mid-century thought on world order. I make no attempt to gauge the popularity of various global schemes, their reception by the general public or politicians, and their political implementation. Rather, I examine the contributions of public intellectuals to shaping the idea of the global within the intellectual and political context of their times, employing a method inspired by Duncan Bell's 'hybrid contextualisation'.[55] The detailed analysis of particular visions of world order provides a nuanced and complex account of the historical development of globalism during the 1940s. The wider thematic explorations of key theoretical perspectives on the 'global' serve to ground the individual visions in their intellectual, political, and cultural context.

Throughout the book, the personal and professional bonds between these thinkers will unfold. For example, Wells's scientific internationalism was a source of inspiration for Aron, Merriam, and Polanyi.[56] Wells sought advice from Wootton in writing his universal declaration of the rights of man.[57] He, like Mitrany, also participated in debates on federalism orchestrated by the British political organisation Federal Union, whose members included Wootton, Curtis, Robbins, and Hayek. Wootton and Curtis were colleagues at Chatham House, and met Lattimore at international conferences organised through the global network of the Institute of Pacific Relations (IPR).[58] The correspondence between Curtis and Polanyi reveals their mutual interest in world politics and faith.[59] Hayek, Polanyi, and Aron met in 1938 at the Colloque Walter Lippmann in Paris and kept in close touch in wartime London.[60] Aron debated political Machiavellianism with Maritain, who, in turn, supported the global constitutionalism of Borgese and McKeon.[61] McKeon and Lattimore spoke in a panel on 'Problems Arising from the Interrelations and Policies of the Great Powers' at a conference on the development of international society, held at Princeton University in 1946. Mumford's correspondence with Borgese dates back to their world constitution project of 1941, revealing a strong convergence of opinion on the future of democracy.[62]

The flexible network of political thinkers that I outline in this study serves to embed the emergence of globalism in the historical intellectual

[55] Bell, *Idea of Greater Britain*, 26.

[56] Michael Polanyi, *The Logic of Liberty: Reflections and Rejoinders* (London: Routledge, 1951); Raymond Aron (René Avord), 'L'universalisme de Wells, Tribute to H. G. Wells on His 75th Birthday', *Adam: International Review* 153 (1941): 6–7; Charles E. Merriam, 'Review of *The New World Order* by H. G. Wells', *American Journal of Sociology* 46 (1940): 402–403.

[57] H. G. Wells, *The Rights of Man: An Essay in Collective Definition* (Brighton: Poynings Press, 1943).

[58] For records of the Chatham House participation in the IPR conferences, see the Records of Royal Institute of International Affairs, Royal Institute of International Affairs, London, box 6, folder 1.

[59] Michael Polanyi to Lionel Curtis, 21 December 1944, Michael Polanyi Papers, Special Collections Research Center, University of Chicago Library (hereafter MPP), box 4, folder 12.

[60] Serge Audier, *Le Colloque Lippmann: Aux origines du néo-libéralisme* (Lomont: Le Bord de l'Eau, 2008); Angus Burgin, *The Great Persuasion: Reinventing Free Markets since the Depression* (Cambridge, MA: Harvard University Press, 2012).

[61] Richard McKeon, 'A Philosophy for UNESCO', *Philosophy and Phenomenological Research* 8 (1948): 573.

[62] Herbert Agar et al., *The City of Man: A Declaration on World Democracy* (New York: Viking, 1941).

fabric in which it developed.[63] The political and philosophical foundation of these intellectual exchanges is an underlying theme in the book, revealing the importance of this transnational Republic of Letters to the building of the interdisciplinary vocabulary of globalism.

OUTLINE OF THE BOOK

The Emergence of Globalism explores the various facets of the theoretical discourse of the 'global' in mid-century Britain and the United States, by uncovering the political assumptions that motivated its proponents, examining the intellectual webs that linked advocates of globalism, reconstructing the cultural conventions that fashioned their ideas, and critically assessing the rhetorical moves that they made. The book is a non-chronological history, a thematic analysis of the diverse conversations in which globalism was developed and shaped.

Two arguments sustain the theoretical claims advanced in the individual thematic chapters of the book. First, the stimulus for thinking about world order and for imagining it as particularly 'global' rose from the perception of epochal crisis that, for mid-century intellectuals, conditioned their world. As I have suggested, the war generated a diffused awareness of the great uncertainty that undermined the foundations of human existence and political order alike. Disquiet about the prospects of democracy in Europe drove mid-century public intellectuals to seek a more stable and resistant form of democratic order that could be applied globally. After the war, trust in international organisations was waning. The failure of the League of Nations to prevent war led many to doubt the new United Nations could operate more effectively. Visions of global order emerged as an attempt to provide a better response to confusion and turmoil.

The second argument is about change. Mid-century thinkers identified the global as an innovative, indeed unprecedented condition of world politics. The crisis they diagnosed as the prime characteristic of their time embodied not only dangerous instability but also flux and fluidity that, for some, could lead to a positive change. Although visions of world order in the 1940s oscillated between ambitious schemes and minimalistic reforms, they shared a common perception of the unique opportunity warranted by the world-changing war to refashion world order. Fear of world destruction by new weapons was accompanied by a cautious optimism about the

---

[63] Usually, the works of some of these thinkers were analysed separately, without reconstructing the intellectual conversations of which they were part. See, for example, Ian Hall and Lisa Hill, eds., *British International Thinkers from Hobbes to Namier* (Basingstoke: Palgrave, 2010); Henrik Bliddal, Casper Sylvest, and Peter Wilson, eds., *Classics of International Relations: Essays in Criticism and Appreciation* (Abingdon: Routledge, 2013); Kenneth W. Thompson, *Masters of International Thought: Major Twentieth-Century Theorists and the World Crisis* (Baton Rouge: Louisiana State University Press, 1980).

possibility to construct a better political order in which liberty, diversity, and peace could be salvaged. The threat of war—and for some the potential annihilation of humanity—endowed the mid-century debate with a novel sense of urgency that had not characterised earlier international thought. Thus, the perception of global crisis and the sensibility of an unprecedented opportunity for global change gave shape to many 1940s visions of world order.

The book is structured around the geopolitical and conceptual notion of political space, a wide theme that runs across the global visions I discuss. Concerns about the desirable spatial dimension of politics formed mid-century globalism. Thus, the historical narrative I frame in this book seeks to reflect the centrality of spatiality for mid-century thinkers. The chapters of the book are organised by spatial scale, progressing from the state to the region, the empire, the federation, and finally the universe. Each chapter examines how past authors reconceptualised different dimensions of political order in the context of the new framework offered by the global space.

Chapter 2 explores perceptions of the state in a global context, arguing that the emergence of globalism encouraged mid-century thinkers to reimagine—but not abandon—the nation-state. My analysis explores Raymond Aron's writings during his wartime exile in London, most of which were published in the journal *La France libre*.[64] Historians have downplayed the significance of Aron's early writings on world politics and focused on his studies of international relations theory in the 1960s.[65] Through an analysis of his proposals to reinterpret the political space of the nation-state in the post-war era, however, I suggest that the war experience formed Aron's conceptualisation of international relations. While the state remained for Aron the main bastion of individual liberty, he acknowledged its conceptual and structural insufficiency in the age of globalism. Aron's interpretation of political ideologies in conversation with the sociologist Karl Mannheim and the philosopher Jacques Maritain led to the development of his loose and pluralistic vision of European unity held together by 'political myth'. A comparison between Aron's vision of world order and that of David Mitrany reveals their shared concern with the need to embed the state in a new global context to guarantee its survival as a political unit in the post-war era. Mitrany's idea of functional relations and Aron's political myth both served to reconceptualise the state in new global settings. I draw on the writings of E. H. Carr to demonstrate that Aron and Mitrany based their proposals

---

[64] Raymond Aron, *Chroniques de guerre: La France libre: 1940–1945*, ed. Christian Bachelier (Paris: Gallimard, 1990).

[65] Raymond Aron, *Paix et guerre entre les nations* (Paris: Calmann-Lévy, 1962).

on two very different interpretations of politics that rendered their global visions politically and intellectually incompatible.

Chapter 3 expands the spatial perspective from the state to the region. In the early 1940s American geopolitical thinkers used spatial concepts to outline the post-war political map, and reimagine the role of the United States in it. Halford Mackinder, Karl Haushofer, and Isaiah Bowman had pioneered the study of the relations between geography and politics. Americans interpreted geopolitics as the dynamic, ever-changing interaction between political government and natural geography. The chapter explores the notion of 'dynamic geopolitics' in the writings of two leading American geopoliticians, Nicholas J. Spykman and Owen Lattimore. Their proposals for tripolar regional world order were grounded in empirical observations and competing interpretations of world politics: Lattimore imagined a post-imperial order based on a global pluralistic democracy, while Spykman wanted to establish the United States as a new player in a world order still organised by the precepts of empire. I analyse the key concepts in their geopolitical visions to distinguish their seemingly similar tripolar world orders, and reveal the conceptual centrality of 'empire' to their global thought. Finally, I explain the marginalisation of geopolitics in the post-war American discipline of International Relations.

Chapter 4 returns to the problem of empires and their position in a new global order. It examines the notion of 'democratic federalism' through the story of the British organisation Federal Union. In this and the following chapter, I uncover an important change in the meaning of democratic federalism as the foundation of mid-century global order. Originally, this structure was proposed as a solution to safeguard the declining British Empire, but by the end of the war it became part of a global scheme for socioeconomic reform. The chapter examines the visions of democratic federalism promoted by Lionel Curtis and Clarence Streit, aimed at creating a democratic world region based on the British Empire and the idea of Anglo-American cultural supremacy. The discussions at Federal Union committees and in the organisation's newsletter reflect the growing resistance to the imperial model of organising the global political space. Finally, the chapter reveals the limits of Federal Union's approach to the European colonies and their future within the new federal system.

Chapter 5 traces a different debate on democratic federalism at Federal Union, which sought to overcome the legacy of empire by emphasising the economic and social emancipatory function of the democratic federation. I outline the rise of a new idea of democratic federalism that shifted from a constitutional structure to safeguard the declining British Empire to a regional scheme for socioeconomic change. This transition was shaped in debates among its members, including William Beveridge, Lionel Robbins, Barbara Wootton, and Friedrich Hayek, in Federal Union meetings and in the pages of *Federal Union News*. This new conception of federalism hoped to meliorate individual social and economic living conditions through transnational unity. However, there was no clear consensus on the desirable and possible political strategies to bring about federal economic democracy, as Wootton and Hayek's debate on free market and social planning demonstrated. This episode revealed the tensions between competing ideas of liberty and democracy, and their implications for global politics, anticipating some of the debates around the European Union.

Perceptions of federal world order are the theme of chapter 6, which shifts the spatial focus from the region to the whole world. I look at a group of American and European émigré intellectuals in the United States who formed the Chicago Committee to Frame a World Constitution (1945–1948). The committee, led by Robert M. Hutchins, Richard McKeon, and Giuseppe Antonio Borgese, united leading intellectuals and scholars concerned with the crisis of world order after the atomic bomb. Theirs was a sustained intellectual attempt to delineate the theoretical foundations for a world federation and global government, and cement them in a constitutional document.[66] The constitution was, in Mark Mazower's words, 'a staggeringly implausible document' that 'sank almost without trace'.[67] Yet the real contribution of the committee rests, I suggest, in the vast unpublished documentation it has produced on key theoretical aspects of the new global condition of world politics like representation, political participation, and moral unity. I examine the theoretical contribution of this project to mid-century conceptualisations of legal, political, and moral universalism. The protagonists of this debate were the philosopher McKeon, who advanced a minimalist form of pluralistic universalism, and the anti-fascist Italian literary critic Borgese, who proposed an all-encompassing constitution grounded in natural law and moral universalism. When Borgese's version was accepted, McKeon retired from the committee and advanced his ideas at the UNESCO preparatory committee on human rights and democracy (1948). However, as the jurist Hans Kelsen noted in his comments on the constitution, by alienating the advocates of the pluralistic approach to world constitution the committee undermined the project's feasibility.

Chapter 7 outlines the interplay of globalism and perceptions of science through a series of debates about the potential contribution of scientific practices and technological innovation to the conceptualisation of the global sphere. The atomic bomb presented a global threat that required, for many mid-century commentators, a global solution. The bomb intensified perceptions of the global impact of science and ignited public debate

---

[66] Robert Maynard Hutchins et al., *Preliminary Draft of a World Constitution* (Chicago: University of Chicago Press, 1948).

[67] Mazower, *Governing the World*, 233.

on its political implications. The *Bulletin of the Atomic Scientists* provided a platform for scientists and politics scholars to discuss world affairs. The chapter charts conversations about the place of science in global politics through the writings of four individuals: H. G. Wells, Charles E. Merriam, Michael Polanyi, and Lewis Mumford. Through this network of thinkers and publications, I explore how mid-century perceptions of global order developed in debates on the philosophy of science, liberalism, individualism, and morality. I examine the different roles assigned to experts and scientists in these global visions, and highlight the hidden assumptions about moral universalism that motivated them. Despite the universal aspiration of these globalist proposals, their philosophical precepts were grounded in an implicit—sometimes explicit—defence of Western civilisation, its moral values and political traditions.

Chapter 8 investigates how religious ideas shaped and constrained mid-century theories of world order. The chapter revolves around Jacques Maritain and Luigi Sturzo, who argued that Christianity—and especially Catholicism—provided the theoretical toolkit for constructing a peaceful and prosperous post-war order for individuals and communities. Charting their interactions with other protagonists of the book, including Raymond Aron, Giuseppe Antonio Borgese, and Reinhold Niebuhr, I discuss their support of federalism as a shape-giving principle for the new order. While both drew on Catholic thought to theorise the various components of a desirable pluralist global order—persons, communities, the common good—their visions differed on a crucial point: the place of democracy in the globalist agenda. The chapter reveals the tensions between the particularistic, inherently Western Christian theological doctrines, and their attempted application as a conceptual foundation for a pluralistic yet united world order. I argue that Sturzo's attachment to social Catholicism led his vision of global order away from the conservative stance that characterised Maritain's proposals, towards a dialectical interpretation of politics. The concluding chapter ties together the various theoretical and historical narratives of global thought in the 1940s, and proposes some reflections on the decline of the globalist ideology at the end of the decade, and its omnipresent return at the end of the twentieth century.

CHAPTER 2

Reimagining the State in a Global Space

THE EMERGENCE OF globalism as a political category did not necessarily entail the disappearance of nationalism, the nation-state, and the idea of national self-determination from mid-century political vocabulary. After the Second World War, the state still retained its relevance in the eyes of many political thinkers, but its conceptual and structural attributes were reimagined to reflect the global dimension of post-war politics.

This chapter explores 1940s perceptions of the state as part of a global political space by focusing on two public intellectuals who made important contributions to thinking about the viability of the state in a new world order: Raymond Aron and David Mitrany. At a time when many intellectuals and political commentators envisaged a new order in which peace, prosperity, and liberty could be guaranteed, Mitrany and Aron developed intellectual strategies for reconceptualising the state through the category of globalism.

Aron and Mitrany considered the state as an important vehicle for advancing people's claims of liberty and autonomy. Their writings in the 1940s aimed at complementing rather than replacing the state as the basic unit of political order in the world. The idea that the state had limited capabilities to address the new challenges of the post-war era emerged, in their writings, from a recognition of the new political space of the 'global', the planetary space that included the entire planet and the whole of humanity. The global space became the new arena for political action, which could no longer be delimited by national boundaries. This transformation was not primarily geopolitical, in their view, but embodied a new political awareness as well. It required to reconstruct political order—institutions, polities, and international relations—in light of the new ideology of the global age.

There are several reasons to explore and compare the international thought of Mitrany and Aron in a common framework. Both interpreted the war as a moment of global crisis with important implications for nation-states. They identified similar tendencies as the possible causes of that crisis: the growing public demand for social welfare that the states failed to address, the deterritorialisation of politics and the rise of universal ideologies, the conflict between myth and reason as the foundation of politics, and the growing threat posed by nationalism to world peace and individual liberty. Both sought to adjust the world's political structure to the global age without resorting to drastic changes of the world system such as establishing regional or world federations. I argue, however, that their similar ambition to safeguard the state in a new world order was based on disparate ideas about the meaning of politics. The comparative framework sheds light on the different political and conceptual strategies they adopted for addressing the mid-century global crisis of the state and adjusting the international system for the global age.

The idea of the 'global' led Aron and Mitrany to reconceptualise the state's function in the political order. The chapter opens with a short biographical note highlighting key moments in the intellectual lives of Aron and Mitrany. I then turn to explore the role of ideologies and nationalism in their writings. The third section focuses on their vision of post-war global order, and the following one assesses their reaction to the idea of European unity. I argue that the wartime international visions of Aron and Mitrany embody two insightful but significantly different attempts to imagine a new global and complex, imperfect, and peaceful order in which the political space of the nation-state could retain a meaningful place. In conclusion, I draw upon the international thought of E. H. Carr to mark the differences between the political conceptions of the global order that Aron and Mitrany proposed.

THE INTELLECTUAL WORLDS OF RAYMOND ARON AND DAVID MITRANY

Raymond Aron (1905–1983) was a French sociologist, philosopher, and political thinker. He read philosophy at the École Normale Superieure, where his classmates included Jean-Paul Sartre, Georges Canguilhem, and Paul Nizan.[1] From 1930 to 1933 he studied sociology in Cologne and Berlin, and discovered the writings of Karl Mannheim, Carl Schmitt, Leo Strauss, and Max Weber. In Germany he also witnessed the rise to power of National Socialism.[2] In the Second World War he served in the French

---

[1] The long-term friendship between Sartre and Aron was undermined by Aron's criticism of Sartre's post-war communism. Raymond Aron, *Memoirs: Fifty Years of Political Reflection* (1983; repr., New York: Holmes and Meier, 1990), 407. The 1997 English-language edition included a preface by Henry A. Kissinger.

[2] Raymond Aron, *La sociologie allemande contemporaine* (Paris: Alcan, 1935), trans. into English as *German Sociology* (Glencoe, IL: Free Press, 1964). Hereafter I will refer to the English edition. On Aron and

army, but after the armistice he escaped to London. He became editor in chief and contributor to an important London-based French language publication, *La France libre*, founded by André Labarthe with General Charles de Gaulle's blessing, who nonetheless did not escape Aron's criticism.[3] *La France libre* was an international success: with over seventy thousand subscribers in 1943, it was the monthly with the largest circulation in Britain and boasted contributions from H. G. Wells, Harold Laski, Paul Éluard, and Julian Huxley, among others.[4]

Aron admired Britain's social and political institutions, but considered himself a French patriot.[5] During his stay in London, from 1940 to 1944, he became part of a community of European expatriates, but maintained close relations with leading British intellectuals including Lionel Robbins and William Beveridge, and renewed his friendship with Friedrich Hayek, Karl Mannheim, and Michael Polanyi. Aron's political essays from that period discussed the crucial themes of the time: liberty, the crisis of democracy, the rise of totalitarian ideology, and the revival of Europe as a political unit. He offered coolheaded philosophical discussion of French and European politics and the post-war settlement, suggesting that the European states, especially Britain and France, should cooperate to bring about a new peaceful and liberal world order in which Western civilisation could flourish.[6]

After liberation, Aron returned to France. He published political commentary in Albert Camus's left-wing *Combat* and in *Les Temps modernes*, which he co-founded with Sartre. From 1947 he was the political commentator of the conservative daily *Le Figaro*.[7] His journalistic career made him a household name. He remained critical of de Gaulle, but in 1947 briefly joined his new party Rassemblement du peuple français.[8] Later he taught at the Sorbonne and the École Nationale d'Administration, and published a well-known study of international relations, *Paix et guerre entre les nations* (1962), which still attracts scholarly interest today.[9]

Schmitt, see Jan-Werner Müller, *A Dangerous Mind: Carl Schmitt in Post-war European Thought* (New Haven, CT: Yale University Press, 2003), 87–103.

[3] On Aron at *La France libre*, see David Drake, 'Raymond Aron and *La France libre* (June 1940–September 1944)', in *A History of the French in London: Liberty, Equality, Opportunity*, ed. Debra Kelly and Martyn Cornick (London: University of London Institute of Historical Research, 2013), 373–391.

[4] Aron was not wholly opposed to propaganda, and hoped *La France libre* could be instrumental to winning the battle of propaganda between Nazi Germany and the Allies. See Raymond Aron, 'Naissance des tyrannies' (1941), in *Chroniques de guerre*, 505–520.

[5] Joël Mouric, *Raymond Aron et l'Europe* (Rennes: Rennes University Press, 2013), 86.

[6] Christopher Flood, 'André Labarthe and Raymond Aron: Political Myth and Ideology in La France Libre', *Journal of European Studies* 23 (1993): 139–158.

[7] Raymond Aron, *Les articles du Figaro. La guerre froide*, vol. 1 (Paris: Editions de Fallois, 1990).

[8] Lucia Bonfreschi, *Raymond Aron e Il Gollismo, 1940–1969* (Soveria Mannelli: Rubbettino, 2013).

[9] Aron, *Paix et guerre*; Raymond Aron, *Thinking Politically: A Liberal in the Age of Ideology* (New Brunswick, NJ: Transaction, 1997), 134–135; for commentary, see the special issue of *Études internationales*,

In the United States and Britain, Aron's thought has been associated with conservative liberalism: opponents and admirers alike have described him as a 'cold warrior' conditioned by his political stance within the Cold War historical framework.[10] He deserves credit for identifying earlier than most the probability of a long-term conflict between the United States and the Soviet Union, but it would be simplistic to read his vast intellectual production in the 1940s as a mere recipe for countering the rise of the Soviet Union to global hegemony: these were not merely preparatory drafts for his later work, but perceptive analyses of the international situation and possible ways to reform it.

Aron's ideas echoed the acute sense of moral, economic, and political crisis in Continental Europe. The vanquished were in search of a new political future, but the French, counting themselves among the victors, were also uncertain of their prospects. With the experience of Nazi occupation and the Vichy regime still fresh in its memory, and the viability of its overseas empire in doubt, France was no longer a great power.[11] French intellectuals were traditionally more attached to the state as a provider of social stability and political order, and sought to address its deficiencies.[12] However, the political, social, and economic decline of the state as a political unit was also recognised by non-French thinkers, including the internationalist David Mitrany.

David Mitrany (1888–1975) was born in Bucharest, Romania. At the age of twenty-four he relocated to London, where, unlike Aron, he found a new homeland. He studied sociology and economics at the London School of Economics with Leonard Hobhouse and Graham Wallas, and met Harold Laski, whose pluralist vision became a source of great inspiration. He worked briefly for the Foreign Office, and later joined the *Manchester Guardian* when, like Aron, he decided to pursue a career in journalism. He became an expert on foreign affairs, held in high esteem by the general readership and the British government alike. In the interwar years he collaborated with various think tanks including the League of Nations Society, the Labour Party

---

Jean-Vincent Holeindre and Jean-Baptiste Jeangène Vilmer, eds., 'Raymond Aron et les relations internationales: 50 ans après Paix et guerre entre les nations', *Études internationales* 43 (2012): 319–492.

[10] See, for example, Stuart L. Campbell, 'Raymond Aron: The Making of a Cold Warrior', *Historian* 51 (1989): 551–573; Jan-Werner Müller, 'Fear and Freedom: On "Cold War Liberalism"', *European Journal of Political Theory* 7 (2008): 45–64; Daniel J. Mahoney and Brian C. Anderson, 'Introduction', in Aron, *Thinking Politically*; Brian C. Anderson, ed., *Raymond Aron: The Recovery of the Political* (Lanham, MD: Rowman & Littlefield, 1997).

[11] On the history of post-war France and its intellectuals, see, for example, Robert Gildea, *France since 1945* (Oxford: Oxford University Press, 1997); David Drake, *Intellectuals and Politics in Post-war France* (Basingstoke: Palgrave, 2002); Tony Judt, *The Burden of Responsibility: Blum, Camus, Aron, and the French Twentieth Century* (Chicago: University of Chicago Press, 1998).

[12] Justine Lacroix, '"Borderline Europe". French Visions of the European Union', in Lacroix and Nicolaïdis, *European Stories*, 107–109.

Advisory Committee (although he refused to join the party), the Institute of Pacific Relations (and befriended its journal editor Owen Lattimore), Chatham House, and Political and Economic Planning.[13]

Like Aron, Mitrany was fascinated with the British and American political cultures. In the 1930s, he spent time in the United States and co-edited the Carnegie Endowment for International Peace book series on the social and economic history of the war. He was a visiting fellow at Harvard, and subsequently accepted a professorship in politics and economics at the Institute of Advanced Study (IAS) in Princeton, New Jersey.[14] When Aron arrived in London, Mitrany was working for the Foreign Research and Press Service, a Foreign Office study group under the direction of Chatham House, where he initially developed his functionalist ideas. His pamphlet, *A Working Peace System*, presented the functionalist world order and was well received in Britain and the United States.[15] It has been described as one of the most impressive books on regional and world order of the period, and was seen as an attempt to detach 'sovereignty' from territoriality and invest functional units with political power.[16] The short pamphlet inspired public debate on international organisations, and later influenced the foundation of certain social and economic agencies of the United Nations.

In 1957, the Treaty of Rome brought a new wave of interest in functionalism, which lasted for the next twenty years. Mitrany's contribution was recognised, although many neo-functionalists, like Ernest Haas and Inis L. Claude, distanced their theories from Mitrany's views. In 1966, his functionalist essay was republished in America with an introduction by Hans Morgenthau, and in 1975 a conference on functionalism, organised by A. J. R. Groom and Paul Taylor, solicited a new interest in Mitrany's writings about functionalism and international order.[17] Yet, as I show in this chapter, the idea of functional order cannot be understood without considering Mitrany's criticism of the state and the ideology of nationalism.

[13] For Mitrany's biography, see Dorothy Anderson, 'David Mitrany (1888–1975): An Appreciation of His Life and Work', *Review of International Studies* 24 (1998): 577–592; on the PEP group and planning, see Daniel Ritschel, *The Politics of Planning: The Debate on Economic Planning in Britain in the 1930s* (Oxford: Clarendon, 1997), 144–180. On Mitrany's liberal internationalism, see Lucian M. Ashworth, *Creating International Studies: Angell, Mitrany and the Liberal Tradition* (Aldershot: Ashgate, 1999), chap. 4. On Owen Lattimore's international thought, see chapter 3.

[14] The first appointment in the School of Economics and Politics at the IAS went to Mitrany in 1933. See Records of the Office of the Director, Faculty Files, box 23, Mitrany, David/1930–1934, in the Shelby White and Leon Levy Archives Center, Institute for Advanced Study, Princeton, NJ. In the United States Mitrany studied the New Deal and published his observations in *American Interpretations: Four Political Essays* (London: Contact, 1946).

[15] David Mitrany, *A Working Peace System* (London: Royal Institute of International Affairs, 1943).

[16] Peter Wilson, 'The New Europe Debate in Wartime Britain', in *Visions of European Unity*, ed. Philomena Murray and Paul Rich (Oxford: Westview, 1996), 39–59.

[17] Anderson, 'David Mitrany', 581–582; A. J. R. Groom and Paul Taylor, eds., *Functionalism: Theory and Practice in International Relations* (London: University of London Press, 1975). For Hans Morgenthau's introduction, see David Mitrany, *A Working Peace System* (1943; repr. Chicago: Quadrangle Books, 1966).

CRITIQUE OF IDEOLOGY AND NATIONALISM

The post-war world order would, for Raymond Aron, be a global political space in which the nation-state's legitimacy could be renewed and guaranteed.[18] The state remained an important political unit in his international thought (alongside the free individual) in virtue of its historical record of political achievements that effectively provided people with the sense of belonging that was the necessary foundation for the political community.[19] However, for Aron, the new post-war order undermined the distinction between 'internal' and 'external' politics, and demanded a reconsideration of the complex relationship between the state and the global political sphere. This idea resonates with Mitrany's interpretation of the problem of the state and nationalism in the 1940s: 'The problem of our time is how to break away from the modern linking up of authority with territory, and in my case especially, how to apply this to the problem of international organisation so as not to do violence to national feeling and at the same time to lay foundation for new developments in a truly world scale'.[20]

Both Mitrany and Aron struggled to reconcile national feelings with individual liberty in a global world order. One of the common aspects of their international writings was the idea that the post-war state would be an open space, constantly shaped and redefined in interaction with regional and global political arrangements. The practices of political interaction beyond the state were not only institutional and organisational, but also ideological. Aron suggested that ideas could be systematically employed to revive nation-states shattered by the war and imagine new multinational political spaces in which existing states could survive and even flourish. Both Aron and Mitrany recognised that the development of new political spaces through novel practices and innovative ideological constructs would not necessarily be a simple and rational process. They highlighted the need to restrain the potentially damaging effects of ideological positions, and shared a commitment to preventing the post-war world from degenerating into a passion-fuelled ideological battle fought globally.

These reflections on the globality of politics did not result of abstract contemplation alone. Aron's international thought in the 1940s emerged

---

[18] A similar interpretation of the European integration project was advanced by economic historian Alan Milward in *The European Rescue of the Nation-State* (London: Routledge, 1994).

[19] Aron used the French term *nation* to denote a polity based on a national community (unlike the less specific *état*). In English the most appropriate translation would be 'nation-state', which I use to indicate a *political* form of national community, in contrast with nonpolitical interpretations associated with the term 'nation' alone. The term 'nation-state' was for Aron more suitable to describe the political reality of Europe, in contrast to multinational (or non-national) states like the Soviet Union and the United States.

[20] Letter from David Mitrany to Mrs I. Hondius, 13 July 1949, in David Mitrany Papers, London School of Economics, London, box 76.

from his personal experience in wartime London, where he dedicated his intellectual energy to envisaging the world order necessary to safeguard individual liberty and political pluralism. Yet the philosophical foundations of his international thought have deeper roots, grounded in his intellectual formation in France and Germany. Before assessing Aron's ideas on nationalism in comparison with Mitrany's, I discuss two key notions in Aron's wartime political thought, ideology and nationalism, which formed the basis of his political reflection at the time.

Aron's mid-century discussion of ideologies built upon the theoretical notions acquired during his visit to Germany a decade earlier.[21] *La sociologie allemande contemporaine* (1935), the outcome of his German studies, explores the relationship between ideology and the sociology of knowledge. In one chapter of the book, Aron discussed the writings of Karl Mannheim, who inspired many political thinkers including Hannah Arendt, Max Horkheimer, Herbert Marcuse, Barbara Wootton, and E. H. Carr.[22] Despite his deep criticism of Mannheim's sociology of knowledge, Aron employed it to reflect on the capacity of ideology to reshape political order.[23] Rather than analysing Mannheim's works, I focus on Aron's interpretation to reveal the interplay between ideologies and politics in his own writings.

Aron considered Mannheim's theory of relativism ('perspectivism') his most significant—though not entirely correct—contribution to sociology. Interpreting the Marxist theory of knowledge, Mannheim suggested that

---

[21] For a historical and conceptual analysis of Aron's years in Germany, see Matthias Oppermann, *Raymond Aron und Deutschland: Die Verteidigung der Freiheit und das Problem des Totalitarismus* (Ostfildern: Thorbecke Verlag, 2008); Evelyn Völkel, *Der totalitäre Staat—das Produkt einer säkularen Religion? Die frühen Schriften von Frederick A. Voigt, Eric Voegelin sowie Raymond Aron und die totalitäre Wirklichkeit im Dritten Reich* (Baden-Baden: Nomos, 2009).

[22] Karl Mannheim (1893–1947) was a Hungarian-born sociologist. He worked in Germany with Alfred Weber, and became a professor of sociology in Frankfurt. In 1933, he moved to London and was appointed a lecturer in sociology at the LSE. He played a central role in the Moot, a Christian intellectual group, whose other members included T. S. Eliot, Michael Polanyi, and J. H. Oldham. For Mannheim's biography and intellectual life, see Geoff Whitty, 'Mannheim, Karl (1893–1947)', in *Oxford Dictionary of National Biography* (2004), www.oxforddnb.com; David Kettler and Volker Meja, *Karl Mannheim and the Crisis of Liberalism: The Secret of These New Times* (New Brunswick, NJ: Transaction, 1995), 3–10; Colin Loader, *The Intellectual Development of Karl Mannheim: Culture, Politics, and Planning* (Cambridge: Cambridge University Press, 1985). For Mannheim's influence on Barbara Wootton, see chapter 5, and Barbara Wootton, 'Review of *Essays on the Sociology of Knowledge* by Karl Mannheim', *Philosophy* 28 (1953): 278–279. On Carr and Mannheim, see Charles Jones, *E. H. Carr and International Relations: A Duty to Lie* (Cambridge: Cambridge University Press, 1998), 121–140. On Mannheim's sociology of knowledge, see Edward Sagarin and Robert J. Kelly, 'Karl Mannheim and the Sociology of Knowledge', *Salmagundi* 10/11 (1969): 292–302; Harvey Goldman, 'From Social Theory to Sociology of Knowledge and Back: Karl Mannheim and the Sociology of Intellectual Knowledge Production', *Sociological Theory* 12 (1994): 266–278. On Mannheim's London exile, see Stina Lyon, 'Karl Mannheim and Viola Klein: Refugee Sociologists in Search of Social Democratic Practice', in *In Defence of Learning: The Plight, Persecution, and Placement of Academic Refugees, 1933–1980s*, ed. Shula Marks, Paul Weindling, and Laura Wintour (Oxford: Oxford University Press, 2011).

[23] Aron, *Memoirs*, 152–156, 259.

each social class had its own perspective on historical knowledge. Knowledge of reality is therefore filtered through one's experience as a member of society.[24] Yet, in contrast to Marxism, Mannheim did not prioritise the workers' perspective over that of the bourgeoisie, but rather accepted a plurality of valid perspectives on reality.

Aron argued with Friedrich Meinecke that historicism was the awareness of mankind's life experience and creations over the centuries and their embeddedness in historical context. Mannheim's historicist approach showed how individual perspectives on knowledge related to each other in a particular historical moment. Aron criticised Mannheim's historicism for giving equal legitimacy and validity to all perspectives. This position, he suggested, could lead to epistemological relativism, which would be incompatible with Mannheim's intention to invest reality with coherent general meaning. It would be impossible to decide which of the various worldviews embodied a truthful meaning. For Aron, this contradiction was an unresolved dialectic. He had misgivings about the ability of relativist sociology to achieve its goal of assessing and comparing ideological viewpoints without expressing a value judgment. Social scientists and historians, who were necessarily confined by their own historical experience, could not overcome their epistemological limits simply by employing a reflective approach.[25] Yet, to a certain extent reflectiveness could help avoid relativism by relating one's own viewpoint to that of others, and accepting the impossibility of objective evaluation of historical reality and its meaning.

Aron's discussion of international order was intertwined with his assessment of the conceptual and political force of ideologies. The Second World War had a decisive effect on the maturation of his concept of ideology. In his earlier writings, he defined ideology as a system of political ideas, representations, acts, and beliefs oriented towards a certain political goal or vision.[26] Yet he did not clarify how ideology was formed and by whom, how it was transmitted in society, and how it related to domestic and international institutions.[27] In May 1942, he wrote that the war was as much about *ideas* as about physical security, territorial conquest, or political independence.[28] Later, he advanced the interpretative category of

[24] Karl Mannheim, *Ideology and Utopia: An Introduction to the Sociology of Knowledge* (1929; repr., London: Trench, Trubner, 1936), 19–39.

[25] Raymond Aron, 'The Philosophy of History', written in 1946 for *Chamber's Encyclopedia* (1950), republished in French as 'La philosophie de l'histoire', in Raymond Aron, *Dimensions de la conscience historique* (Paris: Les Belles Lettres, 2011), 32–49.

[26] Raymond Aron, *Introduction to the Philosophy of History: An Essay on the Limits of Historical Objectivity*, trans. George J. Irwin (1938; repr., London: Weidenfeld and Nicolson, 1961); Aron, *German Sociology*, 58–63.

[27] On Aron's concept of ideology, see Alessandro Colombo, 'L'Europa e la società internazionale: Gli aspetti culturali e istituzionali della convivenza internazionale in Raymond Aron, Martin Wight e Carl Schmitt', *Quaderni Di Scienza Politica* 6 (1999): 256–259.

[28] Aron, 'La stratégie totalitaire et l'avenir des démocraties' (1942), in *Chroniques de guerre*, 569.

praxeology to suggest that ideologies also developed through political practices.[29] As we have seen, Aron's criticism of Mannheim suggested that ideas
and ideologies evolved not in abstraction, but out of a specific historical
spatiotemporal reality. Nonetheless, at this point he did not provide a detailed analysis of the historical emergence of ideologies.[30]

In 1946, Aron argued that the plurality of competing ideologies would
become a dominant post-war theme, undermining universal political visions. Abstract theory could not help make sense of the immense body of
scientifically collected data about the world's political diversity or provide
the necessary tools to overcome the clash of different viewpoints in the
political arena.[31] Aron criticised Mannheim for arguing that reality could
stem from abstract ideologies and for overemphasising the role of ideas
in shaping history while undermining political practices and historical
contingencies. Even if Mannheim understood the advantages of cultural
and political pluralism, his method of identifying different viewpoints in
society was too abstract and vague to offer concrete political insights. In
practice, Aron argued, ideologies were based not on objective truth but on
subjective values, which did not necessarily reflect an accurate reading of
reality. Sometimes, he concluded, ideologies projected particular utopias
on real politics, and therefore embodied 'a refusal to see reality as it is'.[32]
Without evaluating the accuracy of Aron's interpretation of Mannheim's
sociology, which the latter contested, I suggest that Aron's own view of
ideologies and their ambivalent role in politics was an important grounding for his later political writings on nationalism and international order.

In Aron's articles in *La France libre*, ideology was not always used in a
pejorative sense. He agreed that ideologies, and even propaganda, could
retain a positive and desirable—rather than repressive—political role as
an effective means to mobilise popular masses. During the war, he hoped
the Western democracies would use ideological propaganda effectively to
boost public morale and bolster the fight against the Nazi enemy.[33] At the
same time his major concern remained shielding individual liberty from
the threats of tyrannical and totalitarian rule. The war was 'ideological'
because it represented a battle between different subjective systems of
political ideas, each claiming a universal validity. Each of the belligerent
parties envisaged a different political future for humanity: a Nazi world
empire, Soviet republic, or free liberal democratic states. After the war,

---

[29] Aron, *Paix et guerre*, pt. 4.

[30] Raymond Aron, 'L'âge des empires' (1945), in *Chroniques de guerre*, 981.

[31] E. H. Carr also used Mannheim's sociology of knowledge and critique of ideologies as instruments
in his political battle against 'idealism'. While Carr and Aron identified different threats to international
peace, both found inspiration in Mannheim's thought and appropriated it for their own ends. For an
account of Carr's interpretation of Mannheim, see Jones, *E. H. Carr and International Relations*, 122–135.

[32] Aron, *German Sociology*, 63.

[33] Aron, 'Démocratie et enthousiasme' (1942), in *Chroniques de guerre*, 649–660.

he underlined the lack of—and need for—a new political ideology in Europe to lift the masses from their indifference and overcome past conflicts.[34] Aron's attitude to ideologies was dialectical. Necessary but potentially disruptive ideologies inherently tended to seek a universal expression, compromising in consequence an important aspect of humanity: diversity.[35] Promoting a particular worldview as universal was indispensable for accumulating political power and realising the dream of transcending state monism, but by looking at the pluralistic world through a narrow partisan lens, the wider sense of politics could be lost to shallow propaganda.[36]

By the end of the decade, the irreducible opposition between the two ideologies had become evident and Aron's arguments became more polemical. He feared that Europe would be dragged into a global ideological battle, which would blur the distinction between the national and international and challenge the state's territoriality.[37] For Aron, this deterritorialisation of ideological conflict, operating locally and globally, emphasised the need to think about politics in overlapping spatial spheres.[38] He sought to ground world politics in specific historical political practices, against the indeterminate abstraction of universal ideologies. From his London-based perspective on world politics, Aron saw Britain as a leader in the long and complex development of democracy as a political form based on tolerance, pluralism, and individual freedom. Was liberalism another ideology with universal aspirations? Aron's answer was unclear. He had often claimed that liberalism was too tolerant to be considered an ideology, but suggested that it was the desirable alternative to communism in the ideological clash that would characterise the post-war world.[39]

The deterritorialisation of politics was an important theme in Mitrany's writings as well. In 1948, he crystallised his wartime political ideas in an article for *International Affairs*, where he identified an inherent contradiction between the ideology of national statehood that guided political order in Europe as well as in the colonial world and the rise of a new

[34] During the war, according to Aron, the ideologies more capable of mobilising the masses were the totalitarian ones. See Aron, 'Naissance des tyrannies'; Raymond Aron, 'L'Europe peut-elle devenir une unité politique?', *Terre d'Europe* 33 (1947): 12–21.

[35] Aron used the term 'dialectic' to describe his thought, yet emphasised that for him the dialectic usually lacked synthesis. At most, as he suggested, the third moment of the dialectic could be a 'critical reflection', not a solution. See Giulio De Ligio, 'Introduction', in *Raymond Aron, penseur de l'Europe et de la nation* (Brussels: P. Lang, 2012), 6–8.

[36] Aron's thought was not free of this contradiction: he denounced the European communist parties for their ideological dependence on the Soviet Union and political detachment from local reality, while at the same time upholding pluralism as a positive political value. See Aron, 'L'Europe peut-elle devenir une unité politique?', 15.

[37] Raymond Aron, *L'homme contre les tyrans* (Paris: Gallimard, 1946); Campbell, 'Raymond Aron', 551–553.

[38] Aron, 'L'âge des empires', 984.

[39] Raymond Aron, 'Victoire idéologique?', in *Chroniques de guerre*, 913; Anderson, *Raymond Aron*; Daniel J. Mahoney, *The Liberal Political Science of Raymond Aron: A Critical Introduction* (Lanham, MD: Rowman & Littlefield, 1992).

global trend of economic integration.[40] The problem was, in essence, the insurmountable tension between the ideology of national segregation that defined the existing political order and the concrete unity imposed by the economic conditions of the post-war world, or in other words 'the will for national distinctiveness and the need for social integration'.[41] In this clash between abstract ideas and material needs, Mitrany diagnosed that materiality would prevail over ideology, and suggested adapting the former to the latter.

Since Mitrany wanted to combat the conceptual rigidity and dogmatic foundation of ideology with a pragmatic materialistic scheme of political order, he did not engage in a philosophically sophisticated critique of ideologies. He defined ideology as a system of ideas and beliefs shared by a given society or social group. Like Aron, he was wary of the inherent totalising and universalising aspirations of ideological systems. In what he considered his best work, Mitrany denounced Marxism as a rigid and contradictory ideology that undermined social and cultural diversity by promoting ruthless urbanisation over existing agrarian structures in disregard of the practical and material needs of individuals.[42] The underlying message of his social history of agrarian Russia was that ideologies conceal their divisive qualities behind a façade of unity and progress. Ideologies were a potential source of conflict because they prioritised abstract concepts over practical concerns. Like other mid-century thinkers, including Jacques Maritain and Richard McKeon, Mitrany suggested that it would be easier to compromise and agree on common practical interests, such as a railway line, than to achieve a common ground between different ideological systems, such as capitalism and communism.[43] For this reason, he sought to focus his proposals for world order on the practical aspects of international organisation.

Nationalist ideologies, namely the protectionist and exclusive policies of the autarkic nation-states, generated for Mitrany international rivalry that could—and did—lead to world war. The state's failure to deliver on its social and economic promises and the increasingly global scale of economic and social interaction had contributed to the rising doubts about its effectiveness as a political unit. This view was shared by other internationally minded thinkers, like Lionel Robbins and E. H. Carr, who argued in 1945 that 'it is the failure of the nation-state to assure military security

[40] David Mitrany, 'The Functional Approach to World Organization', *International Affairs* 24 (1948): 350–363.
[41] Ibid., 354.
[42] David Mitrany, *Marx against the Peasant: A Study in Social Dogmatism* (London: Weidenfeld and Nicolson, 1951).
[43] David Mitrany to the editor of the *Manchester Guardian*, 2 February 1949, Mitrany Papers, box 77. On McKeon and Maritain, see chapters 6 and 8.

or economic wellbeing which has in part inspired the widespread questioning of the moral credentials of nationalism'.[44] In the same year, Mitrany expressed a similar idea in a letter to H. N. Brailsford: 'Perhaps the only difference is that you are a socialist and so assume that capitalism is the cause of international economic friction, while I am an internationalist and believe that national competition is a cause of international friction. . . . The more we have of national planning the more we must have international planning. . . . I fear that without such international coordination a planned national economy is likely to be even more ruthlessly competitive than was the capitalist national economy'.[45] The state was evidently more than an ideological construct. It represented real historical needs and desires that cannot be denied political expression.

Mitrany distinguished between 'nationality', the historical characteristics of a given society and a 'natural principle governing the formation of states', and 'nationalism', 'the extrovert political phenomenon' that suppresses other forms of expression. Nationalism was an ideological imposition, while nationality was a historical phenomenon.[46] Like Aron, Mitrany recognised the important historical function of nationality but levelled his criticism at the ideology of nationalism. This distinction wrapped, nonetheless, the idea of the nation in a cloud of conceptual ambiguity that did not help decide whether national policy was a legitimate political decision or an embodiment of a repressive nationalistic ideology.

The issue of social and economic planning on national and international scales reflects the difficulty of assessing the influence of ideology on political decision making. Aron's reflection on the progress of liberalism after the war received new impetus from the British public debate on social policy and planning that embodied for him an important moment in the development of liberalism.[47] Despite his reputation as an anticommunist, enhanced after the publication of Le grand schisme in 1948, he was not unsympathetic to some of the avowed aims of socialism.

Aron shared Élie Halévy's critique of totalitarianism as an ideology that limits human freedom, but wanted to depict a more nuanced picture of the impact of totalitarian ideologies on the freedom and well-being of individuals and societies.[48] Thus, he distinguished between the ideologies of Soviet communism, with its humanist aims, and Nazism, aimed at

---

[44] E. H. Carr, *Nationalism and After* (1945; repr., London: Macmillan, 1968), 38. On Lionel Robbins's analysis of national policies as a cause of war, see chapter 5.

[45] Extract from a letter from David Mitrany to H. N. Brailsford, n.d. 1945, Mitrany Papers, box 73.

[46] David Mitrany, 'Nationality and Nationalism' (1948), in *The Functional Theory of Politics* (London: London School of Economics, 1975), 139–140.

[47] See chapter 5 for a detailed discussion of the British debate on social planning and international order.

[48] Élie Halévy, *L'ère des tyrannies* (Paris: Gallimard, 1938).

power alone.[49] He argued that socialism and communism could have a humanistic goal, which the illiberal Soviet ideology failed to represent, and conceded that a degree of social planning beyond spontaneous individual action was necessary. In London, he observed the public discussions on welfare and reconstruction, especially after the publication of the Beveridge Report on the funding of the welfare state in Britain (1942).[50] Aron and Beveridge might have been introduced at the Reform Club or at the London School of Economics by their mutual friends Hayek and Robbins, yet there is no direct evidence for this. Nonetheless, Aron's writings make clear that he was well acquainted with the British efforts to address public claims for better living conditions. He considered this document, as well as other attempts to establish a state-run system of social welfare, as part of the political heritage of liberal Europe, and a positive phase in the progress of liberalism.[51]

Similarly, Mitrany argued that social planning was 'the first ideological programme to lead straight to international community without offending the traditional national liberal attitudes'.[52] He therefore suggested that a transnational ideological system based on need fulfilment would unite people where nationalist ideology divided them. The rise of public awareness of social rights was an important source of support for his scheme for international change. It motivated the foundation of the British Political and Economic Planning group of which Mitrany was a member.[53] Like many others, including the British economist and federalist Barbara Wootton, he thought that planning on a national level alone would not be sufficient to achieve the desirable social and economic change. Limited resources and national competition for markets set limits to social and economic growth and could also undermine international cooperation and pose a threat to world peace.[54]

Mitrany's arguments in favour of international planning were not based on utilitarian reason alone. He thought that individuals recognised the universal nature of their social demands. If the nation-states were to assume exclusive responsibility for addressing social demands, Mitrany feared that the tension between the universal claims and their local and limited realisation would become an unbearable moral strain on the individual. This

---

[49] In his later autobiography he marvelled at his younger self for not appreciating the totalitarian threat posed by Soviet Russia. Aron, *Memoirs*, 210–212.

[50] Aron, 'Victoire idéologique?', 914; Aron, 'Réformes', in *Chroniques de guerre*, 819; William H. Beveridge, *Social Insurance and Allied Services* (London: HMSO, 1942).

[51] Aron, 'Victoire idéologique?', 913.

[52] David Mitrany, 'Note on the New Nationalism and the New Internationalism', submitted to the Foreign Press Research Service, 3 October 1940, Mitrany Papers, box 7.

[53] On the PEP group, see Ritschel, *Politics of Planning*, 144–180.

[54] For a general discussion of national planning as a threat to peace, see Ashworth, *Creating International Studies*, 89–90.

idea, which Mitrany developed in 1949 in his speech at a conference on mental health and world unity, transfers the discussion of the repressive nature of nationalism and ideology to a different level. He argued that the parochial and exclusive nature of national politics, which encouraged social reform only within its boundaries, would not only cause wars and strife but would take its toll on individuals' mental health as well.[55]

The rational structure of Mitrany's functionalist system was aimed at addressing problems related to irrational aspects of human life, such as feelings, sentiments, and emotional stress. He discussed nationalist ideology as a mental illness that should be cured by building rational technical institutions. While the establishment of a rational international order was a goal that Aron and Mitrany shared, Aron was readier than Mitrany to accept that irrationality was not a human pathology (or a mental illness) but part of normal human life. Aron's rational strategy for international change was based on mobilising—not necessarily demolishing—the irrational and mythical aspects of politics to promote a liberal and pluralistic order.

The war experience, Mannheim's sociology of knowledge, and the political role of secular religions and myth led Aron to develop a multifaceted conception of human social interaction, based on the interplay of reason, emotions, and beliefs.[56] The spiritual aspect of social relations, the material conditions of politics, and rational decision making would all play a part, according to Aron, in shaping the post-war world order. Mitrany's attempt to rationalise politics through functional institutions was, thus, incompatible with Aron's approach that highlighted the intricate relations between the rational and the irrational in politics.

Aron accepted that morality was an important motivation for human political action, but—like irrationality—it should not become the guiding power in political discourse. These concerns emerge clearly in Aron's criticism of the Catholic philosopher Jacques Maritain, which I return to in chapter 8. Aron argued that Maritain was wrong in conflating politics and morality and demanding that a political leader should act according to high moral standards.[57] Whereas Maritain wanted to 'distinguish to unify', or in other words to highlight the difference between politics and morality in order to create a new model for moral political conduct, Aron adopted a more sceptical approach. He insisted on separating politics from morality, while accepting that ideas and beliefs—a secular religion—were

[55] David Mitrany, 'Mental Health and World Unity', paper delivered to the International Conference on Mental Hygiene, London, August 1949, Mitrany Papers, box 9.
[56] On Aron's concept of secular religions, see Iain Stewart, 'Raymond Aron and the Roots of the French Liberal Renaissance' (PhD thesis, University of Manchester, 2011), 89–96.
[57] Raymond Aron, 'Sur le machiavélisme, dialogue avec Jacques Maritain' (1982), *Commentaire* 8 (1985): 511–516. More on Aron and Maritain's interpretations of Machiavelli in chapter 8.

necessary components of the foundation of new political arrangements and communities. As we shall see, the interplay between rational order and irrational political impulses remained a critical part of Aron's and Mitrany's international thought in the 1940s.

THE STATE AND A NEW WORLD ORDER

Aron's temporary British viewpoint on European politics encouraged him to think seriously about international relations. He emphasised the need for a comprehensive, global framework to understand political events and evaluate the different powers governing the global and domestic spheres. World war, as well as technological advances, opened up the closed and self-contained political space of the nation-state, and helped Aron reflect on the interplay between internal and external politics. Assessing the new political challenges, he envisaged a new world order where appropriate political, military, economic, and cultural conditions guaranteed the survival and development of the existing states. His interest in international order might have emerged from his concern that France's existence as an independent liberal nation-state would be undermined by a constant threat of war.[58] However, his initial focus on France soon evolved into sustained thinking about the general prospects of global order.

The fundamental message of Aron's wartime international thought was scepticism about abstract and absolute political visions. He underlined the need to take historical heritage seriously when thinking about future political solutions. History—revealed in the stone ruins of the European cities as well as in the patrimony of ideas shared by political communities—would play an important part in defining the political reality of the postwar world.[59] Therefore, a rational, universalising vision of order, based on legal pacts or economic relations, could not take full account of the complexities of the individual and communal sense of identity expressed in the existing system of states. The abstract economic theories of his friends Jacques Rueff or Friedrich Hayek, who invited Aron to join the Mont Pèlerin Society, were the targets of Aron's criticism for their lack of historical specificity and knowledge.[60] Rather than scraping the world map clean and

[58] Richard Gowan correctly attributed the source of Aron's wartime pluralism to the French historians Renan and Thibaudet. Yet Gowan's analysis does not extend to Aron's pluralism in the international realm. Gowan, 'Raymond Aron, the History of Ideas and the Idea of France', *European Journal of Political Theory* 2 (2003): 395.

[59] Raymond Aron, 'Discours à des étudiants allemands sur l'avenir de l'Europe', *Table Ronde* 1 (1948): 63–86. Luigi Sturzo advanced similar historicist ideas; see chapter 8.

[60] In summer 1938, Aron met Hayek, Rueff, Ludwig von Mises, Michael Polanyi, and other liberal economists at the Colloque Walter Lippmann in Paris, where they sought to envisage a new form of liberal economy in opposition to both collectivism and laissez-faire. Aron argued that the theoretical premises

starting anew, Aron's dialectical approach reached to past traditions for legitimacy and inspiration for a new order.[61]

Would the nation-state remain a viable political unit in the post-war era? For Aron, the distinctive element of the victorious powers, the United States, the Soviet Union, and the British Empire, was their internal order as multinational states. They were heterogeneous political units that included a variety of nations, peoples, and communities. What mattered for Aron was not their large territorial scale, but their internal political and cultural diversity.[62] The political structure of the 'Wilsonian' nation-state, based on ethnic and cultural homogeneity and shared language and history, seemed to have come out of the war on the losing side. The universal political ideologies promoted by the large-scale multinational states—which Aron sometimes called 'empires'—would challenge the legitimacy of the nation-state as a political unit, and undermine the cultural and political diversity of the world.[63]

By the end of the war, Aron stopped counting the British Empire among the world powers.[64] This change suggested to him not only the emergence of a bipolar order and the decline of the state as a political form, but also, tragically, the removal of the West from the centre of world politics. Possibly, these tendencies could be halted if Europe were to become a world power alongside the United States and the Soviet Union in a tripolar regional system based on pluralism and cooperation. Evidently, a united Europe and the United States were, for Aron, two bulwarks against the totalitarian ideologies of the repressive imperial powers, which he associated with Nazi Germany and also with the Soviet Union.[65] The three world regions were ideologically, not geopolitically, distinct. The United States embodied the ideology of liberalism that was based on pluralism, tolerance, liberty, and democracy, and therefore was not a rigid universal dogma.[66] Thus, the United States could never be a repressive empire because

---

of many 'classic' economic thinkers did not stand the test of reality. He eventually retired from the Mont Pèlerin Society in the early 1950s. For Aron's criticism of liberal economics, see 'Les limites de la théorie économique classique', *Critique* 6 (1946): 515. On Aron's role in the Mont Pèlerin Society, see Dieter Plehwe, 'Introduction', in *The Road from Mont Pèlerin: The Making of the Neoliberal Thought Collective*, ed. Philip Mirowski and Dieter Plehwe (Cambridge, MA: Harvard University Press, 2009), 13; Burgin, *Great Persuasion*, 123–124.

[61] Raymond Aron, 'Destin des nationalités' (1943), in *Chroniques de guerre*, 608–621.

[62] Aron, 'L'âge des empires', 977. Carr expressed a similar idea in *Nationalism and After*, 38–40.

[63] Raymond Aron, 'Le partage de l'Europe', *Point de Vue*, 26 July 1945.

[64] Raymond Aron, 'Transformations du monde de 1900 à 1950: Déplacement du centre de gravité international', *Réalités* 47 (1949): 70–111, 111.

[65] Ibid. See also Aron, 'Pour l'alliance de l'occident', in *Chroniques de guerre*, 949–959, 950. The comparison with Hitler's Germany appears earlier on, in 1944–1945, while the critique of Soviet expansionism is stronger after 1947.

[66] In this sense Aron disagreed with Schmitt's claim that liberalism was a particular political and economic system oriented towards advancing British and American commercial interests around the world, which, by contrast, for Schmitt, the apparently tolerant liberalism concealed a reality of imperial

of the liberal democratic foundation of its constitution.[67] Liberal pluralism was also, for Aron, a distinct feature of the European political system.[68] If Europe's pluralistic heritage were to acquire the status of a global normative meta-value, the illiberal empires could be restrained and nationalistic ideologies could be suppressed.[69]

Great—and perhaps insurmountable—difficulties faced the European states, but Aron hoped that the tripolar order would announce a new era in the history of Europe, marked by relative independence from direct Soviet or American influence. Well-informed, liberal, and pluralistic political decision making could save Europe from becoming a pawn in a global bipolar order: an alliance or unification was the only way the European states could retain a meaningful role in the international sphere. By reappropriating their political responsibility, and accepting their active role in forging historical change, the peoples of Europe could redirect their political destiny.[70]

Yet there was an important caveat. Even if this utopian scenario of peaceful unification could be realised, Aron argued that war would be a permanent element of world politics. The defining principle of the post-war era was 'impossible peace, unlikely war'.[71] With this emblematic phrase Aron wanted to convey the message that political differences between the victorious powers could not be immediately overcome, but all sides were unwilling to engage in direct warfare again. For him, this principle would be the foundation of the precarious post-war stability, in which ideologies would struggle for greater influence without resorting to actual warfare.

The demise of the nation-state and of nationalism as a political ideology cast doubts on the idea that states should be the microcosmic embodiments of the universal principle of national self-determination.[72] Like

domination through legal and economic universalism. See Carl Schmitt, *The Nomos of the Earth in the International Law of the Jus Publicum Europaeum*, trans. G. L. Ulmen (1951; repr., New York: Telos Press, 2003), 172–177.

[67] Aron's description of liberal democracy as non-ideological, and thus of American intervention as non-imperial and benevolent, is a political statement rather than a theoretical claim. It is easy to argue that liberalism corresponds to Aron's own definition of ideology as 'a system of political ideas, representations, acts and beliefs oriented towards a certain political goal or vision'. Yet, as a supporter of Marshall Aid, Aron deemed it necessary to distinguish between some forms of foreign intervention and others, between Soviet imperialism and American generosity. See Aron, 'L'âge des empires', 983.

[68] Richard Gowan, 'Raymond Aron and the Problems of Sovereignty and Order in International Relations, 1940–1966' (MPhil thesis, University of Cambridge, 2002).

[69] Gowan, 'Raymond Aron, the History of Ideas and the Idea of France', 391. It seems, therefore, that Aron considered totalitarianism an exception rather than a result of the European political tradition of tolerance and pluralism.

[70] By the end of the war, Aron seems to have changed his mind about Europe's neutrality. In the context of the French post-war political debate, Aron's position rejected the neutral 'third way' solution that hoped France could remain independent from both Soviet and American influence. See Tony Judt, *Past Imperfect: French Intellectuals, 1944–1956* (New York: New York University Press, 2011), pt. 4.

[71] Raymond Aron, *Le grand schisme* (Paris: Gallimard, 1948), pt. 1, 14–25.

[72] Aron, 'L'âge des empires'.

Mitrany, Aron thought that the idea of 'nationality' was a necessary stabilising factor for the new world order, but it was no longer sufficient.
He never gave up on the nation-state structure, which he saw as the political representation of a distinct—if often incoherent or fragmentary—
historical political and cultural community. If the nation-state had a historical role, why was it an inappropriate political form for the post-war
era? Aron's treatment of this question was inconsistent, yet I infer from
his writings three possible responses that would be relevant to understand
Mitrany's thought as well.

First, the state's geographic scale influenced its economic and political
stability. In a smaller territorial state, Aron opined, insufficient quantity
or variety of natural and economic resources may undermine the polity's
resistance to crisis.[73] Some small states did not have the military means—
the resources, labour, and organisation—to effectively defend their independence. In this, he repeated earlier internationalist doubts about the
feasibility of small states in the age of empire.[74] Mitrany also agreed on
these points, and associated the critique of small states with 'international
realists' like Carr and Lippmann, who argued that 'some states were too
small for a progressive material life'.[75] A possible solution could be an
alliance or a federation of sorts, where small states could pool together
natural and financial resources and create a joint army.[76] However, both
Mitrany and Aron remained uncertain of the political viability and effectiveness of this scheme.

Second, in the post-war era the rivalry between the two great powers
dented the national sovereignty of smaller states, in particular regarding
the decision to declare and wage war. In 1947, Aron suggested that the
European states were not truly independent if their right to declare war
depended on American consent.[77] A European Union, he argued, would
have greater political leverage than the extant states in determining foreign policy. On this point, Mitrany doubted that a European federation
or union could provide the continent with a much stronger defence than
the NATO alliance or an alternative security pact between the European
states and the United States.[78]

Third, both Aron and Mitrany agreed that the most important reason for
the decline of the nation-state was the ideology of 'nationalism' rather than
the structure of the state. National policies like economic protectionism,

[73] Raymond Aron, *France and Europe* (Hinsdale, IL: Henry Regnery, 1949).
[74] Georgios Varouxakis, '"Great" versus "Small" Nations: Size and "National Greatness" in Victorian Political Thought', in Bell, *Victorian Visions of Global Order*, 136–158.
[75] David Mitrany, 'The Protection of Human Rights' (1947), in *Functional Theory of Politics*, 188.
[76] Aron, 'Transformations du monde', 70–72, 108–111; Aron, 'Victoire idéologique?'
[77] Raymond Aron, 'Conférence Sauvenniere (Loire), 5 August 1947, Semaine étudiantes internatio-nales', Raymond Aron Papers, Bibliothèque nationale de France, Paris, box 89.
[78] David Mitrany, 'Federalism or Functionalism' (1948), Mitrany Papers, box 73.

cultural homogeneity, exclusion, and discrimination were causes of international conflict and internal weakness. This approach suggests that Aron and Mitrany considered pluralism and diversity important political values in the post-war era, particularly relevant in an increasingly interconnected world.

Let me now examine in detail the influence of scale and ideology on the decline of the nation-state according to Aron and Mitrany. Aron's doubts about the political feasibility of small states emerged from the question of ideology rather than from a geopolitical reflection.[79] Larger states might have military and economic advantage in wartime, but for Aron the geopolitical criterion implied in 'la théorie des grands espaces', the theory of 'big spaces', was an insufficient framework to understand global politics: political or economic power did not depend exclusively on scale, or on territorial expansion. In January 1944, he wrote an essay calling for Western alliance, referring to the British geopolitician Halford Mackinder and his thesis of the Heartland, the large strategic land mass in Central-Eastern Europe. According to Mackinder, the power that would dominate the Heartland, a vast area of economic and political importance, would dominate the whole world.[80] For Aron the question was more complex, since political ideas and industrial potential had a deeper impact on world politics than geographic materiality. The question of scale and the viability of small states gave rise to a reflection on the deterritorialisation of politics. This seemed to Aron and Mitrany to be an increasingly relevant—and potentially dangerous—trend in world politics. In this framework, ideological concerns could prompt Continental Europe and maritime Britain to unite in a federation or alliance, despite their geopolitical differences.

Aron's treatment of the idea of the 'big space' highlights its ideological foundation: a 'big space' could become as powerful as Mackinder predicted if it promoted a universal, imperial ideology. The essence of Aron's rejection of this geopolitical category of political analysis was grounded in his wariness of its ideological implications. Mouric explains that Aron associated the theory of 'big spaces' with the German notion of Großraum, which emerged in Carl Schmitt's writings and served the political goals of the Nazi regime.[81] Despite a lack of direct evidence, we can assume that Aron was acquainted with Schmitt's early writings on world order;[82] however, it is worth bearing in mind that the direct reference is to the wider-spread

[79] For a geopolitical interpretation, see chapter 3.

[80] H. J. Mackinder, 'The Geographical Pivot of History', *Geographical Journal* 23 (1904): 421–437; Aron, 'Pour l'alliance de l'occident'.

[81] Mouric, *Raymond Aron et l'Europe*, 101.

[82] Carl Schmitt, *Land and Sea: A World-Historical Meditation*, trans. Samuel Garrett Zeitlin (1942; repr., Candor, NY: Telos, 2015). Aron might have been familiar with an earlier version, originally published in 1939, Carl Schmitt, *Völkerrechtliche Großraumordnung mit Interventionsverbot für raumfremde Mächte: Ein Beitrag zum Reichsbegriff im Völkerrecht* (repr., Berlin: Duncker Humblot, 1991).

geopolitical theories of Mackinder, and to later interpretations by the German geopolitician Karl Haushofer, whom Aron mentioned in his articles in *La France libre*. His opposition to geopolitics embodied, therefore, the idea that political problems were grounded in ideological questions, not geographical factors. The failure of the nation-state structure could not be explained merely by correlating geographical scale and political viability. It was the ideological doctrine of nationalism—characterised by exclusiveness, protectionism, and internal cultural and political homogeneity—that was 'too small' and limited for the global age.

Mitrany arrived at a similar conclusion via a different route. Like Aron he predicted the deterritorialisation of politics in the age of universal ideologies and global economic relations. His solution was not to replicate on a world scale a territorially and historically specific political heritage, like liberal pluralism, but rather to 'break away from traditional political theory, which always linked social activity to some fixed political jurisdiction'.[83] Geopolitical discussions were, for him, too ideological to bring about political change on a global scale. By imagining spheres of influence, strategic frontiers, and regional unity, geopolitical theories projected political and ideological desires on the physical world.

In an attempt to make frontiers politically meaningless, Mitrany turned away from the territorial expression of political order and focused on a global network of deterritorialised administrative agencies. His theory of functional arrangements aimed at transferring some public activities, especially in the social and economic sphere, from the territorial political unit to an international deterritorialised and non-ideological organisation.[84] He responded to the challenge of ideology—and in particular nationalism—by bringing to the fore what he considered to be ideology-free elements of political life: practical human 'needs'. The continuous and fruitless political contentions would be replaced with economic or 'functional' interaction based on specific aspects of public life in which different international players would have a common interest in cooperating.[85]

Like other liberal internationalists, Mitrany pointed to national sovereignty and nationalist ideology as the greatest obstacles to international cooperation.[86] Yet he agreed with E. H. Carr that 'power' was to remain a central part of world politics. Peaceful international cooperation through political debate had little chances of success due to the overarching impact

[83] David Mitrany to François Perroux, 1 December 1948, Mitrany Papers, box 76.
[84] Mitrany, *Working Peace System*, 19–40.
[85] For general discussions about the influence of Mitrany's functionalism on the European Union, see, for example, Martin J. Dedman, *The Origins and Development of the European Union, 1945–95: A History of European Integration* (London: Routledge, 1996); Brent F. Nelsen and Alexander C.-G. Stubb, *The European Union: Readings on the Theory and Practice of European Integration* (London: Palgrave, 2003).
[86] On Mitrany's theory in relation to liberal internationalist ideas of sovereignty, see Ashworth, *Creating International Studies*, 80–91.

of divisive national interests. Understanding power meant, for him, taking into account the pragmatic and ever-changing conditions of political interaction and constructing a system that would be immune to ideological disagreements. A federation based on a transnational constitution would be too rigid to deal effectively with dynamic global power relations. The new system would have to accommodate the constantly shifting political and economic power relations in the global sphere without resorting to ideological arguments or relying on constitutional constraints.[87]

The solution to the challenge of the post-war world was a pragmatic system of 'shared' or 'pooled' sovereignty, which would give rise to a global network of agencies whose responsibility was to manage various social, economic, and technical activities on a world scale.[88] Mitrany was not interested in debunking the existing system of national states because he recognised their political and historical rationale. Instead, he wanted to move away from debates about national political ideology by constructing a network of technical organisations responsible for addressing a specific 'need' like transport, natural resources, trade, agriculture. Some of these agencies had already existed, especially in the fields of communications, transport, and commerce, and could be the models for future arrangements.[89] Although he was not the only promoter of 'functionalist' solutions, Mitrany doubtlessly became one of the most vociferous and influential speakers for this cause.[90]

Functionalism was, for Mitrany, an incremental plan for the establishment of a global system of multilayered authorities involving states, economic agencies, corporations, and administrative organisations. While some degree of unity and political agreement would be necessary for the operation of the system, he thought that by distributing political power across a wide array of state and non-state agencies he could shield individual freedom from the disruptive influence of national ideologies. On this point, Carr wrote to Mitrany in 1943, commending him for his theory of functional organisation, but doubting that functionalism could replace the 'awkward fact of nationalism' with international cooperation.[91] Mitrany responded that nationalism was a 'bundle of interests and sentiments', which he hoped to control and mitigate—rather than replace—by focusing on the practical aspects of cooperation.[92]

[87] Mitrany, 'Protection of Human Rights', 187–190.

[88] Mark F. Imber, 'Re-reading Mitrany: A Pragmatic Assessment of Sovereignty', *Review of International Studies* 10 (1984): 103–123; Cornelia Navari, 'David Mitrany and International Functionalism', in Wilson and Long, *Thinkers of the Twenty Years' Crisis*, 214–246.

[89] Mitrany, *Working Peace System*, 28–29.

[90] Lucian Ashworth discusses other contemporary functionalist thinkers, including Mary Parker Follett and G. D. H. Cole. See 'A New Politics for a Global Age: David Mitrany's *A Working Peace System*', in Bliddal, Sylvest, and Wilson, *Classics of International Relations*, 59–68.

[91] E. H. Carr to David Mitrany, 18 May 1943, Mitrany Papers, box 62.

[92] Mitrany to Carr, 19 May 1943, Mitrany Papers, box 62.

One of the key advantages of the functionalist order was, for Mitrany, its political and cultural pluralism. The idea of functionalism was not married to any historically or geographically situated political and economic system. For Mitrany, functionalism was compatible with pluralism because its institutional structure could accommodate diverse political and economic systems. Aron was similarly concerned with defending pluralism, as a dialogue-based political project facilitated by the creation of institutional spaces to guarantee individual liberty by the rule of law. He adopted, however, a different interpretation of the implication of pluralism on the global sphere. Aron opposed the growing interwar tendency to use 'cultures' or 'civilisations' as rigid and stable meta-historical building blocks for historical narrative and political analysis.[93] For him, the universal histories of Oswald Spengler and Arnold J. Toynbee were grounded in an antiquated nineteenth-century mind-set that assumed that an abstract, universal political category could help understand human history. Their philosophies of history promoted a seemingly pluralistic approach that denied the West any claim to superiority or primacy. However, Aron criticised their attempt to narrate a universal history that encompassed all cultures, civilisations, and epochs in one evaluative framework. From his viewpoint, they not only sinned by ignoring the incoherence and diversity of human existence, but also failed to recognise the impossibility of their position as historians. They claimed objectivity but were in fact bound by historical contingency and intellectual bias.

Aron directed at universal histories the same criticism he levelled at Mannheim's philosophy of knowledge: pluralism implied not only diverse positions but also the lack of universal synthesis. It is, therefore, possible that Aron could have criticised Mitrany's functionalism with a similar argument. Despite the explicit support for pluralism, functionalism depended on the idea that the whole world, with its diverse cultures and traditions, could become part of one coherent and complex system of international agencies. Moreover, it assumed that humanity as a whole could agree on the definition and the means of provision of practical needs, which Mitrany had never clearly defined. While both Aron and Mitrany recognised the tensions between pluralism and order in the post-war era, Mitrany's attempt to reconcile them through a universal principle of functionality was, for Aron, an impossible synthesis.

---

[93] Aron, 'La philosophie de l'histoire', 35–36; Arnold Toynbee, *A Study of History*, ed. Edward D. Myers (London: Oxford University Press, 1934). Toynbee influenced the historical understanding of Owen Lattimore, as well as Carl Schmitt. Oswald Spengler, *The Decline of the West* (1922; repr., New York: Knopf, 1939); Hans W. Weigert, 'Oswald Spengler, Twenty-Five Years After', *Foreign Affairs* 21 (1942): 120.

EUROPE, UNITED AND DIVIDED

During the war, many British political commentators and international thinkers were concerned with the question of European unity.[94] Schemes for federal union became increasingly popular.[95] In this context, Mitrany's functionalism emerged as an alternative to federalism, which he rejected on the basis of his critique of ideology. 'The very number and variety of federal proposals', he wrote in 1948, 'shows that they are not based on any self-evident grouping and self-evident will to unite'.[96] Even if a common political ground, such as a shared belief in liberal democracy or Anglo-American supremacy, could be found, Mitrany feared that a transnational federation based on 'ideology', in his terms, would merely enhance political conflicts in the world. As an example, he referred to one of the best-known proposals for 'liberal democratic federation' advanced by the American journalist Clarence Streit. For Mitrany, this idea of uniting the Western European democracies, Britain, the dominions, and the United States in a federal state was deliberately created as a political and strategic project to defeat the illiberal powers. Mitrany sought an international scheme that would promote world peace, rather than reinforce some powers in the case of a third world war.[97] To his mind, this federation would give rise only to ideologically fuelled international rivalry, preparing the ground for another major international conflict.[98] Mitrany was less than certain that the constitutions of the European states were homogeneous enough to permit easy unification, and suggested that some of Europe's problems, such as economic development and military defence, could be addressed by co-operative action involving various European states, which did not require a federal union.[99] Thus, the question of Europe could be understood by Mitrany only in the context of his system of international agencies to coordinate and administrate specific human needs. He saw no need to imagine Europe as a political entity through a translation of the political imaginary of nationalism into a regional scale.

The political imagery of Europe was, however, a key feature in the continent's political future, according to Aron. He turned to the question of

---

[94] For a detailed discussion, see, for example, Wilson, 'New Europe Debate in Wartime Britain'.

[95] See chapters 4, 5, and 6 for detailed discussion of two proposals for a regional or world federation.

[96] Mitrany, 'Federalism or Functionalism'.

[97] Mitrany's criticism was directed at the famous proposal put forward by the American journalist Clarence Streit to unite all Western democracies in a federation. Clarence K. Streit, *Union Now: A Proposal for a Federal Union of the Democracies of the North Atlantic* (New York: Harper, 1939). More on this in chapter 4.

[98] Mitrany, 'Functional Approach to World Organization'. In particular, see the summary following Mitrany's presentation at Chatham House, and Lionel Curtis's comments on the viability of functionalism and federalism, ibid., 360–363.

[99] Mitrany, *Working Peace System*, 3–18.

European unity after July 1941, when the topic emerged in a discussion with Robbins and Hayek at the Reform Club in London.[100] Throughout the following decade, he sought new formulas to redefine Europe as a pluralistic political unit. Like Mitrany he considered a European political federation premature and unrealistic: the existing states would not give up their independence and their national distinctiveness for an ill-defined federal project. Moreover, he pointed out the lack of political community to support and even justify European unity. He recognised the value of such an enterprise, but argued that a European alliance, federation, or confederation remained improbable because of the continent's historical attachment to the pluralistic political structure of the nation-states.[101] These tensions, typical of Aron's international thought in the 1940s, divided later scholars into those who saw him as a European sceptic, those who reaffirmed his pro-unity positions, and those who identified his prime interests in the recovery of France.[102] While he cautiously supported European unity in the early 1940s, by the end of the decade Aron accepted that Europe would not challenge the emergence of bipolarity as the third world power, alongside the United States and the Soviet Union.[103] Nonetheless, his idea of Europe illustrates the core elements of his international thought: globalism, pluralism, and political myth.

The fundamental premise of Aron's idea of Europe was that post-war politics would be conducted on a global, not continental, scale. There would no longer be a 'concert of Europe' but a 'planetary concert' in which Europe's role was still undefined.[104] The transition from European to 'planetary' or global order implied, therefore, the political marginalisation of Europe, which needed to regain its clear political voice before it could attain a leadership position.[105] Using Hegelian terminology, Aron argued that Europe had never existed as a political entity 'per se', indicating the lack of self-consciousness of European unity among the continent's states.[106] Yet, he assumed that the 'concert of Europe' was an effective politico-juridical transnational organisation, and that the political order it embodied was distinctly 'European'. The comparison of the European

---

[100] According to Aron's own recollection of this conversation in Aron, *Memoirs*, 229.

[101] Aron, 'L'Europe peut-elle devenir une unité politique?'

[102] There has been a growing interest in recent years in Aron's idea of Europe. While de Lapparent depicts him as a Europhile, most other scholars agree that he was sceptical of, or indeed opposed to, European integration. See Mouric, *Raymond Aron et l'Europe*; Nicolas Baverez, *Raymond Aron: Un moraliste au temps des idéologies* (Paris: Flammarion, 1993); Giulio De Ligio, *Raymond Aron, penseur de l'Europe et de la nation*; Olivier de Lapparent, *Raymond Aron et l'Europe: Itinéraire d'un européen dans le siècle* (Bern: P. Lang, 2010).

[103] Aron, 'Transformations du monde', 75–77.

[104] Aron repeated this idea many times, for example in 'La menace des césars' (1942), in *Chroniques de guerre*, 584–595; 'Transformations du monde', 71; *Le grand schisme*, 26.

[105] Georges-Henri Soutou, 'Was There a European Order in the Twentieth Century? From the Concert of Europe to the End of the Cold War', *Contemporary European History* 9 (2000): 329–353.

[106] Aron, 'Discours à des étudiants allemands'.

concert and the post-war global order reflects two of his political assumptions. First, if the goal of the Vienna system was the preservation of the ancien régimes, and not only war prevention, Aron reasoned that the global order would maintain the supremacy of the United States and the Soviet Union unless a third power were to emerge.[107] Second, the Vienna system created a political order based on political agreement between a few strong states, leaving the rest of the world in their periphery. Aron hoped to counter this tendency by constructing a new European system based on public *awareness* of the necessity and value of unity as the basis for military and economic cooperation and eventually a European political decision-making body.[108]

The argument that a shared 'political myth' was an indispensable condition for the revival of Europe became more explicit in Aron's writings of the 1970s, but it was present in his earlier writings as well.[109] He thought that intellectuals should be given the task of creating a sentimental and rational awareness of the shared identity of 'Europe' as a political unit. However, as long as the 'myth of Europe' was absent, European unity remained an artificial Hobbesian project, which Aron in fact excluded for lack of a self-conscious European community.

The political notion of a 'myth' has a long and complex genealogy: the term reappears in political philosophy in various historical moments from Plato to the crisis of rational individualism of the early twentieth century.[110] It would therefore be necessary to understand what kind of 'myth' Aron was referring to, and what its political purchase might be in his vision of world order. Giulio De Ligio suggested that Aron borrowed Georges Sorel's idea that a political myth could effectively mobilise people into action, even without a foundation in historical reality.[111] In the 1940s Sorel became known as the 'posthumous father' of Italian fascism, a political movement founded largely on the mystical and passionate attachment of the individual to the Fascist Party.[112] Thus, the post-war era saw an intellectual rejection of the notion of 'myth', as some identified an intellectual

---

[107] Raymond Aron, 'De la violence à la loi', in *Chroniques de guerre*, 661–666.

[108] Aron, 'Les limites de la théorie économique classique'; Aron, 'Pour l'alliance de l'occident', 958.

[109] Aron's best-known discussion of ideology and political myth is *The Opium of the Intellectuals*, trans. Terence Kilmartin (1955; repr., New Brunswick, NJ: Transaction, 2001), but earlier he discussed ideologies in the context of political myth; for example, see Raymond Aron, 'Europe avenir d'un mythe', *Cahiers Européens* 3 (1975): 8–10; Aron, 'L'Europe peut-elle devenir une unité politique?'

[110] For a general discussion of political myth, see Chiara Bottici, *A Philosophy of Political Myth* (Cambridge: Cambridge University Press, 2010); Antonio Martore, 'Mito', in *Enciclopedia del pensiero politico. Autori, concetti, dottrine*, ed. Roberto Esposito and Carlo Galli (Rome: Laterza, 2005), 545.

[111] Giulio De Ligio, 'Introduzione. La dialettica europea e la vita in comune', in Raymond Aron, *Il destino delle nazioni, l'avvenire dell'Europa* (Soveria Mannelli: Rubbettino, 2013). On Sorel's political myth, see Marco Gervasoni, *Georges Sorel: una biografia intellettuale* (Milan: Unicopli, 1997); Willy Gianinazzi, *Naissance du mythe moderne: Georges Sorel et la crise de la pensée savante, 1889–1914* (Paris: Les Editions de la Maison des sciences de l'homme, 2006).

[112] Jack J. Roth, 'The Roots of Italian Fascism: Sorel and Sorelismo', *Journal of Modern History* 38 (1967): 30–45.

link between the individual attachment to irrationality and passionate sentiments and the mass violence that characterised fascism.

The successful usage of political myth by the fascist regimes during the war revealed to Aron their potential role in forming a cohesive political community. As Chiara Bottici shows, it is not always easy to distinguish analytically between Aron's conceptions of 'ideology' and 'myth'. Despite his discussion of the negative implications of political myth as an ideology in *The Opium of the Intellectuals*, in the 1940s he developed a relatively positive interpretation of the myth of European unity, which was not inherently or inevitably aggressive and totalitarian.[113] In Europe, political myth was instrumental to creating rational and emotional bonds between individuals as the basis for a common political project. Aron was aware of the risk that a political myth would provoke violence, but hoped to avert this scenario by insisting on the vaguely defined value of political moderation. Moderation entails, in this case, an awareness of the repressive and uncontrollable aspects of the irrational political myth. Furthermore, Aron invited the people to participate in building the foundational myth of European unity, rather than leaving the task to leaders alone. In a speech to German students in 1947, Aron argued against 'external education', and suggested that 'internal transformation' would lead to a common future for Europe. By this, he meant that European identity should be voluntarily and individually constructed around a unifying historical narrative, told through Europe's idiosyncratic interpretations of science, truth, and liberty. If every individual were to participate in constructing the European myth through collective grassroots storytelling, Sorel's violent mythology would be 'domesticated' and channelled towards peaceful aims.[114]

The use of history to construct this sense of belonging is symbolic because Aron's political myth did not require a truthful historical foundation. Aron did not base political myth on primordial elements of human social and psychological existence, but, like the sociologists Émile Durkheim and Marcel Mauss, he emphasised the socially constructed functionality of the myth over its historical or physiological 'truthfulness'. Inspired by the Italian philosopher and sociologist Vilfredo Pareto, Aron argued that the individual was not a purely rational being: emotions, passions, and irrational preferences shaped individual and group identities and were instrumental in directing political action.[115] Political myth had the heuristic potential to reinforce the already recognised rational need for European unity.

---

[113] On Aron's negative interpretation of political myth as ideology, see Bottici, *Philosophy of Political Myth*, 186–187.

[114] Aron, 'Discours à des étudiants allemands', 70–84.

[115] Vilfredo Pareto, *Trattato di sociologia generale* (Florence: G. Barbèra, 1916); Stuart L. Campbell, 'The Four Paretos of Raymond Aron', *Journal of the History of Ideas* 47 (1986): 287–298.

The myth was located somewhere beyond the reach of rationality because its functionality depended on its capacity to invoke emotions and passions. While Aron was more confident about the possibility to mitigate the negative and violent impulses of the emotion-based political myth, Mitrany's world order aimed at restricting the space of irrationality in politics. He acknowledged that practical aspects of politics were 'wrapped up' in sentiment or myth, which could, ideally, serve as their justification in the ideological political system.[116] Nonetheless, he was persuaded that myth should be expunged and replaced by practical reason. Since his functionalism aimed at rationalising human interaction on the basis of objective, quantifiable, and scientifically measured human needs, the idea of a political myth of Europe would be completely incongruent with his scheme.

Reason, in Mitrany's interpretation, emerged in opposition to abstract theorisation and to sentimental convictions. It was the embodiment of the calculating common sense, which aimed to attain the best result with the available means. He would have doubted the viability of Aron's attempt to distinguish positive myth from negative ideology. Instead of instrumentalising political myth to promote his own functional agenda, Mitrany aimed at mitigating its impact and emphasising the rational and practical aspects of international cooperation. The idea that a federation could be a viable solution to Europe's problems was, for Mitrany, another myth: an irrational and impractically utopian project. A European sense of belonging was a form of regional nationalism that would merely replicate the destructive exclusionary sentiment of nationalism on a larger geopolitical scale.

In his speech on mental health and world unity, Mitrany discussed nationalism and national sentiments in terms of a mental illness that should concern psychiatrists and psychologists. It would be irresponsible to induce more political and psychological disorder by constructing a new sentimental political myth. Reason was a universal quality shared by all human beings, and could therefore provide the practical approach to overcome the disorder of nationalism and ideology.

The discussion of ideology and global order highlights the different approaches of Mitrany and Aron regarding the precedence of institutions over ideas, and of political elites over grassroots action. Lucian Ashworth suggests that for Mitrany popular consent to the functional system would follow the establishment of international organisations. It was a mirror image of Aron's argument that ideas must precede institutions and organisations. Emphasising the practical aspects of politics, Mitrany wanted to establish international institutions first, and build the global sense of belonging later. The efficacy of the functional system would—hopefully—be sufficient for

---

[116] Mitrany to Carr, 19 May 1943; Mitrany, 'Mental Health and World Unity', 2.

buttressing public support, without resorting to irrational notions like political myth.[117]

An important common aspect of the global visions of Aron and Mitrany was their reliance on political elites as revolutionising agents. For Mitrany the technocratic, corporative and administrative elites would guide the establishment of function-based experts-led agencies across the world. Aron suggested that Europe's intellectuals would play a key role in shaping the political myth on which the continent's unification would be based.[118] The elites should be initiators of political unity in Europe but should not hold an exclusive or disproportionate representative power in the European institutions. Unlike Mitrany, who suggested that the legitimacy of global order would be measured by its success in bringing about peace and prosperity, Aron thought that political legitimacy depended on participation and representation.[119] Yet he left the tension between legitimising popular sovereignty and elite leadership unresolved. If a top-down vision of European political unity had no popular purchase, Aron had little faith in the viability of bottom-up transformation. Evidently, he was impressed by the experience of German and Italian totalitarianism, where mass participation in politics was compromised by manipulative propaganda. Despite the importance he gave to legal, political, and economic institutions in his teachings at the École Nationale d'Administration, the Collège de France, and Sciences Po, in his wartime writings he did not describe the institutional mechanisms to put forth the European myth. His vision of politics in the 1940s was based on the contradictions of power and ideology, elites and grassroots, unity and independence. Only human decision could find a possible, partial reconciliation of these dialectics: the attempt to formulate this decision was for Aron the essence and meaning of politics.

E. H. CARR AND POLITICAL ORDER IN THE GLOBAL AGE

The similar assumptions of Aron and Mitrany about the need to conceptualise the future of the nation-state in a global order concealed a fundamental disagreement about the sense of politics and international relations. Both aimed at preserving the nation-state as a realm of diversity and particularism in a pluralistic world and opposed the universalising tendencies

[117] Ashworth, *Creating International Studies*, 92–94.
[118] Raymond Aron, 'Social Structure and the Ruling Class: Part 1', *British Journal of Sociology* 1 (1950): 1–16. There Aron stated that 'by elite I mean the minority which in any society performs the function of ruling the community'. See also discussion of élites in Raymond Aron, 'États démocratiques et états totalitaires' (1939), reprint in Aron, *Penser la liberté, penser la démocratie* (Paris: Gallimard, 2005), 69–71.
[119] Lacroix, '"Borderline Europe"'.

of political ideologies. But these contemporaneous efforts to defend the state in a changing global order embodied different understandings of the goals and practices of the state as a political unit. The state was valuable, for Aron, as a historical site of controlled conflict through which individual and communal identities could emerge. The state could not be transcended without risking the loss of these human political identities. Mitrany, in contrast, sought to use rational 'functional relations' to defend the social community from disruptive conflicts.

The deterritorialisation of politics implied that the state lost its political primacy as an order-generating political form. Mitrany embraced this tendency and proposed that 'sovereignty should be linked to a specific activity, not to territory'.[120] He wanted to reconfigure the division of political functions between territorial and non-territorial units. His political order was based on two overlapping systems: the historical Western system of independent states extended to the colonial world as well, and a technical, experts-led global network of agencies with specific limited responsibilities. Yet this mechanical division of different aspects of government along 'functional' lines and the detachment of legitimacy from citizenship was evidently incompatible with Aron's view of the post-war order as global political space based on the principles of democracy and liberalism.[121]

Aron saw politics as the art of decision making in a permanent state of conflict. Rational and irrational means could be employed to attain a common—necessarily rational—goal. Political action, whether cooperative or belligerent, necessitated both elite leadership and grassroots support. Perhaps inspired by Schmitt, Aron suggested that political decision making touched every aspect of human life; it could be improved, but not avoided. It would therefore be impossible to transfer some aspects of government to a separate global network of nonpolitical agencies, where decisions would, purportedly, be taken without resorting to conflictual interaction.

Mitrany did not deny that politics was a sphere of debate, conflict, and war. However, for him, other aspects of human relations, especially economics and social interaction, could be governed independently from the realm of politics. Thus, in order to promote cooperation, he looked away from politics towards less belligerent activities, focusing on the idea that other forms of human interaction could complement and maybe eventually replace political relations. Mitrany compared the task of the interna-

---

[120] Mitrany, *Working Peace System*, 49.

[121] For the mid-century intellectual exchanges of Aron and Schmitt, see Jan-Werner Müller, 'Vision of Global Order in a "Posteuropean Age". Carl Schmitt, Raymond Aron and the Civil Servant of the World Spirit', *Ricerche di storia politica* 2 (2004): 205–226; Daniel Steinmetz-Jenkins, 'Why Did Raymond Aron Write That Carl Schmitt Was Not a Nazi? An Alternative Genealogy of French Liberalism', *Modern Intellectual History* 11 (2014): 549–574.

tionalist to a psychologist who diagnoses human irrationality and seeks to limit it through treatment and medication. He recognised the irrational aspects of political life, such as nationalism, ideology, and myth, and thought they could be overcome by building rational global structures.

Aron would have opposed Mitrany's proposal to refashion global politics by focusing on scientific research and administrative consensus as rational and therefore 'neutral' modes of organising the international sphere. No expert could formulate a report to dissolve the tension between competing political ideologies. Aron did not try to deny the role of irrationality in politics, but hoped to channel the sentiments and passions towards a politically desirable end, which in the 1940s would have been European unity. He warned against the attempt to expunge political interaction from the public space, and argued that political discussion based on the precepts of Western liberal democracy—tolerance, the rule of law, individual rights, and parliamentary institutions—could create a secure, perhaps peaceful, equilibrium between different ideological systems.

The main difference between the visions of Aron and Mitrany can be seen in their founding principle: for Aron global or regional cooperation could emerge only from a shared belief in the political functions of myth or ideology. For Mitrany, practical and functional institutions could promote political cooperation, while ideas were of secondary importance. Although the two thinkers wanted to defend the centrality of the state as a unit of political organisation in the post-war world, they disagreed on the means of embedding the state in the global context, thus emphasising their diverse interpretations of politics.

In 1945, E. H. Carr published a short book titled *Nationalism and After*. The book included an historical analysis of the origins of nationalism and the nation-state, as well as a discussion of the 'prospects of internationalism'. The book followed a seminar he co-chaired at Chatham House, in which he discussed the adequacy of the nation-state and nationalism in the post-war era and sought to reconceptualise the state to prevent its decline.[122] He recognised the economic and political shortfalls of the nation-state, but doubted that a world state would be a viable alternative. Rejecting Wendell Willkie's popular slogan 'one world' as the foundation of a new world order, Carr suggested that establishing an intermediate level of political and nonpolitical organisation, between the national and the universal spheres, was the appropriate solution for safeguarding the state in a global political order. His idea of a 'functional' rather than national basis for international affairs resonates with Mitrany's proposal, which he had read and appreciated.[123]

---

[122] Jonathan Haslam, *The Vices of Integrity: E. H. Carr, 1892–1982* (London: Verso, 2000), 117.

[123] Carr, *Nationalism and After*, 47–48; E. H. Carr, 'The Moral Foundations of World Order', in *Foundations for World Order*, ed. E. L. Woodward et al. (Denver, CO: University of Denver Press, 1949), 70–75. For a discussion of Willkie's universalism, see chapter 4.

At the same time, Carr shared Aron's sensitivity to the important role of conflict in world politics and to the rise of the great multinational powers to world supremacy after the war. He envisaged a world order in which three or four vast multinational regional 'civilisations' would dominate world politics. Among these he included the United States, the Soviet Union, China, and Britain. Like Aron, Carr argued that Britain should establish closer relations with Western Europe, in order 'to gain a place among the great multi-national civilisations'.[124]

Carr's analysis sheds light on the similarities and differences of the global thought of Mitrany and Aron. His idea of defending the nation-state by establishing an intermediate organisational level between the state and the global echoes their wartime proposals. Like Aron, Carr predicted that the post-war world would be organised in large, multinational regional units, and thought that Europe needed a degree of unity to obtain a position of power. He agreed with Mitrany that a new global or multinational level of functional organisation could complement the political authority of the state, but opined that functional agencies could not be considered nonpolitical since their authority depended on the political decisions of states. Yet, he suggested that to achieve peace and order the world 'may have to put up with a certain salutary make-believe', and pretend that functional organisations were politically and ideologically neutral.[125] In a sense, Carr shared Aron's awareness of the omnipresence of conflict and debate in human life but conceded that the best possible way out of the international impasse could be based on economic or social rather than political or ideological interests.

Carr's ideas highlight the difficulty of assessing the relationship between ideology and the territoriality of politics. Mitrany, Aron, and Carr recognised the displacement of territoriality by ideology as one of the trends of their time and a possible threat to the world's political structure.[126] However, they were in disagreement on how this tendency affected politics. In the 1940s, Aron warned against the rise of totalitarian and abstract universal ideologies, and discussed a regional order in Europe in an effort to ground politics in a specific and localised historical heritage.[127] Mitrany, by contrast,

---

[124] Carr, 'Moral Foundations of World Order', 72.

[125] Carr, *Nationalism and After*, 49.

[126] The replacement of territoriality by ideology as the defining aspect of politics is suggested in a different context by Neil Smith, *American Empire: Roosevelt's Geographer and the Prelude to Globalization* (Berkeley: University of California Press, 2003), chap. 16.

[127] It is worth noting that a decade later Aron advanced the theory of the 'end of ideology'. Aron, *Opium of the Intellectuals*; 'Fin de l'âge idéologique?', in *Max Horkheimer zum 60. Geburtstag gewidmet, Sociologica Aufsätze*, ed. Theodor Adorno and Walter Dirks (Frankfurt: Europäische Verlagsanstalt, 1955), 219–233. Among the supporters of the end of ideologies thesis, see Daniel Bell, *The End of Ideology: On Exhaustion of Political Ideas in the Fifties* (London: Glencoe, 1960). For a general discussion, see Bottici, *Philosophy of Political Myth*, 186.

thought that the deterritorialisation of politics would favour the establish-ment of functional organisations, which could address the shortcomings of the nation-states. He hoped to establish a parallel dimension of interna-tional cooperation, juxtaposed with the political dimension of ideological conflict. Carr appreciated the role of ideas in politics and the universal aspi-rations of the American and Soviet ideologies.[128] However, like Mitrany, he took a pragmatic approach, convinced that rational political organisation, reinforced by some 'make-believe' and political strategy, could undermine the negative influence of ideological conflict. In this sense, Carr's ideas can be seen as a middle-way approach between Aron and Mitrany, but his at-tempt to reconcile functional organisations with political power also helps to elucidate the challenges of thinking about the position of the state in the global age.

[128] Compare to the interpretation of Carr's reflection on ideology in Haslam, *Vices of Integrity*, 105.

CHAPTER 3

Geopolitics and Regional Order

DURING AND AFTER the Second World War, many geopolitical thinkers in the United States developed their visions of post-war world on the basis of a new sense of the world as a compact, small, closed-space geographic system.[1] For them, the novel awareness of the proximity of states and their close interconnectedness had a significant impact not only on military strategy but also on visions of post-war order. What would be the future of the existing empires and colonies in this new global system? Could democracy be exported worldwide? Should the United States become a world leader, and if so, what vision should it propose? I argue that cartographic representations, geographic knowledge, and geopolitical concepts played a significant role in shaping 1940s visions of globalism as a response to the post-imperial age.

Mid-century American international thinkers used spatial concepts to outline the post-war political map and envisage the role of the United States in it. Geopolitics, which they understood as the dynamic, ever-changing interaction between political government and natural geography, provided both research questions and interpretative tools. Importantly, geopolitical concepts informed their interpretation of democracy, and its relations to the existing imperial order. These geopoliticians would have shared Starr's view that 'geography affects changing perceptions of the possibilities and probabilities provided by the geographic environment'.[2] Spatial representations revolving around a dynamic and complex notion of geopolitics were gaining popularity among scholars of world politics, who used a wide variety of cartographic projections to illustrate their claims about the flexibility and mutability of world order.[3] Cartographic innovations provided new viewpoints on the world that represented it as a compact and closed space, and set the foundation for the theoretical rise of geography and geopolitics

[1] Alan K. Henrikson, 'The Map as an "Idea": The Role of Cartographic Imagery during the Second World War', *American Cartographer* 2 (1975): 19–53.
[2] Starr, 'On Geopolitics'.
[3] Henrikson, 'The Map as an "Idea"', 23.

in the study of international relations. As I suggest in the conclusion, despite offering new conceptual categories for the analysis of world politics, geopolitics did not become the intellectual cornerstone of post-war discipline of International Relations.[4] Nonetheless, my exploration of mid-century geopolitics will shed light on a central debate in the United States that touched upon fundamental aspects of world order—democracy, empire, American leadership—and had a long-lasting influence on American political thought.

The chapter opens with biographical notes of the two main protagonists of this chapter, Owen Lattimore and Nicholas J. Spykman. The following section provides a critical analysis of the development of American geopolitics in the first half of the twentieth century, followed by a contextualised assessment of the geopolitical worldviews of Spykman and Lattimore, through four key geopolitical concepts: 'land, sea, and air power', 'scale', 'frontier', and 'tripolarity'. Furthermore, I examine their policy prescriptions for the United States, which were surprisingly similar despite their very different worldviews. I then turn to discuss their ideas about democracy in the global sphere. Finally, I consider the possible reasons for the marginalisation of the global visions of Lattimore and Spykman within the American discipline of International Relations, and their long-lasting contribution to the emergence of globalism in international thought.

OWEN LATTIMORE, NICHOLAS J. SPYKMAN, AND THE SCIENCE OF GEOPOLITICS

In this chapter, I focus on two influential international thinkers, Owen Lattimore and Nicholas J. Spykman, who took geography seriously when envisaging the post-war order and the role of the United States in it. Both identified the war's potential for international change based on geopolitical relations, yet outlined different political projects of global order. Taking as the starting point of my argument the assumption that implicit spatial representations in political thought derive from concrete experiences of a given society, I explore the spatial representations in their theories.[5] The intellectual links between geopolitical thought and world order

---

[4] The marginalisation of geopolitics within International Relations scholarship is evident in Starr's call for its reintegration in the discipline's conceptual toolbox: 'It is important to stress that despite living in the interdependent, transnational, and globalized world of the twenty-first century, geographic factors such as territory and borders are still integral and meaningful elements of world politics'. Starr, 'On Geopolitics', 439. For a similar argument, see Daniel H. Deudney, *Bounding Power: Republican Security Theory from the Polis to the Global Village* (Princeton, NJ: Princeton University Press, 2007), pt. 1.

[5] On legal conceptions of internationalism and the development of international law, see Martti Koskenniemi, *The Gentle Civilizer of Nations: The Rise and Fall of International Law 1870–1960* (Cambridge: Cambridge University Press, 2002); Martti Koskenniemi, *From Apology to Utopia: The Structure of*

suggest that ideas about political space formed an indispensable part of theorising international relations in the 1940s. Notions of political space offered an alternative to a legal conception of internationalism and a new way of imagining democracy in world politics, in the context of imperialism and regionalism.[6]

In the early 1940s, both Spykman and Lattimore were leading figures in American political debate. They held key academic positions in international studies departments in the United States, contributed to discussion of international affairs in scholarly journals and mass-distribution newspapers, and were appreciated by colleagues and politicians alike. Lattimore (1900–1989) was an American sinologist who grew up in China and made its culture, politics, and languages his expertise.[7] In 1928, he returned to the United States as a graduate student at Harvard, funded by a special grant from the Social Science Research Council. At Harvard, he met the geographer Isaiah Bowman, who became his academic patron.[8] In 1939, Bowman, then president of Johns Hopkins University, appointed Lattimore as the director of the Walter Hines Page School of International Relations. From 1934 to 1940 Lattimore was also editor in chief of *Pacific Affairs*, the journal of the Institute of Pacific Relations (IPR), a well-known nongovernmental study group on Pacific interests with an established global network of research councils including Chatham House.[9] Lattimore sought to counter the American centrism of the IPR, and encouraged scholarly contributions from the Japanese, Chinese, and Russian research councils. William Holland, the IPR research secretary and successive editor of *Pacific Affairs*, thought Lattimore 'rather strenuously promoted Soviet participation in the IPR' to avoid one-sided representation of Pacific politics.[10] This attitude attracted the criticism of the 'China Lobby', a group of American businessmen and opinion makers who promoted American interests in China by supporting the Nationalist government against the Communists. One of them was Alfred Kohlberg, who later denounced

International Legal Argument (Helsinki: Lakimieslüton Kustannus, 1989); Galli, *Political Spaces and Global War*, 5.

[6] Geopolitics is only briefly mentioned in a recent edited volume on the origins of American IR; see Inderjeet Parmar, 'American Hegemony, the Rockefeller Foundation', in Guilhot, *Invention of International Relations Theory*, 182–209.

[7] Robert P. Newman, *Owen Lattimore and the 'Loss' of China* (Berkeley: University of California Press, 1992), 6; Owen Lattimore, 'Preface', in *Studies in Frontier History: Collected Papers, 1928–1958* (London: Oxford University Press, 1962), 16.

[8] Smith, *American Empire*.

[9] John N. Thomas, *The Institute of Pacific Relations: Asian Scholars and American Politics* (Seattle: University of Washington Press, 1974), 12.

[10] William Lancelot Holland, *Remembering the Institute of Pacific Relations: The Memoirs of William L. Holland* (Tokyo: Ryukei Shyosha, 1995), 392.

Lattimore to the Federal Bureau of Investigation (FBI) for anti-American activities.[11]

In the early 1940s, Lattimore's expertise enjoyed the support and appreciation of the political establishment. In 1942, President F. D. Roosevelt appointed him as advisor to Chiang Kai-shek in China. This position offered an opportunity to reflect on world politics beyond the Asian sphere. After the United States had joined the war, Lattimore returned to San Francisco as the director of Pacific Operations for the American Office of War Information and was member of the Council on Foreign Relations postwar planning projects. In 1944, he accompanied US Vice President Henry Wallace on an airplane trip to Russia, China, and Mongolia, where they had a glimpse—although not necessarily an accurate one—of popular life in the Soviet Union.

During his ten-year tenure as director of the Page School, Lattimore tried to shift the academic focus from Europe to Asia, integrating insights from anthropology, geography, history, and sociology.[12] He was considered the foremost American expert on the Far East, and the 'American geopolitical masterhand'.[13] His efforts were appreciated by American scholars of politics and international relations, including Quincy Wright, who invited him to teach courses in politics at the University of Chicago.[14]

Yet, Lattimore's career was cut short when, in 1950, the IPR was targeted by J. Edgar Hoover and Senators Joseph McCarthy and Pat McCarran as a hub for anti-American views. Lattimore's inclusive attitude towards Soviet Russia and his association with the IPR provided the grounds for his prosecution as a 'top Soviet spy', aided by the incriminating testimony of a soviet defector, Alexander Gregory Graf Barmine.[15] Five long years of FBI investigation and trial led to Lattimore's complete acquittal.[16] His biographer Robert Newman argued that the groundless accusations were motivated by personal enmities and the collective hysteria following the rise of Chinese Communism and the Korean War.[17] However, the smear on Lattimore's reputation was indelible; in 1963, he accepted an invitation to establish a new Mongol Studies programme at the University of

---

[11] Thomas, *Institute of Pacific Relations*, 36–42.

[12] See Wright to Lattimore, 3 May 1949, in W. H. Page School of International Studies Relations, Records of Owen Lattimore, Director, Correspondence 1949–1951, Ferdinand Hamburger Jr. Archives, Johns Hopkins University, Baltimore, box 5.

[13] This title was given by no other than German geopolitician Karl Haushofer, cited in Paul Wohl, 'An American "Geopolitical Masterhand"', *Asia* 41 (1941): 601. Haushofer's appreciation for Lattimore is evident in his request that Lattimore be his interrogator at the Nuremberg Trials; see Smith, *American Empire*, 291.

[14] Newman, *Owen Lattimore*, 39.

[15] Ibid., 218.

[16] Ibid., 180–197. For Lattimore's account of the trial, see *Ordeal by Slander* (Boston: Little, Brown, 1950).

[17] Holland, *Remembering the Institute*, 92.

Leeds, and spent the following decades in Britain.[18] Lattimore's name remained associated with communist ideology; his contribution to geopolitical and strategic studies was largely forgotten.[19]

Nicholas John Spykman (1893–1943) was born in the Netherlands and travelled extensively in Asia and the Middle East before settling down in California, where he earned a doctorate from the University of California, Berkeley.[20] He joined the academic staff at Yale, and was among the founders of the Yale Institute of International Studies (YIIS), where he promoted an interdisciplinary approach to international relations with an emphasis on geography and geopolitics.[21] In 1929, he argued that the geographic factor was the most important factor in international relations: 'geography, particularly in the form of political geography seems to me the most basic study in our all field'.[22] His course syllabus included texts by contemporary American geographers such as Bowman, who played a central role in the formation of the American mid-century approach to geopolitics.[23]

As the chairman of YIIS (1935–1940) and director of the Department of International Relations within the Yale Graduate School, Spykman had a significant impact on teaching and research programmes in international relations. His two best-selling books, *America's Strategy in World Politics* (1942) and *The Geography of the Peace* (published posthumously in 1944), won the praise of critics from academia and politics alike, including Bowman.[24] During the Second World War, he joined the Far East Study Group of the Council on Foreign Relations, planning the post-war order in Asia.[25] Later, Spykman was mentioned among the masterminds of Containment

[18] David D. Buck, 'Lattimore, Owen', in *American National Biography* (2000), www.anb.org/articles/14/14-00355.html.

[19] David Harvey, 'Owen Lattimore: A Memoire', *Antipode* 15 (1983): 3–11.

[20] According to some sources, he served as an undercover agent for the Dutch government in the Far East. See Perry Anderson, 'Imperium', *New Left Review* 83 (2013): 12n15; Thompson, *Masters of International Thought*, 92; Nicholas J. Spykman, *The Social Theory of Georg Simmel* (1923; repr., New York: Transaction, 2007).

[21] On the YIIS's contribution to the development of American IR, see Paulo Jorge Batista Ramos, 'The Role of the Yale Institute of International Studies in the Construction of the United States Security Ideology, 1935–1951' (PhD thesis, University of Manchester, 2003).

[22] Edwin M. Borchard, ed., *Proceedings of the Fourth Conference of Teachers of International Law and Related Subjects, Held at Briarcliff Lodge, New York, 16–17 October 1929* (New York: Carnegie Endowment for International Peace, 1930), 40.

[23] Jonathan Haslam, *No Virtue Like Necessity: Realist Thought in International Relations since Machiavelli* (New Haven, CT: Yale University Press, 2002), 179–181.

[24] Nicholas J. Spykman, *The Geography of the Peace* (New York: Harcourt Brace and Co., 1944); Nicholas J. Spykman, *America's Strategy in World Politics: The United States and the Balance of Power* (New York: Harcourt, Brace, 1942); Isaiah Bowman, 'Review: Political Geography of Power', *Geographical Review* 32 (1942): 349–352.

[25] On the Far East Study Group and other CFR initiatives, see Dayna Barnes, 'Think Tanks and a New Order in East Asia: The Council of Foreign Relations and the Institute of Pacific Relations during World War II', *Journal of American-East Asian Relations* 22 (2015): 89–119.

Policy, and acknowledged as one of the founding fathers of the discipline of International Relations in America.[26]

Spykman's analysis of American foreign policy was an original contribution to strategic writings, based on his vast knowledge of geography and history.[27] Similarly, in his geopolitical writings, Lattimore is revealed not only as an influential sinologist, but also as a knowledgeable and original political thinker who based his international thought on concrete political and anthropological experience. Both exemplify the diversified, complex, and interdisciplinary qualities of American scholarship on international relations in the 1940s. By importing concepts and methods from anthropology, history, economics, and geography, they envisaged a more complex and inclusive approach to the study of the international realm than is usually accounted for. The focus on the dynamic qualities of geopolitics permitted them to imagine a world based on pluralism and instability, rather than, as later thinkers characterised the post-war years, on order and division.[28] They envisaged a tripolar international system led by three regional powers, one of which would be the United States, and attempted to account for and accommodate the rise of new powers like China and Russia within the post-war political and economic order by using geopolitical notions. Their visions constructed big geopolitical regions, vast spaces that undermined or replaced the nation-states as the basic components of world order. The questions they posed about international order expressed doubts about the existing system of nation-states, and consequently downplayed the principle of self-determination as a fundamental part of political order.

ISAIAH BOWMAN, KARL HAUSHOFER, AND GEOPOLITICS IN TRANSITION

In their intellectual quest for new conceptual tools for the interpretation of international relations, many American scholars found inspiration in other disciplines, including, importantly, political geography and geopolitics. However, it is notable that American political geographers, or scholars who applied geographic concepts to international relations, were very

---

[26] David Wilkinson, 'Spykman and Geopolitics', in *On Geopolitics*, ed. Ciro E. Zoppo and Charles Zorgbibe (Dordrecht: Martinus Nijhoff, 1985), 77–117; Guilhot, *Invention of International Relations Theory*, 84, 193.

[27] For an analysis of Spykman's contribution to American strategic thought, see Anderson, 'American Foreign Policy and Its Thinkers'. Anderson described Spykman's *America's Strategy* as 'perhaps the most striking single exercise in geo-political literature of any kind' (14).

[28] A recent account of the search for order after the war underplays the importance of pluralism and dynamism to contemporary writers; see G. John Ikenberry, *After Victory: Institutions, Strategic Restraint, and the Rebuilding of Order after Major Wars* (Princeton, NJ: Princeton University Press, 2001).

keen to distance themselves from the German school of *Geopolitik*, which in the American public imaginary was associated with the Nazi new world order of conquest and oppression.[29] At the same time, it is clear that the exchange of geopolitical ideas between the two countries, which went back at least half a century, was crucial to the development of geopolitical concepts.

The interest in geopolitical ideas in the United States emerged at the turn of the century, when Frederick Jackson Turner and Alfred T. Mahan explained the history and politics of the United States in geopolitical terms.[30] Turner's frontier thesis and Mahan's sea power vision became the cornerstones of later geopolitical thinking in America and Germany alike. Friedrich Ratzel's famous notion of *Lebensraum*, the living space of the German people, was elaborated to counterbalance what Mahan described as American naval supremacy.[31] Ratzel's interpretation of politics in organic terms was introduced to an American readership by one of his students, Ellen Churchill Semple, who influenced greatly the younger generation of geographers, including Isaiah Bowman.[32]

At the same time, the relation between the physical environment and political power was also discussed by the British geographer Halford Mackinder, whose 1904 speech to the Royal Geographical Society warned his British audience of the risks that a land-based empire in the Russia could pose.[33] He claimed that for the first time it was possible to reveal the 'geographical causations of universal history'.[34] His theory revolved around the historical notion of the Heartland, or geographical 'Pivot', a wide land mass stretching from the Balkans through Russia to the Arctic Sea. This was the geographic basis of the land power, which was opposed by a technologically savvy and industrially advanced sea power. To illustrate his point, Mackinder used a map, titled 'the traditional seats of power', that divided the world into large regions and ignored all political borders. The aim of his geopolitical thought was to help Britain formulate a new geopolitical strategy in an interconnected closed system where competing imperial powers struggled to attain political and military supremacy.

[29] Smith, *American Empire*, 274; Hans Werner Weigert, *Generals and Geographers: The Twilight of Geopolitics* (New York: Oxford University Press, 1942).
[30] Alfred T. Mahan, *The Influence of Sea Power upon History, 1660–1783* (London: Sampson Low, Marston, 1889); Frederick Jackson Turner, *The Frontier in American History* (1893; repr., New York: Henry Holt, 1947).
[31] Friedrich Ratzel, *Politische Geographie* (1897; repr., Berlin: Oldenbourg, 1923); Friedrich Ratzel, *Anthropo-geographie* (Stuttgart: J. Englehorn, 1882–1912).
[32] Lucian M. Ashworth, 'Mapping a New World: Geography and the Interwar Study of International Relations', *International Studies Quarterly* 57 (2013): 138–149; Andrew Crampton and Gearóid Ó Tuathail, 'Intellectuals, Institutions and Ideology: The Case of Robert Strausz-Hupé and "American Geopolitics"', *Political Geography* 15 (1996): 533–555.
[33] Mackinder, 'Geographical Pivot of History'.
[34] Ibid., 422.

It was only over twenty years later that his idea of the Heartland achieved greater international academic acclaim. In the 1940s United States, Mackinder's ideas set the terms for geopolitical debate.[35] Gerry Kearns claims that Mackinder's legacy was evident in three formulations of geopolitical theory: Nazi geopolitics of the 1930s, American Cold War Containment Policy, and American unipolarism of the early 2000s.[36] However, I argue that in the 1940s many American geopolitical thinkers found in Mackinder a provocative source of inspiration and used his thesis as the foundation for a new world order. Lattimore and Spykman were both influenced by Mackinder's concept of political space, which oriented natural geography towards a concrete political end. Nevertheless, they rejected its cartographic foundations and its spatial assumptions and attempted to elaborate more sophisticated and dynamic accounts of global geopolitics.

During the same period, Mackinder also influenced, to his indignation, the German geographer Karl Haushofer who launched *Geopolitik* as a science and a national foreign policy.[37] Haushofer's geopolitics built on Mackinder's theory, yet also recognised the importance of Bowman's geographical survey *The New World*, first published in 1921 and revised in 1928.[38] It was written following Bowman's participation in the 'Inquiry', the American study group that informed the delegation to the Paris Conference in 1919. The book became an American best-seller, and copies were still distributed to US military libraries in the Second World War.[39] Presented as a scientific study of the geographic conditions of various political units, the book promoted a new understanding of the relation between the natural and the human. As Smith suggests, despite Bowman's claims the book was not a neutral analysis: its implicit aim was to carve up a new geopolitical space for the United States, as a leader of a new economic and political system, which recognised the limits of the state in an interconnected world.[40] The book was part of Bowman's wider educational project in the interwar years aimed at advancing the study of geography in the United States, underpinning American political and moral exceptionalism in geopolitical terms,

[35] Due to public demand, Mackinder's 1919 geopolitical treatise was revised and republished in 1944 as Halford Mackinder, *Democratic Ideals and Reality* (Harmondsworth: Penguin, 1944). Mackinder returned to his earlier ideas also in H. J. Mackinder, 'The Round World and the Winning of Peace', in *Compass of the World: A Symposium on Political Geography*, ed. Hans Werner Weigert and Vilhjalmur Stefansson (London: Harrap, 1946), 161–173.

[36] Gerry Kearns, *Geopolitics and Empire: The Legacy of Halford Mackinder* (New York: Oxford University Press, 2009), 17.

[37] Karl Haushofer, *Geopolitik der Pan-Ideen* (Berlin: Zentral-Verlag, 1931); Kearns, *Geopolitics and Empire*, chap. 1.

[38] Isaiah Bowman, *The New World: Problems in Political Geography*, 4th ed. (Yonkers-on-Hudson, NY: World Book Company, 1928).

[39] Smith, *American Empire*, 441.

[40] Neil Smith, 'Bowman's New World and the Council on Foreign Relations', *Geographical Review* 76 (1986): 438–460.

and highlighting the United States' unique mission as a global leader. By the mid-1940s, Bowman established a new Geography Department at Johns Hopkins that wanted to be an 'American Cambridge', co-founded the Council on Foreign Relations, and was the motor behind the International Geographical Union. He was a close advisor for President Roosevelt, and exerted significant influence on the State Department.[41] Yet, as much as he wanted to distance his scholarship from the *Geopolitik* school, for many he was the 'American Haushofer', an important link in the intellectual chain that connected Germany and the United States.[42]

Haushofer saw Bowman's magnum opus as a challenge: his reply was a geopolitical world vision based on German geopolitical interests. For him *Geopolitik* was a 'science' based on the concepts of *Lebensraum*, Land/Sea dichotomy, autarky, and the idea of pan-regionalism.[43] In the United States, his ideas were often presented, somewhat simplistically, as the 'pseudoscientific' foundation for Hitler's foreign policy.[44] However, the political scientist Robert Strausz-Hupé thought that the study of geopolitics in America was still intellectually worthwhile and politically indispensable. In his book *Geopolitics* he surveyed German scholarship in order to offer his American readership a new way of studying international relations, a 'radical break' from the European legal tradition of nineteenth century diplomacy.[45] As he showed, the development of geopolitical thought was a result of the intense, yet often reluctant, relationship between German and American thinkers. For many Americans the Second World War brought this fruitful exchange to a crisis.

Bowman, Lattimore, Mackinder, Strausz-Hupé, and Weigert were part of a group of scholars sharing a keen interest in geopolitics. As a review article published in 1942 suggested, they shared the theory of geopolitics that saw states as 'dynamic phenomena'.[46] This focus on change, mutability, and instability in the interaction between politics and geography led their theories away from the pitfalls of natural determinism. Geopolitics helped them conceptualise the main characteristic of states as, paradoxically, their instability, which resulted from the constant need to respond to natural, political, and social challenges. Their theoretical contributions were accompanied by cartographic illustrations by the major American

[41] Ibid.

[42] Smith, *American Empire*, 287.

[43] Karl Haushofer, *Wehr-Geopolitik: Geographische Grundlagen Einer Wehrkunde* (Berlin: Junker und Dünnhaupt, 1932).

[44] John H. Hallowell, 'Review Article', *Journal of Politics* 5 (1943): 187–189. See also Robert Vitalis, 'Review of David Ekbladh, "Present at the Creation: Edward Mead Earle and the Depression-Era Origins of Security Studies". *International Security* 36 (2012)', H-Diplo, 15 June 2012.

[45] Robert Strausz-Hupé, *Geopolitics: The Struggle for Space and Power* (1942; repr., New York, Arno Press, 1972) viii.

[46] Charles B. Hagan, 'Geopolitics', *Journal of Politics* 4 (1942): 478.

cartographer of the period, Richard Edes Harrison, whose maps sought to challenge and complicate the traditional American conceptions of world geography.[47] The exchange of ideas between the German and American geopolitical schools culminated in the 1940s when American political geographers used geopolitical concepts like the Land/Sea dichotomy and the frontier to envisage a new global order, often unfolded in anti-imperial terms, in which the United States would have a leading role.[48] The group's two collections of essays, titled *Compass of the World*, manifest well the American intention to distinguish between the 'science' of political geography (which they professed to practice) and the ideologically biased German *Geopolitik*. Yet this distinction should be taken with a grain of salt, since many—but not all—American geopoliticians were motivated by a not less strong ideological drive to recast the United States as a leading actor in world affairs.[49]

Despite not being directly associated with this American geopolitical circle, Spykman had a great influence on its members. In his review of Spykman's *The Geography of the Peace*, Weigert praised the author as a brilliant and original geopolitical thinker, while criticising his basic assumptions which amounted to a 'disillusioned submission to the old balance of powers game'.[50] A critical point of contention was Spykman's interpretation of Asia's political importance. Weigert rejected Spykman's argument that Russia's power concentrated in its western areas and that China's power lay in its coastal regions. He considered Spykman's theory of world politics reactionary and 'outright dangerous' because it ignored the fact that 'a new age is dawning in Asia', an age of local political development that would halt imperialism in the region. He concluded his review by acknowledging Spykman's influence on American geopolitics, whilst in the same breath accusing his last work of despair and nihilism. Weigert's review emphasised explicitly the conceptual similarities between Lattimore and Spykman, who used the geopolitical lens to look at international order, yet at the same time pointed to the fundamental difference of their political and normative commitments.

Lattimore used geopolitical ideas to articulate his political vision of world order, and considered it a neutral, scientific tool of political analysis. At first sight, it seems that his geopolitical theory, centred on the land mass, was an interpretation of Mackinder's Heartland. However, Lattimore

[47] Weigert and Stefansson, *Compass of the World*; Hans Werner Weigert, Vilhjalmur Stefansson, and Richard Edes Harrison, eds., *New Compass of the World: A Symposium on Political Geography* (London: Harrap, 1949).

[48] Ashworth, 'Mapping a New World', 140–142.

[49] Isaiah Bowman, 'Geography vs. Geopolitics', in Weigert and Stefansson, *Compass of the World*, 40.

[50] Hans W. Weigert, 'Review of *The Geography of Peace* by N. J. Spykman', *Saturday Review*, 22 April 1944, 10.

had a different understanding of the relations between politics and geography, or in other words, of the meaning of geopolitics as a social science. Geopolitics indicated an approach to analysing political activity: 'it is a "realist" understanding of a territory and the political powers that control it. It is a unique perspective, a way of studying a political unit, a region or a state, and its position in the world'.[51] Lattimore gave a crude, perhaps naïve, interpretation of geopolitics, which was mainly aimed at distancing his own attempts at spatial theory from the ideological endeavours of the German geopoliticians. He claimed that reality, which could be observed by the senses and studied through intensive fieldwork, set the ground for political theorisation, and not vice versa. He argued that international relations should be studied by rational analysis of the various aspects of human reality encountered in the field. Geographic, anthropological, linguistic, and historical knowledge had to be taken into account when analysing political relations. However, as I will show, Lattimore's historical narratives were also motivated by a normative claim about the obsolescence of 'empire', which he hoped to replace by 'democracy', a term he never clearly defined. Both categories were interpreted in relation to space and political power: empires were ruled by repressive, external domination, while political power in democracies was internal, popular, and participatory. His work highlights that although geopolitics was often based on empirical knowledge of the world, it was never a value-free perspective.

Spykman shared Mackinder's argument that geopolitics provided the conceptual framework to take into consideration geographic factors when formulating a state's foreign policy in peacetime or war.[52] As I have mentioned before, he saw political geography as one of the most important aspects of the study of international (or rather for him, interstate) relations. He recognised that geopolitics was necessarily oriented towards a political goal, and not just a neutral analytical perspective. Spykman's geopolitical thought evolved from the preliminary argument that 'geography is the most fundamental factor in foreign policy of states because it is the most permanent'.[53] Gearóid Ó Tuathail has criticised this claim, arguing that natural conditions were in fact less permanent than Spykman wanted: geological shifts and climate change might affect a territory's geographical conditions even in a short time span.[54] Yet Spykman was not a geographical determinist. His fundamental claim was that a state's specific geopolitical conditions and position in the world system conditioned its relationships with other political powers, but, importantly, these geo-

---

[51] Owen Lattimore, *Solution in Asia* (London: Cresset Press, 1945), 58.
[52] Spykman, *Geography of the Peace*, 6.
[53] Spykman, *America's Strategy in World Politics*, 41.
[54] Gearóid Ó Tuathail, *Critical Geopolitics: The Politics of Writing Global Space* (London: Routledge, 1996), 51.

political attributes were changing rather than fixed. Unlike Lattimore, he saw geopolitics not as a recipe for anti-imperial democratic global change, but as a necessary knowledge to strengthen American foreign policy in the existing imperial world order.

LATTIMORE AND SPYKMAN ON LAND, SEA, AND AIR POWER

The Land/Sea dichotomy was a recurring theme in geopolitical writings on world order in the 1940s, and by consequence the foundation of the international thought of Spykman and Lattimore. In the first half of the twentieth century, Bowman, Mackinder, Mahan, and Haushofer gave a political interpretation to these geographical concepts. Symbolically, the Land and Sea represent two out of the four classic natural elements that make the world: earth, water, air, and fire. However, as the German jurist Carl Schmitt noted, political thinkers usually referred to Land and Sea as conflicting 'powers', not only as natural elements.[55] They acquired a historical significance as methods for ordering and controlling the natural and human world, and subsequently gained a mythical meaning as the fundamental principles of entire civilisations. For Lattimore, the Land/Sea dichotomy described two inherently opposed transport technologies and two different means of bringing about political and economic order to a territory. These also implied two historical and political perspectives on a given territory: the oceanic and the continental gazes. Lattimore used this dichotomy to discuss the role of geography and political power in the transformation from imperial to democratic order. By contrast, Spykman saw Land/Sea as two strategies for national defence, applicable to different geopolitical situations indicated by the state's 'place in the world'. He used this dichotomy to reflect upon his two main geopolitical concepts, the Heartland and the Rimland. Both thinkers argued that the Land/Sea formula was destabilised—but not cancelled—by the increasing relevance of the Air element to political and cultural control over men and nature.

Lattimore's starting point was the assumption that the European and American imperial powers came across the sea to Asia and looked at the vast territory from boats and ports in the littoral zone: 'our thinking about Asia stemmed from the great age of navigation at the beginning of the sixteenth century, when the old caravan routes were surpassed by new

---

[55] Schmitt, *Land and Sea*, 9–10. See also the illuminating introduction by the translator, Samuel Garrett Zeitlin, 'Propaganda and Critique: An Introduction to Land and Sea', lxvi–lxvii. Despite similarities in their interpretation of the Land/Sea dichotomy, there is no evidence that Lattimore or Spykman was familiar with Schmitt's geopolitical writings.

sea routes'.[56] Nonetheless, he recognised the rise of local Asian powers that established their political centre in the land masses, looking outwards from the continental core towards the coasts. Lattimore's analysis endowed these concepts with political meaning: the oceanic gaze was repressive and exploitative, the continental gaze was constructive and collaborative.[57] The oceanic gaze, typical of the European empires, does not penetrate the local territory, and has no grasp of its unique cultural and political characteristics. According to Lattimore's conception of knowledge, a superficial outlook cannot offer detailed information of Asia and its people. A political system based on ignorance cannot be anything other than repressive. A territorial gaze allows a better understanding of local habits and structures. Nonetheless, a territorially based system of control was not, in itself, a guarantee against imperial repression and domination. The advantage it offered was merely a potential political interaction, which could lead to the creation of political space that measured itself with the local populations' recognised political agency.

One of the questions arising from Lattimore's analysis of the Land/Sea dichotomy relates to the implications of these concepts to a general understanding of history. Did Lattimore see the Land/Sea dichotomy as an empirical description of historical change, or as a normative criterion to understand power relations in the world? Rowe claims that Lattimore's view of history was structured by technological determinism because its focus on the land and sea binary implied a vision of historical time as consisting of alternating epochs of maritime and territorial modes of transport technology. He accuses Lattimore of overemphasising the importance of these technologies in forming systems of political control, and in describing the shift from one era to another as unavoidable.[58]

However, it is not so obvious that Lattimore regarded the Land/Sea dichotomy as a 'general law'. Rather, he employed these concepts as a part of his anti-imperial discourse, offering a new key to local development that was independent of the European powers' sea-based intervention. Lattimore's interpretation of land and sea powers was meant not as a teleological conceptualisation of history, but as a political proposal to review power relations in the world, and especially in Asia, in order to give an opportunity to local land powers to oppose European imperialism. Therefore, the 'land mass' has an important prescriptive function, aimed at highlighting fundamental limitations in thinking about world politics from an external vantage point. Lattimore uses the outsider position to argue that superficial knowledge and indirect political involvement have led to the no-longer-

---

[56] Lattimore, *Solution in Asia*, 12.
[57] Ibid., 10–15.
[58] William T. Rowe, 'Owen Lattimore, Asia, and Comparative History', *Journal of Asian Studies* 66 (2007): 759.

desirable imperial domination. The growing international influence of the United States could put it in a position to reverse this trend, and encourage local, direct systems of government.

Lattimore's geopolitics was part of his anti-imperial political project. For him a new interpretation of the political space would be necessary to bring about a postcolonial world order based on freedom and democracy. His geopolitics sought to bring to attention areas of the globe that the Americans and Europeans saw as politically passive, and to give political agency to their populations.[59] He repositioned Mackinder's notion of the Heartland towards the East, undermining the importance of Europe, and argued against the British geographer that the Heartland did not imply conquest or imperial struggle.[60] If, as Kearns argues, 'geopolitical vision is never innocent; it is always a wish posing as an analysis', then Lattimore's wish was to highlight the international and democratic potential of local political power in Asia.[61]

Lattimore's new Heartland was a political project aimed at reshaping the political space of Asia as a large and pluralistic region of democracy, freedom, and popular participation. Since he published his writings in the United States, it is clear that he hoped to convince his readership to take a central role in this political transformation, without, nonetheless, imposing particular interests and values on the nascent democratic region. Lattimore promoted an interventionist position, aimed not at empowering the United States internationally, but at aiding the colonial regions to become 'democratic'.

The complex interaction between the Land/Sea elements was also central to Spykman's geopolitical thought that envisaged a constant struggle between maritime and continental powers to balance their powers and achieve peaceful temporary equilibrium. He further complicated his thesis by adding two new concepts to the world map: Rimland and Encirclement.[62] The Rimland is formed of the littoral areas of Europe and Asia ('Eurasia'), stretching from the North Sea to the Mediterranean, the Red Sea, the Indian Ocean, and the Pacific (see Map 1). The cartographic representation of Eurasia aimed to show that this was the world's area of greatest economic, political, and demographic development, yet the map's ambiguous features undermine the clarity of Spykman's message about global strategy and geopolitics. He located in the Rimland the conceptual and

---

[59] Owen Lattimore, 'American Responsibilities in the Far East', *Virginia Quarterly Review* 16 (1940): 162.

[60] Mackinder, 'Geographical Pivot of History'.

[61] Gerry Kearns, 'Imperial Geopolitics: Geopolitical Visions at the Dawn of the American Century', in *A Companion to Political Geography*, ed. John Agnew, Katharyne Mitchell, and Gerard Toal (Oxford: Blackwell, 2007), 174.

[62] Spykman, *Geography of the Peace*, 40; Michael P. Gerace, 'Between Mackinder and Spykman: Geopolitics, Containment and After', *Comparative Strategy* 10 (1991): 347–364.

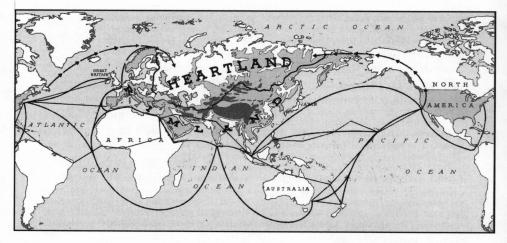

MAP 1 Geopolitical Map of Eurasia. Reproduced from Nicholas J. Spykman, *The Geography of the Peace*, (1944), 38.

geographical meeting point of the sea and land powers, a 'frontier zone' of political struggle and innovation. Modifying Mackinder's dictum on the Heartland, Spykman suggested that who rules the Rimland commands the world.

The Rimland was an independent political zone separated by lack of communication and transport technologies from Mackinder's Heartland, and conceptually contrasted to it. Geopolitical conditions made the Rimland a 'buffer zone', a frontier area between the sea and land powers, rather than an area of independent and autonomous power. Interestingly, all of the 'great powers' that Spykman identified, including the United States, Britain, Russia, Germany, and Japan, were positioned outside the Rimland, but projected their power onto it (see Map 2).[63] This point seems to be the main difference between the Rimland and Lattimore's frontier zone. As we shall see, whereas for Lattimore the frontier population was endowed with political agency, the Rimland population was instrumental to the great powers' geopolitical balance of power and lacked their own decision-making power. Evidently, Spykman perpetuated an imperial view of world order, in which hegemonic power acquired direct or indirect control of areas of strategic interest, largely in disregard of local communities.

Spykman employed maps to show the relations between the Heartland and the Rimland, and their strategic implications for the world states, connected by commercial, diplomatic, and military interests, represented by black lines and arrows. Through these cartographic images, he sought to

[63] Spykman, *Geography of the Peace*, 41.

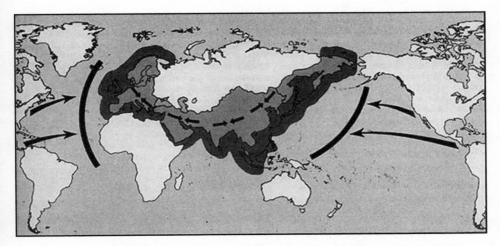

MAP 2 Eurasian Conflict Zone. Reproduced from Nicholas J. Spykman, *The Geography of the Peace*, (1944), 52.

overcome the imaginary divide between East and West, and reflect the compact and interconnected qualities of the new world order. The cartographic imagery that Spykman used to illustrate his interpretation of the Land/Sea relationship remained, however, conceptually and visually confusing. Rather than elucidating the meaning of his conceptual proposals, the maps highlighted their ambiguity and complexity.

In the 1940s, the cartographic imagery of the world underwent significant change when geographers started to use new projections aimed at representing the world from different, previously ignored, geographic viewpoints to important political consequences.[64] The American public's rising interest in world maps reflected President Roosevelt's strong awareness to the crucial rule of geographic knowledge in war strategy and peace planning. New experiments were made to create cartographic representations—usually maps and globes—that embodied the new image of the world as a small, cohesive, compact, and interconnected space.

One of the main features of these new cartographies was the emphasis on the world's unity and continuity. For President Roosevelt, this implied that the United States could not rely on geographic distance and maritime defence as protection from its overseas enemies.[65] Spykman encouraged the United States to adopt a global perspective on geopolitics and political strategy: 'Global war, as well as global peace, means that all fronts and all

[64] Susan Schulten, *The Geographical Imagination in America, 1880–1950* (Chicago: University of Chicago Press, 2002), chap. 9. Derek Gregory, *Geographical Imaginations* (Oxford: Blackwell, 1994).
[65] Henrikson, 'Map as an "Idea"', 28.

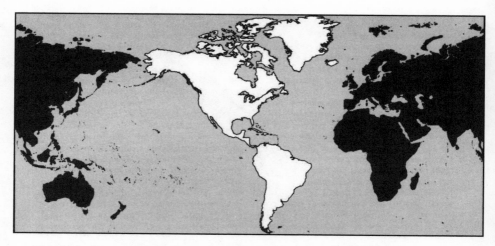

MAP 3 The Western Hemisphere Encircled. Reproduced from Nicholas J. Spykman, *The Geography of the Peace*, (1944), 33.

areas are interrelated. No matter how remote they are from each other, success or failure in one will have an immediate and determining effect on the others. It is necessary, therefore, to see the world as a whole'.[66] This unifying cartographic imagery played a central role in understanding the political world through the concept of Encirclement: if the Old World is placed at the centre of the map, as in the traditional Mercator projection, it is 'encircled' by the American coasts (see Map 3).[67] If, on the other hand, the map is centred on the New World, following the Miller projection as he suggested, the Old World's Eurasian coasts could 'encircle' it. In his eyes, the active position of the embracing power is better than the passive 'encircled': the new cartographic projection served to alert the Americans to their possible 'encirclement' by hostile powers. Spykman employed maps to illustrate the cartographic and political notion of Encirclement and its two alternative strategic implications for the Western Hemisphere (see Map 4).[68]

Spykman argued that the geopolitical position of the United States—facing three oceans, the Atlantic, the Pacific, and the Arctic, and spreading its influence over its two 'extensions' (Canada and Latin America)—endowed it with a special global leadership role. Thus, the United States was 'the most important political unit in the "New World"', and should create the post-war world order according to its own notion of 'balance

---

[66] Spykman, *Geography of the Peace*, 45.

[67] For a historical account of the Mercator projection, see Mark Monmonier, *Rhumb Lines and Map Wars: A Social History of the Mercator Projection* (Chicago: University of Chicago Press, 2004).

[68] On the policy implications of Spykman's Encirclement, see John A. Thompson, *A Sense of Power* (Ithaca, NY: Cornell University Press, 2015), 209–212.

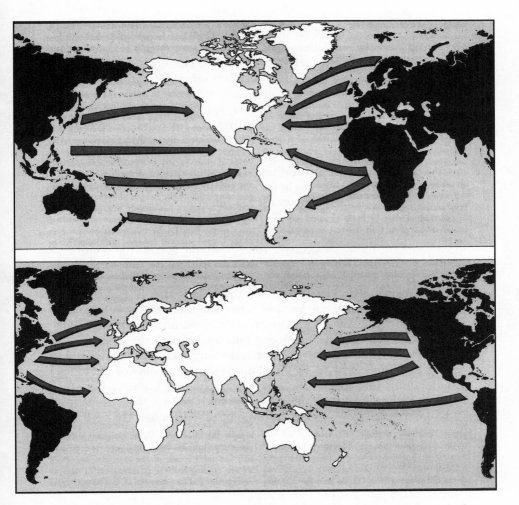

MAP 4 The Future of the Western Hemisphere? Reproduced from Nicholas J. Spykman, *The Geography of the Peace*, (1944), 59.

of power'.[69] The geopolitical notion of Encirclement reinforced Spykman's argument in favour of American interventionist foreign policy. It considered the Monroe Doctrine as a 'total hemispheric defense', underlining the US role as maritime and territorial leader of region extending into the Pacific and Atlantic oceans, to include more than half the globe.[70]

[69] Spykman, *America's Strategy in World Politics*, 46.
[70] Ibid., 88. On the history of the Monroe Doctrine, see Dexter Perkins, *A History of the Monroe Doctrine* (London: Little, Brown, 1941); Jay Sexton, *The Monroe Doctrine: Empire and Nation in Nineteenth-Century America* (New York: Hill & Wang, 2011).

The mid-century rise of air power for military warfare and civil transport destabilised the traditional geopolitical discourse of the Land/Sea dichotomy.[71] Air travel was celebrated for its technological achievements, and the new bird's-eye view of the earth it offered.[72] Yet, air power was also conceived as a new threat to civilisation. The bombing of Guernica in 1937 exacerbated public fear of air raids, but also highlighted the military potential of the new technology.[73] The growing interest in air power gave new impetus to a reconsideration of earlier geopolitical theories. Many thought the 'traditional' Land/Sea dichotomy would be undermined by air power, which would revolutionize the geopolitical perspective of the world.[74] Even Mackinder sought to adjust his famous Heartland theory to a new conceptual view of the earth that emerged from the human experience of flight.[75]

Wendell Willkie, the former presidential candidate and author of the best-seller *One World,* suggested that the aerial perspective emphasised the idea that the world was 'one', an indivisible unit whose inhabitants shared a common humanity that would overcome any political divide.[76] The aerial worldview would not necessarily lead the observer to ignore the details that characterise local societies and their habits; Willkie's comments on specific aspects of foreign politicians and lifestyles aimed at bridging over geographical distance and underlining the common traits of near and far countries that flight technology rendered closer. By employing the aerial gaze he provided an overarching view of the lands he visited, but his travelogue also lingered on minute detail to familiarise his reader with foreign lands, their cultures and leaders: 'strange as it may seem', he observed, 'Stalin dresses in light pastel shades. His well-known tunic is of finely woven material and is apt to be in soft green or a delicate pink. His trousers a light-tannish yellow or blue'.[77] By spicing up his political and economic commentary with personal anecdotes, he outlined a harmonious and cosmopolitan humanity, which reconnected through the velocity and accessibility of air travel.

---

[71] Jenifer L. Van Vleck, 'The "Logic of the Air": Aviation and the Globalism of the "American Century"', *New Global Studies* 1 (2007). Andrew Baker suggests that air power had a decisive impact on the bureaucratisation of diplomacy; see *Constructing a Post-war Order,* 30–37.

[72] Ibid., 248.

[73] On total war and air power, see Ian Patterson, *Guernica and Total War* (London: Profile Books, 2007). There is a vast literature on the reception of air power in Britain, which is largely beyond the scope of this chapter. See, for example, David Edgerton, *England and the Aeroplane: An Essay on a Militant and Technological Nation* (Basingstoke: Macmillan, 1980).

[74] One of the most salient examples of this claim is Schmitt, *Land and Sea.*

[75] Denis E. Cosgrove, *Apollo's Eye: A Cartographic Genealogy of the Earth in the Western Imagination* (Baltimore: Johns Hopkins University Press, 2001), 245.

[76] Willkie, *One World.*

[77] Ibid., 70.

The aerial viewpoint created new cartographic images of the world as a round, compact, smooth, and closed space. Interestingly, Lattimore and Spykman recognised the revolutionary potential of air power, but they thought its impact would be mainly conceptual rather than political. For Lattimore, the aerial representations of the Earth highlighted its natural unity, but obfuscated the nuances of human social existence, giving an illusion of geographic spaces empty of political attributes. The world's territories become pawns in a strategic game, rather than proactive, autonomous political units. The limits of the aerial perspective highlighted the political importance of what happened on the ground.[78] The aerial viewpoint embodied, according to Lattimore, the well-established Western imperialistic approach that saw the Chinese, and the Asian populations more generally, as peoples without politics. Lattimore's work *Inner Asian Frontiers of China* (1940) subsequently influenced Eric Wolf's critical idea of 'people without history', which expanded Lattimore's argument that there were no peoples that inherently lacked political agency. Instead, the capacity for political agency could be expressed under certain conditions, arguably not under the exploitative rule—and flattening gaze—of the Western powers.[79]

In 1946, Lattimore discussed air power, suggesting that it necessitated a new map of the world, in which lines of longitude and latitude were more significant than national territorial borders.[80] The new air technology rendered the Arctic an increasingly important area when flight over the polar region replaced the risky air routes over the Pacific Ocean. Yet for Lattimore the importance of air power lay not in the technological achievement, but in its political implications. Air technology was a revolution *in potentia* rather than in practice, until it affected the world's political structure as a whole. Thus, if only a few Western powers had access to air technology, the imperial world order would not be abolished. A real turning point could be the acquisition of air power by the Asian region, where it could open up landlocked countries to other regions of the world, and facilitate their development as independent political powers. Therefore, he saw air power not as a defining element of a new 'air age', but as a transitional technology that would shift the world's geopolitical balance from empire to democracy. Technology was to be reinforced by shared

[78] See an example of this view in R. E. Harrison and H. W. Weigert, 'World View and Strategy', in Weigert and Stefansson, *Compass of the World*, 74–88; Owen Lattimore, *The Situation in Asia* (Boston: Little, Brown, 1949).

[79] Owen Lattimore, *Inner Asian Frontiers of China* (New York: American Geographic Society, 1940). Wolf defined Lattimore's book as 'remarkable'; see Eric R. Wolf, *Europe and the People without History* (Berkeley: University of California Press, 1982), 33, 398.

[80] Owen Lattimore, 'The Inland Crossroads of Asia', in Weigert and Stefansson, *Compass of the World*, 374–394.

consciousness to the political limits of imperial control.[81] Thus, not only was Lattimore not a technological determinist, he was well aware of the crucial role of politics in defining the meaning of technological innovation.

The problem was one of perception as much as of technological might. Air technology and the spatial imaginary of the aerial gaze exacerbated for Lattimore the pathologies of imperialism, already present in the 'gunboat' era. Imperialism implied not only specific political practices, but an all-encompassing world order that created a common imagination exemplified in colonial mental maps. Europe, and for that matter the United States as well, observed Asia from boats and airplanes as one massive and smooth territory, inhabited by hostile yet indistinguishable tribes and 'races'. This infinite land was 'empty' of politics because from the shore, or from the air, the foreign rulers could not identify the continent's complex political structures. They presumed its population lacked interest in establishing a system of political control, or in participating in politics in the same manner that an educated European or American citizen would.

Lattimore advanced an epistemic critique of Willkie's account, which emphasised shared and universal human values. He highlighted the importance of direct, in-depth, detailed knowledge of the different modes of social organization and political interaction in local Asian societies, to formulating political thought. Despite Willkie's keen eye for detail, Lattimore deemed his quick observations superficial. The profound and truthful form of knowledge was available only to those who travelled and explored the Asian land masses.

Lattimore thus differed significantly from those who announced the coming of the air age. In denouncing the potential of air power to carry on the obsolete practices of empire, Lattimore implicitly criticised the widespread American conception of air power. Influential figures like Clare Boothe Luce, a pioneering air traveller, Republican politician and the wife of publisher Henry Luce, construed air power as a means to extend American influence around the world without resorting to actual imperial conquest.[82] Air power could complement sea power to guarantee American interests worldwide, since there were 'no distant places any longer'.[83] As Jenifer Van Vleck notes, this was not a new approach: since the 1920s air power was seen as a way to facilitate imperial control of the colonial periphery. Some wartime commentators went as far as calling America an 'Empire of the air', which slowly became a catchphrase in the popular

---

[81] Ibid., 382.

[82] On the relations between American aviation and the emergence of the ideology of American-led internationalism, see Jenifer Van Vleck, *Empire of the Air: Aviation and the American Ascendancy* (Cambridge, MA: Harvard University Press, 2013).

[83] Ibid., 9.

imagination of America's global role; this was the precise idea that Lattimore hoped to eradicate.

Spykman was even more doubtful of the political importance of air power as an independent, politically relevant technology. He thought air power was ineffective in connecting the Rimland to the land mass. He accepted that warfare had become 'truly tri-dimensional' but did not think that air power could be more than an auxiliary of land and sea powers. Air technology could be politically revolutionary if it could overcome the natural barriers, which previously hampered transportation and communication and condemned some regions to political isolation.[84] In 1944, he refuted the claims promoted by Lattimore and geographer Vilhjalmur Stefansson that air power could, under certain conditions, radically change world politics.[85] Technical limitations, like the need for fuelling stations and landing bases, encouraged him to overlook the destabilising potential of air power in the framework of his tripolar strategy. Nevertheless, it is surprising that Spykman ignored the potential capacity of air power to connect easily the Rimland and the Heartland, which he considered technologically and politically detached. A closer Rimland/Heartland relationship would have rendered sea-based political control irrelevant and undermined the independence of the littoral zones, challenging much of Spykman's strategy.[86]

Air power brings to the fore the disagreement between Lattimore and Spykman on the issue of empire. Since the war emphasised the decline of the European empires, a new world order would have to take into account the transition towards decolonisation in Asia and Africa. Lattimore's geopolitics emerged as a critique of empire, proposing a more collaborative scheme of interstate relations to eschew the mentality of imperial power politics. By contrast, Spykman sought to replace the European empires with American power, and argued that America's military bases in the Pacific were essential to prevent the ascendancy of Russia and China, the two new rising powers of the 1940s.

Lattimore discarded Spykman's ideas as an old-fashioned approach: 'an inability to get away from the obsessions of the past hundred years. . . . For the last one hundred years, an enormously important area of the world, the Asiatic half of what the German geopoliticians call the "Eurasiatic land mass", the greatest continuous mass of land on the earth's surface, has been dominated, partly for geographical reasons and partly

---

[84] Spykman, *Geography of the Peace*, 16.
[85] Vilhjalmur Stefansson, 'The North American Arctic', in Weigert and Stefansson, *Compass of the World*, 215–265; Lattimore, 'Inland Crossroads of Asia'.
[86] Spykman, *Geography of the Peace*.

for technological reasons, by the nations which had sea power'.[87] The new land-based world order meant for Lattimore that the imperial age of the 'gun-boat' was over and consequently the coastal frontier would be replaced by the land frontier stretching between Russia and China. Spykman argued that the coastal areas, in his words the 'Rimland', would maintain prime importance as a frontier area, and remain a central part of sea- and land-based strategic defence. This difference had an important impact on their global strategy. For Lattimore, once imperialism was eclipsed, 'the things that will happen along [the Russia-China] land frontier, far beyond the reach of any American gunboat or battleship, or airplane carrier or air base specified by the most ambitious American Centuryite, are of greater significance than anything that will happen in the Pacific Ocean'.[88] However, for Spykman, a geopolitical vision focused on either land supremacy or sea domination was unbalanced because the real focal point of international politics was in the area of their encounter. The Rimland became the hub for imperial interaction and the focal point of American foreign policy.

THE GEOPOLITICS OF SCALE

Geography and technology influenced the conception of space in yet another way: by making political thinkers reconsider the notion of 'power' through the geopolitical concept of 'scale'. Considerations of 'scale', in particularly regarding the desirable size of states, had been part of international thought since at least the late nineteenth century.[89] Nonetheless, wartime thinkers argued that a reflection on scale was necessary because technological innovations changed the relations between time and space, potentially influencing the 'balance of power' in the world.

The notion of 'power' played a central role in Spykman's geopolitical writings. For him, 'all civilized life rests in the last instance on power', which he defined as 'the ability to move men'. Politics was concerned with increasing the state's power, and not with 'justice, fairness and tolerance'. He recognised that political power could be a means to an ethical end, but simultaneously tried to divorce the notion of political international 'power' from 'morality', which was for him a 'world of dreams'.[90]

Spykman suggested that 'power' should be discussed not in moral but in geopolitical terms. Both he and Lattimore agreed that 'the ability to move

---

[87] Owen Lattimore, *America and Asia: Problems of Today's War and the Peace* (Claremont, CA: Claremont College, 1943), 35.

[88] Ibid., 37.

[89] Varouxakis, '"Great" versus "Small" Nations'.

[90] Spykman, *America's Strategy in World Politics*, 11–18, 7.

man' could be exercised better in large-scale political spaces, arguing that small states could not resist the pressure from their stronger neighbours and would have to integrate into the larger polity, voluntarily or not:[91] 'a world order that is both progressive and stable must include the concept of large Asiatic states, each of which is politically free and each of which has its political and economic system centred in the heart of its own territory, reaching out from the centre to defend and control the land frontiers and the coasts and ports'.[92] Warning against a repetition of the unsuccessful post-war settlement of 1919, Lattimore and Spykman argued that small states were politically undesirable. Unlike the Wilsonian ethos of national self-determination, these geopoliticians did not underwrite the right of national groups to a state of their own.[93] Rather, their main concern was to create a balanced, peaceful, and safe global system in which national minorities could thrive as part of large regional polities.

In the air age, Spykman argued, only large states could be powerful enough to sustain air-, sea-, and land-based warfare.[94] Smaller states without the demographic, economic, geopolitical, and natural resources to wage tri-dimensional war could exist only as 'buffer states' under the protection of larger states, in a system based on the principle of 'balance of power': 'the existence of a buffer state is an indication of a system of approximately balanced forces'.[95] In 1941, he discussed the international implications of his interpretation of power: the international sphere was characterised by a struggle for power in which each state aimed to protect its independence and the integrity of its territory.[96] The struggle for power was a continuous historical phenomenon resulting from the impossibility of attaining absolute 'order' or 'anarchy' in the intrinsically dynamic and changeable international sphere.[97] The post-war planning should therefore aim at creating a world made of units of equal power: 'Map makers of the post-war world should try to avoid as much as possible great inequality in power potential'.[98] Yet this advice seems to counter Spykman's earlier argument that the struggle for power, independence, and territorial integrity was an inherent part of human nature that could not be simply resolved by geographical arrangements.

Evidently both Spykman and Lattimore proclaimed a regional world order, yet Spykman's was more in line with American priorities at the time,

---

[91] Lattimore, 'Inland Crossroads of Asia', 387; Spykman, *America's Strategy in World Politics*, 19.

[92] Lattimore, 'Inland Crossroads of Asia', 382.

[93] Mazower, *Governing the World*, chap. 8.

[94] Nicholas J. Spykman, 'Frontiers, Security, and International Organization', *Geographical Review* 32 (1942): 438.

[95] Ibid., 441.

[96] Ibid., 437.

[97] Spykman, *America's Strategy in World Politics*, 15.

[98] Spykman, 'Frontiers, Security', 444.

and resonated to a certain extent with the regional plan proposed by Nelson Rockefeller, assistant secretary of state for American republic affairs, at the Dumbarton Oaks Conference in 1944. At the Georgetown meeting, two American visions for world order emerged: a system of regional blocs promoted by Rockefeller, and a universal institutional vision advanced by Brookings Institution's Leo Pasvolsky.[99] Eventually, Pasvolsky's proposal prevailed, and the United Nations was founded on universal, not regional, principles. The discussion between Rockefeller and Pasvolsky reflects a wider American debate on post-war order to which Spykman contributed. Nonetheless, Rockefeller's global vision was based on regional alliances and cooperation pacts, while Spykman's unabashedly focused on extending American power in its geopolitical region, which would for him overlap with the Western Hemisphere.[100]

Spykman used frontiers to parcel the world into states and regions of equal powers, because 'the frontier determines the power potential of the territory it surrounds'. How could this be done? How could 'power' be evaluated and measured in order to parcel territories equally? *America's Strategy* presents quantitative research in politics, based on empirical data and statistics, to evaluate the power potentials of a given territory and formulate political strategy on the basis of calculable parameters like geography, climate, resources, and demography. However, since these factors were not static or equally distributed, an artificial territorial division would be desirable but impractical. A solution could be found only if the political scientist and the geographer joined forces to formulate 'legal provisions for sanctions that harmonize with the distribution of power'.[101] His conclusion, giving the final word in international affairs to geographers and politicians, rejected interwar legalistic internationalism, which grounded collective security in international institutions such as the League of Nations, where legal solutions were prioritised over political ones.[102] Spykman called for a return to a *political* world order overtly based on the existing regional balance of power.

---

[99] Mazower, *Governing the World*, 204. On Rockefeller and Pasvolsky's debate, see Cary Reich, *The Life of Nelson A. Rockefeller: Worlds to Conquer, 1908–1958*, vol. 1 (New York: Doubleday, 1996), 286–296.

[100] Gisela Cramer and Ursula Prutsch, 'Nelson A. Rockefeller's Office of Inter-American Affairs and the Quest for Pan-American Unity: An Introductory Essay', in *¡Américas Unidas! Nelson A. Rockefeller's Office of Inter-American Affairs (1940–46)*, ed. Gisela Cramer and Ursula Prutch (Madrid: Iberoamericana Vervuert, 2012).

[101] Spykman, 'Frontiers, Security', 447.

[102] The historical interpretation of the League of Nations as a legalistic project was recently challenged by Wertheim, who argued that the League was conceived as a political—rather than juristic—international organisation. This, however, was not the way the League of Nations was understood in the 1940s. Stephen Wertheim, 'The League of Nations: A Retreat from International Law?', *Journal of Global History* 7 (2012): 210–232.

AFTER FREDERICK JACKSON TURNER:
THE FRONTIER IN INTERNATIONAL RELATIONS

The spatial concept of the Frontier played a pivotal role in the political imagination of Spykman and Lattimore. Bearing a geographic, symbolic, and political meaning, the Frontier became the political space created by the territorial division and encounter of two different political and social entities. Importantly, each of the thinkers used the geopolitical frontier to justify a different political goal: for Lattimore anti-imperialism and for Spykman American interventionism. The Frontier theory remains Lattimore's most recognised contribution to historical and anthropological scholarship, although its strategic or political importance is now lost.[103] The frontier, an area rather than a line, gives order to the entire political system.[104] It is not a demarcating outline of the political unit, but a physical, conceptual, and political zone of struggle and interaction, of both local and international importance. Since Lattimore thought that sociopolitical ideas and norms penetrated the territory from its frontiers towards the centre, the frontier population became the political vanguard for the entire political unit.[105]

In the American imagination, the Frontier was associated with the thesis advanced by historian Frederick Jackson Turner in 1893, which created the myth of American democracy: the 'moving frontier line' westwards was the practical and political reason for the development of the American conception of liberty, as distinct from the European political traditions.[106] Free from binding social and economic relations, the frontier land was available to be inhabited by the American pioneers. Turner's influential writings paved the way for a long-term American interest in the frontier as geopolitical myth: even Lattimore's friend, Vice President Henry Wallace, published his version of the Frontier Thesis.[107] Lattimore, however, saw Turner's frontier as a symbol of expansion and conquest: after all, the American continent was not an empty space, and it should not be forgotten that

---

[103] Lattimore's frontier theory was applied by historians and anthropologists to various geopolitical realities, including M. Nazif Mohib Shahrani, *The Kirghiz and Wakhi of Afghanistan: Adaptation to Closed Frontiers and War* (Seattle: University of Washington Press, 2002); C. R. Whittaker, *Rome and Its Frontiers: The Dynamics of Empire* (London: Routledge, 2004); James C. Scott, *The Art of Not Being Governed: An Anarchist History of Upland Southeast Asia* (New Haven, CT: Yale University Press, 2009).

[104] Owen Lattimore, 'Inner Asian Frontiers: Chinese and Russian Margins of Expansion' (1947), 134–136, and 'The Frontier in History' (1955), 470, both in *Studies in Frontier History*.

[105] Weigert and Stefansson, *Compass of the World*, 393.

[106] Frederick J. Turner, 'The Significance of the Frontier in American History' (1893), in Turner, *Frontier in American History*. For a historical account of the 'frontier' in American history, see Kerwin Lee Klein, *Frontiers of Historical Imagination: Narrating the European Conquest of Native America, 1890–1990* (Berkeley: University of California Press, 1999), 193. Klein invokes Lattimore's contribution to frontier theory in passim.

[107] Henry A. Wallace, *New Frontiers* (New York: Reynal and Hitchcock, 1934).

its native peoples lost their life and territory in the encounter with the pioneers.[108] Conceptually, whereas for Turner at the end of the westbound expansion process the geographic frontier disappeared into the Pacific Ocean
and lost its geopolitical importance, for Lattimore the frontier would remain a defining political factor because it depended not only on geography, but also on the society and the state which construed it. Lattimore argued that Turner's thesis was limited by its focus on the frontier as the zone
of *geographic* encounter between the European immigrant and the American wilderness. Instead, he suggested a more holistic, structural view, taking into account the institutional and cultural factors that characterised
and motivated the social exchange in the frontier zone. For him, each society required and perpetuated the concept of Frontier, and the necessary
'other' on its opposite side, to define its own identity.

Lattimore's discussion of Turner's thesis gives rise to the question whether
there is a substantial conceptual or geopolitical difference between the
American and the Asian landmasses. Geographically, one can claim that the
American continent also offered a vast landmass where a pluralistic, democratic, and dynamic society could be developed, in a similar manner to Lattimore's vision for Asia. In 1944, Lattimore affirmed that America and China
were both geographically similar 'land masses'. Yet they were not endowed
with the same political qualities and potential. The most important point
of difference was that for millennia China articulated its foreign policy in
territorial terms, while the United States, a much younger state, still based
its foreign relations on sea power and on maritime trade and communication networks with Europe and Africa.[109] Furthermore, the Americans imported their institutions from Europe, creating, for Lattimore, a politically
homogeneous space. The interaction with local populations, which he saw
as an analytically different process from the interaction with the local territory, did not have an important political and cultural impact. American
internal cultural diversity, between different states and migrant communities, was not internationally significant. The higher degree of political
diversity rendered the Asian frontier particularly effective in promoting
change, local agency, and freedom. It remains unclear whether Lattimore
thought that the integration of different local Asian communities in one
polity would reduce the political potential of the frontier to generate freedom and pluralism, or if this spatial concept would remain effective even
when its capacity for political innovation was exhausted.

[108] Lattimore, 'Frontier in History', 489. For a brief discussion of Turner and Lattimore's frontier,
see also Jürgen Osterhammel, *The Transformation of the World: A Global History of the Nineteenth Century*
(Princeton, NJ: Princeton University Press, 2014), 329.
[109] Owen Lattimore and Eleanor Holgate Lattimore, *The Making of Modern China: A Short History* (New
York: F. Watts, 1944), 18–25. On sea power in American foreign policy, see Mahan, *Influence of Sea Power
upon History*; Harold Sprout and Margaret Sprout, *Toward a New Order of Sea Power: American Naval
Policy and the World Scene, 1918–1922* (1940; 2nd ed., Princeton, NJ: Princeton University Press, 1943).

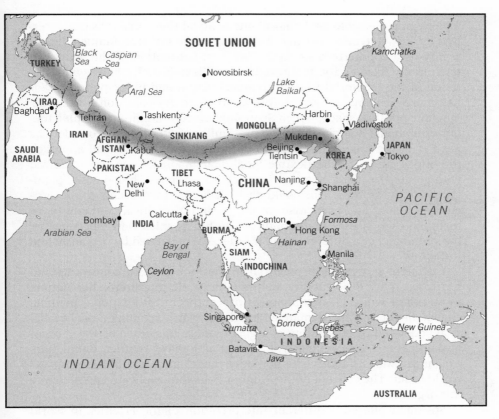

MAP 5 Owen Lattimore's Asian Land Frontier.

The political space of the Frontier is better illustrated, for Lattimore, by the vast Asian Land Frontier, stretching from Turkey to Korea (see Map 5).[110] Unlike the American Frontier, this was a geographic space of cultural interaction and a hub of national movements. James C. Scott's reading of Lattimore emphasises the contention between the sedentary agricultural plane people and the nomadic pastoral hills populations, and the fundamental importance of the relations between the human and the natural in creating the political sphere. Lattimore saw the nomadic social order, which escaped the control of the territorial state, as a complex developed social system, unlike most interpreters who conceived the transition from agriculture to nomadism as social deterioration. The populations of the frontier zone, like the Mongols, Uzbeks, and—in Scott's research—Zomia highlanders, created

[110] On Lattimore's Frontier theory in relation to Asian nationalism, see James Cotton, *Asian Frontier Nationalism: Owen Lattimore and the American Policy Debate* (Manchester: Manchester University Press, 1989), 37–57.

a pluralistic, unstable, and amorphous political space that was characterised by 'low-stateness'. Lattimore and Scott alike saw this unique political reality as a counterbalance to the Western conception of the state as a territorially fixed entity. It allowed a more flexible and versatile interpretation of the territorial space of political action and participation.[111] For Lattimore this entailed an interpretation of liberty based on a versatile, dynamic political space, which Scott later elaborated into a complex theory of nomadic anarchism. Lattimore, unlike Scott, did not consider the peoples of the inner Asian hills as promoters of an anarchical approach to politics, although the flexible landless nomadic system was endowed with greater freedom than the fixed territorial state. The nomadic populations of the frontier zone could decide whether to 'descend' to the agricultural planes and participate in the territorial political community, or maintain their liberty and mobility. The hill peoples were not anarchic but promoters of a different kind of order, characterised by pluralism and instability.

Lattimore saw political potential in the Frontier as a conceptual and territorial space of instability and mutability. He interpreted his lifetime as an era of world crisis, a moment of significant international political change facilitated and demanded by global war. Excluding a new global system defined by institutions or legal organisations based on the concept of political and social stability, he found in areas of conflict, interaction, exchange, and instability the potential model for a pluralistic post-war world order. The concept of the Frontier helped to explicate and illustrate this argument.[112]

Spykman offered a different interpretation of the Frontier in world order. On New Year's Eve, weeks after the attack on Pearl Harbor, Spykman gave a speech at the joint session of the Association of American Geographers and the American Political Science Association, outlining his spatial vision of post-war order, and the role of the United States in it. He argued that the Americans would be given the task of formulating a postwar 'new world order' based on the 'usual components' of world politics: boundaries, territorial security, and international organisation. He rebuffed as outdated the legalistic universalistic notions of 'order', which sought to construct a universal juridical framework applicable worldwide. Political power would continue to reside in territorial states whose dynamic

---

[111] Scott, *Art of Not Being Governed*, 172–173, 210.

[112] In the European context, the preeminent French historian Lucien Febvre developed a similar interpretation of the land frontier as a zone of political and cultural interaction. Like Lattimore, he also thought that conflicts at the frontier zone (in the European case the eastern frontier with Russia) were important for the formation of the political unit's character. See *L'Europe: Genèse d'une civilisation: Cours professé au Collège de France en 1944–1945*, ed. Thérèse Charmasson (Paris: Perrin, 1999). For a general account of Febvre's argument, see Marcello Verga, *Storie d'Europa. Secoli XVIII–XXI* (Bologna: Carocci, 2004), 117–120.

struggle for power would outlive the war. By consequence, war and conflict could not be avoided, only limited.

In these circumstances, his geopolitical theory evolved from what he considered to be the state's most important feature: its territoriality. The state's territoriality gives prime importance to the 'imaginary line' of the 'boundary', which is 'not only a line of demarcation between legal systems but also a point of contact for territorial power structures. From the long-term perspective, the location of that line may indicate the power relations of the contending forces'.[113] Spykman used the frontier theory as an opportunity to discuss power relations because frontiers delimit a state's power potential. The cultural, ethnic, or economic importance of the frontier areas is completely absent from this account that regards frontiers as one of the instruments available to the sovereign state to control the flows of people and goods into and from its territory.

The Rimland could also be seen as an extended frontier zone, the dividing area between the sea and land powers, a geopolitical mega-frontier that complemented the importance of the political frontiers between states. Spykman drew the conclusion that the United States had to project its political influence on the Rimland to achieve a powerful position in the world. He referred to the Monroe Doctrine as the defining vision of American foreign policy and outlined its spheres of influence, which traditionally included North and South America. At a time when many Americans argued for a revision of the territorial reach of the Monroe Doctrine, Spykman wanted to extend it to include Canada and the Arctic.[114] Yet he went further and employed the Rimland idea to include in the American sphere of influence also the Atlantic and Pacific Oceans, and eventually the coastal areas of Western Europe and East Asia. Thus, the impact of contending powers could be limited, and the United States could potentially become a leading international rather than regional power. By redefining the American frontiers, he expressed the idea that in the post-war global, compact, and interconnected world, the distance between the United States and its potential overseas enemies could not provide any reliable defence. For Spykman, the extension of the American frontier beyond the oceans, to Asia and Europe, created a new foreign policy based on active intervention, serving his political goal of ending American isolationism.

In contrast to Lattimore's Frontier, which constructed a zone of interaction, Spykman's strategic and divisive frontier created new impetus for potentially imperial intervention in the name of regional defence. The redefinition and extension of the Monroe Doctrine, an important theme in the American political debate at the time, was not a major concert for

[113] Spykman, 'Frontiers, Security', 437.
[114] Spykman, America's Strategy in World Politics, 40–62.

Lattimore. He considered it as the emblem of the negative and destructive aspects of the imperial order: the paradoxical combination of self-interested intervention in the colonial world, and international policy of isolationism embodied the worst of American foreign policy. This pattern in foreign policy was exactly what his vision of world order hoped to eradicate by employing the discourse of democratic interventionism:

> Democracy by definition is a process of adjusting the demands and interests of all peoples by giving decision to the majority and at the same time protecting the basic rights of the minority. Democracy therefore has an inherent tendency to become a world order. . . . Today we live in a world which, for reasons of communications alone, let alone many other things, is a world in which isolation is physically impossible. The consequences of things done in any part of the world spread to all other parts of the world. The fact that we are a democracy has a tremendous impact on hundreds of millions of people who do not have democracy.[115]

TRIPOLARITY

It is a truism to note that the position of the United States in the Western Hemisphere conditions American foreign policy, and more generally the American outlook on world politics. In the 1940s, a key issue in American public debate revolved around the question of whether the geopolitical conditions of the United States favoured a foreign policy of isolationism or international interventionism.[116] Both Spykman and Lattimore employed their spatial conceptions—as well as ideological motivations—to justify the abandonment of isolationism. Nevertheless, despite characterising the world as a global, small, interconnected space, they did not envisage it as politically unified, and did not think that American interventionism would be accepted worldwide without a challenge. A universal approach would have been undesired for Lattimore, and realistically unattainable for Spykman. Instead, they embraced a regionalist perspective and envisaged a tripolar world order, in which the New World was seen as one power region in the world, the 'Western Hemisphere', while the Old World constituted two power regions: Europe and Asia. Each region

[115] Lattimore, *America and Asia*, 22.

[116] Thompson, 'Geopolitical Vision'; *Sense of Power*, chap. 5. For general accounts of American isolationism and internationalism in the 1940s, see Daniela Rossini, ed., *From Theodore Roosevelt to FDR: Internationalism and Isolationism in American Foreign Policy* (Keele: Ryburn, 1995). On the history of American isolationism, see Brooke Blower, "From Isolationism to Neutrality: A New Framework for Understanding American Political Culture, 1919–1941," *Diplomatic History* 38 (2014): 345–376; Bear F. Braumoeller, "The Myth of American Isolationism," *Foreign Policy Analysis* 6 (2010): 349–371; Reynolds, *From World War to Cold War*, 296–301, 338.

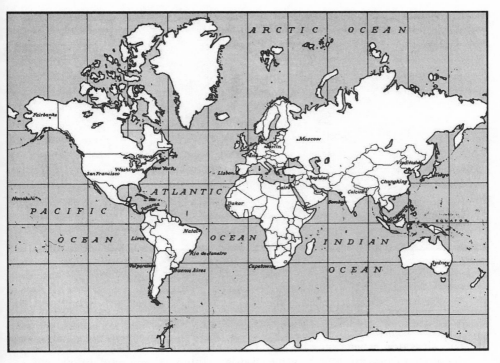

MAP 6 Traditional Europe-Centred Mercator Map. Reproduced from Nicholas J. Spyk-man, *The Geography of the Peace*, (1944), 15.

would be guided by one great power, setting the terms of the political game. Interestingly, Lattimore shared Spykman's commitment to the trip-olar thesis with the United States and the Soviet Union as two power poles, but there was no agreement on the third component: a Chinese-led democratic Asia for Lattimore, or a British-led and American-influenced Europe for Spykman. The rest of the world, including Australia, Latin America, and Africa, was of marginal importance for Spykman, who de-scribed these regions as 'world islands' where there are no great powers. While Asia played a central part in Lattimore's vision, he did not discuss Africa and Australia at all.

Cartographic innovations in the 1940s are important to understanding the turn to tripolarity and regionalism. The Miller and Gall projections became popular as substitutes for the previously dominant Mercator pro-jection, thanks to their purportedly distortion-free perception of the world.[117]

[117] Susan Schulten, 'Richard Edes Harrison and the Challenge to American Cartography', *Imago Mundi* 50 (1998): 174–188; Schulten, *Geographical Imagination in America*, 204–230; Monmonier, *Rhumb Lines and Map Wars*, 1–17, 178–180.

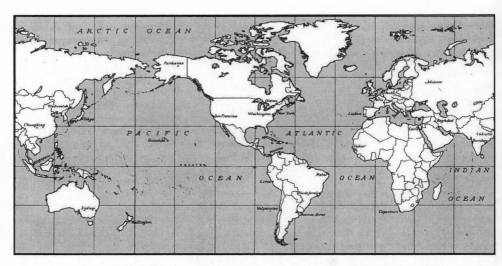

MAP 7 Miller Projection Centred on Western Hemisphere. Reproduced from Nicholas J. Spykman, *The Geography of the Peace*, (1944), 18.

The Mercator projection (see Map 6), developed in 1569 by the Flemish mapmaker Gerardus Mercator, was initially intended as a navigation map and had one major flaw: it failed to show the poles. In 1942, the American cartographer Osborn Maitland Miller invented a new cartographic projection based on the well-established Mercator projection, but showing the North and South Poles. Furthermore, mapmakers like Harrison used different perspectives, focusing their maps on different regions and most famously the Arctic, in order to reveal geopolitical connection hitherto ignored.

These maps provided mid-century thinkers with visual explanatory tools and conceptual grounds for their world-order theories. *America's Strategy* and *The Geography of the Peace* included a range of maps by American cartographers, such as Richard Edes Harrison and J. McA. Smiley. Spykman suggested that the idea of political tripolarity could be understood only by looking at a specific kind of maps, based on the Gall or Miller projections. When the Gall projection was centred on the United States, Spykman argued, the two other power blocs—Europe and Russia—became evident on the map (see Map 7).

Lattimore also included maps of central Asia in his books as an immediate representation of the geopolitical meaning of the Great Frontier as a politically coherent area of exchange between various cultures and societies. He also had a keen interest in Harrison's map series centred on various regions, reflecting the world's roundness and flexibility. This multiplicity of maps matched Lattimore's political visions about the various regional viewpoints on world politics. Thus, the novelty of these maps, and of the geopolitical visions of Lattimore and Spykman, was not necessarily rooted in new physical geographic realities but in a new representation of political space. Denis Cosgrove suggests that in the 1940s new cartographic publications manifested the growing importance of spatial representations in shaping the new role of the United States as a world leader.[118] Similarly, Spykman and Lattimore thought that their spatial conceptions, emerging from new representations of the observable world, implied a normative claim that American isolationism was no longer viable. It is telling that despite their different assumptions on political agency, both argued that interventionism was the only strategy to carve an adequate post-war space for the United States in a new regional setting: as a new kind of imperial power for Spykman, or as an anti-imperial liberator for Lattimore.

Notwithstanding cartographic innovations, some basic elements, such as the division of the world into regions and continents, remained central to the geopolitical writings of Lattimore and Spykman. Martin W. Lewis suggested that the process of formulising incoherent categories into specific world regions took place during the Second World War. The US State Department established the Ethnogeographic Board as an interdisciplinary research group to assist in planning the post-war order. In this forum, the world was redivided into regions, including Russia, Europe, the Far East, South Asia, the Near East, Africa, and Latin America.[119] This American attempt to reconceptualise the world map might have encouraged Spykman and Lattimore to envisage a new tripolar order that reorganised the world's regions around three power poles. The war alliance between Russia, the United States, and the British Empire could be another reason why the idea of a tripolar order gained popularity. Many thought that these three victorious powers would dictate the post-war order. Similarly, Raymond Aron, E. H. Carr, and George Orwell also envisaged a world divided into three regions.[120] By 1977 the 'tripolarity' school of thought, centred on Russia, the United States, and China, has been recognized and

---

[118] Cosgrove, *Apollo's Eye*, 244–251.

[119] This division became the foundation for American 'area studies'. See Martin W. Lewis, *The Myth of Continents: A Critique of Metageography* (Berkeley: University of California Press, 1997), 157–180, 190–200.

[120] George Orwell, *Nineteen Eighty-Four* (1948; repr., Harlow: Longman, 1983); Aron, *L'homme contre les tyrans*. For Carr's ideas, see chapter 2.

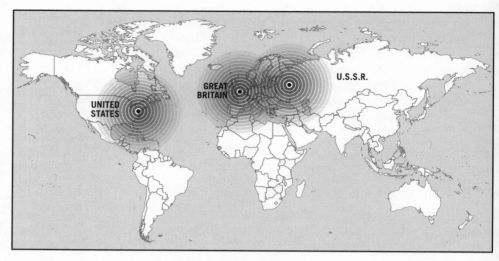

MAP 8 Nicholas J. Spykman's Tripolar World Order.

discussed by political scientists as a viable if complicated political alternative to bipolarity.[121]

However, these ideas of tripolarity lack the conceptual geopolitical background Lattimore and Spykman offered. For them, tripolar order could reflect the post-war geopolitical reality (which Spykman did not see as he died in 1943), but could also guarantee a degree of regional diversity that a universal legal solution would undermine. In 1941, Spykman thought the post-war world would not differ substantially from the pre-war world: a world of sovereign states struggling to maintain their territorial integrity and political independence. Yet, these states would no longer be united in a legal international order governed by a world organisation like the League of Nations. It would be more effective to organise them politically in three great regions of roughly the same geopolitical 'power', each led by one, preferably democratic, hegemonic power.[122] Thus, he suggested that the three regions should revolve around the most powerful states in the world: the United States, Soviet Russia, and the British Empire (see Map 8).

Lattimore's proposal was geopolitically similar but substantially different: he suggested that China, instead of the declining British Empire, should be the third power hub (see Map 9). He hoped the Asian 'Third World' could put an end to Soviet-American antagonism, as well as to im-

[121] Joseph L. Nogee and John W. Spanier, 'The Politics of Tripolarity', *World Affairs* 139 (1977): 319–333.

[122] Spykman, *America's Strategy in World Politics*, 461.

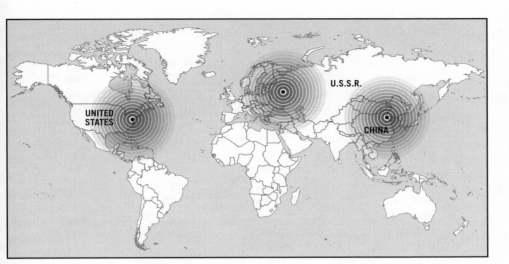

MAP 9 Owen Lattimore's Tripolar World Order.

perial domination, by offering a political and economic alternative 'middle way'. His critique of imperialism led him to see Asia as a potential democratic power. He pointed to a free and democratic China as a future regional leader, alongside Russia and the United States. 'I think China is still perhaps the most important single area. There have been people who have spoken of the years to come after the war as the "American Century". Perhaps it is more likely that the next hundred years will be the Chinese Century'.[123] Although such a statement would not seem out of place today, in the 1940s the major public debate revolved around the idea of an 'American Century', announced by Henry Luce in an influential article in *Life*, just two years before Lattimore proclaimed the 'Chinese Century'.[124] Luce argued, not unlike Spykman, that the American Century ended US isolation, and marked its entrance into world politics as a leading power. It was the beginning of a new age not only in American history, but for the world as a whole.[125]

Lattimore hoped that China's rise to global importance would mark the end of imperialism as the defining category of political space.[126] The Chinese leadership depended not only on factors of power, but also on a moral claim: China would offer a new model for freedom and democracy.

[123] Lattimore, *America and Asia*, 34.
[124] Henry Luce, 'The American Century', *Life*, 17 February 1941; Smith, *American Empire*, 27.
[125] Donald W. White, 'The "American Century" in World History', *Journal of World History* 3 (1992): 105–127.
[126] Owen Lattimore, 'The Fight for Democracy in Asia', *Foreign Affairs* 20 (1942): 694–704.

The idea of the 'Chinese Century' celebrated potentially democratic China as a new partner in a democratic world politics, the leader of the 'Third World', against European and American imperial tendencies.[127] The 'Third World', a term Lattimore first used in 1948, was not only a vanguard plan for regional democracy, but also an experimental playground for a compromise between the American and the Russian models, especially in economics.[128] The local Asian traditions and cultures would develop an autochthonous version of democracy as a midway between capitalism and collectivism, to defeat the American-Soviet binary. Thus, the 'Chinese Century' announced the emergence of a new political age, but also of a new economic system, which differed from imperial traditions by expunging exploitation and inequality. This 'Third World' economic system, interestingly, shared some basic assumptions with early theories of the welfare state, since for Lattimore a semi-regulated free-market state would not 'protect profits at the expense of human rights'.[129]

THE GEOPOLITICS OF REGIONAL DEMOCRACY

Western modernity gave birth to democracy as a world-ordering principle, according to the historical analysis of both Lattimore and Spykman. Lattimore added, however, that modernity also generated a parallel phenomenon, the global principle of imperialism, leading to the geopolitical division of the world between colonisers and colonised. Did this global division undermine modernity's promise of political and human emancipation? The responses that Lattimore and Spykman offered to this question set the foundation for their visions of post-war order, emphasising the relations between democracy and geopolitical interpretations of politics. Their disagreements reveal their competing interpretations of democracy and empire global categories of politics that set the foundations for their geopolitical thought. Both Lattimore and Spykman rejected universalism as an undesired—and unattainable—political ideal. Yet their common support of regionalism could not undermine their profound disagreements on the empirical and normative implications of their geopolitical visions of democracy on a global scale: while Lattimore saw his geopolitical thought as the foundation for a pluralistic regional democratic order,

---

[127] Owen Lattimore, 'International Chess Game', *New Republic* 112 (28 May 1945): 731–733.

[128] The origins of the term 'Third World' are unclear. The conventional account suggests it first appeared in 1952, in an article by the French demographer and economic historian Alfred Sauvy in *L'Observateur*. See B. R. Tomlinson, 'What Was the Third World?', *Journal of Contemporary History* 38 (2003): 307–321. If we accept this narrative, it seems that Lattimore had made an earlier use of the term. In 1948 he wrote of Asia as the 'third world', an alternative to both Soviet Russia and capitalist America, in 'The Chessboard of Power and Politics', *Virginia Quarterly Review* 24 (1948): 185.

[129] Lattimore, *Situation in Asia*, 223.

Spykman considered democracy as the exclusive political heritage of the West, which could not be extended beyond its civilisational sphere.

In 1945, Lattimore attacked the main argument of Willkie's *One World*, that the American concept of political freedom should be applied universally. Willkie's own political convictions, he suggested, prevented him from understanding the local populations and their unique political values. Democracy should represent not an imposed universal concept of 'justice', but a locally specific notion of 'freedom' measured by the society's own standards. 'Justice' meant abolishing the discriminatory bias between internal and external freedom: the democracies that foster freedom at home should not deny democratic self-rule to other peoples.[130] Regional democracy was minimal yet flexible: collective freedom from external imperial domination and a set of individual rights including freedom of political participation, freedom of speech and press, and cultural freedom. For Lattimore, political organisation was the first step towards a just society, in which justice would eventually be administered by a legitimate democratic government.

When envisaging a new world order, Lattimore sought to confront the European and American democratic experience with Asian interpretations. In 1942, he argued 'that Asia will be the litmus paper that reveals the nature of the world order brought about by a victory of the United Nations. For the very reason that the United Nations represent on the whole the democratic world cause, and yet themselves are not equally democratic in all respects, victory will face them with the responsibility of determining the degree of democracy that is to prevail over the world as a whole'.[131] Yet this did not mean that the Western democracies should determine the characteristics of global democracy. Lattimore preferred to maintain the flexibility and inclusiveness of the democratic system, instead of selecting one historical version of democracy as a normative model. He suggested that China would develop its own version of democracy to appeal to traditional Asian communities where values like individual liberty, justice, and equality often did not have the same meaning as in European or American democracies.

Democracy remained an attribute of political progress. It was a scalar not binary concept, which had to be remeasured and readjusted continuously. Lattimore suggested, however, that it could be measured temporally rather than spatially, in comparison with the past condition of the same society rather than with other contemporary societies.[132] Yet by signalling certain values, like freedom, self-rule, and political participation,

---

[130] Owen Lattimore, 'The Issue in Asia', *Annals of the American Academy of Political and Social Science* 243 (1946): 51.

[131] Lattimore, 'Fight for Democracy in Asia', 694–695.

[132] Lattimore, *Solution in Asia*, 138.

as the foundation of democracy, he already indicated a preference for a particular concept of human modernity that possibly limited the inclusiveness of his democratic vision.

The basic assumption that different societies could give rise to different democratic regimes, which would nonetheless be united by shared commitment to freedom, self-rule, and equality, was thoroughly rejected by Spykman, who associated the idea of democracy with one specific civilisation, the Anglo-Saxon.[133] Liberal democracy resulted from the historical trajectory of one cultural and racial group, originally in Europe and then in North America. The exceptionality of the Anglo-Saxon political experience—which did not imply for Spykman a positive political and moral judgment—rendered futile any attempt to export democracy elsewhere. In Latin America, which attracted Spykman's interest for its strategic proximity to the United States, 'the liberal social myth is not as convincing as it was formerly, and it is doubtful whether, in the prevailing type of social structure below the Rio Grande, democratic parties could achieve and hold power. Our analysis has suggested that neither race, climate, economic pattern, social structure intellectual predilection or historical tradition promises a future development for Latin America similar to the Anglo-Saxon pattern'.[134] He excluded the idea that Latin America would develop an idiosyncratic democratic system, different than the Anglo-Saxon example: 'social conditions in Latin America thus preclude a successful revolutionary campaign for the establishment of democratic government, and democracy is a form of government that cannot be successfully imposed from the outside'.[135]

The idea that the liberal democracies—or the Anglo-Saxon people—should set a democratic model for the world was, for Lattimore, embedded in a false conception of the meaning of democracy. He suggested that the Chinese, unlike the Americans, understood that 'democracy was everchanging, a way of "doing things" rather than a fixed political system'.[136] The multiplicity of civilisations in the world, of which China was the oldest, suggested not that democracy was a unique attribute of one civilisation, but rather that each was capable of generating its own version of democracy:[137] 'one of our habitual assumptions is that as backward peoples develop, even though they may demand political independence from Western countries, they must model their thought on the Western countries, hoping eventually to model their institutions on these same countries. This was true. It no longer is true'.[138]

[133] Spykman, *America's Strategy in World Politics*, 215, 230; Anderson, 'American Foreign Policy and Its Thinkers', 15.
[134] Spykman, *America's Strategy in World Politics*, 259.
[135] Ibid.
[136] Lattimore, *America and Asia*, 10.
[137] Lattimore and Lattimore, *Making of Modern China*, 2.
[138] Lattimore, 'Issue in Asia', 52.

A possible inspiration might have been the works of his friend Arnold J. Toynbee, who developed a well-known theory of 'world civilizations' as the historical components of the world's political system.[139] While Toynbee described the historical encounter between civilisations as conflictual, Lattimore built on his interpretation of the frontier dynamics to suggest a more pacific cultural and political exchange.[140]

The inclusive democracy that Lattimore promoted stopped short of religion. His ethnographic research presented religion as an integral part of Asian cultures, but for him it remained a source of conflict to be expunged from the public sphere. The negative view of religion in politics is clear from Lattimore's view of India. Enthusiastic about India's independence, he met with Prime Minister Jawaharlal Nehru to discuss their visions of Asia. However, in 1949, he expressed the hope that the newly founded state would turn away from the 'archaic politics of religion' towards 'modern secular politics'.[141] Secularism, and not only democratic politics, became the standard for civilisation in modern politics and in the international sphere. In his attempt to limit international and domestic conflict, Lattimore circumscribed the action of cultural attributes like religion to the private sphere, compromising the pluralist foundation of his democratic order.

Religion was for Spykman a positive contribution to the formation of the Western democratic ethos, based on individualistic liberalism. In other places, such as Latin America, religion played a different social role, and therefore could not contribute to the emergence of democracy. With sweeping generalisations, Spykman casted the 'values most dear to the Spaniards' as 'religion, honor and courage', which gave rise to an anarchistic individualism that could not be reconciled with the Anglo-Saxon democratic conception of individual rights.[142] Religion, and specifically Protestantism, became part and parcel of the social, cultural, and economic conditions that allowed democracy to flourish in the West, and could not be replicated anywhere else.

The main point of Spykman's reflection on democracy was not to deny that other peoples had political agency to shape their political future. Rather, his argument embodied a deeper critique of democracy in the West as well. For him, non-Western peoples would not choose to construct their post-war order on democratic lines, because they realised that democracy

---

[139] Lattimore praised Toynbee's work in a review, but criticised its teleological historiography and 'mystical' notion of 'civilization'; see 'Spengler and Toynbee', *Atlantic Monthly* 181 (1948): 104–105; Toynbee, *Study of History*; Luca G. Castellin, 'Lo "Sguardo" di Arnold J. Toynbee sulla politica internazionale del XX Secolo', *Filosofia Politica* 25 (2011): 57–70.

[140] The most salient example of this is the first president of the Republic of China Sun Yat-sen (1866–1925), who read and translated the works of many Western political thinkers, including Rousseau, before developing his own ideas.

[141] Lattimore, *Situation in Asia,* 185.

[142] Spykman, *America's Strategy in World Politics*, 228.

could no longer guarantee freedom, welfare, and prosperity. Even in its natural habitat, liberal democracy failed to deliver on its promises of social progress and economic growth. Spykman argued that these failures 'have greatly undermined the hold of democratic liberalism on the people', and weakened the position of the democratic political system in the battle against the 'revolutionary force of National Socialist ideology'.[143] There was no reason to believe that China, or Latin America, would want to democratise, even if they could. Democracy was but a feeble, unappealing myth.

Instead, Spykman envisaged the post-war order as a tripolar system in which different races scrambled for imperial domination. The imperial legacy of racial discrimination had some benefits, especially economic ones.[144] While rejecting the 'Aryan' racial prejudices, Spykman still did not think that the post-war order would transcend racial differences or overcome the discriminatory practices of racial exploitation in the colonies: in Latin America, for instance, 'the social value of being white is very great'.[145] He highlighted the parallels between race and economic achievements, but doubted that the post-war order should propose an alternative. The essence of Spykman's geopolitical thought embodied an attachment to—rather than a reversal of—the geopolitics of empire, proposing concrete ideas to strengthen the American position in an unequal, belligerent world.

Racial discourse lost its political significance for Lattimore, who rejected its use as a criterion for human classification or political domination. After employing racial terminology to describe unique traits of the Chinese society in earlier works,[146] in the 1940s he opposed racial prejudices in Chinese, American, and British political discourse:

> Several of the countries which are democratically organized at home are the owners of imperial possessions in Asia and Africa which not only are not democratically ruled, but are in fact organized on precisely the principle of 'master race' and 'subject' (less-human) race which is a fascist dogma. With the outbreak of war between the established master-races and the claimant master-races all this was changed. There are two important aspects of this change. In the first place, geographically localized demands for an extension of the principle of empire- modifications of the 'old order'—were superseded by an all-inclusive struggle for the 'new order'—the redivision of empire everywhere in the world. In the second place, all the subject-races have acquired a new importance. It is partly for the profit of

[143] Ibid., 217–218.
[144] John M. Hobson, *The Eurocentric Conception of World Politics: Western International Theory, 1760–2010* (Cambridge: Cambridge University Press, 2012), 154–160.
[145] Spykman, *America's Strategy in World Politics*, 221–222.
[146] Rowe, 'Owen Lattimore', 768.

ruling them that the great nations are fighting. Are they simply to acquiesce, paying taxes and in some cases providing troops?[147]

'Race' was no more than a rhetorical tool in political discourse, an antiliberal metaphor that wrongly assumed that biological groups were politically rigid and homogeneous. Wartime geopolitical changes and the acquisition of political agency by previously marginalised groups revealed the manipulative political use of the racial discourse by the imperial powers. The war destabilised the relationships between white and nonwhite populations, and the hegemony of the white populations gave way to a new multipolar order. To the extent that the notion of 'equality' appeared in Lattimore's writings, and it was not often discussed, it was conceptualised from a collectivist viewpoint that saw all communities as equally legitimate as different attributes of humanity, and therefore entitled to have cultural and political voice. The vertical categorisation of human societies along racial lines was incompatible with his global political vision based on a 'flat', non-hierarchical, and diversified space.

Thinking about the future of democracy in a regional order helped Lattimore and Spykman connect their geopolitical visions to the concrete political problems of their days. Neither of them provided a sophisticated or detailed account of democracy, but their reflections on the topic highlight the main aspects of their political thought. In Lattimore's vision of a regional democracy, geopolitical 'large spaces' became 'blocs' of freedom, where various 'nations' or peoples interacted to construct their own democratic system. Asia would be a 'Freedom Bloc', or the 'Third World', an independent and democratic political region with important geopolitical stabilising function. Spykman, by contrast, was wary of the democratising capacities of the colonial populations, and hoped political power remained in the hands of those 'fit to govern'. Despite his criticism of American society, the goal of his geopolitical vision remained enhancing American power in the challenging post-war—yet not post-imperial—era.

GEOPOLITICS AND THE POST-WAR POLITICAL SPACE

The global visions of Lattimore and Spykman used geopolitics to conceptualise post-war political innovations as regional—rather than universal—spaces. One of my objectives in this chapter has been to show that in their proposals geopolitical transformations were intertwined with ideological projects. Ideas about the desirability of empire and democracy on a regional or global scale emerged from empirical and anthropological

---

[147] Owen Lattimore, 'After Four Years', *Pacific Affairs* 14 (1941): 142.

observations, not only from abstract contemplation. They rejected simplistic ideas about universal unity, because, for them, the actual political and geographical order of the world revealed a high degree of diversity and incoherence. However, these empirical observations led Lattimore and Spykman to opposed normative implications. Lattimore replaced empire with democracy as the foundation of a regional order based on self-rule, popular participation, and political liberty. His attempt to address political diversity by defining 'democracy' in a vague and inclusive manner came at the expense of the concept's clarity. Spykman, who had no illusions about the flawed and exclusive nature of democratic politics, sought to refashion the United States as a democratic leader of a world of competing empires. Both thought that decolonisation in Asia gave impetus to their visions, rendering them timely, relevant, and desirable.

Yet others had their doubts about the viability of their regional geopolitical visions. In 1942, Kurt R. Mattusch of the American State Department wrote in the left-leaning journal *Amerasia* a critique of American geopolitics, arguing that regionalist geopolitics was misled because 'in a global war, space has a new meaning': a new universalism based on Roosevelt's Four Freedoms and on economic cooperation.[148] Mattusch's prophetic criticism foresaw the marginalisation of geopolitics in American international thought. It is telling that Lattimore's scholarship is rarely associated with political or strategic studies, and his contribution to international thought has been forgotten. Spykman is better remembered as an early 'realist' thinker (though the term remains vague and contested), who inspired his better-known Yale colleagues Frederick Sherwood Dunn and Arnold Wolfers, but his own writings continue to gather dust.[149]

There are five main reasons for the declining interest in their regional geopolitics after the war. The first cause is personal: Spykman died in 1943 and Lattimore was ostracised from academia and the public sphere when Senator McCarthy prosecuted him for anti-Americanism in the 1950s. The second factor is the atomic revolution, which created a new universal rather than regional perception of politics, emphasising the need for world unity around values like peace, security, and progress.[150] The third reason is the rise of a universalistic political ideology that proposed to overcome the barriers of territoriality and geography through institutions of global management, the United Nations, the Universal Declaration of Human Rights, the World Bank, and the International Monetary Fund. This new international regime was accompanied by the deterritorialised working of global capitalism and free trade. The abstention of the communist bloc

---

[148] Kurt Mattusch, 'Geopolitics—"Science" of Power Politics', *Amerasia* 6 (1942): 236.

[149] Nicolas Guilhot, 'Introduction: One Discipline, Many Histories', in Guilhot, *Invention of International Relations Theory*, 27; Haslam, *No Virtue Like Necessity*, 179–181; Vitalis, 'Review of David Ekbladh'.

[150] Sluga, *Internationalism in the Age of Nationalism*, 87. See chapter 7.

from international capitalism set a practical limit to its aspirations, but the terminology of the international political and economic organisations emphasised their global rather than regional scale.[151]

The fourth reason was the emergence of Cold War ideology and foreign policy, especially after the Korean War and the Chinese Civil War, which particularly compromised Lattimore's idea of a third 'Freedom Bloc'. If in 1947 Lattimore praised Czechoslovakia's democratic regime, the 1948 Czechoslovak coup d'état made him change his mind about Soviet benevolence.[152] Bipolarity was formulated as a clash between two universally aspiring ideologies, leaving little space for alternatives.

The last reason was decolonisation. Despite Lattimore's support for Asian anticolonial movements, he did not foresee their insistence on the political structure of the state as the vehicle of political freedom, and overemphasised the liberating capacities of a regional, supranational world order. Eventually, decolonisation led to the reinforcement of states, not regions.

Nonetheless, the geopolitical visions of Lattimore and Spykman and their intellectual circle make an important contribution to the development of the idea of political space. Cartography and maps helped them give their abstract ideas about empire and democracy a practical, visual foundation. Spykman and Lattimore were both explorers and travellers, who emphasised the importance of connecting international theory to the reality of political practice and power relations. The abstract notions of 'democracy' and 'empire' cannot be comprehended without paying attention to their territorial roots and to their spatial implications. Without providing clear definitions of these terms, Spykman and Lattimore construed 'democracy' and 'empire' by the practices of power and control that emerged through geopolitical perceptions. At the same time, geopolitics necessarily embodied normative and ideological assumptions that gave shape and meaning to geographical observations. Therefore, the writings of Lattimore and Spykman show the complex and intricate process of construction of space through political ideas, and vice versa. The idea of the 'global' emerged in a dialogue with specific geopolitical sites like the frontier, which informed normative assumptions about power relations in the world. The geopolitical thought of Spykman and Lattimore reveals the concrete and conceptual spaces that constructed for them the categories of global order.

---

[151] Smith, *American Empire*, 454–456. On legal, scientific, and religious universalism, see chapters 6, 7, and 8.

[152] Lattimore, 'The Czech Exception Disproves the Rules', *New Republic*, 22 September 1947.

CHAPTER 4

The End of Imperial Federalism?

IN FEBRUARY 1940, the British organisation Federal Union held its first annual conference at the Queen's Hall in London. A year and a half after its foundation, Federal Union faced a critical moment. The discussion in the meeting hall revolved around the need to define more clearly the organisation's aims and the means for their achievement. Although there was no agreement on the geographical boundaries of the desired federation, or on its ideological foundations, there was a consensus about the form of government it should have: the new federation should be democratic.

Arguably, the idea of a federation of democracies gained initial support after 1939 because it was seen as the last bulwark against the totalitarian threat. If the Western democracies could join forces, they might stand a better chance of winning the war. But for many public intellectuals, democratic federalism was more than a wartime weapon: it was a persuasive vision of a long-lasting post-war global order that could guarantee peace, prosperity, and liberty to all its members. The issues that they grappled with touched one of the fundamental aspects of the post-war world order: how would the decline of the European empires influence the international system and the future of democracy?

In this chapter and the following one, I propose to shed light on a transitional moment in the history of twentieth-century federal thought. The debates around Federal Union, an organisation that attracted public intellectuals and scholars from a wide range of political positions, reveal how the political legacy of empire slowly lost its centrality in the federal debate. The alternative was a new federalist approach based on social and economic justice. Existing literature on Federal Union has not dedicated much attention to the conceptual problems emerging from the organisation's publications and debates, focusing instead on the inconclusiveness of their plans, and assessing their influence on political decision makers.[1] At the same

[1] For a history of Federal Union, see, for example, Richard Mayne, John Pinder, and John C. Roberts, *Federal Union, the Pioneers: A History of Federal Union* (Basingstoke: Macmillan, 1990); John Kendle, *Federal Britain: A History* (London: Routledge, 1997), 105–124. For sympathetic accounts, see, for example, Joseph P. Baratta, 'The Internationalist History of the World Federalist Movement', *Peace & Change* 14

time, Federal Union's mid-century attempt to define democracy beyond the state remains largely overlooked by recent studies of global democracy.[2] I argue, however, that the organisation deserves a closer intellectual scrutiny because it provided the institutional platform for a fundamental change in the definition of democratic federalism, from a system to preserve the imperial order to a tool of socioeconomic reform.

The view that empire could and should set the institutional and ideological basis for a future democratic federal order became, at Federal Union, obsolete. Instead, new ideas emerged, anchoring democratic federalism in a debate about economic and social progress. I outline this transition in two chapters. First, this chapter looks closely at the rendering of empire in the writings of two federalist thinkers, Lionel Curtis and Clarence Streit, whose influential visions of democratic federalism set the conceptual ground for Federal Union's debates. It does so by interrogating the political projects that they developed and placing them in the context of the debate on federalism at Federal Union. Their proposals were deeply embedded in the experience of empire and in the idea of Anglo-American exceptionalism, which they considered the desired foundation for a post-war liberal order. Yet, their visions were not received uncritically at Federal Union. In the next chapter I show how the metahistorical narrative developed at Federal Union replaced empire with economics as the appropriate framework for mid-century thinking about democratic federalism. The goal of the federalist visions of economic thinkers like Barbara Wootton, Friedrich Hayek, and Lionel Robbins was to improve the economic and social conditions of the world, rather than safeguard the legacy of Western civilisation.

Imperial federalism was hardly a mid-century invention. Since the nineteenth century, federation had been proposed as a scheme to revitalise and salvage the imperial system.[3] British thinkers envisaged the transformation of the British Empire into a transnational federation, a new British

---

(1989): 372–403; Andrea Bosco, ed., *The Federal Idea*, vols. 1–2 (London: Lothian Foundation Press, 1991, 1992); Andrea Bosco, 'Lothian, Curtis, Kimber and the Federal Union Movement (1938–40)', *Journal of Contemporary History* 23 (1988): 465–502; Wesley T. Wooley, 'Finding a Usable Past: The Success of American World Federalism in the 1940s', *Peace & Change* 24 (1999): 329–339.

[2] For recent theories of transnational and global democracy, see, for example, Anthony McGrew, 'Transnational Democracy', in *Democratic Theory Today: Challenges for the 21st Century*, ed. April Carter and Geoff Stokes, (Cambridge: Polity, 2002); Archibugi and Held, *Cosmopolitan Democracy*; Daniele Archibugi, Mathias Koenig-Archibugi, and Raffaele Marchetti, eds., *Global Democracy: Normative and Empirical Perspectives* (Cambridge: Cambridge University Press, 2012); John S. Dryzek, 'Transnational Democracy in an Insecure World', *International Political Science Review* 27 (2006): 101–119.

[3] Victorian thinkers were also convinced of the advantages of federalism as a liberal political structure, conceived in the framework of 'empire'. As I argue here, mid-century federalists sought to set their ideas apart from Victorian advocates of federal union by emphasising the notion of democracy. On Victorian federal thought, see Bell, *Idea of Greater Britain*; Bell, 'The Victorian Idea of a Global State', in Bell, *Victorian Visions of Global Order*, 159–185. On the history of federalism in British thought, see, for example, Michael Burgess, *The British Tradition of Federalism* (Madison: Fairleigh Dickinson University Press, 1995); John Turner, ed., *The Larger Idea: Lord Lothian and the Problem of National Sovereignty* (London: Historians' Press, 1988).

Commonwealth, as a means to overcome the limits of the declining imperial system while keeping some of its benefits.[4] Yet, as the discussion in
Federal Union demonstrates, by the 1940s this attitude lost its public appeal. The demand for greater autonomy of the 'white' dominions could not
be quelled by the establishment of an imperial federation that would grant
them limited sovereignty. Furthermore, the European grip on the colonies
in Asia and Africa weakened during the war, leading some to consider colonial political emancipation a short- rather than long-term goal. Many Federal Union members became convinced that a truly democratic federation
would have to transcend the institutional and ideological experience of empire and constitute a new order based on equality and participation.

Lionel Curtis and Clarence Streit were two of the most vociferous advocates of democratic federalism. Curtis had spent decades elaborating his
federal vision of a democratic commonwealth, in conjunction with his friend
Philipp Kerr (Lord Lothian). Streit discovered the appeal of federalism in
the 1930s and wrote a best-seller promoting the federation of Western democracies. Their writings proposed two ways to imagine democratic federalism in the post-imperial age: Curtis highlighted the moral heritage of the
British Empire as the core of the new democratic federation, led by Britain
and its dominions, while Streit considered the English-speaking democracies, Britain and the United States, as the political embodiment of a unique
liberal approach to politics that should form the basis for a democratic federation.[5] The imperial dependencies and colonies that had been historically part of the imperial and the Atlantic worlds were silently excluded
from these federal visions.

The significant aspect of the debates at Federal Union is their rejection
of the earlier ideas of both Curtis and Streit, and the emphasis on the economic and social meaning of 'democracy' beyond the state. I argue that
the rejection of the federalist visions of Curtis and Streit can be explained
by their conceptual attachment to the legacy of empire that the British organisation sought to repudiate. Nonetheless, it is worth remembering that
the federalists did not always find satisfying solutions to the problems
that they identified in the visions of Curtis and Streit.

This chapter begins by looking at the history of Federal Union and the
organisation's attempts to elucidate its goals and, especially, the meaning
of democracy in a federal context. The following section discusses Curtis's
idea of a democratic federation as part of his long-term campaign to salvage the British Empire. The third section examines how Streit theorised
the idea of democratic federation in the context of the Anglo-American

---

[4] Jeanne Morefield, *Empires without Imperialism: Anglo-American Decline and the Politics of Deflection*
(New York: Oxford University Press, 2014), chap. 3.

[5] Peter J. Katzenstein, 'The West as Anglo-America', in *Anglo-America and Its Discontents: Civilizational
Identities beyond West and East*, ed. Peter J. Katzenstein (London: Routledge, 2012).

world, and explores some of the limits of his ideas. Finally, I consider Federal Union's response to the legacy of empire by examining how articles and reports written for Federal Union tackled the place of the colonies in the proposed democratic federation.

FEDERAL UNION: LOBBYING FOR A DEMOCRATIC FEDERATION

Federation and democracy had been the two cornerstones of Federal Union since its foundation in 1938. Its founders, Derek Rawnsley, Charles Kimber, and Patrick Ransome, were young Oxford and Cambridge graduates who realised that the world could soon be destabilised by war and elaborated a plan for a world federation to promote peace and cooperation.[6] They sent their petition to opinion makers and intellectuals around Britain, who helped them to formulate a 'statement of beliefs', which was then signed by Ernest Bevin, the archbishop of York (Cyril Garbett), Lord Lothian, Lionel Curtis, William Beveridge, Wickham Steed, Lancelot Hogben, Julian Huxley, Barbara Wootton, Basil Liddell Hart, and many others.[7] Although federalism had long been part of British political thought, Federal Union's success in securing the support of leading British intellectuals and politicians reflects the opportune time of its foundation and the organisation's campaigning skills.

By June 1940, Federal Union counted over twelve thousand members in two hundred fifty local branches across Britain.[8] As the movement expanded, new members became keener to contribute to the lively debate on its premises and goals. These discussions animated the movement's public meetings as well as the pages of its publication, *Federal Union News* (*FUN*). The Federal Union Research Institute, founded by William Beveridge, united public intellectuals including Barbara Wootton, Lionel Robbins, Lionel Curtis, Cyril E. M. Joad, Friedrich Hayek, and others for intense discussions on the future of democratic federalism. However, the initial period of Federal Union's expansion was cut short in the summer of 1940. Many of the organisation's young supporters joined the war effort, and public opinion was more attentive to war news than to schemes of federalism.[9] Despite these difficulties, from 1940 to 1944 *FUN* remained a vehicle

---

[6] Kendle, *Federal Britain*, 105–124.

[7] Sir Charles Kimber, 'Foreword', in Patrick Ransome, *Towards the United States of Europe: Studies on the Making of the European Constitution* (London: Lothian Foundation Press, 1991), 4–6.

[8] Mayne, Pinder, and Roberts, *Federal Union*, 12–18.

[9] On Federal Union's political activities before 1940 and the reaction of the British Foreign Office, see Andrea Bosco, 'Federal Union, Chatham House, the Foreign Office and Anglo-French Union in Spring 1940', in *Federal Idea*, vol. 1, 291–325.

of vibrant debate on the long-term vision of global federal democracy, with contributions by many of Britain's political and intellectual leaders. The newsletter offered the organisation a chance to crystallise its political goals and present them to the public.

Federal Union enjoyed the unqualified support of Labour MP Henry Usborne, co-founder of the Parliamentary Group for World Government, the motor behind the British World Federalist Movement, and later a great supporter of the Chicago Committee's World Constitution.[10] Following the failure of Churchill's plan to federate with France, British politicians were wary of the idea of a federation to unite Britain with other states.[11] Nonetheless, by late 1941 some had changed their mind. *FUN* reported enthusiastically on a speech made by Harold Nicolson, in which the National Labour MP accepted that state sovereignty had to be limited, and withdrew his earlier reservations about federal union if a democratic programme was pursued.[12] In the report, *FUN* replied to some of the questions Nicolson raised in his speech, highlighting the movement's commitment to a *democratic* federation and arguing that federalism was instrumental to achieving a transnational democratic order.

During the war, Federal Union coordinated intense discussions over the meaning of a federal democracy among federalists from Britain and abroad. At the outset, democracy was perceived as the opposite of Nazism; put simply, the war was fought to defend democracy from tyranny.[13] Later, the focus turned to planning a 'New World Order' rooted in freedom and democracy: even the newsletter's motto was changed to 'Spokesman of Freedom's New Order'.[14] Historical studies of Federal Union have emphasised the movement's difficulties in choosing a common political programme that all its members could share: a European, Atlantic, imperial, or world federation.[15] Most members agreed that the federation's chances of success depended on the political experience of the member states, pointing out that some, like Britain, were better placed than others to lead the federal project. Kimber and Robbins represented the strongest faction in favour of a federation of the European democracies without the United States

---

[10] Joseph P. Baratta, *The Politics of World Federation: From World Federalism to Global Governance* (New York: Greenwood, 2004), 159–177. For Usborne's relations with the British Federal Union, see his correspondence with the Chicago Committee to Frame a World Constitution in the Records of the Committee to Frame a World Constitution, Special Collections Research Center, University of Chicago Library, box 30, folder 6. For a detailed account of the Chicago Committee, see chapter 6.

[11] More on Federal Union's involvement with the Anglo-French union proposal in the next chapter.

[12] *FUN*, 20 December 1941.

[13] Federal Union, *How We Shall Win* (London: Federal Union, 1940).

[14] *FUN*, 14 October 1940.

[15] Mayne, Pinder, and Roberts, *Federal Union,* 10–15; Alberto Castelli, *Una pace da costruire: i socialisti britannici e il federalismo* (Milan: FrancoAngeli, 2002), 75–80; Ann Oakley, *A Critical Woman: Barbara Wootton, Social Science and Public Policy in the Twentieth Century* (London: Bloomsbury Academic, 2011), 149; Andrea Bosco, 'Introduction', in Ransome, *Towards the United States of Europe,* 25–30.

and Russia.[16] The political scientist George Catlin argued that the 'Anglo-world', Britain and the United States, had the necessary political and institutional experience to promote a federation crafted after the American federalist model.[17] The philosopher Cyril Joad emphasised the negative aspects of European history—repression, imperialism, wars—to argue in favour of a global federation.[18] Like Joad, Barbara Wootton hoped for a global federation. She was unwilling to limit her vision to specific geopolitical frontiers, but in 1943 admitted that a European federation was likelier than any other.[19] Left-leaning supporters of Federal Union, like Konni Zilliacus, shared the substance of Wootton's vision, namely the three basic federal principles of democracy, equality, and social justice, but were at odds about who should be responsible for designing and leading the federal institution.[20] Frances Josephy saw the war alliance among Russia, China, the United States, and Britain as an opportunity for a more stable collaboration among the 'Big Four', building on diversity rather than on a specific political history.[21] However, other members argued that the Soviet policy of public ownership and control over economic life was incompatible with liberty.

Kimber significantly suggested that the only point of agreement was that the future federation would be democratic.[22] This claim is substantiated by the fact that a large proportion of the pages of FUN was dedicated to outlining the meaning of federal democracy in order to produce a definitive document stating the organisation's policy goals. On 1 June 1940, as the evacuation from Dunkirk was under way, Federal Union published their draft policy statement. Their chief aims were 'to obtain support for federation of free peoples under a common government directly or indirectly elected by and responsible to the people for their common affairs, with national self-government for national affairs; to ensure that

[16] Robbins's ideas emerged in rejection of Clarence Streit's plan (see below). See Bosco, 'Federal Union', 299.

[17] George Catlin, 'Anglo-American Union as a Nucleus of World Federation', in *Studies in Federal Planning*, ed. Patrick Ransome (London: Macmillan, 1943), 299–336. Catlin (1896–1979) was an English political scientist and writer who advocated Anglo-American political union. As a professor at Cornell University, he contributed to shaping the American discipline of political science.

[18] C. E. M. Joad, FUN, 28 March 1942. Cyril E. M. Joad (1891–1953) was the head of the Department of Philosophy and Psychology at Birkbeck College, London, well known for his participation in *The Brains Trust*, a popular BBC radio discussion programme. On his critique of European civilisation, see Luisa Passerini, *Europe in Love, Love in Europe: Imagination and Politics in Britain Between the Wars* (London: I.B. Tauris, 1999), 230–231.

[19] Wootton, 'Socialism and Federation', in Ransome, *Studies in Federal Planning*. See also general discussion on Federal Union and Wootton in Passerini, *Europe in Love, Love in Europe*, 265–280.

[20] Konni Zilliacus (1894–1967) was a British envoy to the League of Nations. During the war he worked for the Ministry of Information and in 1945 was elected an MP (Labour).

[21] F. L. Josephy, FUN, 28 March 1942. Frances L. Josephy (1900–1985) was a graduate of Newnham College, Cambridge. She was a liberal political activist and chair of Federal Union from 1941.

[22] Kimber, 'Foreword', 6.

any federation so formed shall be regarded as the first step towards ultimate world federation; through such federation to secure peace, based
on economic security and civil rights for all'.[23] In this early statement the
word 'democracy' was not mentioned, but two years later, they published
a new policy statement that sharpened their definition of democracy to
include personal freedom of association and speech, freedom from spy-
ing and arbitrary arrest, freedom of access to information, and freedom
from war, from want, from censorship and propaganda, and from abuse of
privilege. Effective popular representation would be ensured by universal
suffrage. Membership in the federation entailed the surrender of arma-
ments to the federal government, and promotion of economic and political
cooperation.

Defining the scope of democracy remained a key challenge for Federal
Union. The implicit question remained political rather than geographic:
What should be the criteria for admission to the federal union? Who would
be included in the new democratic order? In the final report of the Annual
Meeting of 1942, Federal Union insisted on the need for a certain degree
of political homogeneity between the political and economic visions of
the federating states: domestic democratic constitution was construed as
the indispensable minimal condition for admission, and the member states
were required to be 'free'.[24] While the two conditions may seem easy to
assess in the context of the European democracies (Germany, Italy, and
subsequently France would join the federation once they threw the fascist
yoke and became 'free'), they cast a shadow on the future of the colonies.

The vocabulary of imperialism in the British public sphere was arguably
fluid and ever changing.[25] It is however possible to draw a distinction, for
the purpose of our discussion, between various political components of
the modern imperial systems. The dominions were semi-independent polities, under the sovereignty of the Crown. Since their citizens were mostly
white settlers, they were often considered part of the British cultural and
political sphere. The colonies were territories inhabited by settlers from
the imperial country, under immediate imperial rule but sometimes partially self-governed. The dependencies were similarly lacking in political
autonomy, but their population was by and large local and their government was directed by the relevant authority at the imperial metropole (like
the Colonial Office, for the British Empire).

One of the contested questions at Federal Union regarded the proposal
that the colonies, dependencies, and dominions should immediately be-

[23] 'Federal Union Policy', *FUN*, 7 December 1940. The writers of the statement included Wootton,
Josephy, Kimber, Joad, and Zilliacus, among others.

[24] *FUN*, July 1942.

[25] Andrew S. Thompson, 'The Language of Imperialism and the Meanings of Empire: Imperial Discourse in British Politics, 1895–1914', *Journal of British Studies* 36 (1997): 147–177.

THE END OF IMPERIAL FEDERALISM? • 107

come part of the federation as free, democratic, and equal members. Was formal liberation and constitutional democracy sufficient to establish a degree of homogeneity, or should there be a higher degree of cultural and political similarity between the member-states? For thinkers like Lionel Curtis political freedom was built not only by formal declaration of autonomy but also through historical and spiritual experience. Similarly, Streit outlined his federal vision in terms of American political exceptionalism. These approaches evidently undermined the universality of the idea of democratic federation, limited its political space to the Western civilisation and challenged the possibility of the new democratic federation to include new 'inexperienced' democracies. In what follows I sketch the attempts of federalist thinkers within and around Federal Union to address the questions of inclusion and exclusion in the context of the democratic federation, highlighting the tensions between their rejection of the logic of the empire and their quest for a stable, cohesive, and distinctly democratic union.

LIONEL CURTIS'S SERMON ON THE MOUNT

Federal Union attracted the attention of the proponents of imperial federalism, who saw in the new movement encouraging support for their federalist visions. One of them was Lionel Curtis (1872–1955), a political thinker, historian, and advocate of imperial then world federalism. For him, the new organisation could help realise the project he had been propagating for over two decades, a federation based on the institutional and moral model of the British Empire. With Lord Lothian, he joined Federal Union in its early days, and hoped to introduce its three young founders into the intellectual sphere of the Round Table group and the New Commonwealth Society, which were his preferred venues for debating the idea of imperial federation.[26] For Curtis, there was an evident conceptual continuity between his own early proposals of imperial federation and the wartime enthusiasm for a federal union: the connecting link was the British Empire, which embodied the moral and political liberty that the war sought to salvage from totalitarianism.

---

[26] The NCS was founded in 1932 by Lord David Davies to advocate a fundamental reorganisation of the international system through confederation. Curtis was one of the many supporters of the NCS (another was Winston Churchill). On the NCS, see Burgess, *British Tradition of Federalism*, 138–139; Martin Ceadel, *Semi-detached Idealists: The British Peace Movement and International Relations, 1854–1945* (Oxford: Oxford University Press, 2000), 283; Neil D. Bauernfeind, 'Lord Davies and the New Commonwealth Society 1932–1944' (MPhil dissertation, University of Wales at Aberystwyth, 1990); Waqar H. Zaidi, '"Aviation Will Either Destroy or Save Our Civilization": Proposals for the International Control of Aviation, 1920–45', *Journal of Contemporary History* 46 (2011): 150–178. On Curtis's support of Federal Union, see Bosco, 'Introduction', 24–28.

The four keystones of Curtis's global vision were the idea of the Christian commonwealth, the British Empire, American federalism, and democracy. The roots of these ideas can be traced to significant episodes in his life. His evangelical Christian family taught him that since morality was the foundation of social order, the border between politics and religion was often blurred. He became closely acquainted with imperial politics as a public servant in South Africa after the Boer War, and as a member of Alfred Milner's 'Kindergarten', a group of young administrators who changed the political and constitutional map of South Africa.[27]

Back in London, Curtis co-founded with Alfred Milner the Round Table advocacy group to lobby for the transformation of the empire into a federation of self-governing states.[28] In the first half of the twentieth century, the Round Table group elaborated a new conception of the British Empire, now re-christened the British Commonwealth. It was a union of Britain and the white settler dominions that shared, according to the Round Table, Anglo-Saxon culture and political preference for liberalism. The colonies and the dependencies did not feature in this new imperial narrative. The Round Table sought to empty imperial history of its unappealing aspects and transform the empire into a positive political and moral force of international cooperation. Curtis developed his federal thought around the idea that the empire, or commonwealth, should evolve into a democratic federation to give the dominions greater political freedom and prevent their national independence. He continued his imperial federalist crusade as Beit Lecturer in Imperial History at Oxford, and in his treatise *The Commonwealth of Nations*.[29]

After the First World War, he became an advocate for closer British-American relations.[30] As a member of the British delegation to the peace conference in Paris, he underlined the need to foster better political interaction between the United States and Britain. With this end in mind, Curtis

---

[27] Alexander May, 'Curtis, Lionel George (1872–1955)', in *Oxford Dictionary of National Biography* (2004), www.oxforddnb.com; J. Lee Thompson, *A Wider Patriotism: Alfred Milner and the British Empire* (London: Pickering & Chatto, 2007); Saul Dubow, 'Colonial Nationalism, the Milner Kindergarten and the Rise of "South Africanism", 1902–10', *History Workshop Journal* 43 (1997): 53–85.

[28] The best historical account of the Round Table is Alexander May, 'The Round Table, 1910–66' (DPhil thesis, University of Oxford, 1995). May argues that the main characteristics of the group were 'tenacity and adaptability' (11). The same can be said of Curtis. On the Round Table's project to democratise imperial politics, see Jeanne Morefield, 'An Education to Greece: The Round Table, Imperial Theory and the Uses of History', *History of Political Thought* 28 (2007): 330–342. See also Andrea Bosco and Alex May, *The Round Table: The Empire/Commonwealth and British Foreign Policy* (London: Lothian Foundation Press, 1997), 372–375.

[29] Lionel Curtis, *The Problem of the Commonwealth* (London: Macmillan, 1916); Curtis, *The Commonwealth of Nations: An Inquiry into the Nature of Citizenship in the British Empire, and into the Mutual Relations of the Several Communities Thereof* (London: Macmillan, 1916).

[30] Deborah Lavin, *From Empire to International Commonwealth: A Biography of Lionel Curtis* (Oxford: Clarendon, 1995), 166–168.

and the American geographer Isaiah Bowman were among the founders of the Royal Institute of International Affairs (Chatham House) in London and the Council on Foreign Relations in New York.[31] The historical importance of Curtis does not lie in the perceptiveness of his political analysis: he was sometimes mocked as a 'scorned prophet', but he was a prolific and widely read writer on international affairs, whose ideas circulated in diverse intellectual environments including Chatham House, the Foreign Office, Federal Union, All Souls College and the University of Oxford, the United States, and the dominions.[32]

Civitas Dei, Curtis's three-volume magnum opus and his most articulate federalist manifesto, was published in the United States under the title *World Order*. The book was a political proposal based on a metahistorical overview of Western civilisation. Following up on the project of imperial federation he had advocated at the Round Table, Curtis embarked on a politico-theological quest for a 'guiding principle in public affairs'.[33] This was finally identified with the Christian idea of solidarity and the 'infinite duty of each to all'. The British Empire, led by the Anglo-Saxon people, embodied this superior civilisational guiding principle of a new world order because it was oriented, to Curtis's mind, towards liberty and 'the common good'. In Jeanne Morefield's words, 'the British Empire/Commonwealth was both unique and the vehicle for a greater idea as it worked its way toward world historical ends'.[34]

The image of the British Empire that Curtis advanced separated the actual history of empire, with its patterns of exploitation and violence, from the glorious ideal of spreading liberty and democracy that motivated, to his mind, the British presence overseas. Since for Curtis the British Empire embodied a global experiment in spreading freedom globally, he argued that 'experienced commonwealths', Great Britain and its dominions, would have to show leadership and take the first step towards the realisation of a closely knit imperial federation that could, eventually, include the United States or European democracies as well. The book was received with mixed reviews. A British commentator admired the immense scope of the book's historical overview and its 'majestic' vision, and even praised its practicality, but a Canadian reviewer doubted that the dominions would be interested in partaking in the project.[35] American and Japanese reviewers similarly

---

[31] Smith, *American Empire*, 182; Smith, 'Bowman's New World', 449.

[32] May, 'Curtis, Lionel George (1872–1955)'.

[33] Lionel Curtis, *Civitas Dei* (1934–1937; 2nd rev. ed., London: Allen & Unwin, 1950). Hereafter I refer to the 1950 second revised edition.

[34] Morefield, *Empires without Imperialism*, 101.

[35] William Hamilton Fyfe, 'Review of *Civitas Dei* by Lionel Curtis', *International Affairs* 28 (1952): 70–71; James Meston, 'Review of *Civitas Dei* by Lionel Curtis', *International Affairs* 13 (1934): 561–562; D. G. Creighton, 'Review of *Civitas Dei* by Lionel Curtis', *University of Toronto Law Journal* 3 (1939): 249–251.

denounced his views as too religion-bound, conservative, or unrealistic.[36] Their scepticism, however, did not undermine Curtis's enthusiasm for preaching in favour of federation.

The four fundamental notions of federalism, imperialism, Christian theology, and democracy had therefore already found expression in *Civitas Dei*, but in the 1940s they attained a certain rhetorical urgency, when he started to discuss the problem of 'world order'. Curtis's article under this title (1939) neatly summarised his international thought, mentioning his South African experience in 'Milner's Kindergarten', as well as two American texts that inspired him, *The Federalist* and *Union Now*, a political manifesto for democratic federalism by Clarence Streit.[37] In the dramatic climax of his pamphlet, Curtis eulogised the moral superiority of the 'Commonwealth', a political union that he described as the 'sermon on the mount in political terms'.[38] The 'commonwealth' was for him the moral and political building block for a new federal and democratic world order that could extend beyond the British imperial sphere. His world order pamphlet gave rise to a vibrant public debate, leading to the establishment of the World Order Study Group at Chatham House to coordinate the research for a series of new pamphlets on the issue.[39] He rejoiced that the world seemed to finally accept the ideas that he had been advancing for over twenty years: 'the phrase "world order" was now gaining the same kind of currency as the words "self-determination" or "collective security" had obtained in previous years'.[40]

Democracy featured in Curtis's 1940s federalist thought as the exceptional quality of the British Commonwealth, which distinguished it from other imperial systems.[41] His definition of democracy was based not on political participation, but on his moral interpretation of imperial politics. The

[36] Clarence A. Berdahl, 'Review of *Civitas Dei* by Lionel Curtis', *American Political Science Review* 33 (1939): 894–896; Masaharu Anesaki, 'Review of *Civitas Dei* by Lionel Curtis', *Pacific Affairs* 8 (1935): 92–95; Shirley Jackson Case, 'Review of *Civitas Dei* by Lionel Curtis', *Journal of Religion* 18 (1938): 311–313.

[37] More on Streit and his ideas in the next section.

[38] Curtis, 'World Order'.

[39] Ibid. The committee members included Barbara Wootton and Alfred Zimmern. See Lionel George Curtis Papers, Bodleian Library, Oxford (hereafter LCP), box 21. Later in 1940, Curtis entered into a controversy with Lord Astor over the publication of the World Order pamphlets, the fruits of the study group's research. Despite Curtis's insistence, Lord Astor and RIIA General Secretary Gathorne Hardy were sceptical about how the publications would serve Britain's war interests and feared they could compromise official propaganda. It was agreed that the pamphlets, including an influential paper by William Beveridge, would be published independently. Beveridge's pamphlet was eventually published in 1940 by Federal Union as *Peace by Federation?*

[40] Lionel Curtis to Sir John Hope Simpson, 11 February 1940, LCP, box 21, folders 83–84.

[41] Lavin makes no reference to Curtis's interpretation of democracy in her insightful biography, *From Empire to International Commonwealth*. Studdert-Kennedy also makes no reference to ideas of democracy in his articles on Curtis's theology. Gerald Studdert-Kennedy, 'Christianity, Statecraft and Chatham House: Lionel Curtis and World Order', *Diplomacy & Statecraft* 6 (1995): 470–489; Studdert-Kennedy, 'Political Science and Political Theology: Lionel Curtis, Federalism and India', *Journal of Imperial and Commonwealth History* 24 (1996): 197–217. Morefield discusses Curtis's interpretation of democracy in the context of the Round Table group, but does not extend the discussion to the 1940s.

British Commonwealth, he affirmed, was democratic because its leader, England, was 'the heart of freedom', the heir of the Athenian democrats.[42] While the British Empire embodied a particularly strong democratic element, other European societies, including the United States, had also manifested political affinity with the principle of democracy. The democratic ethos was, perhaps paradoxically, unique and universal at once, and the British Commonwealth had the responsibility to create a universal rendering of their unique civilisation. The idea of democracy drew on the British supposedly exceptional moral character, but at the same time served as a criterion to evaluate the degree of 'civilisation' of other societies. While the imperial system played an important role in introducing democratic government to the 'backward peoples', democracy remained, for Curtis, a prize a society obtained when it reached a high degree of moral—not institutional—development.

Importantly, democratic regimes were founded through a long process of *moral* legitimisation. Democracy was a state of mind, a spiritual choice, and a moral way of being, a creed that could help the individuals identify and pursue the greater good. By establishing a federal transnational democracy, Curtis hoped to 'convert' more people to this altruistic morality. He argued that 'majority rule can operate only in so far as citizens have come to recognise the interests of the commonwealth as above their own, and in fact to treat that interest as their highest good'.[43] The recognition of the public good was an inner state of mind, not an attribute of active political participation.[44] A democratic transnational order would, therefore, not be primarily based on rational policy making or on popular participation, but on a universally shared spiritual sentiment: the idea of a greater good that directs the individual towards the right public decision. The British Empire was for Curtis the embodiment of this sentiment of public good on a transnational scale. Thus, throughout the 1940s he continued to repeat the same idea he had advanced before: 'self-governing is primarily a question of character and the ultimate problem of politics is how to develop that character. A commonwealth is simply the sermon on the mount translated into political terms'.[45]

American and imperial exceptionalism merged together in Curtis's writings to construct his political theology of democratic federalism. The American historical experience and political philosophy of federalism served as

[42] Lionel Curtis, *Decision* (London: Oxford University Press, 1941), 59; Curtis, *Civitas Dei*. See also discussion on Greek democracy in Morefield, *Empires without Imperialism*, chap. 3.

[43] Curtis, *Civitas Dei*, 39.

[44] Curtis embraced a Whig Christian position that drew inspiration from the teaching of the Anglican church and considered the British Empire as a moral player in the messianic path to redemption. On Curtis's Christian view of history, see Studdert-Kennedy, 'Christianity, Statecraft'. For the development of this idea in modern Christianity in Britain, see Matthew Grimley, *Citizenship, Community and the Church of England: Liberal Anglican Theories of the State between the Wars* (Oxford: Clarendon, 2004).

[45] Curtis, *Civitas Dei*, 125.

a template for the future, albeit a less persuasive one than the British Commonwealth. The idea of Anglo-American exceptionalism emerged from a politico-theological concept of civilisation, grounded in an idealised historical account of the spiritual development of Britain and its cultural heirs, the dominions and the United States. In this sense, Curtis sought to transcend modern rationality by extracting from the American political achievements their mystical secret of success. The introspective individual moral change would build a new polity by inducing every individual in the world to accept the political theological values of the world federation: commonality, shared destiny, self-sacrifice, and moral brotherhood. For this reason, Curtis rejected the ideas of Streit and Beveridge that the new federal government should have effective economic, political, and social powers. Rather, in 1941 he opined that the moral cohesion of the federation was more important than powerful institutions. The federated states should share a defence policy and budget, but should not subject their internal social structure to centralised federal rule.[46]

Democratic federalism entailed a concept of progress that was not related to technological advances or to geographic interconnectedness. It was based on the belief that a federation would—just like the British Empire—contribute to the moral amelioration of mankind. The universalistic political vision that Curtis proposed did not entail universal participation. When arguing that the British imperial project for agrarian reform in India required the consent of the local populations, he implied that the Indians' political agency was limited to participation in a democratic polity ruled by others.[47] He perceived the right to political self-rule not as a negative freedom from domination, but as a positive right that was neither natural nor universal and was conditioned by the fulfilment of moral duties. He repeated the oft-used Protestant argument that economic power served as a proof of spiritual character and advanced civilisation: material wealth provided an external manifestation of the spiritual superiority of the democratic peoples of Britain, the dominions, and the United States. For this reason, as we will see below, Curtis was keen to base democratic representation on wealth and fiscal capacity.

The attempt to reconcile the particular heritage of the British Empire and the American federation with a universal spiritual ethos of humanity resulted in a conservative stance about the future world order. Curtis was, in essence, a Tory federalist who aimed at restoring traditional communal values and extending them universally. There was no attempt to better people's social, economic, or politic situation, because for Curtis material well-being resulted from spiritual health, which depended, in turn, on accepting a set of traditional moral values grounded in Christian theology

---

[46] Curtis, *Decision*, chap. 3.
[47] Curtis, *Civitas Dei*, 662.

and Anglo-American exceptionalism. Democracy was, for Curtis, a spiritual value.

A world federation would be based on a moral 'sense of duty' and not on a common 'War on Want', as Barbara Wootton put it.[48] This duty sometimes meant, he argued in 1941, sharing the burden of security costs during the war.[49] But, sharing economic burden did not automatically translate into a more equal wealth distribution: 'the end and object of human society is to increase in men their sense of duty to one to another, and not, as a British statesman has told us, to raise the standard of living'.[50] The 'democratic' element of his federation did not embody a prospect of progress. He excluded the desirability of a greater material equality between, for instance, Britain and India. In 1941, Curtis affirmed that 'while I foresee a world government and a stabilised peace in course of time, I do not foresee a human society in which all the racial elements have been mixed into one conglomerate, following one standardised way of life. Such a human society would have acquired the uniformity of a jelly-fish, a one-celled organism, the lowest form of physical life'.[51] Material equality was neither the goal of political unity nor its foundation, which would be forged, instead, on the basis of a spiritual bond of civilisational brotherhood.

The conservative stance of Curtis's thought emerged clearly in the debate around democratic representation. The Federal Union discussion about the possibility of extending the federation to include ex-colonies and non-Western countries highlighted the limits of Curtis's attempt to envisage a post-imperial order. The initial idea of a federal union of Britain, the dominions, and the United States evolved in 1939 into a world federation.[52] The wider geopolitical scope required him to address the tensions between his ideas about the universality of human morality and spiritual brotherhood, and his assumptions about the superiority of the Anglo-American civilisation. Evidently, this idea influenced Curtis's institutional design for the democratic federation. By elaborating a complex representation mechanism, based on taxation and fiscal capability, he hoped to limit the power of more densely populated and poor 'backward' states.[53] The fundamental assumption of Curtis's federal thought was that the new political order would not impact the economic power balance in the world. By setting fiscal capability as the electoral criterion, the hegemonic position of Europe and the United States was less likely to be threatened.

The question of democratic representation was debated extensively yet inconclusively at Federal Union. Major W. L. Roseveare shared Curtis's

---

[48] See chapter 5 for a discussion on Barbara Wootton.

[49] Curtis, *Decision*, 44.

[50] Curtis, *Civitas Dei*, 705.

[51] Curtis, *Decision*, 47.

[52] Curtis, 'World Order'.

[53] Parmar, 'Anglo-American Elites in the Interwar Years', 63–70.

concerns in a letter to *FUN* lamenting that the 'half-starved masses of Asia' would have an advantage over the 'literate well-fed Anglo-Saxons'.[54] However, the official line of Federal Union wanted to link democracy with individual democratic participation, insisting, therefore, on giving equal weight to each voter. The Constitutional Committee of Federal Union Research Institute (FURI), of which Curtis was member, could not find a way out of the conundrum. Conveniently enough, they suggested that the matter of representation would be settled by the federal legislative organ once the federation was established.[55] While Curtis's idea of fiscal representation was rejected unanimously by the Constitutional Committee, Federal Union preferred avoiding controversial new solutions and stayed within the limits of the consensus.[56]

Lionel Curtis did not find in Federal Union an intellectual and political home. In 1943, he wrote a letter to the editor of *FUN* dissociating himself formally from the movement because it promoted a European federation that would, to his mind, ruin the British Empire by alienating and excluding its natural moral allies, the dominions and colonies from its political sphere.[57] His decision to break with Federal Union seems understandable in view of the fact that very few members of the organisation shared his conviction that the British Empire or the American federation embodied an ideal spiritual model for a democratic federation and for a future universal commonwealth of nations.[58] Wootton, Hayek, and Robbins, for example, considered democracy in terms of economic liberty and equal opportunities, and sought to translate this idea into a conception of a political federation. Their vision, as I suggest in the next chapter, emerged from a transnational notion of social and economic justice that was incompatible with Curtis's logic of empire and Anglo-American exceptionalism.

CLARENCE STREIT: 'WE NEED UNION NOW'

The debates at Federal Union were to a degree overshadowed by another proposal for a democratic federation, written in 1938 by American journalist Clarence Streit and published in the United States the following year.[59]

[54] Major W. L. Roseveare, 'Letter to the Editor', *FUN*, 17 January 1942.

[55] The Constitutional Research Committee included William Beveridge, Lionel Curtis, A. L. Goodhart, Patrick Ransome, J. Chamberlain, F. Gahan, W. I. Jennings, and K. C. Wheare.

[56] 'Report on Conferences on the Constitutional Aspects of Federal Union', in Ransome, *Towards the United States of Europe*, 117–130.

[57] Lionel Curtis, 'Letter to the Editor', *FUN*, November 1943.

[58] Martin Erdmann, *Building the Kingdom of God on Earth: The Churches' Contribution to Marshal Public Support for World Order and Peace, 1919–1945* (Eugene, OR: Wipf and Stock, 2005), 220–225.

[59] Streit, *Union Now*. The book was published in Britain by Jonathan Cape in 1939. The references here are to the British edition.

Streit's book was perhaps the most influential vision of democratic union propounded in the interwar years. His main goals were '(1) to provide effective common government in our democratic world in those fields where such common government will clearly serve man's freedom better than separate governments; (2) to maintain independent national governments in all other fields where such government will best serve man's freedom and (3) to create by its constitution a nucleus world government capable of growing into universal world government peacefully and as rapidly as such growth will best serve man's freedom'.[60] Streit envisaged a 'union of the free' based on fifteen democracies that formed, according to him, the core of Western civilisation: Britain, the United States, France, Switzerland, Sweden, Norway, Finland, the Netherlands, Belgium, Denmark, Australia, New Zealand, Canada, South Africa, and Ireland.[61]

In an annex to his book, Streit explained his personal 'road to union' as a reaction against the inaptitude of existing international institutions to deal with political crises.[62] In the interwar years, he was the *New York Times* correspondent to the League of Nations in Geneva, witnessing the discussions about the Italian invasion of Abyssinia in 1936. He later suggested that the League's manifest failure to resolve the crisis led him to believe that only a federal democratic system could safeguard individual freedom and political autonomy in the world. Americans and Britons alike read Streit's book with enthusiasm; thousands joined his political organisation, Federal Union Inc. (founded in 1941), to promote federal union via a closer relationship between democratic states.[63] In the United States, his ideas were received with special enthusiasm, reflecting perhaps the American preparedness to assume a role of political and military leadership in the world.[64]

When Streit organised the Uniting States of the World dinner at the Waldorf Astoria in New York on 22 January 1941, Thomas Mann and Clare Boothe Luce were among the illustrious speakers. Their speeches were heard by the two thousand guests who attended the dinner, and by millions of radio listeners across the country. For Mann, 'the world has become a small and the universal scene of one and the same battle . . . of faith and conviction, a religious battle in which the problem is the same everywhere'. 'The idea of union is alive', he added, and reminded his audience of another American initiative to unite the world's democracies in a common battle against

---

[60] Ibid., 18.

[61] Ibid., 6. For a discussion of Streit's ideas and achievements, see Baratta, *Politics of World Federation*, 50–55.

[62] Ibid., 382ff.

[63] On the reception of Streit's ideas in the United States, see Wooley, *Alternatives to Anarchy*, 87–95.

[64] In parallel to the story I tell in this chapter, in 1940–1941, American policy elites debated how to achieve world leadership through a permanent union or partnership with Britain and its dominions. See Wertheim, 'Tomorrow, the World', pt. 2.

totalitarianism, Giuseppe Antonio Borgese's declaration on *The City of Man*.[65] Clare Boothe argued that Streit's book offered the only peace plan for the future of democracy. It would help the United States and Britain to fight the Nazi threat, and, on the way, extinguish 'creeping statism, growing collectivism, the cancer of centralisation of power'. The union of democracies expressed the idea that 'in a world of man's soul, there are no hemispheres and the spirit of liberty admits of NO Monroe Doctrine'. For this reason, she asserted emphatically, the union of democracies is 'the only thing worth fighting for'.[66]

In Britain, the Round Table group welcomed Streit's ideas with open arms. Philipp Kerr (Lord Lothian), who was a Rhodes Trustee at the time, praised Streit, a former Rhodes Scholar, and compared his work to the American Federalist Papers and to Adam Smith's *The Wealth of Nations*. *Union Now* would be, he hoped, a world-changing book, which expressed in concrete terms the ideas that the Round Table group had sought to advance for over twenty years.[67] Curtis also saw Streit's book as a step forward towards federation, arguing that *Union Now* was a (possibly unintended) reinterpretation of his own project of democratising imperial politics.[68] On his visit to New York in 1939, Curtis was introduced to Streit by Frank Aydelotte, then president of Swarthmore College.[69] He helped bring it to public attention by distributing copies to all his friends and colleagues around the world. Over the following decade, Curtis and Streit continued to meet and approvingly read each other's works, although there wasn't a perfect overlap between their federalist schemes. The fundamental idea that brought them together was that the exceptionalism of the English-speaking countries embodied a promise for a better political order that could salvage freedom from the totalitarian threat.

Although many members of Federal Union saw Streit's campaign as positive support for their cause, it would be wrong to suggest that the British

[65] Giuseppe Antonio Borgese convened the Committee of Fifteen, a group of public intellectuals who wrote the declaration on the *City of Man* in 1940. Other members included Thomas Mann, Lewis Mumford, and Reinhold Niebuhr. On this project, see chapters 6 and 8.

[66] *Democracy's Answer to Hitler*, Program of the Uniting States of the World Dinner at the Waldorf-Astoria, 22 January 1941 under the auspices of Federal Union Inc., LCP, 162.

[67] On the Round Table's reception of Streit's book, see Erdmann, *Building the Kingdom of God on Earth*, 231–232.

[68] Curtis's impression may have been misguided. However, Streit's obituary of Curtis makes clear that their 'basic thought was similar'. After their meeting in New York in 1939, Streit was left with the impression that 'Lionel Curtis well understood that this great transformation could not be achieved with all the world at once, that it must start with a few nations, and that they must be democracies'. See Clarence Streit, 'Lionel Curtis—Prophet of Federal Union', *Freedom and Union* 11 (1956): 11–12. According to Andrea Bosco, Lionel Robbins also noted the similarities between Curtis's proposals and Streit's *Union Now*. See Bosco, 'Introduction', 26.

[69] For an account of their meeting, see Clarence Streit, 'Lionel Curtis—The Federalist', *Freedom and Union* 9 (1949): 8–9. Frank Aydelotte was among the authors of the *City of Man* declaration in 1940.

organisation was founded to promote Streit's ideas in Britain, or that it fully supported the plan that Streit outlined. Nonetheless, given the public success of *Union Now* in the United States, Federal Union members had to measure their own proposals with the American manifesto. Charles Kimber recounted that the three founders of Federal Union received the news of Streit's book from Harold Butler, the director for the International Labour Organisation in Geneva, only after they had already launched their own campaign in London. While they rejected Lothian's suggestion to use *Union Now* as a detailed version of Federal Union's proposals, they adopted some of Streit's terminology, in particular the rhetoric of the 'free peoples' as writers of the democratic constitution.[70]

In retrospect, Kimber suggested that he, Rawnsley, and Ransome saw Streit as a fellow traveller, but considered his proposal as 'quite unrealistic' and even 'undesirable'. Sceptical about English-speaking democratic exceptionalism, they feared that an Atlantic federation would undermine Britain's relations with Europe.[71] This impression was reinforced by Streit's second book, *Union Now with Britain* (1941), which emphasised the positive political implications of the exceptional cultural and political bonds between the United States, Britain, New Zealand, Australia, Ireland, Canada, and South Africa.[72] Like Curtis, he argued that the British Commonwealth was crumbling under the weight of its internal and external conflicts, and thought that the solution would be to inject the Commonwealth with American-style federal spirit. But Streit was not as confident as Curtis that England was the 'heart of freedom'. Instead, he blamed Britain's declining international influence on the political shortcomings of the imperial system that failed to provide freedom and equality to all its members.

Streit's second call for union also marks a slight change in his treatment of the colonies: if in 1939 he advocated a federal trusteeship system arguing that 'transfer of colonies to the Union would not require, of course, upsetting existing administration', in 1941 he added that the union should prepare all 'non-self-governing territory for full membership as rapidly as prudent experiment justifies'.[73] The Federal Union would be less hierarchical than the British Commonwealth, but not necessarily more inclusive: despite Streit's 'admiration and sympathy' for the political achievements of China and Japan, cultural differences prevented their initial admission to the union.

Since India had already been a British 'dependency', and, in a way, belonged to its cultural sphere, he conceded that it be given 'more voice than it has had in its own affairs' and 'some voice in the Union government',

---

[70] Bosco, 'Introduction', 22.
[71] Kimber, 'Foreword', 8–11.
[72] Clarence K. Streit, *Union Now with Britain* (London: Right Book Club, 1941).
[73] Streit, *Union Now*, 250; *Union Now with Britain*, 228.

but definitely not immediate independence.[74] Employing the well-known paternalistic vocabulary of imperial thought, he suggested that the democratic states should treat India and other 'politically inexperienced peoples much the same as we treat politically our own immature sons and daughters'.[75] Letting the 'politically inexperienced masses' partake in the democratic federation was not only impractical but also irresponsible, as it would condemn the project to failure and 'hand the world over to autocracy and war'.[76] The short discussions of the colonies in Streit's two lengthy books suggest that safeguarding the 'free' democracies was for him a separate—and much more important—cause than protecting the freedom of the colonial populations.

The Anglo-American union was a wartime necessity but also 'the safest, surest and best defence of our free principles not only from the foreign but the domestic dangers'.[77] One of these domestic dangers seems to be, for Streit, centralised power. Federalism was not imperialism, he insisted, because it entailed a general restriction of governmental action in both domestic and federal politics. Like Hayek, he envisaged a federal structure that would create a central government with limited powers while decentralising political decision making to state, county, and town administrations.[78]

The intentional rift between the West, where freedom and democracy were championed, and the colonies, where liberation was not an immediate goal, undermined the universal aspirations of Streit's plan but did not diminish its popularity. Other federalist thinkers felt obliged to respond to Streit's plan. In 1939, W. B. Curry, a British schoolmaster and leading member of Federal Union, wrote his own best-selling federalist maifesto, selling over a hundred thousand copies.[79] Originally inspired by H. G. Wells and Bertrand Russell, he shared Streit's vision of a union of the world's democracies as the foundation of a new post-war order. But Streit's federalist solution to the problem of empire, which simply relegated the issue to a federal mandate authority, did not seem adequate to Curry. Instead, he argued that colonial and non-European people could become equal members of the federation. Freedom should not, he suggested, be limited to the European and American democratic states. As soon as the war was over, India and China should become independent and ten years afterwards should join the democratic federation on equal terms.[80]

---

[74] Streit, *Union Now with Britain*, 228.

[75] Streit, *Union Now*, 185–186. Jawaharlal Nehru found Streit's proposals 'attractive' but criticised his disregard of imperialism. See Duncan Bell, 'Before the Democratic Peace: Racial Utopianism, Empire, and the Abolition of War', *European Journal of International Relations* 20 (2014): 649.

[76] Streit, *Union Now with Britain*, 228.

[77] Ibid., 23.

[78] More on Hayek's decentralised federalism in the next chapter.

[79] William B. Curry, *The Case for Federal Union* (London: Penguin, 1939).

[80] Ibid., 193.

The new federation should promote, for Federal Union, the rapid independence of the colonies after the war, not the establishment of a long-term federal system of trusteeship. The Federal Union committee on 'federal powers' similarly confirmed that it was 'urgently desirable' that China, Burma, and India should democratise and join the union.[81] Despite a certain ambiguity at Federal Union regarding the institutional path of the colonial territories and dependencies towards independence, the general assumption was that once free and democratic, they could—if they so wished—join the federation.[82] In this sense, Curry and others at Federal Union sought to complicate the simplistic historical narrative of the West as the 'heart of freedom' and to challenge the view of democracy as a unique and incomparable Anglo-American culture. While a degree of cultural similarity was necessary to foster a stable federal order, Curry suggested that a shared outlook was more important than a common past.

Initially the only precondition for joining Streit's union was a democratic political system, but it soon became evident that for him democracy was shaped by shared values that necessarily emerged from common historical experience.[83] Democracy was a civilisation, a way of life forged by imperial explorations and popular rebellions. This 'civilisation' stood for a political system defending a peculiarly American idea of an individual right to life and liberty. Despite formally including European democracies in his proposed union, Streit pointed to the British and American democracies and especially to the American federal experience as the standards of civilisation for a stable order.

The imperial notions of civilisational hierarchy and teleological progress remained central to the federalist political discourse of Streit and Curtis.[84] There has never been, in their writings, a distinct break with the idea of a global 'standard of civilisation', set by the Western democracies as a universal benchmark for political progress. The conceptual staple of imperial thought, which had already found expression in the League of Nations' Covenant, served as guidelines for Streit's view of the relations

---

[81] 'Report', *FUN*, June 1942, 11. The report was written by Joad, Josephy, Kimber, and Zilliacus.

[82] Some did not see an immediate prospect of colonial liberation, and argued in favour of trusteeship. Reginald Coupland argued that the British policy towards the 'native races' was 'the most advanced in the world' and consisted of 'trusteeship, the assistance of natives towards world government and the recognition that in the meantime native interests should be considered as paramount'. However, his opinion did not find its way to the Federal Union policy statements. See 'Report of the First Colonial Conference, Held at Oxford, January 20 and 21, 1940', in Ransome, *Towards the United States of Europe*, 174–179. Other members of the committee included Beveridge, Curtis, Norman Bentwich, E. E. Evans-Pritchard, Lord Lugard, Sir Drummond Shields, and Ivor Jennings.

[83] Streit, *Union Now*, 56.

[84] For comprehensive accounts of the 'standard of civilisation', see Gerrit W. Gong, *The Standard of 'Civilization' in International Society* (Oxford: Clarendon, 1984); Brett Bowden, *The Empire of Civilization: The Evolution of an Imperial Idea* (Chicago: University of Chicago Press, 2009), 105–160.

between the democratic federation and its colonial outposts.[85] He empowered the democratic states to assume the responsibility—the well-known 'white man's burden'—to administer the new federal tutelage system of the 'politically weak'. The aim of the federation was, evidently, to extend the democratic principle beyond its existing borders until the 'immature' peoples had made the civilisational progress towards 'democracy'.

The rhetoric of Streit's federalist proposal assumed that 'democracy' entailed a particular historical trajectory, grounded in Western culture, but that with the necessary goodwill and political effort it could also be exported around the world. Despite arguing that his federalist proposal was based on a shared political principle and not on imperial or racial supremacy, he preserved the fundamentally paternalist ideology of the 'civilising mission' of the West, depicting the exploitative colonial practices of Western democracies as a legitimate part of their quest for order and stability, which was fundamentally beneficial for the colonial peoples as well. Wrapping the violent history of colonialism in a veil of silence, he motivated the renewal of the mandate system under the auspices of the federation by accusing the non-Western populations of wilful submission: the colonies were 'immature' and not democratic because they *agreed* to be governed authoritatively, 'as children'.[86]

The civilisational divide between 'mature' and 'immature' peoples and the association of democracy with a particular race and culture in Streit's thesis were strongly criticised in 1939 by George Orwell in his essay 'Not Counting Niggers'.[87] Orwell pointed out that Streit's federal vision, albeit practical and possibly even effective to bring about the end of war, positioned the majority of the world's population (except for Europeans and North Americans) beyond the sphere of political agency. Streit's imagined federation was indistinguishable from the political space of imperialism, accepting the political definitions of the imperial discourse, according to which the imperial powers were 'democracies' regardless of their exploitative practices abroad.

Without breaking the divide between the domestic democracy and overseas exploitation, and between the European and non-European races (Orwell discussed both Asia and Africa), the federal union would merely perpetuate the political space of empire, and by consequence give rise to new forms of fascism.[88] While Streit was not a simple apologist of imperial expansion, he failed to transcend the political conceptualisations of inclusion and exclusion that emerged from imperial history. Therefore, it was easy for

---

[85] For a remarkable history of the League of Nations and its mandates system, see Pedersen, *The Guardians*.

[86] Streit, *Union Now*, 128 (my emphasis).

[87] George Orwell, 'Not Counting Niggers', in *The Collected Letters, Essays, and Journalism of George Orwell*, vol. 1, ed. Sonia Orwell and Ian Angus (London: Secker and Warburg, 1968), 360–361.

[88] Ibid.

Orwell to condemn the discussion of democratic federalism as an attempt to ignore the problems of empire and perpetuate the exclusion of the colonial populations. Although Streit explicitly denounced the usage of 'race' as a discriminatory political criterion, his interpretation of the civilising mission of the democracies helped maintain political continuities with the practices of empire, and undermined the universality of his own conception of political freedom.

Federal Union did not join Orwell's public attack on Streit's democratic federalism. *FUN* continued publishing Streit's articles, and his great public success was considered an important indication that the idea of federalism was widely appreciated. Yet, Federal Union criticised Streit's belief that the British Empire and the United States, or the English-speaking peoples, shared a distinct political heritage, rendering them more suitable than others to become the leaders of the transnational federations. This might not have been Streit's intention, since the term 'Anglo-Saxon' does not appear in his book, and his idea of federation included other European democracies, like France, the Netherlands, and Sweden, which did not belong to the Anglo-Saxon cultural and political sphere. Nonetheless, the leaders of Federal Union, like Wootton and Curry, had the impression that Streit's proposals advanced a triumphalist view of the political achievements of Britain and the United States. For them, the federation's cohesion would depend not on an exclusionary common 'civilisation', but on a shared outlook for the future, in which the non-Western peoples must, at least in principle, be invited to partake.

FREDERICK LUGARD, NORMAN BENTWICH, AND THE BOUNDARIES OF THE COMMONWEALTH

The legacy of empire was considered a burden rather than an asset for the new world order that Federal Union sought to propose. The organisation could not, however, ignore the pressing problem of the colonies and dependencies, which remained under direct European sovereignty or indirectly through the mandates system. The crumbling of the imperial order demanded a new strategy for thinking about the relations between domestic and global democracy. For many Federal Union members, the tension between the democratic ethos at home and the illiberal policies of imperial administration abroad could be a potential setback to the realisation of the new federal order. Interwar ideas about preserving the positive aspects of the imperial order as the foundation of a new internationalism had lost their appeal.[89] The idea of imperial citizenship, which

---

[89] For an insightful history of interwar internationalism and its imperial sources, see Morefield, *Covenants without Swords*.

would unite all members of the British Empire including the colonies in a transnational federal polity, was deemed unrealistic.[90] Many felt that the new federal order should offer a brand new interpretation of democracy that would be relevant to both domestic institutions and international relations.

The colonial world gave rise to two dilemmas for supporters of federation. The political dilemma regarded the potential participation of the colonial population as equal members of the federation. The economic dilemma regarded the distribution of economic resources derived from the colonies between the European states and the local population. At Federal Union's colonial committee, Reginald Coupland, Lionel Curtis, Frederick Lugard, and Norman Bentwich recognised that the colonial status quo could no longer hold. Their discussions reveal the struggle of Federal Union to come to terms with the political and economic legacy of empire. The reason for the difficulty was the general impression at the organisation that the outdated imperial order was simply incompatible with the idea of federal democracy, defined in terms of political participation, equality, and freedom. This section surveys the attempts of Federal Union members, and their invited expert contributors, to deal with the intellectual, political, and economic heritage of empire. Their failure explains the turn away from empire as a useful political and historical resource for planning a new order.

In their attempt to overcome Lionel Curtis's vision of post-imperial federation, the members of Federal Union struggled to propose an alternative framework for thinking about the colonies' place in the proposed federation. The most common idea about the future of the colonial world under the federation was the establishment of a federal system of mandates. This unoriginal scheme, inspired by the League of Nations mandate system that the federalists had much criticised, aimed at developing the colonies politically and economically to allow them, one day, to attain political independence.[91] The basic idea was that the federal authority would supervise and direct the administration of the colonies. Yet some doubted that federal tutelage of colonial affairs would be an improvement on the existing system. Frederick Lugard (1858–1945), who was recruited to Federal Union to write a report on the future of the colonies, resented Beveridge's arguments in favour of a federal administration of the 'dependencies'. As a long-time colonial administrator in Africa and a British representative on the League of Nations' Permanent Mandates Commission, Lugard considered himself in a position to shed light on the shortcomings of Federal Union's

[90] On imperial citizenship in the Indian context, see Sukanya Banerjee, *Becoming Imperial Citizens: Indians in the Late-Victorian Empire* (Durham, NC: Duke University Press, 2010); Daniel Gorman, *Imperial Citizenship: Empire and the Question of Belonging* (Manchester: Manchester University Press, 2007).

[91] William Beveridge, *Peace by Federation?* (London: Federal Union, 1940).

colonial policy. While Ransome argued in Lugard's defence that he was no 'reactionary imperialist', the proposals that he advanced served mostly to demonstrate the state of mind that Federal Union hoped to avoid.[92]

In a pamphlet written for Federal Union in 1941, Lugard sought to explain why a federal system of colonial administration would not be a suitable answer to the colonial problem. An opponent of colonial 'self-determination', he shared Curtis's conviction that the moral character of the British Empire and its colonial administrators, who 'have the interests of the Colonies at heart', should be translated into concrete political responsibility for the colonial peoples.[93] This commitment meant, according to Lugard, that special bonds were forged between the colonial populations and the imperial administrators, fostered by a common 'national sentiment' that could create the basis for imperial federal citizenship. However, if full participation in empire as a 'great white republic' was supposed to extend rights to the dominion populations as equals, other racial, historical, or moral communities were categorically excluded, but not completely removed from the protection, and the authority, of colonial governments. Lugard's idealised vision of colonial Africa downplayed the economic benefits derived from the colonies, suggesting that for the European states, the cost of developing the colonies exceeded the financial and commercial gains. He could therefore argue that good colonial administration—following the British example—contributed to the advancement of colonial self-rule and to universal economic progress, despite the evident inequalities between the various racial and national communities.

The concerns about the post-war decline of imperial sovereignty were matched by anxieties about liberty. A democratic federation should set general standards of liberty and democracy in the colonies, Lugard opined, but the actual work of administration should be left in the hands of those who had already manifested their good intentions, like the British. The final point in his analysis of the federal prospects of the colonies was a direct attack against Federal Union's capability to enhance and extend liberty and rights in the colonies. He accused the federalist organisation of denying 'franchise rights for the inhabitants of a Dependency', which would therefore have no political representation in the federal parliament. This, according to Lugard, was an intentional part of Federal Union's proposal of democratic representation, aimed 'to exclude natives since the reason assigned is that their vote would swamp that of the State federal

---

[92] For an account of Lugard's involvement in the league, see Pedersen, *The Guardians*.

[93] Frederick Lugard, 'Federal Union and the Colonies' (1941), in Ransome, *Studies in Federal Planning*, 137. Frederick John Dealtry Lugard (Baron Lugard, 1858–1945) was governor-general of Nigeria as well as 'Britain's most famous African colonial governor in the age of empire, a pre-eminent colonial thinker in the inter-war years'. For Lugard's biography, see A. H. M. Kirk-Greene, 'Lugard, Frederick John Dealtry, Baron Lugard (1858–1945)', in *Oxford Dictionary of National Biography* (2004), www.oxforddnb.com.

electors'. He argued that such racially discriminatory policy was opposed to British policy of granting democratic rights to the colonies through the doctrine of 'indirect rule', which he had outlined twenty years earlier in his classic *The Dual Mandate*.[94]

The language of 'indirect rule' that had enjoyed some success at the League of Nations Mandate Commission was relegated, by 1940, to the margins of the federalist discourse. Instead of fostering a stronger sense of common citizenship across the imperial system, the preferred strategy at Federal Union was to break the bonds of empire in the hope that new cultural and political ties would be created after colonial independence. While Lugard drew on his African colonial experience to argue that political autonomy in the dependencies should be very gradually developed under exclusively British rule, others favoured a swifter change towards colonial independence and democratisation. Federal Union discarded the *moral* legacy of empire as the foundation of democratic federation, but more importantly they rejected the idea that the economic and political structures of empire should be in some form preserved. Nonetheless, they still took it as given that the colonies would need assistance from the federal government in the transition towards independence and democracy.

The British federalists were not alone in their struggle to reconcile the imperial legacy with a vision of a federal union. Historians have suggested that for many planners of European unity, the integration of the continent depended on the maintenance of European formal and informal empire in Africa.[95] The project of 'Eurafrica' gained prominence mostly in German and French political debate in the twentieth century.[96] According to Peo Hansen and Stefan Jonsson, 'efforts to unify Europe systematically coincided with efforts to stabilize, reform and reinvent the colonial system in

[94] Frederick Lugard, *The Dual Mandate* (1922; repr., London: William Blackwood, 1926); Pedersen, *The Guardians*, 108–110. Despite Lugard's apparent confidence in the British colonial mission, his protégé, the African expert Margery Perham, wrote in 1942 a severe critique of the British failure to develop the colonies' economy or democratise their politics. See John Darwin, *The Empire Project* (Cambridge: Cambridge University Press, 2009), 528.

[95] Peo Hansen and Stefan Jonsson, *Eurafrica: The Untold History of European Integration and Colonialism* (London: Bloomsbury, 2014); Marie-Thérèse Bitsch and Gérard Bossuat, eds., *L'Europe unie et l'Afrique: De l'idée d'Eurafrique à la convention de Lomé* (Brussels: Bruylant, 2005); John Kent, *The Internationalization of Colonialism: Britain, France and Black Africa, 1939–1956* (Oxford: Clarendon, 1992). On the African perspective on the idea of French Africa or Eurafrica and post-war African initiatives to reconceptualise a federal citizenship and sovereignty across the two continents, see Frederick Cooper, *Citizenship between Empire and Nation: Remaking France and French Africa, 1945–1960* (Princeton, NJ: Princeton University Press, 2014), chap. 4.

[96] On French interpretations of Eurafrique, see, for example, Papa Dramé and Samir Saul, 'Le projet d'Eurafrique en France (1946–1960): Quête de puissance ou atavisme colonial?', *Guerres mondiales et conflits contemporains* 216 (2004): 95–114; Yves Monarsolo, *L'Eurafrique—contrepoint de l'idée d'Europe: Le cas français de la fin de la deuxième guerre mondiale aux négociations de Traites de Rome* (Aix-en-Provence: Publications de l'Université de Provence, 2010); Charles-Robert Ageron, 'L'idée d'Eurafrique et le débat colonial Franco-allemand dans l'entre-deux-guerres', *Revue d'histoire moderne et contemporaine* 22 (1975): 446–475.

Africa'.[97] The integration of Europe aimed, for them, at consolidating not eroding the European domination of the African colonies. A federal union of Europe and its colonies in Africa would allow a more efficient distribution of natural, economic, and human resources derived from the colonisation of Africa across the European continent. Count Richard Coudenhove-Kalergi, one of the major proponents of the Eurafrican vision, insisted on the importance of Africa as a pool of natural resources for the economic development and demographic growth of Europe.[98] His mid-century followers suggested that European integration could be realised only if the European states would coordinate the exploitation of Africa, thus redressing the perceived injustices of imperial system.

In Britain, one of the main advocates for this short-lived plan was Ernest Bevin, a longtime friend and admirer of Lionel Curtis.[99] As foreign secretary after the Second World War, Bevin sought to advance the federalist vision that Curtis proposed, modified according to his own personal interpretation. He envisaged the loose union of Western Europe, Britain, the Commonwealth, and the bulk of the African continent as a potential foundation for a Third World power that could set an alternative to the binary of the United States and Soviet Russia.[100] A federation of sorts between Europe and Africa not only could provide the declining imperial powers with the resources they badly needed, but also would be beneficial, he suggested, for the development of Africa with the assistance of a United Africa Authority led by experts from all European states.[101]

Against this narrative, the discussions at Federal Union were explicit about their rejection of the practices and legacy of empire in the world, and especially in Africa. Their interpretation of federalism certainly reflected a geopolitical concern about the political and economic decline of the European states, and the hope to consolidate post-war Europe as a leading international power, but the means to achieve these goals included a retreat from empire, not its stabilisation. The alternative approach adopted at Federal Union rested on a shared feeling of anxiety about the future of democracy, in Europe or elsewhere, enhanced by the tensions between domestic democracy and a foreign policy of imperial exploitation. The stabilisation of the European imperial rule of Africa could not, for many federalists, advance the cause of democracy. The main concern remained

---

[97] Hansen and Jonsson, *Eurafrica*, 6.

[98] Richard Coudenhove-Kalergi, *Paneuropa* (Vienna: Paneuropa Verlag, 1923, 1926); Hansen and Jonsson, *Eurafrica*, 28.

[99] Ernest Bevin (1881–1951), a statesman and trades union leader, was foreign secretary in the post-war Labour government (1945–1951).

[100] Anne Deighton, 'Entente Neo-Coloniale? Ernest Bevin and the Proposals for an Anglo–French Third World Power, 1945–1949', *Diplomacy & Statecraft* 17 (2006): 835–852.

[101] Francis Williams, *Ernest Bevin: Portrait of a Great Englishman* (London: Hutchinson, 1952), 208–210.

finding the most efficient and constructive way to disentangle the European empires from their various colonial outposts.

Although the retreat from empire was considered an inevitable part of the post-war order that Federal Union sought to establish, there was no consensus about the process of democratic transformation in Europe and in the colonial world. Norman Bentwich replied to Lugard's proposals in a pamphlet written especially for Federal Union, arguing that the colonies should attain political independence as democratic states and join the federation as soon as possible.[102] Positing that the economic scramble for empire was at the root of the European war, Bentwich reasoned that no post-war order could be maintained without a proper solution to the colonial problem. Europe—or more generally the democratic world—could not be reimagined as a federal region without reconceptualising its formal sovereignty over its overseas colonies, territories, and dependencies. The time-frame for colonial liberation should be measured in years, he suggested, rather than in decades, highlighting the inadequately slow pace of colonial development hitherto. If Curtis and Lugard thought that imperial sovereignty was an important asset for the federal order since it created the much-needed moral bonds to form a global polity, Bentwich saw the European overseas outposts as a liability.[103]

A federation of European states must, for Bentwich, address two critical questions related to the colonial world: the growing support for administrative and economic colonial independence, and the grievances of (European) states without access to colonial resources. However, he insisted that both matters should not be considered exclusively from the European viewpoint. Rather, the democratic ethos of the federation required admitting the colonial population of all races—the white settlers and the native peoples—into the realm of political agency and eventually as equal citizens of the federation. India provided for him an example of a state that could almost immediately after the war attain independence, democratise, and join the federation.[104]

The British Empire did not provide, for Bentwich, a particularly positive example of colonial administration. Lugard's system of 'indirect rule' was obsolete: he argued that the local populations would no longer accept government in which the 'white head thinks and the black hand rules'. He dismissed proposals for 'guided' colonial administration and demanded that the native peoples would have full autonomy in their countries as part and parcel of the newly established federal democratic order. However, when

---

[102] Norman Bentwich (1883–1971) was a barrister, legal scholar and attorney-general in Mandatory Palestine (1922–1929).

[103] Norman Bentwich, 'The Colonial Problem and the Federal Solution', in Ransome, *Studies in Federal Planning*, 110.

[104] Norman Bentwich, 'Federal Union and the Colonies', *FUN*, 11 November 1939.

debating the practical aspects of his proposal, the details boiled down to a new mandates system controlled by the federal government, which would help the colonial people to '"stand by themselves in the strenuous conditions of the modern world" and enter the Federal Union as independent members'.[105] The inclusion of the colonial peoples in the democratic federation still depended on attaining a certain degree of 'civilisation' measured by European standards.

The mainstream opinion at Federal Union reflected Bentwich's conviction that rapid colonial independence and the creation of the democratic federation were two aspects of one global project. The Federal Union 1940 policy statement stipulated that 'the colonies of the State members of the Federation should be part of the Federation. . . . In the administration of all colonial territories and people, the aim should be to promote the utmost material well-being and social progress of the inhabitants, and to provide as soon as possible for democratic self-government for the colonial populations, either inside or outside the Federation'.[106] The colonies were not seen as a token of pride for the European members of the federation, or as a symbol of transnational moral cohesion. The impression left by discussions of colonial policy at Federal Union is that the federalists hoped to rid themselves of the colonial problem quickly, in order to preserve and enhance the democratic ethos of the federation. For this reason, the Australian politician and Federal Union member Ronald Mackay criticised Streit's association of the standard of civilisation with the imperial liberal-capitalistic democracies of Europe and the United States. He highlighted the crucial dissonance between domestic democracy and overseas empire, and hoped that a democratic federation could help overcome the social and economic inequalities that imperialism and capitalism had created.[107]

It remained unclear, however, whether the free and democratic colonies should, eventually, be included in the federation. The unbalanced power relations between the West and the colonial world could become a potential destabilising factor for the federation. Robbins argued that the imperial system could not provide an appropriate model for transnational economic cooperation because of its exploitative characteristics, but was nonetheless wary of including the colonies in the federation. He did not offer a clear plan to overcome the economic, social, and political divide between the advanced European sphere and the exploited colonial world, other than granting the colonies full autonomy in the hope that they would be able to fashion their future according to their own ideas and traditions.[108] In that sense, the prospect of democratic federalism remained limited to the

---

[105] Bentwich, 'Colonial Problem', 136.
[106] 'International Democracy', *FUN*, 7 September 1940.
[107] See, for example, R. W. G. Mackay, 'American Movement', *FUN*, 24 May 1941.
[108] See the next chapter for a discussion of Robbins's ideas.

political space of the advanced, relatively wealthy Western democracies, where, as I show in the next chapter, the federation could help enact social and economic reforms.

The post-imperial democratic federation proposed by Federal Union had clear limits. Democracy became, for them, the key category of politics. It provided the conceptual tools for creating a stratified world order divided into 'backward' and 'civilised' peoples. Many agreed that, in general lines, most colonies should become independent states soon after the war ended. However, Federal Union still held high the idea that the backward colonies and dependencies could join the federal order as independent states only if they followed a specific path towards political maturity guided by the experience of the mature European peoples. 'Backward' people could establish a 'democratic' polity, but the success of their efforts would be judged by the 'advanced' Europeans, who would determine their inclusion or exclusion in the democratic federation. While they rejected the idea that biological race should become a discriminatory criterion of admission to the federation, they applied the cultural criterion of 'democracy', which circumscribed the geopolitical and cultural scope of their project. Thus, it was always the 'West', embodied in Europe, the United States, and the dominions, that was to set the road map for political progress, giving up on imperial rule but retaining a range of informal means of imposing their worldview on the colonial populations. The insistence on cultural, social, political, and economic homogeneity as a key element in the success of the federal vision rendered it less pluralistic and universal than they had initially hoped.

As members of Federal Union increasingly interpreted the idea of 'democratic federation' in economic terms, arguing that social and economic welfare were the fundamental requirements for a peaceful and stable polity, the development of the European colonies became a marginal concern. Even Lionel Curtis was ready to admit that the European overseas empires offered a meagre economic gain at a very high maintenance and defence cost. Furthermore, many were aware that the need to improve the standard of living of the native colonial population would incur even higher administrative cost and financial investment. The imperial ethos, which Curtis upheld as the moral foundation of the democratic federation, was dismissed by other members of Federal Union, who sought a different unifying factor as the motivation for federation.

While Curtis was unmoved by the suggestion that the federation should establish a common—and higher—standard of living across national borders, this was one of the main aims of other federalists. The new unifying federal factor was, for Robbins, Hayek, and Wootton, a shared concern with economic and social living conditions, which some articulated in terms of 'justice'. This marks a shift away from an idea of federation grounded in the imperial experience, towards a federal vision aimed at social and economic amelioration. Equality was primarily interpreted not in terms of political participation, but in terms of access to economic and social resources and opportunities, which should be extended in equal measures to all federal citizens. In this sense, Federal Union focused on debating the economic advantages of federation, which in turn entailed political advantages as well. Whether the colonial populations could, eventually, democratise and benefit from the higher standard of living established in the federation remained an open question.

The debate on the legacy of empire at Federal Union highlighted the potential tensions between the attempt to reinforce democracy on a transnational or global scale, and the hope to establish a new and stable 'world order'. Curtis and Streit hoped that their proposed world order would embody familiar elements, like their idealised version of Anglo-American democracy, while also preserving the global power relations of the imperial system. Yet their different justificatory languages had lost their rhetoric effectiveness at Federal Union. The new economic conception of democratic federation that emerged in this organisation is the focus of the next chapter.

CHAPTER 5

Federal Democracy for Welfare

IN JUNE 1940, on the eve of the armistice, British Prime Minister Winston Churchill proposed to French Prime Minister Paul Raynaud a federal union of France and Britain. The proposal had the support of Clement Attlee, Ernest Bevin, and Charles de Gaulle.[1] In the previous months, members of Federal Union have been advocating such a plan behind the scenes. In April 1940, a group of them, including the economists Lionel Robbins, Barbara Wootton, Friedrich Hayek, and William Beveridge, travelled to France to meet with local economists to promote the realisation of the federation.[2] However, the transition from theory to practice came too late, and the proposal reached France at the eleventh hour before Nazi Germany invaded the country. The French rejection of federal union with Britain dealt a blow to the London-based federalists who had spent months elaborating and perfecting their idea of a political, economic, and military union. Yet the disappointment only enhanced their zeal to develop a more nuanced interpretation of 'federal democracy', which would not prevent war, but would, hopefully, present a viable blueprint for the post-war order.

In *Union Now*, Streit described the Western democracies in rosy colours as precursors of 'modernity' and 'progress', focusing on the unifying qualities of democracy as an ideology rather than a political structure. As we have seen in the previous chapter, his vision relied on the idea that a democratic federation would bolster the Western democracies' power against totalitarianism. It is important to remember that the idea of democratic federalism became increasingly popular in the early 1940s because, for many, it seemed a promising way to guarantee peace. However, many members of the London-based movement Federal Union had already engaged in planning the economic, political, and social structures of the peaceful world order. For them, a democratic federation had another advantage: it offered a platform for socioeconomic change. In this sense, one of the

---

[1] Avi Shlaim, 'Prelude to Downfall: The British Offer of Union to France, June 1940', *Journal of Contemporary History* 9 (1974): 27–63.

[2] Andrea Bosco, *Federal Union and the Origins of the 'Churchill Proposal': The Federalist Debate in the UK from Munich to the Fall of France, 1938–1940* (London: Lothian Foundation Press, 1991).

Federal Union manifestos asserted that 'in terms of the real values of contemporary life, and in terms of the probable post-war situation, the economic element in democracy is second to none'. In this chapter, I discuss the social and economic foundation of Federal Union's idea of democratic federalism as a global change towards peace, welfare, equal opportunities, and prosperity.

In their 1942 policy statement, Federal Union declared that economic democracy meant feeding, clothing, housing, educating, and providing medical care for every citizen. Global standards of living would be determined by the central federal authority, but their realisation would be delegated to national governments. The member states would include Britain, along with any democratic or democratising state committed to partake in this new socioeconomic structure.[3] However, some issues remained contested, including the local and global institutional design, the means to defend liberty in a federal order, and the extension of the federal socioeconomic vision to the global—and colonial—sphere.

This chapter traces the development of democratic federalism as an idea aimed at global socioeconomic transformation. Economists like Barbara Wootton, Lionel Robbins, William Beveridge, and Friedrich Hayek supported the idea of democratic federalism because, they argued, it would provide the necessary political framework to guarantee peace and, importantly, to enact socioeconomic change beyond the state. For them, the ideological heritage of democratic federalism and its roots in imperial experience were a burden rather than an asset. They sought to differentiate their position from that of Curtis and his followers, depicting their vision in global and inclusive terms. However, the relations between individual liberty and state power remained a point of disagreement between the economists at Federal Union.

While the geopolitical reach of their socioeconomic federal vision was often described in global or at least transnational terms, the idea of economic democracy was modelled on the British political experience. Proposals such as guaranteed social services and a certain standard of living clearly reflected domestic political trends in Britain, where the state was expected to assume greater responsibility towards the citizens' economic welfare. Democratic federalism meant, therefore, both political and economic change on a global scale. The federalists envisaged a range of political institutions including federal citizenship, popular parliament, army, and government. The global 'War on Want' would be the common goal of the federated states, which could be attained more effectively through centralised economic, fiscal, and commercial policies.[4]

---

[3] Federal Union, *Federal Union Official Policy* (London: Federal Union, July 1942).
[4] Ibid.

In 1942, a few months before the publication of the Beveridge Report on *Social Insurance and Allied Services*,[5] Federal Union emphasised the central role of planning in the future federation: 'Planning, that is public ownership and control in economic life directed to the maintenance of certain social standards, has come to stay. Planning in the hands of those who believe in political democracy will be directed at achieving economic democracy'.[6] However, the advantages of social and economic planning were strongly contested by some, like Robbins and Hayek, who feared that a planned economy would set an excessive and illegitimate restriction on human freedom of choice. Therefore, the Federal Union debate on the social and economic attributes of democratic federalism provides an opportunity to explore important political questions related to the advantages and risks that global prestructured organisation of the economy—or planning—could pose to individual liberty.

This chapter focuses on the federal democratic thought of three major economic thinkers in 1940s Britain: Lionel Robbins, Barbara Wootton, and Friedrich Hayek. The following section discusses the economic federal thought of Robbins in the late 1930s, as a precursor to the ideas debated at Federal Union. I then present the rise of 'welfare' as a key feature in the economic federalism of Wootton. The fourth section looks at Wootton's debate with Hayek, who built on and expanded Robbins's ideas on economic federalism at Federal Union. Finally, I argue that the insistence of mid-century British federalists on the economic and social benefits of democratic federalism expressed a turn away from previous federal conceptions grounded in the experience of the discriminatory and exploitative imperial order.

LIONEL ROBBINS AND THE POLITICS OF ECONOMIC FEDERALISM

In June 1939, Lionel Robbins received a letter from Lionel Curtis, thanking Robbins for sending him a copy of his recent book.[7] Curtis admitted that he was 'simply astounded' to read that Robbins's conclusions in the last three chapters of his book were very similar to his own opinion about the desirability of a world federation. He added that, with the publication of Streit's best-seller *Union Now*, the cause of federalism would gain international momentum. He suggested that Streit's approach was

---

[5] Beveridge, *Social Insurance and Allied Services*.

[6] 'Political and Economic Democracy', *FUN*, June 1942.

[7] Lionel Curtis to Lionel Robbins, 6 June 1939, in Lionel Robbins Papers, London School of Economics, London. Curtis referred to Lionel Robbins, *Economic Planning and International Order* (London: Macmillan, 1937), composed in 1935 as a series of lectures given at the Graduate Institute of International and Development Studies in Geneva.

political, Robbins's was economic, while his was moral and religious; yet all three shared, for him, essentially similar views. He saw Robbins as a fellow traveller in the federalist path, and encouraged him to join the new London-based organisation Federal Union to help actualise their ideas.

Curtis rightly diagnosed Robbins's enthusiasm for federalism, but he was wrong to suggest that their ideas about federation were similar. In fact, although Robbins conceded that Curtis reached 'substantially the same solution' as himself, his federalism marks a clear turn away from previous federal visions, of which Curtis was the most vociferous representative.[8] As we have seen in the previous chapter, Curtis saw federalism as a means of preserving the integrity of the British imperial system. His tireless advocacy for federation was motivated by the idea that the British Empire represented a high moral achievement, a standard of civilisation that should be the basis for a new world order. Robbins's writings about federalism in the 1930s and early 1940s, and his activities in Federal Union, embody a new version of federal thought. For him, empire and federation were mutually exclusive: 'either there must be empire or federation: on a long view, there is no alternative'.[9] Federation was the preferred form of political order because, for Robbins, it 'took over from the states of which it is composed, those powers which engender conflict'.[10] Since clashes of economic interests between states can be important causes of war, Robbins argued that the powers to form and enforce economic policies should be transferred to wider organisations that can eliminate disharmony.[11] Thus, unlike Curtis, Robbins focused on the economic and social aspects of federalism.

Lionel Robbins (1898–1984) was a professor of economics at the London School of Economics (LSE), where he had previously studied the history of political ideas with Harold Laski and economics with Hugh Dalton and Edwin Cannan.[12] Cannan, alongside Ludwig von Mises and the Austrian school of economics, inspired Robbins's early economic thought. Robbins made an important contribution to economic theory with the publication of *An Essay on the Nature and Significance of Economic Science* (1932), but his main interest was applying economic theories to 'real' problems.[13] In the late 1930s, he dedicated his attention to international economics

---

[8] Lionel Robbins, *The Economic Causes of War* (London: Jonathan Cape, 1939), 10.

[9] Ibid., 107.

[10] Ibid., 105.

[11] Lionel Robbins, *Economic Aspects of Federation* (London: Macmillan, 1941). This pamphlet was written in 1940 for Federal Union and published in the volume edited by Melville Chaning-Pearce, *Federal Union: A Symposium* (London: J. Cape, 1940), 77–106.

[12] For Robbins's intellectual biography, see Susan Howson, *Lionel Robbins* (Cambridge: Cambridge University Press, 2011).

[13] Lionel Robbins, *An Essay on the Nature and Significance of Economic Science* (London: Macmillan, 1932).

and the economic causes of war. It was in this context that he started to consider federation as a solution to the problems of international strife and conflict. His later involvement in Federal Union was relatively brief: he left the organisation in 1940 when he joined the public service. Yet, as we shall see, his ideas on economic federalism continued to inspire the debates at Federal Union, led by Hayek and Wootton.

For Robbins, a federation was a pact of political and economic union between independent states, aimed at advancing common goals—such as peaceful cooperation and economic well-being—while preserving a degree of national sovereignty. He perceived federation as 'an architectonic idea', a skeleton structure for world order, in which different political, economic, and social policies could be realised.[14] Since, for him, the problems of war could not be separated from those of poverty, inequality, and stagnation, a federal structure should have the powers to act in both the economic and political spheres. Although he conceded that economic advantages were not the 'raison d'être' of federation, a stable economic foundation was a condition for its success.[15]

The federal idea was present in Robbins's *Economic Planning and International Order* (1937), and later in *The Economic Causes of War* (1939).[16] In 1939, he penned an article in favour of Anglo-French federation in the *Spectator*, arguing that historical conjuncture provided an opportunity for the union of Britain and France as the first step towards a wider federation.[17] In March 1940, *Spectator*'s editor Wilson Harris wrote a sceptical critique of the proposals of the organisation Federal Union, leading to a published debate between him and Robbins on the viability and desirability of the federalist vision.[18] In 1941, Robbins published his pamphlet *Economic Aspects of Federation*, summarising his main views on the issue.[19]

The geographic boundaries of the federation mattered for Robbins only in terms of their contingent contribution to the project's feasibility. Thus, for instance, in 1939 he proposed an Anglo-French federal union, while in *The Economic Causes of War* he advanced a more ambitious 'United States of Europe', recognising nonetheless the theoretical merits of Streit's proposal to federate the 'Atlantic democracies'.[20] The decision to focus on a regional

---

[14] Lionel Robbins to Ronald Mackay, 15 August 1941, Lionel Robbins Papers, 3/1/5.

[15] Robbins, *Economic Aspects of Federation*, 77.

[16] Robbins, *Economic Causes of War*.

[17] Lionel Robbins, 'An Anglo-French Federation?', *Spectator*, 24 November 1939, 12.

[18] Wilson Harris, 'Federal Union Examined I', *Spectator*, 14 March 1940, 10; 'Federal Union Examined II', *Spectator*, 21 March 1940, 8; Lionel Robbins, 'Federal Union Examined III', *Spectator*, 28 March 1940, 9; Wilson Harris, 'Federal Union Examined IV', *Spectator*, 4 April 1940, 9; Lionel Robbins, 'Federal Union Examined V', *Spectator*, 11 April 1940, 9.

[19] Robbins, *Economic Aspects of Federation*.

[20] Robbins, *Economic Causes of War*, 106n1.

European federation was motivated by the contingent urgency created by the war, as well as by the facilitating conditions that Robbins identified in Europe: similar culture, history, and political institutions characterised most of the European countries, despite linguistic differences. The inclusion of the United States seemed to him a desirable yet unrealistic goal since the American people and leadership did not seem supportive enough of this scheme. Russia was excluded for lack of 'like-mindedness' and political traditions. Only a European federation had the required preliminary advantages that could permit its immediate realisation, yet other federal unions remained theoretically acceptable.

Robbins's writings about federalism emerged in the context of public and academic debates about the tensions between economic planning and individual liberty. He is sometimes described as a free-trade liberal who supported private-sector enterprise and limited state power.[21] Yet, his federalist writings reveal a more complex and nuanced interpretation of the economic meaning of planning and its impact on individual liberty. In 1937, Robbins wrote that 'planning is the grand panacea of our age', a vague and undefined remedy to all economic problems. All economic life, he reminded, was based on planning as a premeditated and rational disposal of scarce goods for a certain purpose.[22] This interpretation of economic planning built on his definition of economics as 'the science that studies human behaviour as a relationship between ends and scarce means which have alternative uses'.[23] Planning was an act of economic rational choice between the various means to attain a political goal. The choice was never between order and chaos, but between different plans, different interpretations of political and economic order.

Robbins argued that economic liberalism was one of many possible economic plans, preferable to others because it defended individual liberty while harmonising diverse individual economic plans. The necessity—and legitimacy—of harmony in politics was justified by Robbins's idea that citizens of different states were also members of one general world community.[24] Yet Robbins did not develop in detail the implications of this vaguely defined global humanism for political order. The challenge that he focused on instead was responding to the multiple and infinite wants of individuals around the world, without imposing a unifying morality or succumbing to aggressive war. A federation based on the precepts of economic liberalism provided for Robbins the means to eliminate disharmony

---

[21] For example, in his recent book about economics, Ha-Joon Chang refers to Robbins as one of the founding fathers of neoclassical liberalism. See *Economics: A User's Guide* (London: Penguin, 2014), 20.

[22] Robbins, *Economic Planning*.

[23] Robbins, *Essay on the Nature and Significance of Economic Science*.

[24] Robbins, *Economic Planning*, 239.

through the construction of a system of rational economic planning for the common good.

Liberal economic federalism was set to prevent war by addressing the frictions created by national sovereignty in the political and, importantly, in the economic sphere. Not every federation could succeed in preventing war and generating prosperity. Robbins's 1937 book was evidently a polemic against socialist and communist economists who envisaged a federal world order based on a planned economy. For him, international communism was a 'totalitarian plan of the world', which demanded the establishment of an international authority with sole ownership of natural resources and full control of labour.[25] Despite the political power of this idea, Robbins gave two main explanations for its inadequacy. First, by limiting the function of the free market through protectionist measures, international communism hampered the market's main function as 'the best means of discovering preferences and wants'.[26] He saw the continuous need to make economic decisions in a socialist economy as a cause for democratic deficiency and a potential for increasing intervention by a central despotic authority. Unlike Barbara Wootton, he did not consider bottom-up democratic control of the central planning authority a sufficient solution to this problem. The second shortcoming of economic communism was its inefficiency. Robbins insisted that 'the criterion for a rational plan is not that different commodities should be produced by the instruments most efficient for producing them, but that the different instruments should be each used to produce those things which have the highest value'.[27] If the market was controlled by a single authority, it would have lost its capacity to create competition and therefore guarantee efficient production. The result would be wasteful production on the one hand, and unsatisfied needs of individuals on the other.

The solution, for Robbins, was evident. There was a need for 'an apparatus to register the strength of demand and the relative capacity of the different instruments of production to satisfy it'.[28] In a liberal federation, he envisaged 'institutions of decentralised initiative operating in such way as to involve a continuous tendency to apply productive resources at the point of highest return'. There was only one known economic plan that could comply with these demands: 'the essentials of such organization are provided by the free market and the institution of private property'. By buying at the lowest prices and producing at the highest, the citizen contributes to enforcing 'the maximum division of labour which is compatible with given tastes and given technique'. Robbins suggested that interna-

[25] Ibid., 188.
[26] Ibid., 192.
[27] Ibid., 197.
[28] Ibid., 223.

tional liberalism was a flexible plan, aimed at a clear goal and particularly adequate as the architectonic structure of a federation of states to guarantee prosperity, democracy, and peace. He envisaged a future in which such a liberal federation could address the problems of economic inequality and poverty across its territory without resorting to aggressive or protectionist measures.

The emphasis on economics distinguished Robbins's position from that of other British federalists. For Robbins, the establishment of a federation 'must not merely involve the surrender of the right to make war, it must involve also the elimination of those disabilities which make war appear to be worth while'.[29] He identified national protectionist policies that imposed restrictions on trade and migration as important—though sometimes unintentional—economic motivations for war. Thus, he argued that federation would minimise the risk of conflict by creating a federal space of free trade and free movement of people and capital. His idea of a federation was based on removing the barriers of national economies, improving economic cooperation, and guaranteeing liberty of movement regardless of the 'historical chance' of birth and citizenship.

One of the characteristics of federation that contributed to its economic efficiency and desirability was its large scale compared with the smaller scale of its member states. However, its 'heterarchical' structure mattered more than its territorial attributes. The political theorist Jean Cohen uses this term to describe the political and legal institutional structure of a federation, which makes possible a diversified distribution of political and economic power across different agencies and territorial units.[30] Without deploying this vocabulary, Robbins shared the idea that economic decision making should happen on different levels of power, between the local communities, the states, and the federal government. This power distribution was, to his mind, essential to maintain a structure of checks and balances on the world economy, to preserve its liberal character, and to limit the disrupting effect of national policies.

The goal of Robbins's heterarchical federal structure was not the weakening of the existing political entities—the states—in favour of the free market. Unlike Hayek, Robbins did not support federalism as a means to transfer political and economic power from states to individuals and local communities. Rather, the heterarchical federal order that he envisaged included a strong centralised authority with specific powers. The federal authority would hold the right to wage war and manage the army as well as, importantly, the right to determine economic policies in three fields: trade,

[29] Robbins, *Economic Aspects of Federation*, 80.
[30] Jean Cohen, *Globalization and Sovereignty* (Cambridge: Cambridge University Press, 2012), 52, 70–72.

migration, and money. These aspects of economic policy making were particularly sensitive to the influence of nationalistic, sectional interests, and thus embodied a higher risk for generating disharmony and war. By attributing the decisional power on these matters to the centralised federal authority, Robbins highlighted the importance of economic matters to the political well-being of the federation and its member states.

Free trade was, for Robbins, the economic guarantee of political liberty. In opposition to 'the sectional, monopolist, restrictions' of the early twentieth century, he called for a return to free trade as formed in the 'age of liberal legislation' of the nineteenth century, which remained, for him, a yet unrealised plan. His main objection was to various forms of protectionism: the establishment of government *monopoly* on production or trade, protectionist tariffs, or government control on industry. While Robbins favoured complete freedom of interstate trade, he accepted necessary restrictions but demanded that these be devised and applied by the federal authority, not the member states.[31]

Robbins was well aware of the problem of inequality and suggested that a democratic federation, unlike empire, could mitigate economic differences.[32] A federal structure could remove the commercial barriers set by national governments, and improve the working of the international economy by rendering production more efficient and distribution of capital and goods more equal. This idea that free trade—regulated by a central authority—helps overcome economic inequality comes out not only in Robbins's reflection on European federation but also in his earlier writings on a post-imperial world order. In 1934, he joined James Meade as member of the Economists Committee of the League of Nations Union in London, where he endorsed the redistribution of natural resources as part of the league's economic policy. Three years later, Meade and Robbins published a pamphlet based on their work in the committee, explaining the advantages of reducing trade barriers around the world.[33] They argued that 'a thorough and very delicate investigation' should be conducted to discover the ideas of the native populations and ensure a more equitable distribution of the economic advantages of the colonies. A policy of free interstate trade should be aimed at overcoming the exploitative practices of the existing imperial order but also at integrating the colonies as active participants in the free world economy.

A more innovative addition to Robbins's federal theory is free migration. He considered the individual's freedom to settle and work in any

[31] Robbins, *Economic Aspects of Federation*, 88.

[32] Robbins did not consider the British Empire an adequate role model for the democratic federation. See Robbins, 'Federal Union Examined V', 9.

[33] Meeting of 25 May 1937, Lionel Robbins and James E. Meade, 'Economic Steps towards World Peace', Records of League of Nations Union, LSE, 7/20. See also Howson, *Lionel Robbins*, 312–315.

part of the federation an indispensable economic tool. Free migration was also linked to the problem of inequality: 'the main argument for permitting migration is that it is the only way of eliminating inequalities which are due to position'.[34] At a time when public debate in Britain turned to the problem of unemployment as one of the major concerns of the national economy, it is understandable that Robbins considered the issue of migration mainly from the point of view of labour economics. His idea of lifting any barrier for migration within the federation followed, in his words, suggestions made by his mentor Edwin Cannan. To his mind, immigrants rationally followed demand, thus contributing to the economic development of places where labour was needed. Furthermore, he suggested that movement of people was often accompanied by capital; states should fear emigration more than immigration. He dismissed objections to free migration as prejudice and xenophobia, yet conceded that concerns about overpopulation should be taken in consideration when framing the federal migration policy.

In 1927, Robbins repeated Cannan's argument for limiting the migration of people 'showing chronicle incapacity to restrain their multiplication' into other territories that were less densely populated. While doubting that such people indeed existed in a world where birth control was easily available, Robbins still upheld the seemingly Malthusian argument that overdensity would bring about a general reduction in the standard of living in a given territory.[35] By 1940, he was mainly concerned with the impact of migration on economic growth in a given territory and with the political conflicts that could be caused by the exclusion of migrants from a given territory. Conceding that the problem of migration could generate international conflicts, he concluded that the federal authority should be allowed to regulate the movement of people as long as it transcended sectional and national interests and acted for the common good of all members. Again, Robbins was certain that a central authority could generate policies in line with the common good, and would gain the legitimising support of all individual citizens and member states.

Where free migration and free trade would fail to address the problem of inequality, which for Robbins was a key concern, he proposed the implementation of a system of inheritance taxation to mitigate economic divergences across the federal territory.[36] Despite the possible application of government-led corrective measures, a degree of inequality would necessarily remain part of the federal economy and society. Robbins suggested that 'the toleration of inequality is surely a small price to pay for the reduction

[34] Robbins, *Economic Aspects of Federation*, 86n1.
[35] Lionel Robbins, 'The Optimum Theory of Population', in *Essays in Economics: In Honour of Edwin Cannan*, ed. T. E. Gregory and Hugh Dalton (London: Routledge, 1927), 103–133.
[36] Robbins, *Economic Planning*, 265.

of poverty', which he foresaw as a direct outcome of the opening of the market and the national borders to free trade and migration.

The third aspect of Robbins's federal economic vision is international money. Arguing that a common federal currency was preferable to the national moneys, he conceded that this solution was not accepted by all the supporters of a federation. Variations in exchange rates were sometimes considered an easier way of maintaining financial equilibrium than the expansion or contraction of debt. Robbins found this argument unsatisfying because it failed to provide sustained economic justification for defining the territory of the national state—rather than the city, the region, or the continent—as the optimal currency area. The existence of national moneys seemed, following his account, a political rather than a rational economic decision, which should be reconsidered after the foundation of the federation.[37]

Robbins's support for federal money should also be understood in light of his earlier opposition to the abandonment of the gold standard. His argument was based on the idea that an international standard was key in maintaining a harmonious and equilibrated international economy.[38] In his 1937 discussion of international money, he addressed the objections to the international monetary system, based on the assumption that in various moments the quantity of capital available in different parts of the system might differ, change, and fluctuate. The monetary nationalists argued against sacrificing local industry to the gold or standard parity, but Robbins considered this scenario a natural part of economics. A contraction of incomes expresses decline in demand, which is part of the free market and does not express a negative symptom of disequilibrium. The mobility of production must be tied to demand, and therefore should not be recompensed with monetary changes.[39]

The most important point for Robbins in favour of international currency was that the supporters of national currencies wrongly assume that the fluctuations of free exchange would have an equilibrating tendency. The more frequent result, he argued, was protectionism, deflation in prices, inflation in other prices, and upset of the liquidity preferences of the public.[40] Later, he added also a political argument, suggesting that national monetary policies were not always motivated by economic reasoning, such as the need for stable equilibrium. Rather, sometimes monetary fluctuations were 'deliberately designed to snatch trade from competitors', thus giving rise to potential causes of international conflict.[41] A federal currency would reduce

[37] Robbins, *Economic Aspects of Federation*, 94.
[38] On the gold standard, see Robbins, *Economic Planning*, chap. 10.
[39] Ibid., 282.
[40] Ibid.
[41] Robbins, *Economic Aspects of Federation*, 95.

the risk of conflict by controlling sectional interests and regulating monetary fluctuations according to the common good of the federal economy. Furthermore, a common currency held for Robbins a symbolic meaning as a unifying factor of 'a common market and a common welfare'. Nonetheless, he avoided prescribing a definitive solution to the problem, and contended with affirming that the control of money and capital movements should be a function of the central federal authority, rather than the member states.

Robbins envisaged the federation as a realm of peace, economic prosperity, and growth, a new model for political and economic order. The federal authority should be, therefore, empowered to tax, borrow, subsidise, carry out public works, and regulate monopolies. 'The prospects of superior market advantage within the federal area may indeed be one of the main attractions to new adherents', he suggested. The external relations of the federation should also be managed by the central authority, which, he accepted, would have to impose some limitations on external trade and migration. However, 'a European federation would be a supreme example of a "have" state and if its economic policy vis-à-vis the "have-nots" in other parts of the world were markedly illiberal, it might rise up against formidable combinations'.[42] This affirmation highlights the distance between Robbins's federal vision and Curtis's imperial order. The foundation of the federation on values of justice and freedom was not a mark of exceptionalism but a promise for inclusion. The liberal ethos of the federation should condition its relations with other parts of the world to permit, potentially, its future extension beyond the European or Western space.

The real obstacle for the realisation of the federation was, for Robbins, national sentiment. He conceded that nationalism reinforced individual sense of belonging and enhanced political cohesion across the polity, but reasoned that patriotism was not a 'very fruitful' form of emotion at the present stage of history because it caused economic damages. Therefore, he wished to separate national sentiments from the locus of political decision making, without demanding emotional allegiance to the federal political and economic institutions. International liberalism does not bid to love all humanity: 'it seeks only to persuade us that co-operation between the different members of humanity is advantageous for the furtherance of individual ends'.[43] Robbins upheld the liberal rational ethos of politics, while granting space for emotions and sentiments in a limited sphere. This separation of economics from patriotism can be sustained only by far-ranging political change, which for Robbins implied the establishment of a new economic and political union, a democratic federation.

[42] Ibid., 106.
[43] Robbins, *Economic Planning*, 326.

BARBARA WOOTTON'S DEMOCRATIC PLAN FOR FREEDOM

In the pages of *Federal Union News*, the economist Barbara Wootton suggested that democratic federalism meant a 'plan for plenty'.[44] The establishment of a federation was, for her, a political project with important economic implications. It was the first step towards the foundation of a welfare-oriented economic order that would transcend the state. Therefore, she suggested that the political space of the federation should be determined not geographically but by the commitment of the peoples and their institutions to political and economic democracy. Importantly, she disagreed with Robbins and insisted that political union was not about shared history, language, race, or borders; it was about a common democratic political and economic outlook. Her concern with welfare and economics shaped the spatial dimension of her thought, emphasising the local and the transnational dimensions of politics. Since her main interests were political and economic relations not *between* states, but across state boundaries, in a horizontal network of agencies and institutions, Wootton could be defined a 'transnationalist'.[45]

One of Wootton's major goals at Federal Union was to promote the cause of economic and social planning on a federal—ideally, global—scale. As we have seen, Robbins advocated economic federalism for its economic policies of capital, trade, and migration that would, he hoped, help undermine the economic causes of war. However, Wootton underlined the federation's benefits for transnational socioeconomic planning for welfare. This conviction implied that the transnational federal spaces were more adequate for planning because a supranational authority would be capable of impartially regulating the economic interests across state borders. Moreover, the federal authority would be able to set and implement a transnational or federal standard of living, thus advancing the goal of global socioeconomic equality. Finally, the federal authority would have a greater variety of industrial and natural resources under its jurisdiction, and would therefore be

[44] Barbara Wootton, 'Plus Plan for Plenty', *FUN*, 6 July 1940. For a general discussion of Wootton's role in Federal Union, see Oakley, *Critical Woman*, chap. 9.

[45] While acknowledging the imprecision of the term 'transnational', I use it here to indicate a political system incorporating more than one existing state, and operating not only through intergovernmental agreements but also through a network of agencies, institutions, and communities active across national borders. I follow Patricia Clavin's definition of transnationalism as 'border-crossing', without implying that these borders also break down. Moreover, transnational arrangements, unlike global ones, are not necessarily universal and could be limited to a regional dimension. In the 1940s federal debate, the term 'international' was often given a similar meaning to today's 'transnational', indicating political, social, and economic arrangements operating through a complex horizontal network of agencies, institutions, and communities, on a regional or world scale. For recent definitions of transnationalism, see, for example, Patricia Clavin, 'Defining Transnationalism', *Contemporary European History* 14 (2005): 421–439; Laura Briggs, Gladys McCormick, and J. T. Way, 'Transnationalism: A Category of Analysis', *American Quarterly* 60 (2008): 625–648.

more capable than the national government of efficiently coordinating the economy. As we shall see, this project of federal planning was based on the assumption that scientific research and democratic political participation— rather than the free market—would enable the identification of humanity's basic needs and the economic solutions to satisfy them.

Barbara Wootton (1897–1988), later Baroness Wootton of Abinger, was born, raised, and educated in Cambridge. She graduated in classics and economics from Girton College, then turned from classics to economics and sociology in order to address the central problems of her times.[46] Alfred Marshall's writings provided an early inspiration to reconcile the scientific and public aspects of economics. John Maynard Keynes was a family friend, and Wootton shared the concerns that lay behind *General Theory of Employment, Interest and Money* (1936), which helped foster the idea that political institutions should have some role in regulating the economy.[47] In the interwar years she became interested in socialism, uniting elements of Fabian economic reformism with a particular emphasis on the importance of trade unions and popular participation. Mark Bevir suggests that the Fabian thesis focused on fiscal and redistributive reform measures in a democratic system based on representative government.[48] Wootton had slightly different concerns, emphasising popular participation at the grassroots level and state intervention to regulate and reshape the market for the common good.

Her long career struck a balance between extensive intellectual activities and public commitment. In 1926, at the age of twenty-nine, she was appointed a justice of the peace. In 1927 she was a delegate to the League of Nations World Conference. Between 1938 and 1964 she served on four Royal Commissions and from 1950 to 1955 was a governor of the BBC. In 1958 she was the first woman to become a life peer and used her position as a deputy speaker of the House of Lords to promote her socialist vision. Later in life, she became well known for her contributions to criminal law and penal reform.[49] In the early 1940s she took part in initiatives and proto think tanks to develop plans for post-war social and economic reconstruction and explore new possibilities for domestic and international socioeconomic order. She divided her time between various teaching posts, War Office activities, and Chatham House, where she was

---

[46] A. H. Halsey, 'Wootton, Barbara Frances, Baroness Wootton of Abinger (1897–1988)', in *Oxford Dictionary of National Biography* (2004), www.oxforddnb.com; Oakley, *Critical Woman*, 45–47.

[47] John Maynard Keynes, *The General Theory of Employment Interest and Money* (London: Macmillan, 1936). Despite the inspiration he provided, Keynes's interpretation of regulation and intervention was much 'thinner' than Wootton's.

[48] On mid-century Fabian political thought, see Mark Bevir, *The Making of British Socialism* (Princeton, NJ: Princeton University Press, 2011), 301–307.

[49] Oakley, *Critical Woman*, 1–5.

secretary to the 'Study Groups on Reconstruction', which aimed to provide a social, economic, and political vision for post-war Britain.

In 1938, Wootton joined Federal Union, and two years later became a member of the Executive Committee, president, and chairman of the FU National Council, a role she held until 1944. At Federal Union, she strengthened her relations with Beveridge, who in 1919 had offered her a studentship for social research at the LSE. Both thought the war offered an opportunity to establish a new social order to be planned on an international rather than merely national scale.[50] In 1942, Beveridge invited her to join a research group on unemployment in Britain.[51] In the same year, she became a member of the committee of intellectuals who helped H. G. Wells to formulate his universal declaration of the 'Rights of Man'.[52] She was also a member of the New Fabian Research Bureau, directed by G. D. H. Cole, and the Federation for Progressive Societies and Individuals, led by Wootton's Federal Union colleague, the philosopher Cyril Joad, and was appointed the Trades Union Congress representative at Chatham House Council.

Wootton despaired about the abstract theorising, which dominated British economics at the time, preventing economists from offering practical, scientific, and useful economic policies. Her critique of classical political economy motivated her intellectual turn towards sociology, a discipline that she consequently helped shape and define. In her *Lament for Economics* (1938), she responded to Robbins's definition of the aim of economic science, condemned the theoretical pretences of British classical economists, and suggested a methodological turn away from grand theory and complex calculations towards policy-oriented scientific research of concrete social and economic problems.[53] The universality of science meant that both natural and social sciences were established on the same empiricist methodologies, and differed only in the degree of precision their research could attain.[54] She deplored the excessive weight classical economic theory gave

[50] Beveridge became honorary president of Federal Union in 1944. For a general discussion of Beveridge's activities in Federal Union, see Jose Harris, *William Beveridge: A Biography* (Oxford: Clarendon, 1997), 355–357.

[51] Harris, *William Beveridge*, 434–437; Paul Addison, *The Road to 1945: British Politics and the Second World War* (1975; repr., London: Pimlico, 1994), 242–243.

[52] Wells, *Rights of Man*; Oakley, *Critical Woman*, 153–154. See also chapter 7. For a short account of Wells's project, see Simpson, *Human Rights and the End of Empire*, 160–171. Simpson also refers to the competing visions of a universal or European bill of rights proposed by Federal Union members Ronald Mackay and Ivor Jennings. Moyn mentions Wells's project very briefly in his recent history of human rights, *Last Utopia*, 55, 75.

[53] Wootton misunderstood some of Robbins's arguments about the nature of economics, downplaying his insistence on the distinction between economic science and political economy as two separate spheres of research.

[54] These ideas were in line with the British scientists' campaign for socially useful scientific research, whose leaders included the biologist Lancelot Hogben. Wootton knew Hogben at the LSE, admired his

to individual rational choice, and claimed that a more complex under-standing of human nature and social interaction, based on empirical data and statistical analysis, was necessary to assess and meliorate social and economic interactions.[55] However, Wootton's heretical approach was not appreciated at the time, and leading economists, including Keynes, Bever-idge, and Robbins, did not engage directly with her criticism. Despite the lack of institutional and academic recognition of her work, Wootton's ideas were often praised and discussed in the popular press.[56]

Wootton's international thought sought to reconcile democracy and so-cialism. Her interest in federalism and its impact on economics was rein-forced by the public campaign for federation led by Federal Union in 1938. For her, federation meant 'the establishment over more than one previously independent state of a supra-national government with strictly limited functions'.[57] The most fundamental of these functions was war prevention. She argued—with many other British internationalists—that international control of armed forces and foreign policy could guarantee world peace. The idea that rational contemplation could, eventually, drive people to overcome differences and achieve a common political ground was a pop-ular theme in British liberal internationalism. For Wootton, the pacifying qualities of federalism were only one aspect of its advantages. The other benefit of world or regional federation would be its vast territorial scale, which lent itself to more complex and sophisticated economic planning and the powerful centralised government capable of enforcing its policies. In the nation-state system, economic planning was limited by the difficulty of addressing economic issues beyond the reach of individual states. The world's growing interconnectedness rendered federal planning a necessity, but the exact geographic dimensions and location of the federation were of secondary importance.

In *Socialism and Federation* (1941), Wootton argued that a large canvas for planning was necessary to raise the standard of living for people across national boundaries, fostering a global—or at least transnational—concept of social justice. She based her vision on a universal idea of the public good, which could not be confined to the political space of the state. Effective eco-nomic planning had two conditions: it required extensive territorial space, and a stable balance between centralised government and popular partici-pation. She argued that federal economic planning would be more effective

sharp intellect, and dedicated to him her book on freedom and planning, *Freedom under Planning* (London: Allen & Unwin, 1945). For a discussion of the British scientists' campaign, see chapter 7.

[55] Barbara Wootton, *Lament for Economics* (London: Allen & Unwin, 1938).

[56] For example, positive reviews of her books were printed in the *Manchester Guardian*, including J. J., 'A Critic of Economists', *Manchester Guardian*, 25 February 1938, 7; 'Planning', *Manchester Guardian*, 7 September 1945, 3.

[57] Wootton, 'Socialism and Federation'.

if the central authority had decision-making power over matters of immigration, trade, currency, credit, tariffs, employment, and production. In the 1940s, the notion that currency, trade, and tariffs should be internationally regulated became more readily accepted.[58] Wootton, like Robbins, thought that a unified economic and social policy had a greater chance of success because it would eliminate excess by better coordinating the various aspects of consumption, production, and trade. For her a federation would be a means to increase social wealth and prosperity universally, in both the private and public spheres, and would therefore be a 'socialist' cause.

Wootton read *Union Now*, but did not share Streit's idea that federation should be centred on the Western democracies, preferring a vision of a world federation. Her most substantial criticism was directed at the lack of 'actual blueprint applicable to the complex economic world'.[59] Streit's vision pertained to what she defined as 'modified capitalism': a laissez-faire approach to the market economy, based on freedom of trade and migration.[60] He endorsed a federation in which the central authority would have very minimal decision-making powers over economic affairs, besides managing the common currency and regulating commerce, but 'trade and migration should become immediately free through the Union territory'. Wootton attacked Streit's free trade policy as 'unrealistic', believing his view that lifting tariffs and quotas would boost trade and increase prosperity to be unfounded. She predicted that local workers would be impoverished by the competition with imported goods and services: 'the first effect of a complete abolition of all trade restrictions throughout the Union would unquestionably be to fling millions out of employment'. She argued that the central authority should have extensive powers to regulate commerce, immigration, and employment for the 'welfare of the whole'.

In her discussions of planning, Wootton had not always attached to the term the same meaning. For example, in 1939, she suggested that the world federation should follow the American New Deal experience and establish a central authority for economic planning that would gradually

---

[58] Martin Daunton, 'Britain and Globalization since 1850: The Rise of Insular Capitalism 1914–1939', *Transactions of the Royal Historical Society* 17 (2007): 1–33.

[59] Barbara Wootton, 'Economic Problems of Federal Union', *New Commonwealth Quarterly* 5 (1939): 150–156. H. G. Wells levelled a similar criticism at the economic precepts of Streit's federalism. He added to Wootton's critique the argument that Streit perpetuated the imperial economic order in which a select few benefited from keeping the world's masses in a state of poverty and ignorance. Wells proposed a democratic world order based on the universal 'rights of man', including social and economic rights. For a discussion of Wells' universalism, see chapter 7.

[60] Wootton, 'Economic Problems of Federal Union', 152. Her view was supported by Harold Wilson, member of FURI and the future British prime minister, in his article 'Economic Aspects of Federation', in Ransome, *Towards the United States of Europe*, 205–212.

grow 'up to the Russian level'.[61] However, if initially she endorsed centralised regulation and direction of the economy, six years later, in *Freedom under Planning*, she argued that planning need not entail centralised authority following the Soviet model, which, to her mind, sacrificed individual freedom for vague economic goals.[62] This means that initially she advanced an idea of a centralised federal authority responsible for setting plans for economic outputs, but also for controlling the means of production and coordinating the whole economy. Later her vision of planning was more limited, endowing the state with the responsibility to set plans for economic growth, and to regulate the economy accordingly. She denied that this idea of planning meant a centralised control of the means of production. Why did Wootton change her mind? There are several possible reasons. First, observing the political and economic situation in the Soviet Union, she might have reconsidered the desirability of the Soviet model. Second, the debates in Federal Union might have persuaded her that many federalists opposed the Soviet economic model because it was repressive and illiberal. Finally, Wootton might have been influenced by the criticism levelled at her arguments by Friedrich Hayek. As we shall see in the next section, Wootton took seriously Hayek's concerns over the illiberal aspects of economic planning, and sought a non-repressive form of planning, which focused on setting plans, regulating the economy, and providing subsidies and similar measures for individual welfare.

Popular control over economic planning was also a main feature of her federal vision. Unlike earlier liberal and radical thinkers like J. A. Hobson and H. N. Brailsford who envisaged world federation as a panacea against war and imperialism, she insisted on the importance of popular political participation and discussed the institutional framework to allow and encourage individuals and small communities to be active partners in controlling the central planning authority.[63] Addressing the issue of the relationship between the governing and the governed, Wootton argued that

[61] Wootton, 'Economic Problems of Federal Union', 153. Some American thinkers, like Rexford Tugwell and Charles Merriam, who were inspired by the New Deal, proposed similar ideas without taking the Soviet Union as their model. In that, they shared the view of Franklin D. Roosevelt, who believed that the US and Soviet systems were moving closer together. See chapter 6 for a discussion of Tugwell, and chapter 7 on Merriam.

[62] Wootton, *Freedom under Planning*, 5–12.

[63] Hobson is sometimes described as 'liberal internationalist', but his vision of federalism revolved around a core of social reform. Wootton met Hobson when both served on the Colwyn Committee on National Debt in 1924. Oakley, *Critical Woman*, 85. For Hobson's internationalist writings, see essays in the recent volume *Selected Writing of John A. Hobson, 1932–1938: The Struggle for the International Mind*, edited by John M. Hobson and Colin Tyler (London: Routledge, 2011); Hobson, *Democracy after the War* (London: Allen & Unwin, 1917); Hobson, *Democracy and a Changing Civilisation* (London: John Lane, 1934). Brailsford is more often described as a radical or socialist thinker. He had been interested in federalism since the First World War, and later became an ardent supporter of Federal Union. Henry N. Brailsford, *Olives of Endless Age: Being a Study of This Distracted World and Its Need of Unity* (New York: Harper, 1928); Brailsford, *The Federal Idea* (London: Federal Union, 1940).

popular participation in politics should be extended beyond casting a vote every few years, but accepted that lack of education or information could hamper citizens' capacity to form political opinions. For the election of public representatives, she argued that people are better judges of personality rather than of ideas and policies. The political parties should therefore focus on the personal qualities of individual candidates, alongside precise and simple policy plans. Local political and civil associations should initiate the shift of political activities from the centre to the periphery. The relationship between government and civil society should be based on democratic associations endowed with power to control government agencies and bureaucracy. Some of these associations could have executive powers as well, for example in food administration. Civil courts would give individuals the opportunity to assume public responsibility as referees for the settlement of disputes. Other associations could be merely advisory, aimed at informing the government of public opinion. New means of measuring public opinion, like polls, surveys, and statistical analysis, could help transform widely shared ideas into policies.[64]

The real advantage of the federal centralised global authority was, for Wootton, its capacity to address the genuine public demand for welfare and social security. The government should employ new methods of social research to discover what individuals considered as 'freedom' and how better living conditions could be achieved. Top-down policies could be corrected by bottom-up intervention. The central authority should leave political space for local initiatives. Popular political participation meant giving more power to those who would be directly influenced by the decisions, and educating individuals to accept greater responsibilities in the public sphere and express their criticism of public policy through local committees and representatives.[65] Wootton did not provide many details of this system's functionality, yet her active involvement with the Trades Union Congress indicates one means of connecting the private and the public spheres through bottom-up action.[66]

Wootton anchored her federalist views in her economic theory. In the 1930s and 1940s, she elaborated a social-democratic economic vision aimed at allowing public authorities to balance the commitment to freedom with the need to address the social demands of the impoverished population of Britain. Clearly, during the interwar years Wootton was not the only one to voice this opinion.[67] In the late 1930s, similar ideas were approved

---

[64] Wootton, *Freedom under Planning*, 150.

[65] Ibid.

[66] Wootton, 'Socialism and Federation', 297.

[67] For Paul Addison, the post-1918 growing social awareness signified a 'swing to the left'; see *Road to 1945*, 127–155.

as the official policy of the Labour Party.[68] However, it is rarely acknowledged that Wootton was an active and vociferous contributor to this leftist mid-century debate on liberty, equality, and planning. As Ben Jackson convincingly shows, in the interwar years British social thinkers increasingly accepted that equality was complementary to liberty, and economic inequality created uneven conditions and opportunities for self-development. The growing participation of the working class in politics encouraged more thinkers on the left to reinterpret equality through the notion of an increasingly active and interventionist state apparatus.[69] Wootton's socioeconomic vision drew inspiration from a variety of sources: Laski's pluralism, Fabian reformism, Keynesian economic interventionism, guild pluralism, and liberal individualism. However, her interpretation of the relationship between economics and politics stood apart. The interplay between liberty and equality, which was fundamental to social progress, had to be conceived on a global rather than national scale. She criticised socialists who thought that resolving the issue of inequality within national boundaries was sufficient, and challenged those who took equality seriously as a political goal to expand the reach of their desired policies to the whole world.

Returning to Wootton's most comprehensive federalist treatise, *Socialism and Federation*, helps us understand the multiple sources of inspiration for her federalist thought. She started by giving a general definition of a socialist: someone who 'wishes to see available resources used in the way that will provide the best possible life and living for everybody; who sets a particularly high value upon economic and social equality for its own sake'.[70] Therefore, socialism was not about public ownership of the means of production, but about a measure of economic and social equality, a universal minimum standard of living. Furthermore, she held that socialism was politically acceptable only in a democratic system upholding civil and political liberties as its basic values.

It would be too easy to classify Wootton's view as 'socialist', as Hayek did in 1944.[71] In fact, she changed her mind about the meaning of planning and about the balance of social planning and liberty in a democratic federation. If in 1939 the attraction of establishing a federation was for her

---

[68] Elizabeth Durbin, *New Jerusalems: The Labour Party and the Economics of Democratic Socialism* (London: Routledge & Kegan Paul, 1985); Duncan Tanner, 'The Politics of the Labour Movement, 1900–1939', in *A Companion to Early Twentieth-Century Britain*, ed. C. Wrigley (Oxford: Blackwell, 2003), 43–44, 52. On the Labour Party and international relations, see Lucian M. Ashworth, *International Relations and the Labour Party: Intellectuals and Policy Making from 1918–1945* (London: Tauris, 2007).

[69] Ben Jackson, *Equality and the British Left* (Manchester: Manchester University Press, 2007), 23–25.

[70] Wootton, 'Socialism and Federation', 137.

[71] Hayek later conceded that she was a liberal-socialist, and their views on planning and federation were indeed not so different. See Barbara Wootton and Friedrich Hayek, 'Economic Planning: Road to Serfdom or Freedom?', *Left* 121 (1946): 255–261.

the possibility of central economic planning according to the Soviet model, a year later she had explicitly rejected the idea that Federal Union should promote extending the Soviet model of socialism on a global scale.[72] After 1940, she highlighted the federation's commitment to minimising the limitations and restrictions on individual political, civil, economic, and cultural liberties. Liberty meant very simply 'being free to do what we want to do, whatever that may be'.[73] She deliberately used a crude definition of liberty to prevent politicians and political thinkers from imposing their particular definition of liberty on society: the substance of freedom should be defined by each and every individual, while the public authorities should only scientifically and rationally 'discover'—and not dictate—what individual freedom might mean for specific people at a specific time.

Wootton's interpretation of freedom was one's ability to do as one wanted, as absence of constraints or restrictions on one's actions. She argued that there was no one definition of freedom; each individual could interpret the meaning of freedom according to his or her worldview. As we shall see below, there may be a conflict between her dynamic concept of 'freedom' and the demand that the state should take an active role to defend it. The public sphere she envisaged was characterised by a strong intervening public authority, capable of 'discovering' the shared meaning of freedom and public good and actively promoting it through specific policies. She implied that this 'discovery' could be made by employing scientific and empirical methods for social research, revealing her unfaltering belief in the change-inducing abilities of human reason, which could not only identify social and economic needs but also direct the political authority towards an efficient solution.

Wootton adopted the concerns Laski expressed in *Liberty in the Modern State* over the state's double function as the provider of the conditions for individual happiness and as the main threat to it. However, if for Laski 'liberty is an inescapable doctrine of contingent anarchy', beset with insoluble tensions between political authority and free individuals, Wootton proposed a more hybrid and optimistic view of the potential balance between political power, popular participation, and individual freedom.[74] The centralised authority would be assisted by the people at the grassroots level, who would participate actively in shaping public policy through local committees, delegations, campaigning, and lobbying.[75]

Another important influence on Wootton's idea of freedom were the writings of the Hungarian sociologist Karl Mannheim, who from 1933 held

[72] Barbara Wootton, 'Socialism and Federal Union', *FUN*, 25 May 1940.

[73] Barbara Wootton, 'Liberty and the Individual' (radio broadcast, High Midland Service, 11 December 1946), in Barbara Wootton Personal Papers, Girton College Archive, Cambridge, GCPP Wootton 3/2.

[74] Harold J. Laski, *Liberty in the Modern State* (Harmondsworth: Penguin, 1937), 250.

[75] Wootton, *Freedom under Planning*, 144–153.

a lectureship at the LSE.[76] Her intellectual debt to Mannheim was not mentioned in her recent biography, despite the many references to his work in her writings, and her positive review of his essays on sociology of knowledge. She was inspired by Mannheim's attempt to reconcile freedom with social planning, a goal that Laski had already abandoned but Wootton still tried to achieve. In his earlier sociological works, Mannheim explored the meaning of scientific truth and the limits of historical knowledge from a post-Marxist position, arguing that human knowledge is characterised by a plurality of perspectives.[77] Nonetheless, he refuted relativism and argued that a meaningful, objective, and truthful understanding of the world was possible.[78] In *Man and Society in an Age of Reconstruction* (1935), he outlined a vision of social democracy based on planning for welfare and individual freedoms.[79]

In London, Mannheim continued to elaborate his analysis of the crisis of contemporary liberal democracies, whose epitome was the Weimar Republic, and suggested possible reforms to prevent the degeneration of democracy into tyranny. His investigation encompassed political, social, and economic issues, and his conclusion that laissez-faire could not provide the social conditions for political liberty was shared by Wootton. If this conviction was already present in the German edition of *Man and Society* (1935), it was significantly emphasised in the English edition of 1940, which could be seen as 'almost a new work', complete with new chapters focused on his personal experience in a liberal-democratic state, Britain.[80] The idea that the state could—and should—engage in rational and well-studied planning of its economic and social structures and services to provide better living conditions for its citizens without compromising their liberty to live according to their choices seemed to Wootton extremely relevant to 1940s Britain.[81]

---

[76] On Mannheim and his work, see chapter 2; for bibliographic references, see note 22 there.

[77] Mannheim, *Ideology and Utopia*.

[78] Compare to Raymond Aron's interpretation of Mannheim's sociology of knowledge: Aron, *German Sociology*. See chapter 2 for a discussion of Aron's critique of Mannheim.

[79] Karl Mannheim, *Man and Society in an Age of Reconstruction: Studies in Modern Social Structure*, trans. Edward Shils (1935; repr., London: Routledge, 1940).

[80] Kurt Wolff, *From Karl Mannheim* (New Brunswick, NJ: Transaction, 1993), 525.

[81] While Mannheim's earlier writings embodied a critique of reason, in the 1940s he turned to rational planning as a possible solution for the crisis of liberal democracies. This explains Wootton's disapproval of the English edition of Mannheim's earlier essays on the sociology of knowledge that appeared posthumously in 1952. In her review of the collection, Wootton suggested the author would have 'radically rewritten' these essays in view of his later theory of politics. Karl Mannheim, *Essays on the Sociology of Knowledge* (1952; repr., London: Routledge, 1997); Barbara Wootton, 'Review of *Essays on the Sociology of Knowledge* by Karl Mannheim. Edited by Paul Kecskemeti', *Philosophy* 28 (1953): 278. For an analysis of the changes between Mannheim's early and wartime political thought, see Ira Katznelson, *Desolation and Enlightenment: Political Knowledge after Total War, Totalitarianism, and the Holocaust* (New York: Columbia University Press, 2003), 162–168.

Wootton and Mannheim knew each other personally. She invited him to participate in events and meetings of Federal Union, including the August 1940 Federal Union conference on 'The New Europe' at Lady Margaret Hall, Oxford. His lecture, later published in FUN, provided Wootton with theoretical support for her vision of social planning in a federal democracy. Mannheim suggested that the experience of the planned war economy showed that planning was possible and sometimes necessary to achieve common goals. He argued that this experience showed that the principle of freedom would not be in contradiction with a new international order based on social and economic planning. For him, the 'concrete situation' in 1940 showed that the public was disappointed with the inability of the free market to provide the promised social goods. The Nazi or Soviet models of the planned economy promised some social welfare at the costly price of individual freedom. Nonetheless, the emergence of mass society emphasised the need for innovations in 'social, economic and political techniques', which are the 'sum of improvements which aim at influencing human behaviour' and can become tools of 'social control' in the government's hands. Positing that the new 'social techniques' could both enhance and restrict freedom in society, Mannheim suggested that democratic planning should be limited to the fields where without it chaos would govern.[82] As before, he asserted that freedom meant lack of deliberate interference in the individual's life and choices. His critique of liberalism called for the establishment of a planned society based on the empirical study of humanity's social behaviour.[83]

Wootton embraced Mannheim's idea that rationalism, scientific methods and individual liberty were three key elements of a new economic world order.[84] She added a layer of complexity to Mannheim's 'perspectivism' arguing that there were multiple individual perspectives on the meaning of freedom, a variety of legitimate freedoms constantly reinterpreted and articulated by all members of society. She demanded that a democratic polity be flexible enough to accept these changing and evolving—and sometimes irrational—ideas of freedom, and allow their expression within the collective political structure. However, as Raymond Aron argued against Mannheim's perspectivism, there is not necessarily a way of arbitrating between the various ideas of 'freedom'. The variability of 'freedoms', and their irrationality, also cast doubt over Wootton's requirement that the state rationally and scientifically discover individual freedom, and defend it against tyranny.[85]

[82] Karl Mannheim, 'Transition from Laissez-Faire to Planned Society', FUN, 7 September 1940.
[83] Mannheim, Man and Society, 30–45; Hall, Dilemmas of Decline, 78–80.
[84] On Mannheim's influence on Wootton, see Alberto Castelli, 'Pianificazione e libertà', Il Politico 3 (2001): 399–431.
[85] Aron, German Sociology, 56; for a detailed discussion, see chapter 2.

Wootton's vision was characterised by a fundamental dualism: various individual liberties were constantly reshaped and redefined, while individual needs were essentially universal and eternal. This dualism imposed a double role on public authorities: to intervene in public life while safeguarding individuals from such intervention. For Wootton, as for Mannheim and in a certain sense for Laski, this meant that mass democracy could no longer exist in an economic system based exclusively on the capitalist free market. The democratic state had to take an active economic role in regulating and organising the market in order to guarantee a predefined living standard to all citizens. The political reality of the 1940s showed her that states either failed to do so, or promoted planning at the expense of freedom. Accordingly, a global democratic federation was indispensable. The federal arrangement would be desirable because economic planning would be more efficient and profitable on a large scale, while maintaining the space of individual liberty at the local, national, or even municipal level. The challenge of Federal Union was not to preserve the balance of powers or to safeguard the imperial status quo, but to promote democracy and social welfare on a global scale without undermining individual liberty.

Wootton was keen to persuade Federal Union that social and economic issues had to be taken seriously when thinking about a democratic world federation. In 1940, she was invited to represent the Federal Union Executive Committee at the FURI economists' committee, whose other members included Robbins, Beveridge, and Hayek.[86] Beveridge, at the time master of University College, Oxford, asked the committee to write a report on the economic consequences, limits, and advantages of federal union. However, the fundamental difference between Wootton's federalist economic thought and that of the other members soon emerged. They circulated a summary paper of their activities before Wootton joined the committee, stating that a federal economy should be endowed with a common currency and a strong central authority to regulate monetary and trade policies also within the member states. Although these ideas essentially repeated the proposals that Robbins had advanced in 1937, the committee added that such a 'radical solution would probably have to be abandoned' because the existing states would not give up their economic sovereignty and independence. The economists sought a compromise, which consisted of applying the principle of free trade at the federal sphere, and leaving the fiscal, monetary, and planning decisions to the national governments. They asserted that 'free trade may be taken to be the fundamental basis

[86] Ransome, *Studies in Federal Planning*, vi.

for the international relation of the nations constituting the International Organisation'.[87]

At the committee, Wootton underlined the close relations between economic policy and social rights on a global scale, and suggested that the new economic policy for Federal Union should be based on planning. Her decisive position undid the fragile consensus within the committee, which polarised into two distinct positions—free market versus social planning—with Hayek and Wootton representing the two extremes. As Robbins noted in his interim report on the committee's activities, the final solution was to avoid any decision and concentrate on envisaging a federation with substantial economic powers that could be used only in exceptional cases.[88]

The report's inconclusiveness beset also the Anglo-French economists' meeting in April 1940. Wootton, Hayek, Beveridge, Ransome, and Robbins travelled to Paris just two months before it surrendered to the Germans to discuss with their French colleagues proposals for European economic federalism. A sense of urgency characterised the meetings, in the hope to elaborate more effective machinery of economic government than the interim report offered. Yet even in this mixed forum, the economists could not agree on the fundamental principle of the federal economic authority—planning or free market—and contended with asserting the general importance of federation.[89] For Wootton this conclusion represented a political compromise, but also clear evidence of the French interest in strong economic federal authority. Robbins was similarly enthusiastic about French support for the federal idea. For Hayek, the conference offered yet another confirmation of his view that no agreement on the nature and scope of federal economic regulation and planning could be reached.

Despite the federalists' failure to prevent war by federation, they continued to discuss federalism as the necessary framework for post-war economic reconstruction. For Wootton, federalism could provide not only economic prosperity, but also a more equal redistribution of wealth. In a series of articles in *FUN*, 'Plus Plan for Plenty' and 'Plan for Plenty', she discussed the political advantages of economic well-being.[90] In order to avoid abstract conceptualisation, Wootton defined planning as 'a recognition of certain elementary needs and of the fact that, if it were not for the war and war preparation, the satisfaction of those needs would be entirely possible'.[91] This definition presupposed—rather than explained—that pub-

---

[87] 'Economic Problems of International Government', in the Records of Federal Union and Federal Trust for Education and Research, London School of Economics, London, 2/B/1.

[88] Lionel Robbins, 'Interim Report on Economic Aspects of the Federal Constitution', in Ransome, *Towards the United States of Europe*, 91–97.

[89] 'Anglo-French Economists' Conference', in Ransome, *Towards the United States of Europe*, 98–103.

[90] Barbara Wootton, 'Plus Plan for Plenty', *FUN*, 6 July 1940; Barbara Wootton, 'Plan for Plenty', *FUN*, 1 March, 15 March, and 29 March 1940.

[91] Wootton, 'Plus Plan for Plenty'.

lic authority and not private individuals had responsibility to satisfy these 'elementary needs'.

Wootton's vision of a global socioeconomically just society was based on two assumptions: First, economic planning can create prosperity and redistribute it more equally across society. A more equalitarian and prosperous society would be politically beneficial because strife and poverty lead to political radicalisation and war. Second, since the war budget showed that the state could finance large-scale projects, in the post-war era these funds should be diverted towards social causes to prevent future war. Her vision included not only social services to the poor and unemployed, but also free or subsidised nutrition and housing for all. Wootton's proposals received a lukewarm reception. While some federalists approved of her ideas, others accused her of paternalism and overemphasising irrelevant details, which could obstruct the federalist cause. Others still preferred social policies based on economic incentives rather than subsistence provisions.[92]

In her subsequent three articles on 'Plan for Plenty', Wootton sought to explain Federal Union's policy guidelines on economic democracy, suggesting that the universal cause of living standards should be the fundamental principle of economic democracy. Her global welfare system would be financed according to the British model, where the system of social services was paid for by taxation. However, public subsidy of basic goods and services was only one way of serving a universal living standard, which also required bolstering local economies and industries. Thus, the means of providing individual needs were diverse and contingent, embodying a commitment to social equality and to private enterprise alike.

When theorising the global economy, Wootton touched upon the economic gap between states. She suggested that global economic inequality could embody a real difficulty for realising the federalist project. Yet tackling the problem of global inequality was in the interest of the rich states as well as the poor ones. The better off the poor states would be, the more they could contribute to the federal treasury through taxation. Therefore, Wootton proposed a global fiscal reform to narrow economic gaps and finance social provisions. Her reform included three main elements: individual—rather than corporate—taxation, tax on inheritance up to a maximum of 60 percent, and finally fixing an 'absolute upper limit' to individual income or inheritance.[93] Such measures were rejected by her fellow federalists who considered them as too severe a limit on private enterprise.[94]

Wootton's fiscal measures would have been accompanied by institutional reform. She approved of some of Keynes's institutional ideas, although her

---

[92] For a collection of letters replying to Wootton's argument, see *FUN*, 20 July 1940.

[93] Barbara Wootton, 'Plan for Plenty (2)', *FUN*, 15 March 1941.

[94] For Robbins, some form of inheritance tax could be used to mitigate extreme cases of inequality, but not as the source of funding for a welfare system.

notion of economic planning was significantly more radical. She was particularly interested in his idea of an International Clearing Union (ICU), a global banking institution that Keynes presented to the British government and the Treasury in 1941.[95] The ICU was to regulate currency exchange and trade using a new international currency, 'Bancor'. By penalising creditor states, Keynes hoped the ICU would encourage states to use their capital to purchase foreign goods and improve the world economy as a result.[96] These were the sort of institutions Wootton hoped could facilitate the transition to a transnational federal economic—and political—system. By stabilising and controlling economic markets, these institutions could contribute to a more balanced distribution of wealth and industry. Yet, by 1943, she despaired of the lack of political willingness to undertake federal and transnational reforms, and proposed to use some—not well specified—political authority to impose these schemes on reluctant states. Indeed, Keynes's idea was never accepted internationally, although in recent years it has attracted some interest and support.[97]

The commitment to social and economic welfare went, according to Wootton, hand in hand with a democratic political system based on freedom and 'the rights of man'. In 1940, when Charles Kimber published the first Federal Union policy pamphlet *How We Shall Win*, she praised his assertion that 'man has certain rights and certain needs, and the business of the political machine is to fulfil [sic] the needs and safeguard the rights'.[98] Her interpretation implies that 'needs' like 'rights' can be discovered and agreed upon by political decision makers. Although their meaning could be interpreted in various ways, it was still possible to lay down standards as the basis of state—or federal—laws. In the *FUN* issue of March 1942, she referred to the importance of Roosevelt's 'freedom from want' in the post-war world order. While acknowledging that Federal Union could not, at that point, outline a consensual economic plan for the future, she underlined her commitment to economic security and social well-being as the foundation of a democratic world order. Federalism was a means to achieve a democratic socialist society in which equality was not merely legal and political but also economic. Hence, as Ransome wrote in a letter to Beveridge as early as 1940, Wootton represented the interventionist faction in Federal Union, who sought to create a 'new economic policy'

[95] At Bretton Woods, Keynes and Harry White presented the British-American joint plan for an international monetary fund that included elements of Keynes's earlier plan. Steil, *Battle of Bretton Woods*, 143–144.

[96] Barbara Wootton, 'The Keynes Plan', *FUN*, June 1943.

[97] See, for example, George Monbiot, *The Age of Consent: A Manifesto for a New World Order* (London: Flamingo, 2003).

[98] Barbara Wootton, 'Standards for a Federal Government', *FUN*, 7 September 1940.

based on planning and state action.[99] However, Robbins, Hayek, and other federal economists blocked her initiatives, which they considered a menace to democracy.

Concerns over the impact of economic planning on freedom were common in social-democratic circles. Wootton's commitment to individual liberty, independent of communal or political association, reflects the mixture of liberal and socialist ideas that characterised the British left. However, within the range of shared views, Wootton put more emphasis on the importance of individual freedom over universal economic equality. Economic equality embodied equal opportunities, rather than 'mathematical' parity.[100] Her innovative contribution was in underlining the global relevance of her egalitarian socioeconomic vision, and its applicability to a federal polity that extended beyond the boundaries of the nation-state.

FRIEDRICH HAYEK AND THE CHALLENGE OF LIBERAL FEDERALISM

The interplay between federalism, economics, and liberty replaced the theme of imperial relations as the central concern of the wartime federalists. Democratic federalism was formulated in social and economic terms, but there was no consensus on the desirable strategies to achieve better living conditions. At Federal Union, the main protagonists of the debate on liberty and welfare were Wootton and Hayek, yet the ideas of Lionel Robbins loomed over their debates. During the 1930s, the conditions and implications of social and economic planning were key concerns for Wootton and Hayek. Their discussion on planning reached its apex with the publication of Hayek's *The Road to Serfdom* and Wootton's *Freedom under Planning*. In between, Hayek replied to the articles on federal planning that Wootton published in 1940–1941 in *Federal Union News*. He argued that economic planning on a federal scale imposed a double threat. First, the rich states may be reluctant to pay for the increase in living standards in the poorer states. Second, democratic institutions were not adequate for discussing and deliberating decisions on which there was no preexisting widespread agreement. For him, one of the chief causes of the Second World War was the failure of German democracy, which was unable to operate effectively due to fundamental disagreements. Similar disagreements would necessarily hamper the functioning of any federal democratic

---

[99] Patrick Ransome to William Beveridge, 19 June 1941, in William Beveridge Papers, London School of Economics, London, box 7, folder 63.

[100] Barbara Wootton, *End Social Inequality: A Programme for Ordinary People* (London: Kegan Paul, Trench, Trubner, 1941).

government.[101] Despite his criticism of Wootton's interpretation of democratic federalism, Hayek was committed to the idea of establishing a supranational political and economic unit to shield individual freedom, a democratic federation.[102]

Friedrich A. Hayek (1899–1992) studied law and economics at the University of Vienna with Ludwig von Mises. In 1923, he obtained a research assistantship in statistics and economic theory in New York, and later became the director of the Austrian Institute for Economic Research in Vienna. Lionel Robbins discovered his work in 1929 and suggested to Beveridge to invite Hayek to give a set of public lectures at the LSE in 1931. Following the success of the lectures, Beveridge came up with the idea to offer Hayek a one-year fellowship, and later the university appointed him Tooke Professor of Economic Science and Statistics. Hayek considered his time at the LSE particularly productive and exciting, despite the fact that his economic views were not widely accepted.[103] In those years, Hayek and Robbins made the LSE an important centre for economic research and theory, counterbalancing the influence of the Cambridge economists, and in particular of Keynes.[104] During those stimulating years, Hayek contributed to the influential academic journal, *Economica*, dined at the Reform Club with Beveridge and Robbins, and befriended other European émigrés, like Mannheim, Michael Polanyi, Karl Popper, and Raymond Aron.[105]

Hayek's economic and political theory was in part a reaction to what he perceived as the growing—and negative—influence of socialist thought on Britain's social policy and theory.[106] The publication in 1944 of *The Road to Serfdom*, which he dedicated to 'socialists of all parties', was a political response to all he believed was wrong in British economic policy.[107] Yet, his approach also emerged from a sustained reflection on the epistemological foundations of social and economic interaction.[108] As Ben Jackson shows, Hayek's critique of national planning emerged in the 1930s in relation to

---

[101] Friedrich Hayek, letter to Federal Forum 'Plus Plan for Plenty', *FUN*, 13 July 1940.

[102] On Hayek's federalism, see Edwin René van de Haar, *Classical Liberalism and International Relations Theory: Hume, Smith, Mises, Hayek and International Society* (Basingstoke: Palgrave, 2009), 106–109.

[103] Friedrich A. Hayek, *Hayek on Hayek: An Autobiographical Dialogue*, ed. Stephen Kresge and Lief Wenar (Indianapolis: Liberty Fund, 2008), 43.

[104] Samuel Brittan, 'Hayek, Friedrich August (1899–1992)', in *Oxford Dictionary of National Biography* (2004), www.oxforddnb.com; Alan Ebenstein, *Friedrich Hayek: A Biography* (Chicago: University of Chicago Press, 2003), 49–75; Bruce Caldwell, *Hayek's Challenge: An Intellectual Biography of F. A. Hayek* (Chicago: University of Chicago Press, 2004), 169–172.

[105] Daniel Stedman Jones, *Masters of the Universe: Hayek, Friedman, and the Birth of Neoliberal Politics* (Princeton, NJ: Princeton University Press, 2012), 31, 74.

[106] Wootton and Hayek, 'Economic Planning'.

[107] Friedrich Hayek, *The Road to Serfdom* (1944; repr., London: Routledge, 2001).

[108] For a recent analysis of Hayek's epistemology, see Theo Papaioannou, *Reading Hayek in the 21st Century: A Critical Inquiry into His Political Thought* (Basingstoke: Palgrave, 2012), 30–69.

Walter Lippmann's writings on the New Deal.[109] His writings in the 1940s made an important addition to his reflections on planning by discussing the implications not only of national planning but also of international planning on liberty and peace.

Possibly, Robbins or Beveridge encouraged Hayek to join Federal Union. From 1939 to 1941, he was an active member of Federal Union and the FURI economists' committee, where he promoted the vision of economic federalism articulated previously in 'Economic Conditions of Inter-state Federalism'.[110] In this article, which echoed the earlier federalist ideas of Robbins, Hayek expressed his unqualified support for federalism, both political and economic as a means to prevent wars and advance individual liberty. In 1944, his interpretation of federalism was further explored in the last—and least discussed—chapter of *The Road to Serfdom*.[111] The chapter opened with a quote of Lord Acton stating that federalism was 'the most efficacious and the most congenial' method to curb the power of the state and of the whole people.[112] For both Hayek and Acton, federalism had the merit of protecting individual freedom from state power. Hayek accepted Robbins's views, expecting federal union to contribute towards economic prosperity and growth by improving trade, communication, immigration, and financial relations across national borders. In addition, he held that federalism would be politically desirable as a guarantee of peace and security: 'wisely used, the federal principle of organisation may indeed prove the best solution of some of the world's most difficult problems'.[113] Like Wootton, Hayek opined that political and economic federalism must develop in parallel, and that the functionalist idea of a transnational economic system run by unbiased and apolitical experts would be a danger to liberty. Economic decisions should be the result of political discussion, not the elaboration of an administrative international agency.

While Hayek shared Robbins's views about the economic benefits of federalism, he envisaged a more limited scope for the federal authority. In this sense, Robbins represents a middle way between the federalist ideas of Hayek and Wootton. Whereas Wootton saw political discussion on the federal dimension as the source of legitimacy for economic planning, Hayek took a less optimistic approach. He assumed that on the federal level the 'similarity of standards and values among those submitted to a unitary plan diminishes', and thought that proposals for international or

---

[109] For Hayek's view of planning in the 1930s, see Ben Jackson, 'Freedom, the Common Good, and the Rule of Law: Lippmann and Hayek on Economic Planning', *Journal of the History of Ideas* 73 (2012): 47–68.

[110] Friedrich Hayek, 'Economic Conditions of Inter-state Federalism', *New Commonwealth Quarterly* 5 (1939): 131–149.

[111] Hayek, *Road to Serfdom*, chap. 15.

[112] Ibid., 224.

[113] Ibid., 243.

federal planning entailed even greater dangers than national planning.[114] Hayek's discussion of federal planning brought to the fore the relations between his critique of human epistemology and his idea that liberty should set the foundation of political order. His rejection of planning predicted that federal economic planning could have two outcomes: the destruction of individual liberty and economic inefficiency. The main argument for excluding planning on the federal level was the impossibility of attaining the necessary political agreement on the goals and the scope of any widespread economic plan. The lack of shared cultural, political, and moral values rendered impossible any agreement on the desirable purpose of society. Human reason per se could offer no guarantee of cooperation, agreement, or even mutual understanding. He agreed that in domestic politics the decision to pursue an economic plan despite its negative impact on some members of society was motivated by morality and solidarity, but these were absent from the international sphere. A consensual economic policy could not be drafted without the backing of a shared system of values and beliefs, which served as the basis of a common feeling of solidarity within the state. Evidently, Hayek opposed the cosmopolitan view that humanity as a whole shared common traits, needs, and desires that could give substance to the common cause. Thus, he repeated his 1939 argument that lack of common morality and social solidarity on the international plane would render any scheme of economic planning an unacceptable and coerced economic sacrifice.[115]

Moreover, Hayek doubted that centralised planning could achieve better economic results than individual decisions in the free market. The limits of human reason undermined the capacity of individuals to objectively evaluate complex economic information, to process large quantities of data, and to predict the long-term outcomes of economic design.[116] Due to the epistemological limits of the planners, who could not rationally predict the outcomes of their plans in a complex world economy, he suggested that planning would be less efficient than individual action in the free competitive market. Like Robbins, he argued that on principle, the actions of many individuals in the free market, based upon limited knowledge but with a similarly limited impact, could construct a more efficacious and prosperous economy than a system directed by a misguided centralised plan.[117]

[114] Ibid., 227.
[115] Ibid., 228. For an interpretation of Hayek's thought as a critique of liberal internationalism, see Hall, *Dilemmas of Decline*, 77–80.
[116] Papaioannou, *Reading Hayek in the 21st Century*, chap. 2. Hayek elaborated these ideas in more detail in *The Sensory Order* (London: Routledge & Kegan Paul, 1952).
[117] Hayek, *Road to Serfdom*, 232.

Hayek's solution was to avoid any kind of federal economic policy beyond this fundamental principle: providing a permanent rational framework within which individual initiative would have the largest possible scope and would be made to work as beneficently as possible. This idea resonates with his discussion of the rule of law as a guarantee of political and economic freedom on the national level. In 1939, Hayek argued that he supported two systems that he referred to as 'planning'. The first was a 'system of general rules equally applicable to all people'.[118] It would be a system based on the rational rule of law rather than specific prohibitions and orders, which would set the background for individual decision making. Second, Hayek made clear that he was not a supporter of the a priori application of laissez-faire, by suggesting that within the federation some degree of economic regulation could be organised on a local level, by interested small communities, with limited impact.[119] Elsewhere he conceded that a centralised plan set by the government could be desired to provide, for example, a comprehensive system of social insurance and 'a minimum income for every person in the country'.[120]

Hayek's rare concession to federal planning resonates with Robbins's position, which remained, however, more flexible than Hayek's regarding the role of the central federal authority. Unlike Hayek, who constructed a federal order to limit the power of the political authority to influence the economy, Robbins wanted to create a new federal public authority to satisfy collective economic needs that were previously undermined by national interests. If for Hayek any federal intervention in the economy should be a rare exception, for Robbins such intervention should be the rule, if aimed at the common good of the federal citizens as a whole.

In the last chapter of *The Road to Serfdom* Hayek levelled a fierce attack at 'socialism' in international politics. Earlier on, he had already defined 'socialism' as 'social justice, greater equality and security' but also 'the abolition of private enterprise, of private ownership of means of production, and the creation of a system of planned economy' in which the 'entrepreneur working for profit is replaced by a central planning body'.[121] This definition helped him to crystallise the opposition between 'socialism' and 'liberalism' as the foundation of a new world order. The rise of socialism represented not only the decline of liberal political economy, but also the crumbling of Western civilisation under the tide of German and Italian fascism. The experience of the war meant, for Hayek, that the democratic

---

[118] Friedrich Hayek, *Freedom and the Economic System* (Chicago: University of Chicago Press, 1939), 194–195.

[119] Hayek, 'Economic Conditions of Inter-State Federalism'; Hayek, *Road to Serfdom*, 227.

[120] See Friedrich A. Hayek, Maynard C. Krueger, and Charles E. Merriam, *The Road to Serfdom: A Radio Discussion*, University of Chicago Roundtable 370 (Chicago: University of Chicago Press, 1945), 4.

[121] Hayek, *Road to Serfdom*, 34.

system could not sustain centralised economic planning without giving up on individual liberty and adopting an illiberal collectivist system on the fascist model. Therefore, if liberal democracies followed the Soviet idea of centralised planning, the result could be restriction of liberty, and subsequently fascism and totalitarianism.[122]

These challenges did not make Hayek give up his federalist vision. He supported federalism as the 'application to international affairs of democracy', the most effective way to achieve world peace.[123] His federalism followed the precepts of political devolution: the division of political authority between the spheres of the federation, the state, and the small community would serve as a check on political intervention in the economy. A federal authority would have a decisive role in reinstating international liberalism if it could effectively shield the individual's freedom of action from any political interference. He argued that 'the need is for an international political authority which, without power to direct the different people what they must do, must be able to restrain them form action which will damage others'.[124] This confirmed Hayek's earlier suggestion that a world economic authority with overwhelming power was undesirable. Thus, he differed from Robbins, who considered a centralised federal authority to be the necessary requisite of an effective federal structure. Hayek suggested that the federal political space would include entrepreneurial self-governing small communities within existing states, united in a federal 'international community' with a central organisation endowed with minimal powers to prevent any other political unit from issuing restrictive economic measures that would undermine free competition and trade. Yet, it remains unclear what incentives individuals and states would have to unite in a federation. It seems that individuals would be motivated to federate in order to limit the authority of the states, but it is far from obvious that states should submit to the people's will and give up power and authority.

When Hayek published *The Road to Serfdom*, suggesting that economic planning could lead to totalitarianism, Wootton was quick to pick up its controversial arguments and write a detailed reply aimed at proving Hayek wrong. Her book, *Freedom under Planning*, was a meticulous critique of Hayek's theory, arguing that economic liberty and public planning could be reconciled in a democratic state.[125] She pointed out that Hayek's thesis

---

[122] While Hayek did not consider socialism and planning as equally dangerous to liberty, and levelled his criticism only at a specific kind of centralised illiberal planning, his *Road to Serfdom* was understood as an attack of any form of planning as 'socialism' and was not welcomed by American New Dealers, like Charles Merriam. See also chapter 7.

[123] Hayek, 'Economic Conditions of Inter-State Federalism'.

[124] Hayek, *Road to Serfdom*, 238.

[125] Wootton, *Freedom under Planning*, 5–6.

was built on the assumption that effective economic planning would necessarily entail public ownership of the means of production, resulting in loss of individual economic freedom. Her goal was to convince her readers that a measure of public planning was compatible with individual freedom. Yet their writings retained some ambiguity around the meaning of 'planning', leading, in 1946, to Hayek's affirmation that 'Mrs. Wootton . . . will be driven to confine her support of planning to that of "planning for competition" (and to supplement competition where it cannot work) which I myself favour'.[126]

Wootton's book sought to address the two points of criticism that Hayek levelled against planning: economic inefficiency and the destruction of liberty. The fundamental assumption of her critique reveals the distance between her view and Hayek's. For Wootton the binary between private and public could be obfuscated in favour of a more integrated system in which individuals, governments, and civil society organisations work together for a shared goal without compromising their distinct functions. Their shared goal would be improving social and economic conditions in society on a global scale. Wootton thought that governmental planning could influence the private sphere while leaving sufficient space for individual freedom of initiative. For Hayek, this shared private-public space was impossible. Political power had an inherent tendency to expand its authority at the expense of individual initiative, and any attempt at blurring the boundary between the private and public spheres would put too much power in the hands of the government, invariably resulting in tyranny and fascism.

The disagreement of Hayek and Wootton on the economic efficiency of planning emerged from their incompatible theories of human knowledge. We have seen previously that Hayek strongly doubted that human reason could provide a reliable foundation for economic planning. Wootton, by contrast, believed in the ability of scientific research to discover universal human needs that could be satisfied by the collective authority. Her argument in favour of planning was based on the capacity of human reason to identify the goals of collective human action by rationally analysing empirical data. States would accept federal economic planning if it could be rationally proven as the best method to facilitate the achievement of common social and economic goals. Although in her view not all human activity was rational, it was still humanly possible and desirable to employ reason in contemplating social, political, and economic affairs. Wootton hoped to extend this model of rational planning to the world as a whole, in order to provide a basic standard of living for all. In this sense, she was the intellectual heiress of liberal internationalists like Hobson, Brailsford,

[126] Wootton and Hayek, 'Economic Planning', 259.

and Norman Angell, who grounded their vision of a peaceful world order in the assumption of human rationality.[127]

Hayek compared legitimate and illegitimate planning to 'laying down a Rule of the Road, as in the Highway Code, and ordering people where they are to go'.[128] The advantage of a general legal framework over specific laws was the limited need to predict specific outcomes of the law. The rule of law represented a very vague and abstract level of legislation as the foundation of a liberal society. For Wootton, this could not be sufficient to address society's needs and demands. The free market was, for her, 'incapable of registering preferences which could not be reflected in consumers' demand for particular articles', such as unemployment.[129] To her mind, rational legislation aimed at treating a specific social malaise, like unemployment, could attain positive results if well grounded in facts and concrete knowledge of reality.

Importantly, both Hayek and Wootton thought that private individuals and civil society organisations should play a role in the new federal system of politics. However, these groups fulfilled different roles in their visions. Hayek saw local self-government as the unmediated expression of the community's political and economic preferences. As part of his proposal for the devolution of state authority to the supranational and subnational levels, he suggested that small communities be given the possibility to do economic and social planning on a local level. Wootton had a different interpretation of grassroots activities, centred on the importance of public consent to and control of government decisions. She saw popular participation as a means of connecting the top and bottom levels of federal politics and suggested that the relationship between the governed and the government should be based 'on partnership and not on fear'.[130] Federal Union might have been for her an example of such bottom-up political partnership, in which individuals united to draft their policy proposals, which could later be sent for discussion in parliament. Both Wootton and Hayek praised grassroots political initiative as a check on the political power of the centralised authority.[131] They recognised that governors and 'planners' often had more limited knowledge of practical and specific issues than the 'common man', and hoped that a system of popular participation could overcome

---

[127] On interwar theories of liberal internationalism, see Casper Sylvest, *British Liberal Internationalism, 1880–1930: Making Progress?* (Manchester: Manchester University Press, 2009); Long, *Towards a New Liberal Internationalism*; Ceadel, *Living the Great Illusion: Sir Norman Angell, 1872–1967* (Oxford: Oxford University Press, 2009); Gorman, *Emergence of International Society in the 1920s*.

[128] Hayek, *Road to Serfdom*, 56.

[129] Wootton, *Freedom under Planning*, 123–125.

[130] Ibid., 155.

[131] Ibid., 152; Hayek, *Road to Serfdom*, 236–237.

this deficiency by putting individuals' practical and specific knowledge to common use.[132]

Ultimately, federalism was for Hayek the best guarantee of democracy because it was the most effective check on political power.[133] He thought that political devolution could enhance freedom by weakening and disintegrating the too-powerful nation-state without transferring its powers to the federal authority.[134] In that, he differed from Robbins, who endowed the central federal authority with extensive political powers in directing military, monetary, trade, and immigration policies. But Hayek disagreed most evidently with Wootton, who saw federalism as a guarantee of democracy because it was a means of involving the individuals in the system of planning directed by the federal state. She envisaged private individuals and associations, including the trades union and local civil organisations, as capable of exerting control over policies elaborated by federal experts. Therefore, the debate on economics revealed that democratic federalism had two different meanings for Hayek and Wootton. If Hayek underlined the individual's freedom of economic initiative, Wootton focused on the individual's capacity to safeguard public freedom by checking and correcting policies elaborated by the state or the federation. This difference reflects the diverging outlooks of the 'democratic federalism' of Wootton and Hayek: while the former hoped to construct a new global public sphere where individual claims for better living conditions were effectively addressed, the latter focused on expanding globally the sphere of individuals' freedom to improve their lives at the expense of both national and federal public authorities.

THE EMANCIPATORY HOPE OF DEMOCRATIC FEDERALISM

The history of Federal Union underlines the ambiguities and inconsistencies embodied in the project of federal democracy. The 1940s mark the transition from an imperial interpretation of democratic federation, advanced by Curtis and to some degree by Streit, to a federalist vision aimed at advancing the social and economic welfare of all individuals, which was proposed by Wootton, Robbins, and Hayek. The shift from empire to socioeconomic principles and imperatives happened within Federal Union but also beyond it. The political reality of decolonisation and the decline of the European empires, along with the public demand for better living conditions, motivated the quest for a new conception of democratic

---

[132] Wootton, *Freedom under Planning*, 150–155.
[133] Andrew Gamble, *Hayek: The Iron Cage of Liberty* (Cambridge: Polity, 1996), 142.
[134] Hayek, *Road to Serfdom*, 240.

federalism. Despite the movement's failure to attain its goals, it shows the direction that 'democratic federation' took after the Second World War, as a framework to provide economic growth and social prosperity beyond the state.

The difference between the economic federalism of Federal Union and the economic concerns of imperial thinkers relates to the non-discriminatory and non-exploitative character of Federal Union's federal order. For Hayek, Robbins, and Wootton, an economic order based on discriminatory labour and production relations contradicted the democratic ethos of their movement. The distinctive inclusiveness of their economic democratic federalism was grounded in the economic efficiency of the market, for Robbins and Hayek, or in the moral equality of all humans, for Wootton. In this context, it is important to remember that the impact of Federal Union outlasted the organisation's lifetime, and inspired the 'founding fathers' of the European Union, like Altiero Spinelli and Luigi Einaudi.[135] The Italian federalists embraced the idea of democratic federalism and the social and economic proposals of Federal Union for a post-imperial world.[136]

Federal Union's intense discussions on the social, economic, and political implications of democratic federalism reveal the organisation's effort to provide a sustained blueprint for a viable democratic federation. Competing visions of democratic federalism implied not only different geographies but also alternative political spaces: the exclusive space of the Anglo-Saxon or Western civilisations, the universal space of planning for individual welfare, and the no less universal space of free trade and enterprise. These visions were united by the claim that democracy could become a global political principle. However, they were undermined by their relative disregard for the non-Western world, despite the growing awareness of the declining imperial global order and the colonial demand of political independence. While Wootton and Robbins clearly rejected the imperial order, they did not propose how to end it. The geopolitical space of the democratic federation was conceptually restricted to the West, and was not yet truly global. Although the democratic federalism of Wootton, Hayek, and Robbins depended on a universal economic system, they did

---

[135] John Pinder, 'Introduction', in Altiero Spinelli and The British Federalists: Writings by Beveridge, Robbins and Spinelli, 1937–1943, ed. John Pinder (London: Federal Trust, 1998), 1–15.

[136] In the early 1940s, as a prisoner on the Italian island of Ventotene, Altiero Spinelli read the writings of Robbins, Beveridge, and Wootton on federalism, which he received from the economist Luigi Einaudi, a friend of Robbins. These authors inspired Spinelli and Ernesto Rossi to write, with Ursula Hirschmann, a treatise titled Per un'Europa libera e unita. Progetto d'un manifesto, better known as the Manifest of Ventotene. See Oakley, Critical Woman, 150; Burgess, British Tradition of Federalism, 173–174; Charles F. Delzell, 'The European Federalist Movement in Italy: First Phase, 1918–1947', Journal of Modern History 32 (1960): 241–250. On Spinelli's international thought, see Cornelia Navari, 'Spinelli, Functionalists and Federalism', in Public Intellectuals and International Affairs, 229–260; Umberto Morelli, ed., Altiero Spinelli: il pensiero e l'azione per la federazione europea (Milan: Giuffrè, 2010); Daniela Preda, ed., Altiero Spinelli e i movimenti per l'unità europea (Padua: CEDAM, 2010).

not dedicate much attention to the prospects of the colonial world, assuming its effortless integration into the federal system by independence and democratisation.

The conceptual shift in the history of 'democratic federalism' in the 1940s exemplified the intricate, nonlinear history of the term. Today, many theorists still struggle to define democracy as the foundation for a new global order, and offer a range of cosmopolitan, republican, or communitarian interpretations.[137] The mid-century debate underlines the importance of social and economic aspects of global, transnational, and federal democracy. I have highlighted the emphasis given in Federal Union to democratic federation as a motor of social and economic change. The goal of the federalists was no longer to perpetuate the imperial order by new means or to defend existing democracies in their battle against totalitarianism. While there were disagreements over the desired methods—planning or individual initiative—Federal Union developed a distinct view of federation as a vehicle of democratic social and economic improvement on a transnational, perhaps global level.

Federal Union members considered global democracy as a necessary condition—but also a challenge—to safeguarding cultural diversity, economic opportunity, and individual liberty. The tensions between unity and diversity exacerbated the lack of decision regarding the geopolitical boundaries of the democratic federation as a world region. Arguably, in the 1940s 'democracy' had not yet achieved the status of universal political standard. Nonetheless, it is clear that Wootton, Robbins, and Hayek sought to identify, define, and elaborate a form of democracy that could serve as a global model for a new political—but also socioeconomic—post-war world order. The history of Federal Union and its members remains a useful reminder of the varied and sometimes confusing meanings of a concept that has inspired many competing political projects, and continues to do so today.

---

[137] See, for example, Archibugi and Held, *Cosmopolitan Democracy*; Archibugi, Koenig-Archibugi, and Marchetti, *Global Democracy*; James Bohman, *Democracy across Borders: From Dêmos to Dêmoi* (Cambridge, MA: MIT Press, 2007).

CHAPTER 6

Writing a World Constitution

The Chicago Committee and the New World Order

ON 18 AUGUST 1945, a few days after the United States dropped atomic bombs on Hiroshima and Nagasaki, the president of the University of Chicago, Robert Hutchins, participated in a radio discussion on 'Atomic Force: Its Meaning for Mankind'. In his speech, he argued that the global control of nuclear weaponry would be indispensable to prevent 'world suicide'.[1] Hutchins's enthusiastic words were heard by two of his Chicago colleagues, literary critic Giuseppe Antonio Borgese, and philosopher Richard McKeon, who, like Hutchins, thought the international moment bore unique danger, but also a potential for initiating global change. The atomic bomb created a political void from which a new order could emerge. They suggested to Hutchins to establish at the university a centre for 'synthetic and structural' research in the humanities, aimed at providing the intellectual foundation for a new world order.[2] Instead of a research centre, Hutchins agreed to form a committee of intellectuals and academics, who would draft a world constitution as the first step towards global change. The publication of this constitution in 1948 was accompanied by a vibrant international debate between its authors and other political observers including Albert Einstein, Quincy Wright, Louis Wirth, Hans Morgenthau, Jacques Maritain, Winston Churchill, Léon Blum, Henry Usborne, Altiero Spinelli, Jan Smuts, Louis B. Sohn, John Boyd Orr, and many others. The British Federal Union also sent a letter of support and appreciation.[3]

This chapter looks at the intellectual experience of the Chicago Committee to Frame a World Constitution Draft from December 1945 to July 1947. While existing scholarship sometimes mentions—briefly and uncritically—the existence of the 'Hutchins Constitution' or considers the committee's

---

[1] 'Hutchins' Radio Discussion (with R. Gustavos and R. Ogburn) on "Atomic Force: Its Meaning for Mankind" (August 18, 1945)', Records of the Committee to Frame a World Constitution, Special Collections Research Center, University of Chicago Library (hereafter CFWC), box 46, document 1.

[2] 'Borgese-McKeon Memorandum to Hutchins (September 16, 1945)', CFWC, box 46, document 2.

[3] See Keith Killby to Giuseppe Antonio Borgese, CFWC, box 8, folder 6.

work as an example of failed utopianism, I focus on the controversies and debates between the committee's members during the two years that led to the draft's publication.[4] This project represented the extension of federal ideas to the global sphere, in continuation with the federalist thought explored in previous chapters. However, there are significant thematic differences between the committee and Federal Union, including the geopolitical scope of the project, its theoretical ambition, and its political motivation. For example, while at Federal Union 'democracy' was accepted as the normative foundation of political union, at the Chicago Committee this position was accepted only after a long debate on the moral value of political pluralism. The history of the constitution sheds light on the complex— and often contradictory and incompatible—theoretical ideas that set the foundation of visions of world order in the 1940s. As I show, the failure of the constitution to attain a concrete political goal depended not only on international diplomatic and geopolitical conjectures, but also on the philosophical assumptions about the moral desirability of pluralism and universalism advanced by the authors of the constitution.

There are three main reasons for rethinking the Chicago Committee. First, its members were influential figures with well-established intellectual authority, including Mortimer Adler, Richard McKeon, Charles Howard McIlwain, James M. Landis, Reinhold Niebuhr, Wilber G. Katz, Rexford Tugwell, Robert Redfield, William E. Hocking, Breadsley Ruml, Albert Leon Guérard, Stringfellow Barr, Harold Innis, and Erich Kahler. Lewis Mumford, Norman Cousins, Jacques Maritain, and Don Luigi Sturzo provided 'external' support. The committee members considered themselves as 'public intellectuals' and 'builders of Utopia'. Their explicit aim, however, was to offer a practical and realistic vision for global political change. Therefore, I investigate their interpretation of the public role of intellectuals through their attempts to bridge the gap between practice and theory in international relations.

Second, the committee's two-years-long discussions are a valuable source for understanding mid-century debates on world constitution. The debates around the constitution reveal two distinct approaches to world order: universalism and pluralism, represented by Giuseppe Antonio Borgese and Richard McKeon. I show the conceptual tensions between Borgese's universal and moralistic constitution and McKeon's attempt to preserve particularism and diversity. Third, the themes they discussed remain central to international theory today, including global constitutionalism, transnational democracy, sovereignty, representation, and distributive justice.

---

[4] Baratta, *Politics of World Federation*, 248; Mazower, *Governing the World*, 232–233; Wooley, *Alternatives to Anarchy*, 44.

In this chapter, I explore the main controversy that beset the committee's deliberations between the minimalist and pluralistic projects of McKeon and Landis (supported also by Niebuhr), and the maximalist constitution of Borgese based on a universalistic political theology. I suggest that the committee's failure to make the desired impact relates to the abandonment of its earlier commitment to pluralism and flexibility, promoted by McKeon and Landis, in favour of Borgese's more ambitious plan. The final draft followed Borgese's version, intentionally obfuscating the disagreements within the committee and creating a false impression of unanimity. I will challenge this impression by reconstructing the main points of controversy, showing that the committee touched upon contentious topics in world affairs, sometimes offering innovative solutions.

The chapter includes five sections. The opening section (following this introduction) briefly outlines the history of the committee, its members, and its goals. I then discuss the conflicting visions of world order within the committee—the universalistic and the pluralistic approaches—through controversies on sovereignty, global representation, and human rights. I then turn to analyse the final constitution. The following section assesses the reactions to the constitution, as published in the committee's journal, *Common Cause*. Finally, I discuss the committee's views on the role of intellectuals in shaping world order.

RICHARD MCKEON, GIUSEPPE ANTONIO BORGESE, AND THE ESTABLISHMENT OF THE CHICAGO COMMITTEE

The Chicago constitution became known as the 'Hutchins Constitution', associated with the prominent humanist's educational and political philosophy.[5] Yet the chancellor's role in the drafting was minor since Borgese and McKeon set the tone of the project. They were close friends despite coming from very different intellectual and personal backgrounds, and their charismatic personalities dominated the committee. However, their visions of world order emerged from substantially incompatible philosophical positions, leading eventually to McKeon's withdrawal from the committee and refusal to sign the final draft.

---

[5] On Hutchins's educational project at the University of Chicago, see Mary Ann Dzuback, *Robert M. Hutchins: Portrait of an Educator* (Chicago: University of Chicago Press, 1991); William H. McNeill, *Hutchins' University: A Memoir of the University of Chicago, 1929–1950* (Chicago: University of Chicago Press, 1991). On the reception of his reforms, see Andrew Jewett, *Science, Democracy, and the American University: From the Civil War to the Cold War* (Cambridge: Cambridge University Press, 2012), 221–224; Robert S. Thomas, 'Enlightenment and Authority: The Committee on Social Thought and the Ideology of Postwar Conservatism (1927–1950)' (PhD dissertation, Columbia University, 2010).

Richard McKeon (1900–1985), the committee's chairman, was a pluralist philosopher and distinguished scholar of classics. He was a disciple of John Dewey and Frederick J. E. Woodbridge at Columbia University, and completed his doctoral thesis on Spinoza and metaphysics.[6] After graduating, he spent a few years conducting philosophical research in Paris, where he studied Descartes under Étienne Gilson at the Sorbonne. Through Gilson, he discovered neo-Thomism and medieval philosophy, which he, in turn, introduced to his friend Mortimer Adler. In 1934, McKeon joined the University of Chicago as dean of the Division of Humanities and helped Hutchins realise his educational reform to break down disciplinary barriers and undermine the excessive pre-professional emphasis of previous undergraduate curricula. The new curriculum focused on critical analysis, broad understanding, and interdisciplinary knowledge of Western civilisation.[7] During the war, he directed the Army Specialized Training Program, whose Area and Language Studies unit aimed at providing military men and woman linguistic and cultural tools to serve abroad. This new approach, founded on comprehensive cultural and literary knowledge and not on grammar-based techniques, set the ground for the development of the post-war 'Area Studies Program'.[8]

In philosophy McKeon is celebrated for his contribution to the 'renaissance of rhetoric', which influenced Marshall McLuhan, George Steiner, and Richard Rorty, who was his student in Chicago.[9] McKeon's pluralism was rooted in Greek philosophy. He described four philosophical types based on Aristotle, Plato, the Sophists, and the Atomists, and defined four basic philosophical questions about the selection of subject matters, the interpretation, the method, and the way the argument was founded (its principle). Each philosophical type would respond differently to the four philosophical questions, yielding a schema of sixteen options, which McKeon called 'philosophical semantics'. He assumed that later thinkers might imitate any of the four Greek philosophers in answering any of the four questions. His basic schemata therefore yielded 256 possible patterns of philosophical thought.[10] This schema grounded his reflection on pluralism, suggesting that there were many legitimate expressions of the truth. While some modes of thought sought to refute other interpretations, McKeon's schema wanted to show that each philosophical approach was irrefutable in its own terms. By comparing various modes of thought, he

[6] Zahava K. McKeon, 'Introduction', in Richard McKeon, *Selected Writings of Richard McKeon*, ed. Zahava Karl McKeon and William G. Swenson (Chicago: University of Chicago Press, 1998), 3.

[7] Richard McKeon, 'Spiritual Autobiography' (1953), in *Freedom and History*, ed. Zahava Karl McKeon (Chicago: University of Chicago Press, 1990), 20.

[8] Ibid., 26.

[9] For Rorty's impression of the Chicago Division of Humanities under McKeon, see Neil Gross, *Richard Rorty: The Making of an American Philosopher* (Chicago: University of Chicago Press, 2008), 95–99.

[10] Walter Watson, 'McKeon's Semantic Schema', *Philosophy & Rhetoric* 27 (1994): 85–103.

McKeon

underlined the rich and complex history of concepts like truth, justice, and freedom.

McKeon's method aimed at clarifying the points of agreement and disagreement between different theories in order to reveal their unity.[11] Similar to Mannheim's 'perspectivism', McKeon's pluralism was grounded on the assumption that 'different objects result from various ways of considering the same object'.[12] Like Mannheim, he assumed that there was one truth attainable by reconciling different, even opposing, viewpoints through discussion and comparison. At the committee, McKeon used his semantic schema to distil the essential inner structure of determination— the main ideas and aims—of a political viewpoint or ideology. Once understood, these differences could be overcome by discussion or compromise, because, for McKeon, all theories boiled down to one fundamental truth. Thus, 'for McKeon world peace was within reach given open and sincere international intercommunication'.[13]

David Depew suggests that McKeon's pluralism was inspired by pragmatism and realism, the two major strands in early twentieth-century American philosophy.[14] Woodbridge taught McKeon that 'what philosophers mean might be comparable or even identical, despite differences in their mode of expression'.[15] Dewey taught him 'to suspect distinctions and separations which remove the process of thinking from the experience in which they originated'.[16] Nonetheless, McKeon's pluralism differed from the positions of Dewey and Woodbridge. He accepted the prevalence of theory over practice, but at the same time, embraced pragmatic conceptual pluralism, which—in contrast to Dewey—meant that pragmatism was just one possible approach of many. While philosophy remained a contemplative activity, it could still acquire an applied function and help policy makers disentangle substance from form. At the committee, his position was characterised by willingness to accept a variety of positions, and reluctance to endorse any particular worldview. As we shall see, however, other members considered his inclusive pluralism politically weak and inconclusive.

---

[11] Richard McKeon, 'Richard McKeon', in *Thirteen Americans: Their Spiritual Autobiographies*, ed. Louis Finkelstein (New York: Institute for Religious and Social Studies, 1953), 80; George Kimball Plochmann, *Richard McKeon: A Study* (Chicago: University of Chicago Press, 1990), chap. 1.

[12] Richard McKeon, 'A Philosopher Meditates on Discovery', in *Moments of Personal Discovery*, ed. R. M. MacIver (New York: Institute for Religious and Social Studies, 1952), 105–132.

[13] Joseph Betz, 'Review of *Pluralism in Theory and Practice: Richard McKeon and American Philosophy* by Eugene Garver and Richard Buchanan', *Transactions of the Charles S. Peirce Society* 37 (2001): 437.

[14] David J. Depew, 'Between Pragmatism and Realism: Richard McKeon's Philosophic Semantics', in *Pluralism in Theory and Practice*, ed. Eugene Garver and Richard Buchanan (Nashville: Vanderbilt University Press, 2000), 30–39.

[15] McKeon, 'Spiritual Autobiography', 8.

[16] Ibid.

9 · Borgese

McKeon's involvement in the committee is absent from his autobiography and rarely mentioned by his biographers, where a significant weight has been given to his role as advisor to the US delegations, to UNESCO and first acting counsellor on UNESCO affairs at the American embassy in Paris. He collaborated with Julian Huxley, Jacques Maritain, and other prominent public figures in a research project on human rights, which set the foundation for the Universal Declaration, and in an inquiry into the various meanings of 'democracy'.[17] In his 1967 essay on the theoretical basis of human rights, McKeon discussed the advantages of ambiguous definitions in philosophical discussions on social and political order. To his mind, the UNESCO committee deliberately employed ambiguous definitions of 'rights', 'democracy', and 'liberty' in order to accommodate as many viewpoints as possible. Philosophical and political pluralism therefore meant an open discussion of practical questions (putting aside ideological positions) to 'uncover and verify common principles and to test them by the falsification of proposed formulations and systems'. Following Dewey, McKeon's pluralism paid close attention to practical problems, assuming that different ideological systems included—despite their apparent incompatibility—a common grain of truth, which could be discovered by mutual recognition of diverging positions and common aims.[18]

Giuseppe Antonio Borgese (1882–1952) arrived at the University of Chicago shortly after McKeon. By then, he was one of the best known Italian intellectuals of his age, active in academia and the liberal press, a famous anti-fascist militant, and a unique voice in Italian literature.[19] Born in a small Sicilian village, Borgese was educated in Florence and Palermo. Benedetto Croce published his doctoral thesis on Neapolitan romanticism, and became his intellectual mentor until they fell out when Borgese criticised Croce's work on Giambatista Vico. He was a successful professor of Italian and German literature in Rome and Milan and journalist for *La Stampa* and *Il Corriere della Sera*. During the First World War, he took an interventionist position in favour of alliance with Britain and France.[20] When Italy failed to achieve its goals in the post-war peace settlement, Borgese was among those blamed for Italy's 'mutilated victory'. He retired from the public scene, and accepted a professorship in aesthetics at the University of Milan. He published well-received poetry and novels, and undertook diplomatic missions abroad for the Italian Foreign Office. His

[17] Ibid., 31. See also the Universal Declaration of Human Rights, passed on 10 December 1948, Paris, France; Richard McKeon, 'The Philosophic Bases and Material Circumstances of the Rights of Man', *Ethics* 58 (1948): 180–187.
[18] Richard McKeon, 'Philosophy and History in the Development of Human Rights' (1967), in McKeon, *Freedom and History*, 61.
[19] Salvatore Cataldo, *Giuseppe Antonio Borgese* (Messina: Sicania, 1990), 79.
[20] Giuseppe Antonio Borgese, *L'Italia e la nuova alleanza* (Milan: Treves, 1917).

174 • CHAPTER 6

career thrived until 1931 when he refused, along with a handful of Italian academics, to give the Fascist oath of loyalty, and immigrated to the United States, where he stayed until 1949. He explained the reasons for his exile in public letters to Mussolini, published in 1935 by the anti-Fascist movement Giustizia e Libertà.[21] He settled at the University of Chicago in 1936, but kept publishing in Italy essays about his political experience in his adopted home.[22] In Chicago, he married Elisabeth Mann, daughter of his friend Thomas Mann, who became a key figure in the Chicago Committee as the editor of its journal *Common Cause*.

In the United States, Borgese developed his idea of a world republic, a global state aimed at reinstating peace and harmony as a liberal panacea against totalitarianism and war.[23] His claim that a shared human morality was possible and indeed desirable exemplified his holistic view of politics. As I will show, Catholic political and social thought played a key role in shaping Borgese's ideas about the human person's moral value, which should be respected and protected by political institutions. Luciano Parisi's analysis of Borgese's literary works suggests that the author's non-confessional interest in religiosity emerged from his existential quest for redemption.[24] I suggest that Borgese's interest in the moral precepts of Catholicism found its expression in his literary and political works, rather than in religious zeal.

Borgese and McKeon selected the other members of the committee according to their commitment to the idea of world government, political impartiality, and intellectual or practical knowledge of world affairs. They hoped to include representatives of all continents, but logistical constraints limited membership to American-based academics (including many European émigrés).[25] Friedrich Meinecke, Lewis Mumford, Arnold J. Toynbee, Jacques Maritain, and Luigi Sturzo declined the invitation but followed the committee's work. The original group included Chicago-based philosopher and editor of the *Encyclopaedia Britannica* Mortimer Adler, Harvard constitutional historian Charles Howard McIlwain, dean of Harvard Law School James M. Landis, theologian Reinhold Niebuhr, Wilber G. Katz, New Dealer and governor of Puerto Rico Rexford Tugwell, anthropologist Robert Redfield, Harvard idealist philosopher William E. Hocking, statistician and economist Breadsley Ruml, Stanford French historian Albert Leon Guérard, and Robert Hutchins.

---

[21] Republished in Gandolfo Librizzi, *'No, Io Non Giuro': Il rifiuto di G. A. Borgese, Una storia antifascista* (Marsala: Navarra Editore, 2013).

[22] Matteo Billeri, 'Introduction', in Giuseppe Antonio Borgese, *Imbarco per l'America e altre corrispondenze al* Corriere della Sera (Cuneo: Nerosubianco, 2012).

[23] Giuseppe Antonio Borgese, *Common Cause* (London: V. Gollancz, 1943).

[24] Luciano Parisi, *Borgese* (Torino: Tirrenia, 2000), chap. 3.

[25] Letter from Giuseppe Antonio Borgese to R. McKeon, 24 December 1945, CFWC, box 18.

The first meeting was held in December 1945 at the Harvard Club in New York City. The main concern was identifying the philosophical foundation for a politically feasible constitution. The debate outlined the main difficulties that the committee would face in its two years of deliberation. Tugwell, the Columbia University agricultural economist who helped Roosevelt to develop the New Deal and later became the governor of Puerto Rico, wanted to theorise the constitution from scratch without prior ideological commitment, but he failed to convince the others. McKeon argued that any new order would necessarily utilise existing ideas and arrangements. Niebuhr and Ruml rejected visions of world order differing substantially from the existing system of sovereign states, which, they argued, would be unlikely to renounce their power.[26] Their challenge was to bring about global change without unsettling the status quo.

A significant discussion revolved around the legitimacy of the attempt of American or Western intellectuals to write a world constitution. Niebuhr was particularly hesitant about writing a global constitution, pointing out the Eurocentrism of Mortimer Adler and Robert Hutchins, who, in those years, established their educational project, the Great Books Foundation.[27] Adler's interwar undergraduate courses in Chicago on the West as the birthplace of philosophy gave rise to this publishing project that proposed to collect the very best of human knowledge and make it accessible to the American reader. However, the project and the logic behind it were criticised as Eurocentric, dogmatic, and haughty.[28]

The committee considered the universalisation of Western culture an inappropriate basis for world government. The American federal constitution ignited their imagination, but they agreed not to replicate it on a world scale.[29] This global-oriented attitude reflected the changing zeitgeist of the late 1940s. The idea that American leadership was the ideal solution of the world's problems, which seemed out of place in 1947, was precisely the message that Borgese's previous political manifesto tried to convey. In 1939, he led a group of intellectuals who joined forces to write a declaration on world democracy. The 'Committee of Fifteen' included seventeen American and émigré intellectuals: Borgese, Thomas Mann, Niebuhr, Mumford, Hermann Broch, Herbert Agar, Oscar Jászi, Frank Aydelotte,

[26] 'Proceedings of the Committee to Frame a World Constitution, Harvard Club, New York, 17–18 Dec. 1945', CFWC, box 51.

[27] 'Preface', in Mortimer Adler, *How to Think about the Great Ideas: From the Great Books of Western Civilization* (Chicago: Open Court, 2007).

[28] Dzuback, *Robert M. Hutchins*, 221.

[29] 'Proceedings of the Committee to Frame a World Constitution, Shoreland Hotel, Chicago, 4–5 Feb. 1946', CFWC, box 51.

Van Wyck Brooks, Alvin Johnson, Christian Gauss, William Allan Nielson, Hans Kohn, Ada L. Comstock, William Yandell Elliott, Dorothy Canfield Fisher, and Gaetano Salvemini.[30] Alarmed by the rise of fascism and Nazism, they called for American intervention in the European war and proposed to establish a world federal democracy under American leadership. Despite the apparent commitment to democratic politics, the published manifesto embodied a conservative worldview that saw Western civilisation as the epicentre of humanity, criticised the conceptual and political weakness of liberal democracies, and called for the establishment of a new order based on Christian values.

Borgese was the intellectual and organisational motor behind this enterprise. Even the manifesto's title, echoing St Augustine's 'City of God', resonates with his earlier book on the moral duty of democracies to defend justice and order in the world.[31] Borgese, and many members of this group who escaped fascist Europe, argued that the United States' privileged position as a future world leader—even a world empire—was morally justified by the duty to establish world peace. The manifesto shared the views of many British imperial apologists who endowed the empire with a moral role as a global defender of peace and order. For the manifesto's authors, the democratic constitution of the United States and its Judeo-Christian cultural tradition fostered the American moral right to world leadership.

In Chicago, these ideas were no longer explicit. Borgese's intellectual and moral reference point remained the American Constitution, yet the allusions to theological concepts and to American empire were limited. The change could have been motivated by the failure of the 1940 manifesto to capture public attention, or by the realisation that the insistence on American exceptionalism as the motor for world change could cost him the support of Russian and non-Western peoples. Unlike the imperial federalists and the Atlantic federalist Clarence Streit, who set the American federal constitution as their model, the committee's shared intention was to avoid Euro- and American-centrism in order to create an inclusive and globally acceptable constitution.[32] Nonetheless, some still harboured doubts about the feasibility of the constitutional project: Niebuhr, Hocking, and Ruml withdrew from the committee because they had misgivings about its potential success. They were soon replaced by three new members: 'Great Books' educator Stringfellow Barr, Canadian historian Harold Innis, and Jewish literary scholar Erich Kahler. However, their qualms

[30] Agar et al., *City of Man*; Adi Gordon and Udi Greenberg, 'The City of Man, European Émigrés, and the Genesis of Post-war Conservative Thought', *Religions* 3 (2012): 681–698.
[31] Giuseppe Antonio Borgese, *Goliath: The March of Fascism* (New York: Viking, 1937).
[32] See chapter 4 for a detailed discussion of Streit's ideas.

shed light on the limits of the constitution and help understand the philosophical assumptions that motivated its compilation.

For two years, the committee discussed the themes that emerged in its very first meeting: the meaning of sovereignty and consent in relation to the notion of representation, the place of existing states in the new constitutional framework, the potential acceptance of the constitution by non-Western states, and the public role of intellectuals. I now turn to expanded discussions of these themes.

THE UNITY AND DIVISION OF SOVEREIGNTY

The most contentious problem on the agenda was the nature of sovereignty in a democratic world order. National sovereignty was often considered by prophets of the international state as the main obstacle for the realisation of their vision.[33] British internationalists of various creeds, including Curtis, Wootton, Robbins, Hobson, Angell, and Brailsford, decried self-interested sovereign states as the cause of war, suggesting that the abolition of the state's right to declare war and manage its affairs independently would peacefully lead to the establishment of a world federation.[34] Although the committee proposed a more sophisticated theoretical treatment of sovereignty than many earlier internationalists did, they shared the view that sovereignty should be reconceptualised to guarantee global security and peace. The constitution intended to weaken the link between territory and authority by grounding sovereignty's source of legitimacy in universal morality.[35]

McKeon advocated a nebulous definition of 'sovereignty' as independent government, and posited that the committee should 'set up an instrument of government by which we will provide for the settling of disputes'. But his attempt at circumventing the problem only intensified the disagreements about the sources of sovereign power and its limits. Niebuhr argued that sovereignty rested with the people, who could, and historically did, abolish their government. Without popular agreement, no constitutional changes could be enacted. 'Ideal' constitutions, he reasoned, could not generate change because transformations happened through historical processes at the grassroots level. Mortimer Adler replied that political

---

[33] 'Borgese's Fifteen Cursory Remarks on Views A and B on a World Constitution', CFWC, box 47, document 38.

[34] See, for example, Brailsford, *Olives of Endless Age*; Brailsford, *Federal Idea*; Hobson, *Democracy and a Changing Civilisation*. Nonetheless, a disillusioned Brailsford argued in his letter to the committee that their proposal to 'abolish sovereignty' went too far and would not be politically acceptable. See H. N. Brailsford to Committee, 15 January 1948, CFWC, box 35.

[35] See discussion of territoriality in modern politics in Galli, *Political Spaces and Global War*, chap. 3.

institutions, and not only history, had a hand in changing the meaning of 'sovereignty' both in practice and in people's minds.

Despite Niebuhr's long-term interest in the idea of world democratic federation, exemplified in his contribution to *The City of Man* manifesto and participation in the Chicago Committee's meetings, he remained sceptical about the idea of writing a global constitution. He rightly identified the committee's intellectual debt to the American Constitution and Federalist Papers, which the other members tried to undermine to preserve the project's unbiased universality, and pronounced his misgivings about expanding American constitutionalism worldwide.[36] However, his main doubt emerged from what he perceived as a lack of world community to ratify the constitution. In absence of a world community with shared values, there would be no new order.[37]

Notwithstanding disagreements about the practice of reallocation of sovereign power, the committee continued to scrutinise the essence of 'sovereignty' as a political concept. While vagueness was a virtue for McKeon, Landis argued that sovereignty was not precise enough to be used in constitution writing. Both 'national sovereignty' and 'popular sovereignty' were misleading because they did not endow the people and the state with specific political roles or actual political prerogatives. Similarly, his Harvard colleague McIlwain reasoned that the legislative aspects of sovereignty had to be clarified to make the constitution an effective *legal* document. In defence of the traditional meaning of sovereignty, he proposed a compromise. Sovereignty was an 'actual thing', indivisible, but its meaning had two aspects: constituent and governing. Constituent sovereignty had a practical and theoretical importance in creating and legitimating the polity, and maintaining a strong political relation between the governing and the governed, who held the right to reclaim their decisional power and abolish the government. Governing sovereignty was a practical concept, characterised by a greater degree of flexibility. It enabled making day-to-day decisions according to the general terms outlined by the constituent act of the people. In the world constitution, constituent sovereignty resided in the people of the world, while governing sovereignty could be given to the people's representatives on local, national, or global levels. Of the two aspects of sovereignty, the more important was, no doubt, the constituent power of the people that initially established the political community.

The power of individuals to unite in a polity and give themselves a government was fundamental to assert the democratic nature of government

---

[36] 'McIlwain's "Some Considerations of Sovereignty Especially in Its Relation to World-Federation", January 1946', CFWC, box 46, document 13.

[37] See 'Proceedings of the Committee to Frame a World Constitution, Harvard Club, New York, 17–18 Dec. 1945'. In 1944, Niebuhr published his critique of democratic politics and the international realm, *The Children of Light and the Children of Darkness: A Vindication of Democracy and a Critique of Its Traditional Defenders* (New York: Charles Scribner's Sons, 1944).

and legitimise its authority. McIlwain argued that governing sovereignty could not be divided theoretically, but could be shared in practice by different organs of government. The following debate revolved around the desirable division of sovereignty in the world. The committee concluded that a world federal state would be preferable to the ineffective league of independent states and to an unfeasible unitary world state. The foundational popular constituent sovereignty remained indivisible and legitimated the political organisation, in which local and centralised political institutions held the sovereignty to govern.[38]

Despite the committee's conscious focus on practical solutions to the problem of sovereignty, Guérard and McIlwain still thought that the issue necessitated a philosophical elucidation to render the constitution politically acceptable. They wanted to overcome the conventional conception of sovereignty as absolute and indivisible—which for them excluded a federal state—but felt that the authority of a past philosopher would add seriousness and respectability to their own efforts. The sixteenth-century French jurist Charles Loyseau was the intellectual source that furnished them with an appropriate concept of sovereignty.[39] Rejecting Bodin's absolute sovereignty, measured by the state's external independence, Guérard and McIlwain embraced Loyseau's 'internal sovereignty', measured by the government's ability to rule within the state. Thus, if sovereign states joined the federal system, their sovereignty would not be lost.[40] By advocating a federalist-friendly concept of sovereignty, they intended not to safeguard the independence of the extant states, but to encourage them to unite in larger political units under a legitimate centralised authority.[41]

The discussions on the possibility of shared sovereignty resulted in two draft constitutions, written by Borgese and Landis. These drafts became the committee's fundamental working papers that signalled the main controversy among its members.[42] On one end of the spectrum, Borgese's constitution assumed that sovereignty rested with the central federal authority that generated individual rights and duties, transcending national boundaries and creating new mechanisms of representation to enable the world federation to evolve gradually into a world unitary state. On the other end,

---

[38] 'Proceedings of the Committee to Frame a World Constitution, Harvard Club, New York, 17–18 Dec. 1945'.

[39] Charles Loyseau, *A Treatise of Orders and Plain Dignities*, ed. Howell A. Lloyd (Cambridge: Cambridge University Press, 1994). On Loyseau's political thought, see Howell A. Lloyd, 'The Political Thought of Charles Loyseau (1564–1627)', *European Studies Review* 11 (1981): 53–82.

[40] Jean Bodin, *On Sovereignty: Four Chapters from the Six Books of the Commonwealth*, ed. Julian H. Franklin (Cambridge: Cambridge University Press, 1992); 'Proceedings of the Committee to Frame a World Constitution, Shoreland Hotel, Chicago, 4–5 Feb. 1946'.

[41] 'Landis Memorandum on "The Minimum Amount of Power That Must Be Delegated to a Central Government", December 1945', 'Adler-McKeon "Review and Summary", March 1946', CFWC, box 46, documents 5, 18.

[42] 'McKeon's "Notes on the Basic Issues between Two Conceptions of a World Constitution" (April 1946)', CFWC, box 46, document 30.

Landis wanted to formulate a 'politically relevant' constitution based on shared sovereignty between a central government inspired by the nascent United Nations organisation and the extant states as units of representation. Borgese thought that the new constitution should give legal prerogatives—expressed as political sovereignty—to the federal government, but Landis preferred a solution more in line with the existing political status quo. Legal revolutions depended, for him, on political sanctions, the lack of which was the main setback of the United Nations.

When debating the competition for sovereignty in the international arena, the committee assumed that *within* states a government had effective sovereignty to initiate legislation, enforce the law, and maintain order and peace, de jure and de facto. They hoped to lock political power in institutions with a greater territorial scope than the state, but they still built their conception of authority and sovereignty on the traditional articulation of centralised power. Neither Landis nor Borgese gave any political power to non-institutional agents (although, as we shall see, cultural organisations would have consultative functions in the global senate), or accepted that economic, religious, or civil associations could participate in sovereign decision making. From this viewpoint, even Borgese's plan, which underlined the insufficiency of territorial states in guaranteeing peace and affluence, was not revolutionary in its conception of politics. It merely sought to transport the existing political structure to the global political space. However, as Agnew has recently suggested, effective sovereignty is not always easily territorialised since political decisions are often taken or executed in relation to factors beyond the state's borders.[43] The committee's plan to maintain the conceptual traits of 'sovereignty' while extending its territorial reach would have given only partial solution to this problem. They focused on the transition of power from one territorial sovereign state to another (possibly extending the scale of the new state's territory to the whole globe), without considering alternative complex political relations between the various agents in the global arena.

THE PROBLEM OF REPRESENTATION

The Chicago Committee envisaged not only new legislative chambers, but also a novel principle of representation for each assembly.[44] The fundamental question was whether a universal and egalitarian representative system was preferable to a flexible and pluralistic one, which would take

---

[43] Agnew, *Globalization & Sovereignty*, 6.
[44] 'Draft II (Hereafter Designated as Borgese's Draft or Draft B)', 'Draft V (McKeon's)', in CFWC, box 47, documents 42, 48.

into account the political, economic, demographic, and cultural discrepancies between different communities, regions, and states. The committee dismissed the idea advanced at the Congress for World Federation in Dublin, New Hampshire, assembled in October 1945 by Streit, Grenville Clark, and former justice of the US Supreme Court Owen J. Roberts.[45] The Congress aimed at overcoming the UN's structural and constitutional weaknesses by turning the international organisation into an effective world government. One of the proposals they advanced was the establishment of a system of 'weighted representation' to replace the 'one state, one vote' principle. The new system would be based on demographic proportional representation with coefficiencies to allow less populated Western states to have more representatives at the world assembly at the expense of more populated non-Western states. The committee opposed this attempt at maintaining Western political hegemony at the cost of global justice and equality. This proposal embodied, for them, obsolete concepts of civilisational hierarchy originating in the imperial world order they hoped to transcend. The discussions highlighted the tension between the inclusive aspiration of the new constitutional project and the awareness that such a solution could undermine the project's political feasibility.

Borgese's main concern was formulating a just system of representation to reflect the global and cosmopolitan foundation of the new polity.[46] The federation would represent all human beings as equals and undermine the political power of nation-states. Borgese hoped that inventing new regions and constituencies—rather than states—as electoral colleges would weaken the states' power and enhance the global spirit that Niebuhr called 'world community'. Borgese parcelled the world's territory into nine electoral regions: North America, Europe, South America, Russia and East Europe, North Africa, Black Africa, Sahara, East Asia, and India. He then divided each region into fifty smaller constituencies.

However, when it came to distributing the world parliament's seats between the various constituencies, Borgese was troubled. He opposed the idea of a system of weighted representation aimed at preventing densely populated countries from overpowering Europe and the United States. He imagined a more equalitarian representative system, but the 'economic status and status of production' and 'contribution to mankind' should be taken into account in the distribution of global political power. Despite doubting the morality of weighted representation, he proposed a complicated system of parameters, including population, taxation, and literacy, to distribute seats in the world legislative council.[47] His proposal, which

---

[45] Baratta, *Politics of World Federation*, Appendix F, 'World Federalist Declarations, Declaration of the Dublin NH Conference, 16 October 1945'.

[46] 'Draft II'; 'Borgese's Draft One Hundred Eleven', CFWC, box 48, document 111.

[47] 'Borgese's Constitution', CFWC, box 48, document 9.

did not differ in substance from the Dublin Declaration, was rejected by the committee. But Borgese did not despair, and elaborated his principle of representation by creating new electoral colleges, each based on a similar number of citizens electing a similar number of seats. The modified system would maintain the universalistic principle of giving equal value to each individual vote across the world.

In coherence with his universal political vision, the basic political unit in Borgese's system was the individual, not the national citizen. The advantage of this system was, as Adler noted, that it created a pure and equal representation, free from nationalistic prejudice. The disadvantage was its complexity: it added to the world's system of states not only the federal world state but also electoral regions and constituencies. This scheme doubled the spaces of political action: it maintained the traditional territorial state as the political space of local government, and invented new political spaces of representation on regional and global scales. Intentionally, there was little overlap and interaction between the two levels of politics. From the viewpoint of sovereignty and representation, the world state was not a pure federation, because the federated states were completely separated from the political apparatus at the global level, which would be based on newly forged local and regional groups. Moreover, the national polities could not serve as a check on the global government because they had no impact on electoral procedures. This system spelled a distinct departure from the existing relations between national governments, citizenships, and international organisations at the time. Therefore, it met with ardent resistance from the committee. Despite this opposition, as we shall see below, after July 1947 this system was integrated into the final draft.

The opponents of Borgese's plan had a simple solution in mind. Landis envisaged a double assembly with one federative chamber representing the states and one world assembly elected directly by the world's population. The principle for their election could be decided by the first chamber. Landis argued that it was both unfeasible and undesirable to transcend politically the existing states, which maintained historical value and practical efficacy. Since, he reasoned, only a few scholarly made constitutions become accepted law, the committee should maximise its chances by staying as close to reality as possible. His reformist, rather than revolutionary, approach empowered the UN with an active legislature capable of enacting laws without the consent of member states. The world state would be a 'community of sovereigns', and not a community of peoples. Landis argued that the detailed features of the world organisation, like representation, institutions, elections, and administration, would have to be determined democratically by the constituting states after the constitution was ratified. Government actions, he posited, would be based on majority rule and power delegation, and the constituting states would decide how much power to delegate to the central government. Therefore, the principle of representation in the council would remain 'one state, one vote'.[48]

In 1946, Landis left the committee to become the head of the American Aviation Board and McKeon replaced him as the dominant voice of the 'minimalist' faction. Following his motto that constitutions should not set ideals but provide institutions to deal with political problems, McKeon created a more sophisticated version of Landis's draft, aimed at granting the federation limited powers to guarantee peace and improve living conditions of people around the world. An advisory council of nations, modelled on an extended and reformed UN Security Council, would represent larger states (smaller states could federate to elect a representative). This system would, McKeon argued, maintain the political principle of equality without inducing major artificial political changes. He added another condition: world citizens are only those who have political rights in their local polity. His aim was to encourage local governments to enact universal suffrage in order to have more voting rights in the world's assembly.[49] Nonetheless, this scheme could limit the world federation's ability to act against discrimination by leaving the locally disenfranchised without a voice on the global level as well.

Since the committee agreed that discrimination and prejudice were sources of global conflict, they sought to outline constitutional means to oppose racism. Adler and Redfield proposed the idea of 'exogenous representation', which encouraged interaction and cooperation across constituencies and electoral regions.[50] They suggested that in an 'exogenous' representative system, each constituency would have to elect at least some nonresident delegates (for example, the constituency of Rome would have to elect some delegates who are residents of London). It was an extreme interpretation of the British selection of delegates for parliament, suggesting that close electors-elected interaction was unnecessary and potentially negative. They ignored, evidently, the fact that in the British system the party headquarters elected the exogenous candidates, thus rendering them ideologically acceptable to their voters. Alternatively, Adler suggested that each electoral college would nominate its own candidates, which would then be elected by members of other constituencies, or vice versa. A more radical proposal was that residents of one constituency would elect the

---

[48] 'Landis' Memorandum on a Double Assembly', CFWC, box 47, document 15.

[49] 'Draft V (McKeon's)', CFWC, box 48, document 48.

[50] As an anthropologist, Redfield promoted the Chicago Area Studies Program for expanding American knowledge of 'Third World civilizations'. However, his views about the universality of Western values were close to Adler's. See Andrew Sartori, 'Robert Redfield's Comparative Civilizations Project and the Political Imagination of Post-war America', *Positions: East Asia Cultures Critique* 6 (1998): 33–64.

political leaders of another, for instance, the Italians would elect the British government. In support of this idea, Redfield argued that such a system would require the voters to acquire a better knowledge of another community's political system and encourage fraternal cross-boundary relations.[51] However, McKeon insisted that this system would exclude certain minorities from being rightfully represented in the legislative. Others merely doubted the plan's feasibility.[52]

In line with their commitment to political feasibility, the committee criticised both the 'maximalist' and 'minimalist' drafts for their excessive idealism. In their discussions, they seem oblivious to the inherent idealistic nature of their very project. Borgese's constitution was rejected as utopian, Western-centric, and impractical. They thought that his project lacked an account of the interaction between the proposed local government, electoral regions and constituencies, and world government. The minimalist proposals of Landis and McKeon were accused of lack of detail and enthusiasm, and targeted for the assumption that the world was already perfectly divided into independent and sovereign territorial states.[53] Despite the criticism, until late 1946 the majority of the committee preferred this minimalist proposal because it seemed more easily acceptable around the world.

The tension between idealism and feasibility remained a constant concern. The need for decisive global change did not undermine the committee's wariness of politically impracticality. In March 1946, the publication of the *Report on the International Control of Atomic Energy* (also known as the Acheson-Lilienthal Report) raised the committee's hopes for an agreement between the United States and the Soviet Union as a first step towards a world constitution.[54] But between March and June 1946 it became clear that President Truman's envoy to the United Nations, Bernard Baruch, had failed to convince the assembly and in particular the Soviet Union that this was a viable and unbiased plan for global pacification. The committee members condemned the evident one-sidedness of the Baruch Plan, and were unsurprised by its rejection.

This was a crucial moment in the history of the constitution. It reinforced the committee's doubts about the feasibility of their project, but did

---

[51] 'Exogenous Representation by Adler and Redfield', CF WC, box 48, document 44.

[52] 'Proceedings of the Committee to Frame World Constitution, Roosevelt Hotel, New York, 16–17 May, 1946', CFWC, box 52, 177.

[53] 'Proceedings of the Committee to Frame a World Constitution, Shoreland Hotel, Chicago, 4–5 Feb. 1946'.

[54] *A Report on the International Control of Atomic Energy* (Washington, DC: Department of State, 1946). For the history of the US Atomic Energy Commission, see Richard G. Hewlett and Oscar E. Anderson, Jr., *The New World, 1939–1946: A History of the United States Atomic Energy Commission*, vol. 1 (University Park: Pennsylvania State University Press, 1962). On the Baruch Plan, see Larry G. Gerber, 'The Baruch Plan and the Origins of the Cold War', *Diplomatic History* 6 (1982): 69–96.

not encourage them to abandon it. In March 1946, Landis suggested that even if the constitution could not 'avert the clash' between the United States and the Soviet Union, it would 'influence all alignments during the clash in a way favourable to the general interests of mankind and provide for a liveable pattern after the clash'.[55] But three months later, they agreed that their constitutional project had become irrelevant to the world's political reality, and decided, following Borgese, to abandon the modest and limited—but perhaps more viable—project outlined by Landis and McKeon, in favour of a more ambitious—'maximalist'—constitution.[56]

At this point, the committee took a turn away from one notion of 'acceptability' based on 'the world as it is', towards a more flexible and permissive notion of 'acceptability' based on 'the world as it ought to be'. Adler's decisive intervention, suggesting that the constitution had already been weakened by too many compromises, soothed some members' doubts about the outlook of their project. McKeon, who thought that a maximalist constitution was both impractical and undesirable, remained in a permanent minority position as most members supported Borgese's grand vision as the only one worth writing. The constitution became for them a declaration of universal human values, an instrument of revolutionary change. McKeon remained alone in his dissent.[57]

DECOLONISING THE NON-WEST

Borgese's book *Common Cause* (1943) ended with an enthusiastic appeal to the English-speaking world, mainly to Americans and Britons, to live up to their character and establish a world republic.[58] Since the late 1930s, Borgese was convinced that intellectuals should join forces to convince the general American and British public that they had a special responsibility for establishing a world democracy.[59] By 1945, he understood that the unique political experience of the English-speaking peoples would not be sufficient without the willingness to join forces with the Russians. In *Common Cause*, Borgese's poetic prose highlighted the particular history of the English linguistic—rather than racial or political—community, describing its political ethos through literary examples. As much as these

---

[55] 'Proceedings of the Committee to Frame a World Constitution, Harvard Club, New York, 29–30 March, 1946', CFWC, box 52.

[56] 'Proceedings of the Committee to Frame a World Constitution, Shoreland Hotel, Chicago, 16–17 June 1946', CFWC, box 53.

[57] Ibid.

[58] Borgese, *Common Cause*, 80.

[59] This idea motivated Borgese's previous attempt at organising a group of intellectuals to think about a new democratic order. See Agar et al., *City of Man*; Gordon and Greenberg, 'The City of Man, European Émigrés', 681.

claims recall earlier Anglo-Saxon utopias, Borgese did not endorse British-American federal unity and indeed opposed similar schemes proposed at the time.[60] He disliked the term 'Anglo-Saxon', for its exclusiveness obfuscated the real racial diversity of the United States, and gave racial claims of superiority a pseudo-scientific appeal. Clarence Streit's federalist best-seller was, for Borgese, a prime example of a racially discriminating vision, despite the fact that Streit never actually used the term 'Anglo-Saxon' in his book.[61]

Nonetheless, Borgese found political inspiration in the English linguistic heritage. He argued that the English language was imbued with a set of politically desirable ideas and concepts, including democracy, liberalism, and prosperity, which could be globally exportable by individuals and smaller communities without preserving the political hegemony of the United States and the British Empire. The English language, he suggested, was easily understood and learnt—giving as an example the spread of English in India—and could potentially become a universal language, if only the English-speaking peoples recognised their responsibility and abandoned their political isolationism. He was apparently unaware of the discriminatory and exclusionist implications of his argument.

The political imagery of the United States as the homeland of freedom and democracy was perpetuated in the committee's discussions through references to the American Constitution and the Federalist Papers. However, they precluded the idea of replicating the American Constitution or the 'Anglo-Saxon democracy' on a global scale.[62] They criticised the proposal of Ely Culbertson for perpetuating Western hegemony and imperialism by law or by force. For the committee, exclusionist visions of world order that extended one country's political experience to the entire globe were a danger to world peace because they prolonged the abusive practices of the imperial order.[63] Their challenge was to merge the American heritage with a new, just political vision.

Alongside the conviction that the British and the Americans had a special global responsibility, the committee surveyed international public opinion about world constitution. They corresponded with international public figures and, highlighting the importance of Russia's participation, commissioned studies from academic experts and Russian expatriates in the

[60] Borgese, *Common Cause*, 90, 134–140. Compare to other Anglo-American utopias in Duncan Bell, 'The Project for a New Anglo Century: Race, Space, and Global Order', in *Anglo-America and Its Discontents: Civilizational Identities beyond West and East*, ed. Peter Katzenstein (London: Routledge, 2012), 33–56.

[61] Streit, *Union Now*. See chapter 4.

[62] 'Borgese's Letter to Hutchins on the Assumption and Principles Underlying His Draft of a World Constitution (December 30, 1945)', CFWC, box 46, document 10.

[63] Ely Culbertson, *Summary of the World Federation Plan: An Outline of a Practical and Detailed Plan for World Settlement* (London: Faber and Faber, 1944); Baratta, *Politics of World Federation*, 69–73.

United States.[64] Since many new and old states were writing (or rewriting) their post-war constitutions, the committee assembled an inspirational pool of constitutions, corresponded with their makers, and analysed legal traditions in India, France, Japan, Italy, India, China, Ceylon, the Philippines, Israel, and Czechoslovakia.[65] They were keen to prove to the world, and especially to the Russians, that they 'meant business, not to show the West's superiority'.[66]

McKeon promoted the idea that the world state should also include non-Western philosophical elements. The positive contribution of the American and British political traditions to the realisation of a world republic would be counterproductive if not balanced by a wider variety of ideas. Mc-Keon's rhetorical schemata suggested that multiple philosophies were not mutually undermining, but contributed to the human quest for truth. The American federalism represented only one among many possible manifestations of the truth. Through participation in global politics, people could understand each other, accept a plurality of ideas, and thus advance world peace. Other members showed sincere—if less philosophical—interest in political diversity, which emerged from their professional and personal knowledge: Tugwell discussed his experience as governor of Puerto Rico, where he vouched for local self-rule. Redfield shared his anthropological insights about Central America. Guérard expressed his admiration for the cultures of the Maghreb and the 'Negros' of Central Africa and wanted to see them adequately represented. Their concern was to ensure that their constitution would not preserve the discriminatory, Western-centric political order of the world.

The committee expected that decolonisation, which started gaining pace after the war, would give impetus to their constitution if they could persuade the colonial peoples that joining the world federation would be their best chance to throw off the imperial yoke. By acknowledging the political agency of people of all races and traditions, the world constitution would spare the colonial populations from waging a costly and bloody liberation war. Yet a fundamental problem remained. The authors of the constitution supported colonial independence only within the context of the global democratic federation.

---

[64] The committee commissioned research into the Russian attitude towards world federalism from the Slavic scholar Bernard Guillemin; see 'Mr. Guillemin's "Russia and World Federalism: Slavic Approaches to Internationalism", Nov 6 1946', CFWC, box 50, document 105. The research ended with the encouraging affirmation that 'even in isolation, Russia has not lost her sense of human unity. Isolation might even have acerbated an inborn longing for universal brotherhood. Never did Russia feel aloof from mankind. An emotional kind of universalism had grown up in spite of her severance from the West. At least on the emotional level, world federalism can be sure to find a response in the Russian soul'.

[65] Elisabeth M. Borgese, 'Constitutional Trends', 13 June 1946, CFWC, box 48, document 60.

[66] 'Proceedings of the Committee to Frame a World Constitution, Shoreland Hotel, Chicago, 16–17 June 1946'.

The committee saw the world constitution as an opportunity to shift the political balance in favour of liberating the colonial world by giving it a place in the democratic world federation. Therefore, one of the key questions related to the principle of representation. Borgese's system of weighted representation was initially rejected because it seemed excessively pro-Western, but his proposal to ground representation in new regional electoral colleges was accepted. This electoral system, as he admitted, might not guarantee an overlap between political communities and electoral colleges. Since he strongly opposed national sentiments, Borgese considered this an evident advantage of his federal voting system. Guérard, who was keen to endow Africans with political freedom, supported Borgese's proposal and argued that constituencies could overcome the imperial territorial division of the continent and allow the tribes of Central Africa to be represented separately from South African white communities. Yet, he ignored the fact that the local populations could perceive the proposed division of Africa into federal electoral regions as a top-down imposition, unrelated to their own political claims.

McKeon and Landis hoped to gain the support of the European empires for their constitution by tacitly accepting the imperial status quo. They proposed a system of state-based representation, which attracted the committee's criticism for ignoring the fact that the world was not neatly divided into free and independent states, but included colonies, dominions, dependencies, and mandated territories, and other geopolitical by-products of imperialism. The state-based electoral system did not offer an appropriate solution for the disenfranchised colonial populations. Furthermore, rather than encouraging political change towards decolonisation, this system gave federal voting rights only to those who could vote for the local parliament. While McKeon and Landis hoped to induce the empires to gradually renounce their discriminatory policies and give equal votes to all, their proposal risked preserving existing inequalities.

There were evident continuities between previous conceptions of international organisation and the committee's perception of the colonial world. In some areas, the committee proposed to replicate the system of mandates and trustees, suggesting the 'immature' territories would be managed democratically as 'federal territories' under the direct rule of the world government. The local population would still be allowed to elect representatives to the world assembly, which would have to ratify their independence. Although ex-colonies would no longer be administered by the European 'Great Powers', the conception of political 'immaturity' remained relevant.[67] The tension between the committee's intellectual pledge to democ-

---

[67] 'Guérard's "Should the Units of the World Federation Be 'Regional Unions and Constituencies', or Should They Be the Existing National States?" (April, 1946)', CFWC, box 47, document 26. For an

racy and freedom, at the expense of empires, and the need to render the constitution 'acceptable' to the world 'as it really is' added another layer of complexity to their discussions. The political scientist Quincy Wright, who followed the Chicago project closely, also identified the conflict between anti-imperialism and political acceptability in his comments on the final constitution draft. Interestingly, the conclusion he drew—that the global constitution should remain closely linked to extant political reality—was very close to McKeon's.[68]

PLURALISM AND HUMAN RIGHTS

The committee's discussions express a strong commitment to political and cultural pluralism. Diversity was not only a descriptive characteristic of the world, but a prescriptive value that the world federation should preserve. This approach gave rise to inevitable practical and conceptual tensions, such as the incompatibility between the proposed democratic global constitution and the mixed constitutions of the federated states. As much as some members found the pluralist ethos appealing, they insisted to fit the plurality of existing constitutional systems (some not democratic) within the universal constitutional democratic government. The committee's research group had shown in 1946 that the overwhelming majority of the world's states had monarchic or despotic constitutions, defined as 'rule by man and not by law'.[69] Moreover, as McKeon reminded his colleagues, the meaning of 'democracy' was not universal, and it would therefore be wrong to apply it as a discriminatory criterion of admission. But even if the constitution would accept a flexible interpretation of 'democracy', Adler, Hutchins, and Borgese doubted that a democratic world government could rightfully ignore obvious infringements of political rights within nondemocratic federated states. If, as McKeon suggested, only free citizens of local governments should be considered world citizens, what would be the status of the non-free, twice-disenfranchised peoples? Saudi Arabia was a frequent example of a despotic, antidemocratic, yet 'willing' state that might join the world federation if its internal constitution was respected. Yet the committee doubted whether democratic states should

---

analysis of the mandate system as part of Wilsonian internationalism, see Michael D. Callahan, *Mandates and Empire: The League of Nations and Africa, 1914–1931* (Brighton: Sussex Academic Press, 1999); Susan Pedersen, 'The Meaning of the Mandates System: An Argument', *Geschichte und Gesellschaft* 32 (2006): 560–582.

[68] Quincy Wright, 'Constitution Making as Process', *Common Cause* 2 (1948): 284–285; Quincy Wright to Elisabeth Mann Borgese, 17 October 1950, CFWC, box 33.

[69] 'Mr. Dux's "Of Democracies and Autocracies in the World Today, with Particular Regard to the Problem of the Executive"', 22 October 1946, CFWC, box 50, document 102.

agree to have fewer representatives in the world assembly than more populated despotic states.

After a heated discussion, the committee agreed that the federated states
should not be compelled to democratise, and could select their representatives to the world state in a nondemocratic procedure. Borgese hoped that
people under despotic rule would be inspired by the world federation to
rebel against oppression and establish domestic democratic regime. He suggested that imposing *formal* democratic elections would have an educative
value, even if the electoral process would not be 'free' according to Western
standards. By organising elections with only one candidate, he argued, the
local population would get used to the practice of democracy and would
later add democratic substance. McKeon opposed this as an unnecessary intervention in local constitutions. However, for Borgese, formal measures to
direct people towards democracy granted the constitution its revolutionary
potential.[70]

Borgese proposed other institutional means to enhance pluralistic democracy, such as a 'syndical assembly', a consultative parliament uniting
representatives of cultural, religious, professional, and linguistic associations from all over the world.[71] This chamber had no law-giving powers but could pass recommendations to the legislative assembly, based
on the wide-ranging knowledge of its members. 'Experts' in a variety of
fields should have, for Borgese, an advisory capacity in the legislative,
but should not have actual political power. His syndical parliament represented industrial and professional corporations, and superficially resembled the Italian Chamber of Fasci and Corporations that embodied, for
him, an insulting caricature of the idea of expert knowledge in politics.[72]

Side by side with celebrating human diversity, the committee discussed
Borgese and Guérard's proposed bill of universal human rights. Borgese
distinguished between 'human rights' and 'citizen rights': human rights are
of primary importance because they are based on the universal 'law of reason', while citizen rights are secondary because they depend on positive
state law. Human rights should be respected on a global scale, while citizen rights depended on membership in a particular state. He argued that
the protection of 'human rights' of all individuals was not conditioned by
national affiliation. This distinction became less relevant in the sphere
of the world federation because all individuals were 'world citizens' and
could claim human and world citizen rights alike.

[70] 'Proceedings of the Committee to Frame World Constitution, Roosevelt Hotel, New York, 16–17 May,
1946', 53–75.

[71] E. M. Borgese, 'Functional Representation and Syndical Chamber, January 17, 1947', CFWC, box 50,
document 117.

[72] On fascist corporatism, see Alessio Gagliardi, *Il corporativismo fascista* (Rome: Laterza, 2010); Gianpasquale Santomassimo, *La terza via fascista: Il mito del corporativismo* (Bologna: Carocci, 2006).

Borgese insisted on including in the constitution a specific set of rights and duties of the world citizens. He intended the description of human rights to be as detailed and precise as possible, but as his critics showed, he only partially succeeded.[73] His draft bill of rights of January 1947 was not, in McKeon's terms, a legal document but an amalgam of legal norms and 'pious declarations'. It included 'the right to be protected in the exercise of such responsibilities and privileges of political citizenship' and the 'right to be protected in the fulfilment of his inalienable claims to life, liberty and the dignity of human person'. It mentioned the 'golden rule' of reciprocity, but also a series of universal rights to 'claim and share': freedom from want, freedom from fear of war and of arbitrary justice, freedom from servitude and exploitation and from discrimination.[74] Other rights, like secret ballot and free press, were left to the discretion of the single states. According to his vision of social planning on a global scale, Tugwell wanted to add social and economic rights, such as housing, nourishment, employment, and a universal living standard, but others did not consider welfare provision as a foundational human right.[75]

Alongside the discussion about the necessity of a bill of rights, the committee debated the possible—and desirable—intellectual sources for universal human rights. Adler sought a shared conception of freedom and justice as a basis for human rights, and found it in Western political culture. McKeon and Landis opposed the very idea that a bill of rights should be included in the constitution. A well-specified and articulated declaration of universal rights would pretend to be based on global consensus when in fact there was none, and would therefore widen the discrepancies between the federated states, rendering agreement more difficult. As McKeon later stated in his report on his activities in UNESCO, an ambivalent and vague definition of rights was preferable for its inclusiveness and pluralism. Above all, he refused to commit the constitution to a specific—Western—conception. It would be unrealistic to expect the whole world to share a common idea of justice as the indispensable foundation of human rights. McKeon was no relativist: for him pluralism did not mean discarding all values and moral evaluations. Yet he argued that the committee lacked the necessary universal moral and intellectual backing to elaborate a complex scheme of rights that could be accepted worldwide. Evidently, he thought UNESCO did enjoy such global consensus and thus agreed to write its declaration of human rights.

[73] 'Proceedings of the Committee to Frame World Constitution, 1–2 April, 1947', CFWC, box 55, 290–300.

[74] 'Constitution One Hundred Thirteen', CFWC, box 49, document 113.

[75] Tugwell's vision resonated with Wootton's idea of orchestrating global production, consumption, and trade to provide a universal standard of living. See discussion in chapter 4.

The specific problem with Borgese's bill of rights, according to McKeon, was its antiquated and anachronistic approach, grounded in the historical experience of the French Revolution. It was a rationalised universal version of 'the law of nature', which might have been an appropriate foundation for the modern democratic state, but no longer reflected the global political values of their time. McKeon argued that while the eighteenth-century concept of rights provided legal limits to the government's power over the individual's life and property, a new bill of rights should address the positive claims of every individual by adding a function or a duty to the world government. He insisted that human rights should be enforced by existing organs of government, with the possible help of the new global institutions.[76] Thus, it would be a 'formal statement of what could be accomplished' through positive legal means and adequate political institutions. McKeon's proposal to reinvent human rights for the postwar global era did not find many followers in the committee. After intense discussions, he gave up and agreed to include a general description of human rights in the constitution, hoping that its vagueness would render it emotionally inspirational and legally innocuous. When McKeon's final resistance was removed, Borgese turned to completing the constitution.

The committee's debate on the bill of rights encourages a reflection on the meaning of human rights in the 1940s. In his revisionist history of human rights, Samuel Moyn argues with Hannah Arendt that during and after the Second World War, human rights were conceived as prerogatives of states; the United Nations introduced the notion of human rights but subjected it to state sovereignty, according to its institutional structure. Thus, in that period human rights did not represent, for Moyn, a break with state sovereignty or with the imperial world order. He goes on to affirm that 'in the 1940s human rights were never at any point understood as a break with the world of states'.[77] Moyn's main argument is that the mid-century conception of human rights depended on earlier ideas of the 'rights of man', which served as the foundation and justification for people to incorporate in a state. The idea of individual rights was bounded by the frontiers of the state, which gave it its political and legal legitimacy. Therefore, for Moyn, 'the central event in human rights history is the recasting of rights as entitlements that might contradict the sovereign nation-state from above and outside rather than serve as its foundation'.[78] This change, he argues, happened in the 1970s, with the decline of other political utopias.

It is beyond the scope of this study to assess in detail Moyn's argument, but his interpretative framework could help understand whether the com-

---

[76] 'Proceedings of the Committee to Frame World Constitution, 1–2 April, 1947', CFWC, box 55.
[77] Moyn, *Last Utopia*, 38–43.
[78] Ibid., 13.

mittee's conception of human rights represents a conceptual break with previous traditions or not.[79] First, it is important that the terminology used in the final constitution focuses on the 'rights of man' rather than 'human rights', intentionally grounding the discussion in the long-standing tradition of rights given rise by the French Revolution. In this sense, the 'rights and duties of man' remain the prerogatives of citizens, but not of the citizens of the nation-states. They are citizens of the world federation, which according to the committee's ideas would include humanity as a whole. Second, this bill of rights constructs new spaces of citizenship that override any nation-state legislation. There was no reference to the space of the state, but an attempt to make the global forum a scene of innovation or reform in human rights. At the same time, this global forum was not an abstract, un-institutionalised space, but a new federal state endowed with electoral regions that replicated the organs and procedures of state government.

The debate on rights and duties at the committee embodied ideas emerging from Catholic theology about the primacy of human person and dignity. The vocabulary of Catholic 'personalism', which Borgese often deployed, reflects the important impact of social Catholic thought on the constitution. Many members of the committee, including Adler, Hutchins, and Borgese, saw Jacques Maritain's (and to a lesser extent Luigi Sturzo's) reflection on personalism as an important contribution to political thought, underlining the fundamental role of morality and religion in shaping the post-war world order. Moyn pointed out the key role of 'personalism' in articulating the modern interpretation of human rights, yet as we shall see, the intellectual vocabulary of social Catholicism had a wider effect on mid-century visions of world order.[80] This context is essential for understanding why the Catholic notion of the human person provided an effective foundation for the intellectual and political development of human rights, and I will return to it in more detail in chapter 8.

The committee's debate on the universal bill of rights reveals two distinct approaches to the problem of human rights in the 1940s. Borgese, like Maritain and Sturzo, grounded the idea of rights in natural law, the 'person', and human dignity. Thus, he was able to give rights a universal dimension detached from the prerogatives of the state. As Moyn notes, since the 1930s this conservative Christian interpretation of rights had received growing attention in the United States. Yet for Borgese, human rights were part of a geopolitical innovation—the democratic world federation—and not merely an efficacious instrument in the battle against

[79] In chapter 8, I discuss Moyn's argument about Christian human rights in more detail.
[80] See Samuel Moyn, 'Personalism, Community, and the Origins of Human Rights', in *Human Rights in the Twentieth Century*, ed. Stefan-Ludwig Hoffmann (Cambridge: Cambridge University Press, 2010), 85–106.

totalitarianism. The global application of Borgese's notion of personal rights and duties was in some aspects innovative, but, as McKeon argued, it embodied a conservative Western stance that undermined pluralism and diversity. McKeon identified and rejected the Catholic foundation of Borgese's thought, which demanded a strong relation between the person and the community, assuming that these social ties embodied also moral obligations. Individuals not only were entitled to rights, but carried a duty to participate and uphold their community, on the local and global levels alike. For McKeon, this holistic vision of social relations forced individuals to follow a certain predetermined road map of social and political order, which could be potentially oppressive. His criticism resonates with Moyn's thesis: doubting the existence of a universal agreement on what specific entitlements should be considered as human rights, McKeon was wary of introducing a strong system of rights and duties. He thought that the protection of individuals should be the responsibility of existing states, with possible assistance from new global institutions. Indeed, this idea was later expressed in the Universal Declaration.

The committee's debates reveal that it would be inaccurate to say that in the 1940s human rights were never understood as a break with the system of states. The constitution embodied an intention to create a global regime of human rights, which would allow criticising and sanctioning states for their wrongdoing. However, this plan was anchored in a conservative Catholic interpretation of the human person, which lacked attention to public consent or legal means of enforcement. Despite these limitations, the committee's discussions shed light on a transitional moment in the complex and nonlinear history of human rights.

The Preliminary Draft of a World Constitution

In 1948, the final and amended constitution was published in the committee's journal *Common Cause* and in the *Saturday Review of Literature*.[81] The *Review*'s editor, Norman Cousins, was a world federalist who praised the constitution as a 'work of tremendous importance' that should be discussed in regional conventions across the world.[82] But as we shall see, not everyone was similarly enthusiastic.

[81] Hutchins et al., *Preliminary Draft of a World Constitution*; also published in *Common Cause* 1 (March 1948).

[82] Norman Cousins to Giuseppe Antonio Borgese, 6 January 1948, CFWC, box 35. Cousins (1915–1990) was the president of the World Federalist Association and a great supporter of the constitution and published it in the popular *Saturday Review*. In 1945 he published a pamphlet, *Modern Man Is Obsolete* (New York: Viking, 1945), that launched his public antinuclear campaign.

The constitution opened with a poetic preamble, a declaration of values and rights, grounded in the tradition of natural rights assuming that state law derived from a pre-political shared conception of justice.[83] The preamble claimed the world's people agreed that their common cause was the advancement of the spiritual and physical well-being of humankind. In pursuit of 'universal peace and justice', the governments 'ordered their separate sovereignties in one government of justice' since 'the age of nations must end and the era of humanity begin'. The constitution would found the federal republic of the world, a new order based on universal recognition of preexisting human values and not only on popular democratic decision or on legal procedure.[84]

The first section of the constitution breaks down the idea of shared values into a declaration of duties and rights. It opens with the duty of every citizen, or resident of mandated territory, to serve 'physically and mentally' the cause of the advancement of humanity, to abstain from violence, and to keep the 'golden rule' of reciprocity. Borgese's voice emerges clearly from the statement that the constitution guarantees rights 'in conformity with the unwritten law which philosophies and religions alike called the Law of Nature and which the Republic of the World shall strive to see universally written and enforced by positive law'. These entitlements included 'release from the bondage of poverty and exploitation of labour, with rewards according to merit and need', freedom of association and assembly, protection against tyrannical rule and discrimination, self-determination for minorities, and any other freedoms 'inherent in man's inalienable claims for life, liberty and the dignity of the human person'.[85] The final section states that 'the four elements of life, water, air, earth and energy, are common property of the human race'. Their management, whether public or private, would be subordinated to the 'common good'.

Borgese's impact on the final shape of the constitution is most evident in this section, which reflects the secularised Catholic foundation of his political thought that perceived political constitutions as the structural expression of preexisting morality.[86] It is not surprising, therefore, that Sturzo and Maritain, with whom Borgese frequently corresponded, approved of the constitution's ideals.[87] Like Borgese they thought that the

[83] On natural law and natural rights, see Richard Tuck, *Natural Rights Theories: Their Origin and Development* (Cambridge: Cambridge University Press, 1979). On natural law in relation to human rights and European imperialism, see Anthony Pagden, 'Human Rights, Natural Rights, and Europe's Imperial Legacy', *Political Theory* 31 (2003): 171–199.

[84] Hutchins et al., *Preliminary Draft of a World Constitution*, 3.

[85] Ibid., 5–7.

[86] On social Catholicism in constitutional thought, see Gustavo Zagrebelsky, *Il diritto mite* (Turin: Einaudi, 1992), 49.

[87] Sturzo and Maritain commented enthusiastically on the constitution; see Maritain to the Committee, 26 November 1947, CFWC, box 37.

rights of men were natural—God-given—and inalienable by the state or any other political organisation. Sturzo, a leading social Catholic politician in interwar Italy, inspired Borgese to see social and economic entitlements as natural pre-political rights. Borgese was more critical than Sturzo of the ecclesiastic institutions of the Catholic Church, and considered faith a private matter. Nonetheless, on a more theoretical level he accepted Sturzo's social Catholic vision of a universal social space of reciprocal responsibility and solidarity and insisted upon man's natural *duties* as precondition for rights. The individual's duty to 'serve' humanity was intended to undermine political allegiance to the nation-state, which embodied for Borgese an inherent threat of totalitarian repression, but came at a price of conditioning human rights to compliance with the demands of the political community.

The constitution then turned to describe the world government's vast sphere of power to enforce the constitution, guarantee the rights and duties of man, maintain peace by law, settle conflicts, supervise the alteration of boundaries, administer 'immature' territories, intervene in interstate violence, organise armed forces and limit local possession of weaponry, control physical and economic resources, establish a world bank and fiscal agencies, regulate commerce and transport, supervise immigration and grant federal passports, and appropriate property where necessary. Nonetheless, as Brailsford noted, the economic powers and responsibilities of the world government were not outlined.[88] From this critique, we learn that to a certain extent the committee ignored the universalising potential of economics, a notion that became central to mid-century thinking about world order. As we have seen in chapter 2, Mitrany based his idea of a new world order on the universality of social economic needs, which he addressed by inventing a global network of economic agencies. Wootton founded her federal thought on the idea that only a world federation could provide a universal standard of living; without it, social and economic inequalities could undermine the political cohesion of the federation.[89] The universality of economics was a key aspect of world order for Hayek and Polanyi, who argued that free competition in the global market was a fundamental guarantee of freedom. The world's existing economic interconnectedness could be the model for other—also political—global arrangements. Yet the impact of economics on global politics escaped the committee's attention, with the notable exception of Tugwell, who hoped, in vain, to establish a global version of his New Deal.

The constitution's largest representative assembly was the Federal Convention, elected directly by the people. The electoral colleges were not

[88] Brailsford to Committee, 15 January 1948.
[89] On economics and federalism according to Wootton and Hayek, see chapter 5.

states but new constituencies uniting 'kindred nations and cultures' in nine regions: Europe (possibly with the United Kingdom, the Commonwealth, and the French colonies), the United States (possibly with the United Kingdom), Russia (with east Baltic or Slavic states), the Near East and North Africa, South-Saharan Africa (with or without South Africa), India (with or without Pakistan), China (with Korea and Japan), Indochina and Indonesia, and South America. The constitution adopted with some minor changes Borgese's vision of electoral regionalism, in which the new regions would not necessarily become administrative or political units. The committee hoped to overcome the common dilemma of representation that haunted other mid-century theorists of global order: while a demographic representation would give more power to Asia than to Europe, weighted pro-European representation seemed antidemocratic and unjust. Indeed, as the influential international lawyer and UN supporter Louis B. Sohn wrote in his comments on the constitution, their representative system offered a viable solution to a problem he had been unable to resolve.[90]

Despite the enthusiastic reception, this elaborate representative system challenged both democracy and popular sovereignty. The popularly elected convention had no direct political powers or clear responsibilities and would convene for one month every third year. Its main role was electing the members of the legislative and executive organs. For example, unlike the American president, the world president would not be elected directly by the people. Each region would nominate candidates for the presidency, elected by the convention. The convention would also elect the ninety-nine members of the council, the main legislative body that held the powers to initiate and enact law. Eighty-one councillors would be elected by and from the convention, and the additional eighteen would be nominated 'expert' councillors of intellectual and professional acclaim. The people's direct political influence was therefore limited to electing a large and ineffective body of representatives, whose main mission was to elect other representatives. This two-step system manifests the committee's intention to avert what they considered as the main threat to their project's success: that the elected representatives would act as members of their national states, rather than in the interests of the world as a whole. The obvious risk was evacuating the democratic principle of its contents by distancing the world's peoples from their representatives and limiting their powers to influence directly the political shape of their government. The idea of appointing a fifth of the council by merit and not through

---

[90] Louis B. Sohn to the Committee, 27 December 1947, CFWC, box 36. Sohn later resolved this problem in his own way, and published a book with the federalist Grenville Clark. Grenville Clark and Louis B. Sohn, *World Peace through World Law* (Cambridge, MA: Harvard University Press, 1958).

democratic procedure embodies the committee's interpretation of 'mixed constitution' with democratic and aristocratic components. Borgese succeeded in convincing his colleagues that intellectuals and experts could bring additional value to politics. If, as the committee feared, the public was unable to elect worthy parliamentarians, the constitution should introduce appointed parliamentarians to balance off misguided popular choice. This idea symbolises the committee's dual view of democracy: democracy was the best political constitution to safeguard the people's freedom, but the people could not be trusted to build and defend it.

The limited democracy of the world federation is evident in the design of the executive branch of government. The executive power would be vested in the president, who could initiate federal legislation, which would then be approved by the council. The president held a right to veto any council-initiated legislation. Unlike the American president, the world president would be elected by the legislative and therefore would, ideally, benefit from its support. However, the system of checks and balances would be weaker than the American one. The president would appoint the chancellor, who would form the cabinet, whose members would not be members of the council. This provision would give the chancellor a greater degree of independence in appointing the cabinet, but would represent a limit to the power of the people to elect their political leaders. The president and the council would establish a series of smaller administrative and political orders with limited powers. These would include a House of Nationalities and States, representing local communities and governments, a Syndical Senate, representing professional and corporate interests, and an institute of science and culture. Every twelve years, the president would appoint a planning agency to propose the budget and provide long-term economic plans. Apparently, this multiplicity of institutions suggests that the committee wanted to express a range of political ideas in the federal institutions, but the legislative and executive bodies would remain relatively small and centralised. The other agencies would remain effectively toothless, given that neither the president nor the cabinet would be liable to take their recommendations into account.

The constitution also designed juridical and military institutions. The juridical power included a network of regional tribunals, headed by the global Grand Tribunal that would include sixty justices, appointed by the president, in five benches: constitutional court, disputes between the world government and local governments, disputes between the world government and individual citizens, disputes between local governments, and disputes between individuals and private corporations. The military was controlled by the Chamber of Guardians, which commanded the federal army and determined local weapon quotas. This organ aimed at international control of weaponry as proposed by the *Report on the International Control of*

Atomic Energy. The physicist Robert Oppenheimer, scientific consultant for the Acheson-Lilienthal Report, contributed greatly to shaping the report's conclusions, which suggested putting all fissile material under the control of an international agency, the Atomic Development Authority. For the Chicago Committee, the Acheson-Lilienthal Report marked a serious step towards the idea—if not the realisation—of world unity. Its international rejection motivated the committee's turn away from 'acceptable' but limited constitution towards more audacious proposals. Designing the Chamber of Guardians as a political not professional organ may reflect the committee's disillusionment with the ability of external experts to influence weapon control in a world ruled by political interests.

Finally, the constitution established a Tribune of the People as spokesman for minorities. The election procedure for this position also aimed at granting a voice to the minority: the successful candidate would have obtained the second largest vote. Borgese argued against his critics—who suggested that the losing candidate for presidency should be appointed tribune—that although this method was opposed to democratic majority rule it gave voice to the oft-silent minority. The tribune would have no vote, but could have the privilege of the floor before the Grand Tribunal to defend the rights of individuals and groups.

The constitution outlined the general principles for future legislation: no law could discriminate against a religion, sex, creed, caste, or doctrine; no interest group could obtain privileged access to natural resources; slavery, torture, arbitrary seizure, and capital punishment were banned. A series of socioeconomic provisions would be included in future legislation according to local circumstances: old age pensions, unemployment relief, health and accident insurance, provisions for maternity and infancy, free education. Finally, the constitution suggested that the global political power was better placed to bring about 'justice' and 'progress', and should therefore overrule both private and local initiatives.[91] Yet there is little discussion about possible clashes between the local and the global governments, interests, and institutions.

The postscript, which was not an integral part of the constitution, drew much of the criticism. It stated the committee's four assumptions: war must and can be outlawed, world government is the only alternative to world destruction, 'World Government is necessary, therefore possible', and the outcome of world government would be peace and justice. The committee sought to justify their detour from the reality of politics by presenting the constitution as 'a realistic proposition taking into account the extant realities and forces, against the utopian assumption of a minimal

---

[91] On the relationship between political power and local initiative from a constitutional perspective, see Maurizio Fioravanti, *Costituzione* (Bologna: Il Mulino, 1999), 145–159.

world government, a security world government, practically a police world state. . . . Maximalist then must be understood as the real minimalism, namely, the search for the minimum common denominator over which all people can meet'.[92] This common denominator was, for the committee, the shared belief that the constitution was 'necessary and therefore possible'. The critics who ridiculed this declaration attacked in fact Borgese's legal and moral vision, which presumed that just world order could be reinstated if only the world's peoples would decide to establish it.[93]

On the constitution's list of signatories, two names were significantly absent: James Landis and Richard McKeon. In August 1947, McKeon wrote a letter to Borgese explaining why he could not sign the constitution: its Western-centric ideological bias would make the document universally unacceptable. He rejected the reference to the law of nature as the foundation of human rights as incongruent with the language of human rights in the twentieth century. The constitution's centralising tendency and the artificiality of the electoral regions were antidemocratic. He reasoned that the constitution's strong executive was outlined after the unfounded assumption that all strong leaders would follow the moral and political example of the wartime charismatic leaders, Roosevelt and Churchill. Instead of a strong executive, he preferred reinforcing the legislative and the judiciary, and proposed to establish a closer link between political and economic rights by giving specific agencies the power to enforce them.[94]

Borgese and McKeon represented two different constitutional approaches. Borgese grounded the constitution in the assumption that a just order of being is both desirable and possible, and that its establishment was humanity's moral duty. The democratic principle was undermined by his centralised universalistic vision. McKeon's constitution, by contrast, supported the decentralisation of political power in a pluralistic federal structure that maintained its complex distribution of authority among various political, social, and economic agencies. He would determine only the necessary concepts and functions to allow a global federal union, avoiding clear statements about human rights, economic planning, and social policy.

Why did the committee steer away from McKeon's realistic pluralism towards what Thomas Mann defined as 'revolution, utopia, the intelligent will to readjust reality to truth'?[95] Possibly, the German writer's letter to the committee provided one answer: 'in the main [the constitution] shows the spirit of one man, Giuseppe Antonio Borgese'. Mann, who was Borgese's

---

[92] Hutchins et al., *Preliminary Draft of a World Constitution*, 42–43.
[93] Wooley, *Alternatives to Anarchy*, 42–46.
[94] Richard McKeon to Giuseppe Antonio Borgese, 26 August 1947, CFWC, box 18. Landis, who withdrew from the committee in 1946, did not provide a reason for not signing the constitution.
[95] Thomas Mann to Giuseppe Antonio Borgese, 2 September 1947, CFWC, box 19.

longtime friend and later father-in-law, saw the constitution as the brain-child of one person. Borgese's power of persuasion had won the committee over by stating the obvious: constitutions faced great practical challenges. The conclusion he drew, and the committee accepted, was that given the limited prospect of realisation, it would be morally and theoretically bet-ter to propose an ambitious, groundbreaking world order. Borgese's reply to Mann makes exactly this point: 'the objective conditions of the world during this last year has [sic] improved the chances of lofty planning and willing. . . . Extreme remedies are required for extreme evils and therefore what may have seemed utopian or nearly so in the past should seem today more realistic than all the realisms that have failed'.[96]

HANS KELSEN AND THE CRITICS OF THE CONSTITUTION

In July 1947, at the committee's last formal meeting, Hutchins agreed to sponsor a monthly publication, *Common Cause*, to continue the intellectual and scholarly debate on the constitution. The journal's editor was Elisa-beth Mann Borgese (1918–2001), a biologist, Borgese's wife, and Thomas Mann's daughter. She worked ceaselessly to convince the American and international audience of the merits of the constitution, and wrote articles to justify the constitution's ambitious 'maximalist' approach.[97] She liaised with federalists like Cord Mayer, Tom O. Griessemer, Grenville Clark, and Henry Usborne, and solicited prominent intellectuals to comment on the constitution. Many picked up the challenge, including George Catlin, Ed-ward Teller, Albert Einstein, Lewis Mumford, Piero Calamandrei, Norman Cousins, Violet Rawnsley, and Altiero Spinelli.

The political scientist John Herz wrote in his 1950 review that from the 'standpoint of world federalism this draft certainly embodies a good deal of careful thinking'. He criticised, however, its excessive rationalism: the constitution ignored human irrationality, which formed the major setback to the project's realisation. His scepticism regarded the Soviet Union's adherence to the project, since he doubted that the Russian people would be able—as the committee expected—to persuade their government to join a world federation. He concluded quoting the German philosopher Ernst Jünger: 'Our hope is only in an inner transformation of man—not in evolution but in mutation, in a generatio spontanea, a complete new beginning; looking at it rationally, we are lost'.[98]

[96] Borgese to Mann, 2 November 1948, CFWC, box 19.
[97] Elisabeth Mann Borgese, 'Why a Maximalist Constitution', *Bulletin of the Atomic Scientists* 4 (July 1948): 199–203.
[98] John Herz, 'Review of World Constitution Draft', *Western Political Quarterly* 3 (1950): 267–268. On Herz's international thought, see Peter Stirk, 'John H. Herz: Realism and the Fragility of the International

The constitution's excessive rational and theoretical attitude was criticised also by John N. Hazard, expert in Soviet law at Columbia University, who accompanied Vice President Henry Wallace to China and the Soviet Union during the war (Owen Lattimore was another member of Wallace's entourage). Hazard suggested that Soviet scholars and intellectuals might support the constitution because it reflected some Marxist principles, like the distribution of natural resources. But he feared that the Soviet people, as well as the government, would resent the 'too American' constitution, where the president was closely modelled on the American leader.[99] The challenge remained how to convince people to support a constitution that differed from their own 'way of life'. Like Herz, Hazard thought that the solution was emotional inspiration, not rational argument.

The tension between ideal desirability and political practicality was a fundamental part of the committee's discussions. Although Borgese considered public intellectuals as the spearheads of a future world order, he knew that they often failed to convince the public to support their ideas. Intellectuals could not lead the revolution: 'no one would unhesitatingly intrust [sic] the aristocratic principle to the community of PhDs as such, for, to put it mildly, aristocracy and academy are not one and the same thing'.[100] Following Hazard's idea that the constitution needed the support of a distinctly *political* aristocracy, Borgese sent copies to politicians, ambassadors, and opinion makers around the world, including in India, Israel, Russia, Japan, China, and South Africa, in hope that they would rally in favour of a world revolution.

For some commentators, the difficulty to reassemble popular support emerged from the internal deficiencies of the constitution, rather than a lack of persuasive arguments or emotional connection. The Austrian legal theorist Hans Kelsen, who developed the influential theory of the 'purity of law', criticised the constitution based on his interpretation of the idea of law as a system that exists only as a social reality, consisting in the fact that people actually follow certain norms. Laws necessitated both social support and clear sanctions to become valid and efficacious. Various norms form a coherent legal system if they all derive from the same 'fundamental norm', which has to be presumed (rather than derived from another source of legitimacy such as human reason or nature) in order to give the system its validity. Hence, the legal system is 'pure' in the sense that its coherent, logical legal structure is independent of moral, religious,

---

Order', *Review of International Studies* 31 (2005): 285–306; Casper Sylvest, 'The Conditions and Consequences of Globality: John H. Herz's *International Politics in the Atomic Age*', in Bliddal, Sylvest, and Wilson, *Classics of International Relations*, 89–98.

[99] John N. Hazard to Giuseppe Antonio Borgese, 5 November 1947, CWFC, box 36.

[100] 'Dux and Borgese "Of Education as the Standard for Weighted Representation in a World Assembly"', 3 June 1946', CFWC, box 52, document 55.

political, or ideological groundings. The substance and specific content of legal norms are irrelevant to the efficacy and validity of the legal system.[101] In the international sphere, Kelsen called for the development of a positivist, coherent, and self-contained international legal structure, independent of ideology and political controversy. He also advocated the establishment of a political structure to enforce the new legal order.[102] Although Kelsen emphasised the importance of global political structures to create a peaceful world order, he argued that these should not be conflated with the normative international legal system.

Despite his support of the general idea of a world constitution, Kelsen pointed out the juridical and political weaknesses of the Chicago project. To his mind, the committee confused a prescriptive juridical document with a theoretical treatise about human nature. From the viewpoint of international law, he argued that the draft misguidedly sought the source of sovereignty in external entities: the member states, nations, people of the world, or the human person. For Kelsen the solution to the sovereignty problem was much simpler: the source of sovereignty was internal and not external to the legal system. It was the law itself that gave the political authority—in this case the world federation—the sovereign power to act.[103] He rejected the constitution's moral claim for universal validity because it was a juridical agreement forged between specific states—not 'nations' or 'peoples'—that should have been listed in the preamble. He rejected Borgese's proposition that natural law—interpreted as universal human reason and the basis of morality—should provide the 'fundamental norm' of the world constitution. Kelsen argued that human morality could not provide reason for action, and therefore a legal norm would be meaningless without a specific sanctioning agency to enforce it. This was also his criticism of the constitution's treatment of the notion of 'rights'. The right 'not to be poor' would be legally void without a global economic system to exclude poverty. Similarly, the right of personal protection from subjugation has no content if the constituent states are not compelled to accept a democratic form of government.

Kelsen's solution to these ambiguities was simple: the world government should appropriate its authority to define 'rights' and express them in positive law. To establish the claim that the 'four elements' were property of the human race, the constitution should provide specific legal and institutional means for management and control of natural resources (which had nothing to do with the mystical notion of Borgese's 'four elements'). Detailed provisions were necessary to endow the federal government with

[101] Hans Kelsen, *Pure Theory of Law* (1934; repr., Clark: Lawbook Exchange, 2008), chap. 1.
[102] Jochen Von Bernstorff, *The Public International Law Theory of Hans Kelsen* (Cambridge: Cambridge University Press, 2010), 2.
[103] Koskenniemi, *From Apology to Utopia*, 231.

juridical power to enforce its laws. Kelsen tried to 'translate' parts of the constitution into positive juridical terms, but reminded the committee that the essence of their constitution remained legally unclear because it conflated legal norms with moral and sociological claims.[104]

However, the absence of legal provisions was not always considered a flaw. For some commentators, the committee provided an inspiring moral vision by translating the idea of natural right into a legal-political document. The Italian jurist Fernando Della Rocca, one of the founders of the Italian Christian Democratic Party, was well versed in social Catholic political and legal theory. In the post-war era, the Christian Democratic Party became one of the most powerful political parties in Europe and an important contributor to the foundation of the European Union.[105] In an article on natural law, Della Rocca praised the constitution for its contribution to the reinforcement of the law of nature by emphasising the moral aspect of human rights. The constitution stated the essence of human rights and transformed their subject, the universal man, into a universal citizen with specific political relations to the world government trusted with guaranteeing his rights. He saw no need to construct a positivist prescriptive framework for human rights beyond what the constitution offered: human values and morality would contribute to their enforcement more than any sanction.[106]

One of the main channels through which the committee hoped to influence world politics was the nascent international organisations. In 1947, Jacques Maritain received a copy of the constitution as he was travelling to Mexico as head of the French delegation to the Second Session of the UNESCO General Conference. In a letter to the committee, he wrote that his impression of the constitution was 'excellent'. He also suggested two additions to the document: concrete procedures for the admittance of states to the federation and the establishment of a clearly defined supranational status of citizenship.[107] In an unstable post-war world, he found in the constitution inspiring insights for peaceful change. Yet even Maritain was not persuaded that the constitution could be implemented: it was a spiritual manifesto, an inspirational intellectual project aimed at highlighting the moral value and dignity of the human person as part of a world community. Despite the high hopes of some committee members to

---

[104] Hans Kelsen, 'Some Remarks on the Preliminary Draft of a World Constitution', CFWC, box 36.

[105] On social Catholicism, see chapter 8; Antonio Parisella, *Cattolici e Democrazia cristiana nell'Italia repubblicana: Analisi di un consenso politico* (Rome: Gangemi, 2000); Gerd-Rainer Horn and Emmanuel Gerard, *Left Catholicism, 1943–1955: Catholics and Society in Western Europe at the Point of Liberation* (Leuven: Leuven University Press, 2001).

[106] Fernando Della Rocca, 'Natural Law and the World Constitution', CFWC, box 36.

[107] Undated excerpt of a letter of Jacques Maritain to the Committee, CFWC, box 37. On Maritain, see chapter 8.

create a practical political document, Maritain posited that the constitution could—at most—serve as an ideal project to reinforce a new sense of moral globalism and universal goodwill.

The Limits of Constitutionalism

In April 1948, McKeon published an article on the philosophy of human rights. He discussed contemporary interpretations and strategies for their implementation, and argued that the debate about rights revolved not around different opinions regarding which rights should be considered 'human rights', but around divergent philosophical assumptions in which these rights could be grounded.[108] This assertion reflects the major conflict at the Chicago Committee. There was widespread agreement that a world government was necessary to guarantee human rights, peace, and prosperity on a global scale. There was relative consensus about the meaning of human rights, if not overwhelming agreement on their specific articulation. However, I suggest that the main disagreements regarded the philosophical assumption underlying the project. Borgese's universalism and McKeon's pluralism were incompatible, despite the fact that both envisaged similar goals for humanity. In his article, McKeon suggested that these discrepancies could be overcome by focusing on the practical and institutional aspects of world order and maintaining an intentional degree of ambiguity about its philosophical foundation. Perhaps this conclusion was based on his experience at the committee, where the attempt to reach a general agreement on the philosophical foundation of world government led, for him, to a universalising form of cultural imperialism. For McKeon, the question whether humanity could and should share a common vision of the truth was irrelevant. For Borgese, however, this question stood at the core of his political project, and the answer was necessarily affirmative.

International historians who have discussed the history of the committee have tended to downplay the importance of this internal debate, but I suggest that the disagreement between McKeon and Borgese embodies two significant and competing mid-century interpretations of the idea of political universalism. The first approach, represented by Borgese, is inspired by social Catholic thought and natural law. It grounds the constitution in the universal faculty of human reason, but articulates it in spiritual terms. The idea of a world government emerged to protect humanity from evil rule, atomic destruction, and war, yet, importantly, it also sought to reinforce the sense of duty that all men should feel to each other. Thus,

---

[108] McKeon, 'Philosophic Bases and Material Circumstances'.

the world constitution project became an educational mission, a political catechism for the whole world.

The second approach, taken by McKeon, was based on a different sort of universalism. He argued there was one, definite truth to be discovered, but saw more importance in the quest than in the discovery itself. The pluralistic and inclusive discussion between various philosophical and political positions was for him the basis for a post-war human rights regime. A world government would create a universal political space, without filling it with particular meaning, prerogatives, and directions beyond the mere institutional framework necessary for discussion. McKeon envisaged a global political structure where different political traditions, units, and philosophies could coexist. His conception of human rights evolved from this minimalist idea, suggesting that through discussion, different groups could arrive at a common political decision without necessarily sharing the reasoning, motivation, or general worldview. If for Borgese shared values were the foundation for international cooperation, for McKeon procedure and practice were equally important. McKeon's opposition to Borgese's scheme was directed not mainly against the substance of his proposals, but against the extension of any particular philosophy on a world scale.[109]

Two issues were relatively absent from the constitution: economics and technology. Barbara Wootton's criticism of the lack of 'economic blueprints' in Streit's proposal can also highlight a significant limit of the Chicago constitution.[110] Despite Tugwell's intentions to operate a global New Deal, the committee considered economic planning a contentious issue that might taint the constitution in ideological colours, and hoped to avoid controversy by ignoring the whole debate on economics despite its centrality to public policy at the time. McKeon's suggestion to plan specific economic institutions for international cooperation was rejected. The committee followed traditional ways of thinking about politics separately from the economic sphere of human interaction, in spite of the contemporaneous attempts of UNESCO to bring these spheres together.

The interplay of technology of politics was also narrowly interpreted, despite the fact that technological innovations—the atomic bomb—provided the original stimulus for the project. While the committee doubted the contribution of technology to world government, they were certain that it posed a threat to world peace. Unlike H. G. Wells's vision, their world government did not build upon the benefits that cutting-edge technology could offer to humanity, but represented a grimmer vision of a humanistic plan

---

[109] McKeon is similarly critical of Julian Huxley's proposal of scientism as a universal philosophy for UNESCO; see McKeon, 'Philosophy for UNESCO', 573.

[110] See chapters 4 and 5.

to save humanity from technology.[111] Without discussing the positive potential global benefits of nuclear energy, transport, or communication technologies, they formulated their proposal in the traditional terms of institutional politics and law.

The history of the Committee to Frame a World Constitution and its rich archival documentation call for a reflection on the role of intellectuals in the public sphere. Its members were deeply convinced that 'Humanities scholars' should contribute to policy making and public affairs. They felt committed to moving beyond their professional duties and to shift their activities from the realm of theory to that of practice. The experience of the Second World War encouraged them to take a more decisive political stance. Since most of them were beyond the age of conscription, they felt morally compelled to make at least a post-war contribution to peace. It is implicit in their efforts that they assumed the role of intellectuals was not necessarily to govern but to theorise practical plans for world revolution (according to Borgese) or legal reform (according to McKeon). Intellectuals were in a better position to formulate theoretically substantial yet concrete political plans because of their broad understanding and non-partisanship. Intellectuals, they thought, should be active members of society because they had responsibility to apply their knowledge to social improvement. As some constitutional provisions made clear, there was institutional space in the new world order for intellectuals to offer their insights, but they shied away from arguing that intellectuals could or should form a global aristocracy of expertise: they saw their own role in politics as external ideologues of globalism.

The committee made no reference to Borgese's previous attempt to unite intellectuals to write a world constitution, a project that had a more limited success than the 1947 constitution. Perhaps the disregard for the earlier proposal reflected the awareness that the pre–Pearl Harbor concept of the 'City of Man', as an American-centred, Christian, and conservative vision of world order, was no longer relevant to the post-war era. The early project of Borgese, Mann, Mumford, and others resembled the Anglo-American global visions of Curtis and Streit. Yet, the Chicago Committee sought to advance a more inclusive, post-imperial global proposal. This objective was reached only to a limited degree. The final document based global order on universal political philosophy, which left little political agency to non-Western, colonial, or disenfranchised peoples. The constitution did not provide a persuasive vision of autonomy, democracy, and independence for the colonial people, who rightly remained doubtful of its contribution to their fight for liberty.

---

[111] This political humanism resonates with the ideas of Lewis Mumford; see chapter 7.

Rather than an instrument of colonial liberation, the 1940s idea of a global constitution was a universal protective shield against totalitarianism, political centralisation, and abuse of human rights. The final document reflects a wider trend of mid-century constitutionalism to reconcile democratic legalism with the rising—and changing—logic of human rights. For many, this conception remains relevant today.[112] However, the committee's discussions shed light on the complex and intricate history of global constitutionalism. The controversy between Borgese and McKeon shows that this historical episode should be read not only as a story of political failure, but as a telling example of the theoretical, political, and juridical challenges faced by those who attempt to write a global constitution.

[112] The foundation in 2012 of the journal *Global Constitutionalism* (edited by Mattias Kumm, Anthony F. Lang Jr., Miguel Maduro, Antje Wiener, and James Tully) reveals the centrality of these arguments to current political and juridical debates. The journal's subtitle, 'Human Rights, Democracy and the Rule of Law', suggests that many mid-century concerns remain relevant today.

CHAPTER 7

Perceptions of Science and Global Order

ON 2 MARCH 1946, the American cultural critic Lewis Mumford published an article in the *Saturday Review of Literature*, a widely read liberal publication edited by the world federalist Norman Cousins.[1] 'We in America are living among madmen', Mumford affirmed in the outset of the article: 'Madmen govern our affairs in the name of order and security. The chief madmen claim the titles of general, admiral, senator, scientist, administrator, Secretary of State, even President. And the fatal symptom of their madness is this: they have been carrying through a series of acts which will lead eventually to the destruction of mankind, under the solemn conviction that they are normal responsible people, living sane lives, and working for reasonable ends'. Humanity was, for Mumford, hijacked by an 'infernal machine', the outcome of technological achievements that had lost touch with the 'sane' moral values of unity and common faith. He called scientists and politicians to dismantle the atomic bomb and 'be men once again'. Those, like himself, who were already conscious of the global dangers that technology posed to mankind should whisper in the leaders' ears the unifying moral values of 'humanity' and 'one world' as an antidote to global belligerence and destruction. The illustration accompanying the article left little room for misunderstanding: an exploded globe was torn apart by 'new engines of destruction'.

Mumford's dramatic outburst depicted science and technology, along with politicians who had 'ceased to obey the laws of life', as the enemies of humanity and 'civilisation'. His earlier optimism about the positive contribution of technology to human progress, outlined in *Technics and Civilization*, had withered.[2] Mumford was evidently not alone in pointing out the contribution of science to the crisis of humanity in general, and Western civilisation in particular. His writings were part of a larger debate that predated the atomic bomb and its devastating implications. Scientific

---

[1] Lewis Mumford, 'Gentlemen: You Are Mad!' *Saturday Review of Literature*, 2 March 1946, 5–6.
[2] Lewis Mumford, *Technics and Civilization* (New York: Harcourt, Brace, 1934).

research was perceived as a global activity—harmful or beneficial—that transcended national borders; the technological applications of science similarly had global implications for humanity at large, beyond racial, cultural, and political divides. Therefore, mid-century commentators developed their perceptions of 'science' as a response to the question 'what is the global order capable of doing?'

In this chapter, I discuss competing perceptions of 'science' in the 1940s as part of a political project to construct a new and better global order, often under American or Western guidance. The protagonists of this story— Mumford, H. G. Wells, Charles E. Merriam, and Michael Polanyi—were not undertaking a merely meditative existential exercise. While some of them might have seen the 'crisis of man' as a defining aspect of their era, their writings aimed at more than philosophical and sociological analysis: they shared a commitment to thinking politically about science as a potential ordering principle for the post-war world.[3] They identified a new condition of political globalism that required a reconceptualisation of political order. 'Science' and its proxies were seen as threatening devastators of humanity, but also as its potential saviours. Thus, the various perceptions of 'science' advanced in the 1940s shared the idea that humanist values—rather than state control or political power—could salvage the positive aspects of 'science' as the foundation of a new liberal global order.

The public intellectuals whose work I explore in this chapter perceived both morality and science as global phenomena. The post-war global order would intertwine, they posited, scientific universalism—understood in terms of the universal validity and impact of scientific discoveries—with moral universalism grounded in a notion of common humanity. Political boundaries could not resist the global flow of scientific ideas and discoveries, and could not disengage the moral bonds that connected humanity together.

The conceptualisation of science and morality as profoundly 'global' gives rise to an important problem: does globality imply defence of unity or respect of diversity? In the nineteenth century, international thinkers perceived science as a potent unifier that could bring together people from different political, cultural, and ethnic backgrounds.[4] Mid-twentieth-century thinkers oscillated between a defence of the perceived unity of human values (like freedom, tolerance, and justice) and a recognition of the exceptional heritage of Western civilisation. Positing the unity of human values, they envisioned a global order aimed to defend Western exceptionality precisely because they saw Western civilisation as the birth-

---

[3] On the American discourse of the crisis of man, see Mark Greif, *The Age of the Crisis of Man: Thought and Fiction in America, 1933–1973* (Princeton, NJ: Princeton University Press, 2015).

[4] Mazower, *Governing the World*, chap. 4.

place of both scientific and moral universalism. I argue that by attributing a global value to a particular interpretation of humanity, these thinkers developed a range of implicit and explicit strategies to limit the space for diversity within their proposed global order.

The reception of the atomic bomb in the United States (and to a lesser degree in Britain) as a shocking and unprecedented experience of human destruction should be understood in the wider context of theories of universalism of science. One response to the challenge of the universality of science, which I explored in chapter 6, was advanced by public intellectuals from the University of Chicago who set up a committee to write a world constitution. Hutchins, Adler, and Borgese thought that the universality of science should be counterbalanced by a universal moral ethos embodied in a world constitution for a global federation.[5] Others, however, attempted to find in science the foundation for a new political order, by appropriating concepts derived from the natural sciences to describe and explain world politics. One strategy for employing scientific concepts for political thought was offered by the new 'scientism', an approach to the study of politics and society that applied scientific concepts and practices to social research, assuming that all knowable phenomena could be analysed and understood using scientific, mathematical methodologies.[6] Science has been seen as an arbiter of truth, an objective approach to the social sphere.[7]

This chapter opens with an overview of the mid-century global thought of H. G. Wells, who envisaged a socialist, legalistic world state administered by scientists and technicians. I shed light on the relationship between Wells and Merriam, Polanyi, and Mumford as the chapter progresses. The next section explores Charles Merriam's idea of a universal democratic world order informed by the expertise of social scientists. The third part analyses how Michael Polanyi perceived science as a global liberal 'dynamic order' of individuals and communities who shared unformulated knowledge and traditions. I compare his early interpretations of liberal order and philosophy of science with the ideas of Karl Popper, Friedrich Hayek, and Edward Shils. In the final portion of the chapter, I return to Lewis Mumford, who responded to the universal menace of the atomic bomb by emphasising humanity's universal commitment to shared values. In conclusion, I suggest that the universality of science led these figures to advance a range of

[5] Jewett, *Science, Democracy*, 218–223. The University of Chicago was, during those years, an important—but not exclusive—stage for debates on the social sciences. Harvard was another important centre. See Joel Isaac, *Working Knowledge: Making the Human Sciences from Parsons to Kuhn* (Cambridge, MA: Harvard University Press, 2012).

[6] An influential critique of 'New Scientism' was advanced by the philosopher and psychologist Eric Voegelin in 'The Origins of Scientism', *Social Research* 15 (1948): 462–494.

[7] Duncan Bell, 'Beware of False Prophets: Biology, Human Nature and the Future of International Relations Theory', *International Affairs* 82 (2006): 493–494.

global political projects—Wells's world government, Merriam's jural order, Polanyi's dynamic order, Mumford's world federation—united by an attempt to defend 'humanity', perceived as the preexisting, Western-centred order, that totalitarianism, global war, and the nuclear bomb threatened to exterminate.

WORLD GOVERNMENT OR WORLD DESTRUCTION: H. G. WELLS RESPONDS TO THE CRISIS

A key figure in the Anglo-American debate on science and world politics is H. G. Wells (1866–1946), whose vision of a scientific world government inspired later discussions of science-centred political order. Wells's universalism emerged from a conception of scientific knowledge as a shared human asset that could overcome political, geographical, or cultural barriers and set the technical and conceptual foundations for a new centralised world order. In early twentieth-century Britain, and by the 1930s also in the United States, scientific ideas played an important role in shaping political and international thought.[8] During Wells's lifetime, social Darwinism fashioned ideas about human communal life in Victorian political thought. He witnessed its replacement in the late 1930s by the Marxist interpretation of science as a methodological instrument for social progress and, in the mid-1940s, saw the rise of physics as the model science of the global nuclear age. Nonetheless, he maintained a relatively consistent view of the interplay between science and politics, suggesting that scientific progress could create a unified, homogeneous, and peaceful political order to overcome war and strife on a global scale.

In 1940, he participated in a conference on the New World Order organised by the British National Peace Council to discuss his book on the topic.[9] In his address, he argued that technology abolished the distance between places and increased military power, and thus rendered states 'too small for contemporary conditions'. Global destruction could be averted, he posited, only by the establishment of a rational global political system: 'this war storm which is breaking upon us now, due to the continued fragmentation of human government among a patchwork of sovereign states, is only one aspect of the general need for a rational consolidation of human affairs'.[10]

[8] Jewett, Science, Democracy, 59–64, 240–245; Pemberton, Global Metaphors, 27–30.
[9] Other participants in the event included Cyril Joad, Salvador de Madariaga, and J. Middleton Murry. The proceedings were published as National Peace Council, On the New World Order (London: National Peace Council, 1940). For a detailed discussion, see chapter 5.
[10] Wells, New World Order, chap. 2; W. Warren Wagar, H. G. Wells and the World State (New Haven, CT: Yale University Press, 1961).

In the 1940s, the soaring popularity of technology-infused visions of global order magnified the reputation of Wells as a visionary science fiction author and political thinker, even though his public and literary career had long passed its peak.[11] Yet his arguments about the infeasibility of small states were not new or original. The idea that technological innovation rendered the world a smaller place had been a common trope in Victorian political thought.[12] Since the turn of the twentieth century, Wells himself, as well as other international thinkers, had argued that technological innovations could—and should—unify the world.[13] As we have seen, Lattimore, Spykman, Wootton, and Aron considered small states politically inadequate for the post-war era, because they lacked the military and economic means to defend their independence or sustain economic growth. Such arguments, however, did not necessarily translate into support for a world state. In Wells's case, the critique of geopolitically small states was anchored in his normative universalistic political stance that prioritised social and political monism over pluralistic diversity.

Wells is one of the pioneers of 'one-worldism', the idea that the world was a closely knit unit, an organic whole.[14] Often, the political implications of one-worldism were world government and the abolition of the extant system of states. Science and technology provided a theoretical and practical grounding for this radical vision. As we have seen in chapter 3, Wendell Willkie encouraged his American readers to adopt the aerial perspective, facilitated by the experience of flight. This viewpoint emphasised the world's interconnectedness, suggesting that the superficial continuity of the planet was stronger than the cultural, political, and social borders that divided it. Wells advanced a similar interpretation of the political implications of flight technology in a short story written in 1907.[15] His pioneering vision of imaginary innovations emphasised, like Willkie, the declining importance of political boundaries in the age of air power. But Wells was more attuned than the American politician to the dangerous military applications of flight technology, which could lead to world destruction, as he explored in his 1914 speculative account of the atomic bomb.[16]

The response to the global threats that technology posed was, for Wells, a world state. Throughout the first half of the twentieth century, he had

---

[11] Vincent Brome, *H. G. Wells* (London: House of Stratus, 2001), 199–215; Pemberton, *Global Metaphors*, 60.

[12] On Victorian technological utopias, see Bell, *Idea of Greater Britain*, 81–90.

[13] On the influence of technology on perceptions of the abolition of distance, see, for example, Van Vleck, *Empire of the Air*, chap. 3.

[14] On 'one-worldism', see Wooley, *Alternatives to Anarchy*, 22; Baratta, *Politics of World Federation*, 2; Lawrence S. Wittner, *One World or None: The Struggle Against the Bomb* (Stanford, CA: Stanford University Press, 1993), 10–18; Pemberton, *Global Metaphors*, 152–164.

[15] H. G. Wells, *The War in the Air* (London: George Bell & Sons, 1908).

[16] H. G. Wells, *The World Set Free* (1914; repr., London: Hogarth, 1988).

been an indefatigable promoter of world state, administered by elite of experts.[17] In 1940, the content of his world order vision focused on scientifically planned and directed 'world socialism', a legal order based on a bill of rights of man, and freedom of education and expression to all. 'World socialism' entailed collective economy guided by a permanent socialist government of administrative and technical experts rather than party politicians. The global socialist government was, for Wells, an alternative to rather than extension of the Soviet political system, which, he argued, lacked legal respect for individual freedom.[18]

In 1940, Wells launched a public campaign to author a universal bill of rights. In the pages of the Labour *Daily Herald*, Wells, other commentators, and the readers debated which rights should be included in the universal bill: right of nourishment, free trial, housing, education, and medical care, and freedom of association, discussion, worship, work, and movement.[19] A committee that included Barbara Wootton then set about to revise the bill of rights in view of amendments proposed by readers, yet a final version was attained only in 1943.[20] For Wells, the bill of rights provided the necessary defence for individual freedom in a world order based on socialist economic policies and informed by rational scientific research. Those who criticised Wells, expressed misgivings about the revolutionary ethos of his proposals that lacked democratic control.[21]

The idea that education should play a key transformative role in forming the citizens of the world state was central to Wells's vision, as well as to the interwar proposals of world government, advanced by internationalist thinkers such as John A. Hobson and Alfred E. Zimmern.[22] The difference was that Wells prioritised a formative programme based on scientific and technical expertise over political or governing skills. Scientists

[17] H. G. Wells, *Anticipations of the Reaction of Mechanical and Scientific Progress upon Human Life and Thought* (London: Chapman and Hall, 1902); *A Modern Utopia* (London: Chapman and Hall, 1905); *New Worlds for Old: A Plain Account of Modern Socialism* (London: Archibald Constable, 1909); *What Is Coming? A Forecast of Things after the War* (London: Cassell, 1916); *The Open Conspiracy: Blueprints for a World Revolution* (London: V. Gollancz, 1928); *Guide to the New World: A Handbook of Constructive World Revolution* (London: V. Gollancz, 1941); *Phœnix: A Summary of the Inescapable Conditions of World Reorganisation* (London: Secker and Warburg, 1942).

[18] Wells had previously expressed his support for an amalgam of Western liberalism with the Soviet political and economic project in an interview with Joseph Stalin. 'Marxism vs. Liberalism: An Interview with H. G. Wells' (23 July 1934), www.marxists.org/reference/archive/stalin/works/1934/07/23.htm.

[19] Simpson, *Human Rights and the End of Empire*, 163–166.

[20] Wells, *Rights of Man*; John S. Partington, *Building Cosmopolis: The Political Thought of H. G. Wells* (Aldershot: Ashgate, 2003), 125–130.

[21] See, for example, the essays of Salvador de Madariaga and J. Middelton Murry in National Peace Council, *On the New World Order*.

[22] See, for example, J. A. Hobson, *Towards International Government* (London: Allen & Unwin, 1915); Alfred E. Zimmern, *The Third British Empire* (London: Oxford University Press, 1926). I have discussed these themes in detail in 'L'impero della libertà: imperialismo e internazionalismo nel pensiero liberale inglese, 1914–1936', *Contemporanea* 17 (2014): 31–58.

and engineers would have a unique role in the new order, providing the indispensable scientific research and technological innovation for global social progress. The unified, homogeneous world state that Wells envisaged rested on the assumption that people around the world had similar capacities, needs, and preferences that scientific research could discover and translate into policies. The global scope of scientific knowledge did not determine the universality of politics; but by providing the intellectual and technical expertise for creating a global political order, science facilitated the 'world revolution' that Wells described.

Scientific methods of enquiry promoted objectivity and prejudice-free judgment of political and social problems, two values central to his meritocratic, universal vision of world order. The only way to unite societies and traditions in one political framework, a world state, was to judge their claims and habits in an objective, unbiased, and scientific manner, and thereby integrate the best aspects of each into an objectively good culture for the world. Wells oscillated between cautious optimism and flagrant pessimism. Scientific research could potentially advance humanity towards a universal system of peace and human rights, but if applied to particular interests (like the defence of the state) it could also speed up human society's degeneration into totalitarianism, abuse, and slavery. As some of his dystopian science fiction works revealed, the dark side of science was always close at hand.

The world government, operated by global elite of trained scientists, experts, engineers, and technicians, left little space for cultural, political, or social diversity. Globalism meant, for Wells, social monism. Any 'reasonable man, of any race or language anywhere, should become a "Western Revolutionary"' and participate in the creation of the world state, he suggested.[23] Yet by anchoring the political order to a pre-political, scientific conception of the common good, that transcended political, cultural, and racial differences, Wells created a political synthesis that permitted only a minor degree of diversity to be expressed.

Within Wells's vision of a united world, some ties were stronger than others. In 1940, he opposed the idea of European federation, because, for him, Europe's states and empires had stronger cultural, political, and economic relations beyond the continent than with their neighbouring states. Europe could not generate as robust a sense of identity as the imperial systems. Personal experience motivated his views: 'I find the idea of cutting myself off from the English-speaking peoples of America and Asia to follow the flag of my Austrian-Japanese friend [Count Coudenhove-Kalergi] into a federally bunched-up European [sic] extremely unattractive'.[24] Reluctant

---

[23] Wells, New World Order, 121.
[24] Ibid., 66.

to define himself as a 'European', he felt a stronger commitment to a 'great English-speaking community' that included the United States and the dominions. Associating Britain with Europe, he feared, would untangle its non-European identity bonds.

Yet Clarence Streit's proposed union of democracies was no more appealing to Wells than a European union. Like Orwell and Mitrany, he pointed out that the member states of the Streit's democratic federation were not, in fact, democratic. He argued that democracy could not serve to define the common identity of the federation, especially if the colonial possessions of member states would be transferred in bulk to federal administration without appropriate democratic consultation of their inhabitants.

Instead of gradually uniting the existing states in regional or transcontinental federations, Wells optimistically suggested that the final goal of a world state should be realised immediately, in one revolutionary move: 'it would be far easier to create the United States of the World, which is Mr Streit's ultimate objective, than to get together the so-called continent of Europe into any sort of unity'. Rather than emphasising particular identities, such as European or Anglophone, Wells preferred focusing on the widest common denominator—humanity—as the foundation for a truly global world order.

Despite his visionary accounts of technological innovations and his perceptive predictions of their political implications, Wells's idea of a new world order was limited by a conservative conception of statehood based on stability, social and cultural homogeneity, and elitist nondemocratic leadership. The centralised global state embodied liberal principles, such as civil and legal rights, as well as a socialist idea of welfare and equality. However, it was grounded in a monistic conception of order defined by the allegedly objective and unconfutable outcomes of scientific research. Under the auspices of the universality of science, the world state extended on a global scale the specific historical experience of Western civilisation, leaving no space for diversity, pluralism, or dissent.

CHARLES E. MERRIAM, SCIENTIFIC OBJECTIVITY, AND POLITICAL JUDGMENT

H. G. Wells lived to see the Manhattan Project scientists realise the 'atomic bomb' he had described and named thirty years earlier. Yet by 1945, his deteriorating health and declining public influence left him at the margins of the debate on atomic energy. When he died the following summer, the international discussion about the advantages and perils of the atomic bomb was at its peak. The scientists who developed the American nuclear weapons returned to their universities amid growing concerns with the implications of their scientific knowledge for international politics and the future of humanity. At Chicago, Manhattan Project physicists Eugene Rabinowitch and Hyman H. Goldsmith decided that scientists needed to be more actively involved in the public sphere by reaching out directly to the general public and intervening in the debate on the applications of their inventions.[25] In 1945, they founded the *Bulletin of the Atomic Scientists* as an educational project for a lay readership. Contributors included leading scientists like Hans Bethe, J. Robert Oppenheimer, Leó Szilárd, and Edward Teller, but also social scientists and philosophers including John Boyd Orr, Michael Polanyi, Bertrand Russell, Charles E. Merriam, and Edward Shils.

The *Bulletin*'s objective was to bring to the fore the complex interaction between politics and science and encourage scientists to leave their laboratories and express their views on the political uses of science and technology.[26] In its early years, the *Bulletin* sought to persuade the public that atomic weapons (sometimes atomic energy in general) embodied grave social dangers and should be banned.[27] However, the journal eventually became a platform for a wider reflection on the relationship between science and international politics. The atomic bomb exacerbated preexisting tensions about liberty and authority between the scientific and political spheres. The pressing question of international control of atomic weapons was perceived as part of a more general discourse on the universality of science, which unfolded in the nexus of scientific objectivity and political decision making.

The *Bulletin* gave an opportunity to Charles E. Merriam (1874–1953), the prominent professor of political science at the University of Chicago, to participate in the discussion on politics and science. Merriam's appropriation of the rhetoric of a scientific world order was coupled with a strong emphasis on the importance of political judgment. Despite his favourable opinion of the science-motored world order outlined by Wells, Merriam was more interested than Wells in salvaging a central place for political decision making in the post-war global order. Both Merriam and Wells highlighted the important role of experts in bringing scientific knowledge to the realm of politics, but if for Wells these experts were natural and physical scientists, technicians, and engineers, for Merriam they were social and political scientists. The conjuncture of social science expertise and value-grounded political decision making could potentially,

[25] Patrick David Slaney, 'Eugene Rabinowitch, the *Bulletin of the Atomic Scientists*, and the Nature of Scientific Internationalism in the Early Cold War', *Historical Studies in the Natural Sciences* 42 (2012): 114–142.

[26] Alice K. Smith, *A Peril and a Hope: The Scientists' Movement in America, 1945–47* (Chicago: University of Chicago Press, 1965).

[27] Paul S. Boyer, *By the Bomb's Early Light: American Thought and Culture at the Dawn of the Atomic Age* (New York: Pantheon, 1985), 49–59.

according to Merriam, overcome the global disorder enhanced by atomic warfare and establish a peaceful global order.

During his long career, Merriam left a long-lasting mark on the discipline of political science, which he hoped to render more empirical and 'scientific'.[28] After graduating from Columbia University, where his teachers included John W. Burgess and William A. Dunning, he moved to Germany to study the history of political thought with Otto von Gierke and Hugo Preuss.[29] His dissertation, 'A History of the Theory of Sovereignty since Rousseau' (1900), became a seminal study in the field. Soon afterwards, he joined the University of Chicago's Political Science Department. He attained an influential position in the discipline as one of the founders of the American Political Science Association and the Social Science Research Council. Through these institutional connections, he worked to secure funding for new empirical and politically neutral research agenda in political science.

The study of political behaviour had been on the rise in American political science since the First World War. The main aim of this new approach was to shift the topical focus of political science away from institutions and the formal structure of government towards other themes including political parties, public opinion, and interest groups. Behaviouralism also encouraged importing new methodologies and quantitative techniques from other disciplines, like sociology and psychology.[30] In this context, Merriam suggested that normative and historical studies should be integrated with a present-oriented examination of political relations, guided by 'objective scientific attitude' and 'standards of impartial intelligence'.[31] The study of politics, he opined, should explore new themes, like voting patterns, pressure groups, and political parties, and employ new methodologies, like interdisciplinary collaborations and quantitative techniques.[32] Empirical methods provided, he argued, factual value-neutral findings that could inform—yet not necessarily determine—public opinion and administrative

[28] For Merriam's biography, see Barry Dean Karl, *Charles E. Merriam and the Study of Politics* (Chicago: University of Chicago Press, 1974); Mark G. Schmeller, 'Charles E. Merriam', in *American National Biography* (2000), www.anb.org/articles/14/14-00408.html. On Merriam's role in shaping political science, see Dorothy Ross, *The Origins of American Social Science* (Cambridge: Cambridge University Press, 1991), 450–469; Raymond Seidelman, *Disenchanted Realists: Political Science and the American Crisis, 1884–1984* (Albany: State University of New York Press, 1986), 109; Jewett, *Science, Democracy*, 178.

[29] Karl, *Charles E. Merriam*, 25–35; John G. Gunnell, *The Descent of Political Theory: The Genealogy of an American Vocation* (Chicago: University of Chicago Press, 1993), 82–92.

[30] Robert Adcock, 'Interpreting Behavioralism', in *Modern Political Science: Anglo-American Exchanges since 1880*, ed. Robert Adcock, Mark Bevir, and Shannon C. Stimson (Princeton, NJ: Princeton University Press, 2007), 187–189.

[31] Charles E. Merriam, *New Aspects of Politics* (Chicago: University of Chicago Press, 1925), 237. These ideas echo the views of Wootton on the social sciences; see chapter 5.

[32] Karl, *Charles E. Merriam*, chap. 1; Merriam, *New Aspects of Politics*; Merriam, *Systematic Politics* (Chicago: University of Chicago Press, 1945).

policies of elected representatives.[33] Later on, the prominent American political scientists Harold Lasswell and Gabriel Almond, both University of Chicago alumni, found inspiration in Merriam's methodological explorations for their own post-war systematic studies of foreign policy and political communication.[34]

Merriam shared with other mid-century social scientists, including Wootton and Mitrany, the idea that scientific research could supply the factual basis to inform good and effective social policy.[35] If scientists aimed at discovering the truth about the natural world, political scientists should strive to uncover the powers that controlled the human world. Ideally, he suggested, scientific studies of society and politics should inform public policy and facilitate decision making. Like Mitrany, he celebrated the New Deal as a successful example for a national project that made good use of accurate, scientific knowledge about social, economic, and political conditions. As vice chairman of the National Resources Planning Board, a federal agency for coordinating between various planning agencies across the United States, he argued that political scientists should not determine public policy, but have an advisory function, collecting and analysing data, and providing policy recommendations to the executive administration.[36]

In a democratic regime, the interplay between science and politics was especially important. In 1939, Merriam defined democracy as 'a form of political association in which the general control and direction of political policy of the commonwealth is habitually determined by the bulk of the community in accordance with appropriate understanding and procedures providing for popular participation and consent'.[37] Citizens held, for Merriam, a duty and responsibility to participate directly and indirectly in the act of government. Therefore, he argued, factual, value-neutral knowledge about politics should ground their political decisions and opinion. Drawing on a variety of sources including Jean-Jacques Rousseau, Hans Kelsen,

[33] Charles E. Merriam, The New Democracy and the New Despotism (New York: McGraw-Hill, 1939); Merriam, Political Power: Its Composition and Incidence (New York: McGraw-Hill, 1934); Mark C. Smith, 'A Tale of Two Charlies: Political Science, History and Civic Reform, 1890–1940', in Adcock, Bevir, and Stimson, Modern Political Science, 130.

[34] John G. Gunnell, 'Continuity and Innovation in the History of Political Science: The Case of Charles Merriam', Journal of the History of the Behavioral Sciences 28 (1992): 133–142.

[35] In the interwar years, the American internationalist and under secretary general of the League of Nations, Raymond B. Fosdick, advanced similar ideas on the potential contribution of the natural sciences to developing sociology, economics, and political science in the United States. See Raymond B. Fosdick, The Old Savage and the New Civilization (Garden City, NY: Doubleday and Doran, 1928). For a discussion of Fosdick and other theorists of internationalism and science in the interwar years, see Waqar Zaidi, 'Liberal Internationalist Approaches to Science and Technology in Interwar Britain and the United States', in Laqua, Internationalism Reconfigured, 27–30.

[36] Charles E. Merriam, 'The National Resources Planning Board', Public Administration Review 1, no. 2 (1941): 116–121. On the National Resources Planning Board and public intellectuals, see Ira Katznelson, Fear Itself: The New Deal and the Origins of Our Time (New York: Liveright, 2013), 373–375.

[37] Charles E. Merriam, 'The Meaning of Democracy', The Journal of Negro Education 10 (1941): 309; Merriam, New Democracy, 11.

Abraham Lincoln, James Bryce, Thomas Mann, and John Dewey, Merriam outlined the basic principles of democracy: 'the essential dignity of man', the 'elimination of privilege', the 'perfectibility of mankind', distributive justice, procedures to convey popular opinion to political decision makers, and policy-based social change. Scientific research and education provided empirical means to help the public and the politicians alike to identify the best policies that would 'produce more units of material and spiritual good'.[38]

At the epistemological level, Merriam was convinced that in a democracy, knowledge about the common good was attainable through rational systematic research in the natural and political sciences. In spring 1941, shortly before the United States entered the war, he gave the Godkin Lectures at Harvard.[39] The topic, 'On the Agenda of Democracy', allowed him to explore the domestic and international prospects of democracy, and suggest that statistical, empirical, and experimental research could inform a prosperous, peaceful democratic post-war order. It was not up to science to define the common good—which Merriam articulated in terms of security, order, justice, welfare, and freedom—but scientific research could pour factual, precise meaning into these general terms.[40] 'Scientific methods' were analytical tools for discovering the truth by distinguishing between facts and opinions towards the political realisation of an abstract pre-given value like human dignity, freedom, or welfare. Thus, Merriam could suggest that 'the combination of scientific possibilities and the increasing sense of human dignity make possible a far more intelligent form of government than ever before in history'.[41] The value of human dignity did not require scientific proof, yet statistical studies, opinion polls, and quantitative analysis could help find the adequate means to express human dignity in politics. Notwithstanding Merriam's strong conviction about the effectiveness of scientific research for political change, he never provided detailed examples to substantiate his claims that remained, therefore, in the realm of general strategy rather than concrete action guide.

Reflecting on 'democracy and world order', Merriam suggested that technology made politics more 'global'. A new global concept of democracy was needed, based on social justice, the rule of law, and global redistribution of 'the gains of civilization' among all the peoples of the world. Initially, rather than proposing a world federation or a world state, Merriam's universal order was based on collaborative planning aimed at erasing social

---

[38] Merriam, 'National Resources Planning Board', 121.

[39] Charles E. Merriam, *On the Agenda of Democracy* (Cambridge MA: Harvard University Press, 1941), 7–21.

[40] Charles E. Merriam, 'The Ends of Government', *American Political Science Review* 38 (1944): 21–40.

[41] Merriam, *Systematic Politics*, 332.

and economic contradictions in the world.[42] Doubts about the effectiveness of national politics in the age of globalism thus led to his rejection of state monism.[43] There are evident similarities between Merriam's proposals and David Mitrany's functional order. The New Deal administration inspired both to envisage multilayered universal administrative planning above and across existing states.[44] Yet Merriam was far less critical of political ideologies and nationalism than Mitrany, and more confident about the people's capacity to control effectively the political authorities through democratic participation.

By the end of the war, Merriam was convinced that the next stage in political order would be a global democracy.[45] Rather than a world state, he theorised a 'jural order of the world', a global system based on democratic relations between states, social justice, joint economic planning, and popular consent. The positive reception of his idea encouraged Merriam to focus his efforts on the systematic study of world politics, which led eventually to bolder suggestions for world government.[46]

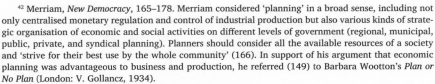

One of the motivations for Merriam's support of a world democracy was the atomic bomb, which, he argued, demanded groundbreaking political transformation: 'we are now confronted by revolution, dimming in meaning all human revolutions rolled into one'.[47] The bomb's invention did not necessarily spell the self-defeat of humanity or that 'modern man is obsolete', as the world federalist Norman Cousins suggested.[48] In his address of 29 March 1946 before the American Political Science Association, Merriam described the atomic bomb as a manifestation of humanity's great intelligence: 'the mind is king, not the atom'. The atomic bomb reinforced— rather than weakened—the importance of political judgment on a global

---

[42] Merriam, *New Democracy*, 165–178. Merriam considered 'planning' in a broad sense, including not only centralised monetary regulation and control of industrial production but also various kinds of strategic organisation of economic and social activities on different levels of government (regional, municipal, public, private, and syndical planning). Planners should consider all the available resources of a society and 'strive for their best use by the whole community' (166). In support of his argument that economic planning was advantageous to business and production, he referred (149) to Barbara Wootton's *Plan or No Plan* (London: V. Gollancz, 1934).

[43] For Mitrany's view of global order, see chapter 2.

[44] For a discussion of the New Deal as the inspiration for the post-war world order, see Borgwardt, *New Deal for the World*.

[45] Merriam, *Systematic Politics*.

[46] Hans Kohn, 'Review of *Systematic Politics* by Charles E. Merriam', *American Journal of Sociology* 51 (1946): 575–576; H. McD. Clokie, 'Systematic Politics', *Canadian Journal of Economics and Political Science* 13 (1947): 123.

[47] Charles E. Merriam, 'Physics and Politics', *American Political Science Review* 40 (1946): 445–457; Merriam, 'Physics and Politics', *Bulletin of the Atomic Scientists*, 1 May 1946, 9–11. The article in the *Bulletin* was an extended and revised version of the original address, published in *American Political Science Review*.

[48] Cousins, *Modern Man Is Obsolete*. Cousins was probably less pessimistic than Merriam was led to believe because he actively supported world federalism as a viable solution for international affairs. See chapter 6 for his comments on the Chicago constitution draft.

scale as the key for channelling value-free scientific knowledge towards positive goals. Without the guiding hand of political decision making, the world would become a repressive 'whirling mechanism of fantastic power and speed'.[49] Here Merriam was in significant disagreement with Mitrany. Despite their similar view of the need for scientifically informed economic and social planning on a global scale as the foundation for a democratic world order, Mitrany hoped to circumvent politics altogether, while Merriam highlighted the importance of politics in the creation of global order.

Reviewing Wells's *The New World Order*, Merriam hoped to see more 'Wellsian thinking' in politics, more ambitious plans to 'reconsider and readjust' social and political institutions on a world scale.[50] Yet for him Wells's writings were 'feeble' and lacked precise policy recommendations. Possibly, Merriam was concerned with the limited space dedicated to democracy in Wells's political order. Democratic decision making was, for Merriam, the only remedy to the disruptive consequences of scientific innovations like the atomic bomb. Like Wells, Merriam thought that the discovery of nuclear energy redefined the spatiality of politics in global terms. Yet for Merriam, the future challenge for political scientists was to reconceptualise the relations between political authority and the governed in the age of global politics. Democratic participation remained necessary as a guarantee of equal distribution of resources, political and social rights, and individual freedom.[51]

If in 1941 Merriam envisaged a limited world democracy aimed at social and economic planning, by 1947 he expanded his vision to a world federation founded on a universal bill of rights based on 'cultural, fraternal and human' feelings.[52] The 'bill of rights', he argued, was required by the 'revolutionary moment' generated by the atomic bomb. The war and the deteriorating economic situation brought to the fore the recognition that the eternal and universal 'dignity of man' deserved institutional defence across different political regimes and systems.[53] He used the terms 'human rights' and 'the rights of man' interchangeably, to express the 'common conscious-

---

[49] Merriam, 'Physics and Politics', *Bulletin of the Atomic Scientists*.

[50] Charles E. Merriam, 'Review of *The New World Order* by H. G. Wells', *American Journal of Sociology* 46 (1940): 402–403.

[51] Merriam, 'Physics and Politics', *American Political Science Review*.

[52] Ibid. Merriam claimed, perhaps improbably, that his ideas on world government were picked up by Richard McKeon, who played a central part in the UNESCO preparatory committee on human rights in 1946–1947. McKeon made no reference to Merriam in his writings on the subject, but they probably knew each other as colleagues at the University of Chicago. Merriam was aware of McKeon's membership in the Committee to Frame a World Constitution, and in his sixth Walgreen lecture (1947, in Records of the Atomic Scientists of Chicago, Special Collections Research Center, University of Chicago Library, box 32) predicted that the constitution would be 'of very great significance and utility'. Yet he was not invited to join the committee, perhaps because he and Hutchins had 'contrary ideas about what constituted legitimate scholarship in political science'. See Dzuback, *Robert M. Hutchins*, 161.

[53] Merriam, 'Physics and Politics', *American Political Science Review*.

ness of rights and wrongs as a basis of humanity'. This universal bill of rights was a declaration of intents, a fundamental set of political liberties to individuals around the world that all states should agree to enforce. It was based on the universal 'right to life of the individual personality', from which stemmed civil rights, political rights, social and economic rights, and the right of communication. The bill of rights would undermine the place of the state as the main political forum for individuals and communities, and provide a global arena for assessing the authority of states and defending individuals from their power.[54]

Despite the overt commitment to value pluralism, Merriam oriented his vision of world order towards a defence of unity on a global scale. Science was, for him, a universal system for understanding and ordering the world. Its universality emerged from the natural capacities for rational thinking of all human beings. He wanted to apply the methodology of scientific research to the study of social and political phenomena to discover the unifying—rather than the exceptional—factors that could bring together individuals and communities around the world. In this sense, he espoused the well-known internationalist trope of science as a unifier, highlighting its application in political science in general, and in democratic planning in particular. Nonetheless, as Reinhold Niebuhr argued in his positive review of Merriam's book *On the Agenda of Democracy*, the inherent conflict between liberty and authority in Merriam's visions of world democracy remains unresolved.[55]

MICHAEL POLANYI AND THE LIBERAL DYNAMIC ORDER

If Merriam utilised science to inform and plan democratic order on a global scale, the scientist and social philosopher Michael Polanyi saw science as a communal activity that could set a conceptual rather than functional model for a liberal order of the world. For Polanyi, science had more to offer than techniques, information, and methods for understanding the natural and human worlds. Science was a system of dynamic and spontaneous order, based on the shared faith of all individual members in the validity of generational traditions. The unrestricted dynamics that characterised the processes of scientific research could, Polanyi suggested, inspire the construction of a post-war liberal global order, based on a fiduciary

[54] Merriam, 'A World Bill of Rights', fifth Walgreen Lecture on Physics and Politics, Records of the Atomic Scientists of Chicago, box 32.

[55] Reinhold Niebuhr, 'Authority and Liberty', *Nation*, 21 March 1942, 347.

consensus about shared values and traditions including the rule of law, individual freedom, tolerance, and justice.

Michael Polanyi (1891–1976), a Hungarian physical chemist turned social scientist and philosopher, developed a critique of liberal democracy through a communitarian interpretation of the universality of science. He drew on his experience as a scientist to reflect on the meaning of liberty, rationality, and faith in the post-war world. After the First World War, he worked as a researcher in physical chemistry at the Kaiser Wilhelm Institute, Berlin. Like many Hungarian intellectuals of his generation, he was attracted by the city's vibrant cosmopolitanism, but with the rise of Nazism he decided to settle down in Britain, as professor of physical chemistry at the University of Manchester.[56] In the 1930s, he was drawn into public debate about the relations of science and politics, in conversation with Karl Mannheim, T. S. Eliot, Friedrich Hayek, Karl Popper, and Edward Shils.[57] By the end of the decade, he decided to study social rather than scientific problems.

Science embodied for Merriam and Polanyi a universal truth that could be translated into the realm of politics. The universality of science reflected the universal human capacity to reason, and the global, sweeping impact of scientific innovations on human life. Did the universality of science imply political centralisation or pluralism, greater order or anarchic liberty? As I suggested, Wells developed a paradigmatic account of universal science as facilitator of world government, which was grounded in a monistic view of politics and society. Wells's writings provided important inspiration for Polanyi as a scientist and political commentator. Looking back at his youth, Polanyi recounted that with Wells he became 'impatient with traditional statesmanship', and like him wanted to bring about a 'new world order on scientific lines'.[58] Yet the experience of world wars and revolutions changed his mind. By the 1940s, he rejected the idea that technological innovations should define and direct global political order.[59] He did not believe that 'the decisive problems of our world can be solved by applying the methods of science. Our troubles today are political and not technical'.[60] Science could not offer political thinkers expert technical guidelines to govern the world, yet could furnish methods for conceptualising global order.

---

[56] Mary Jo Nye, 'Michael Polanyi and the Social Construction of Science', *Tradition and Discovery* 39 (2012): 7–17.

[57] William T. Scott and Martin X. Moleski, *Michael Polanyi: Scientist and Philosopher* (Oxford: Oxford University Press, 2005), 175–189; Mary Jo Nye, *Michael Polanyi and His Generation: Origins of the Social Construction of Science* (Chicago: University of Chicago Press, 2011), 183–200.

[58] Michael Polanyi, 'Can Science Bring Peace?', in *The Challenge of Our Time* (London: P. Marshall, 1948), 41–43.

[59] Polanyi often referred to Wells as an early influence on his scientific and social thought, but in a letter to Karl Mannheim he suggested that he overcame Wells's 'materialism' and adopted a more 'religious' approach. See Polanyi to Mannheim, 19 April 1944, MPP, box 4, folder 11.

[60] Michael Polanyi, 'Introduction', in *Logic of Liberty*.

Polanyi's sociology of science highlighted the importance of the practices and costumes of the scientific community for discovering universal truths, as opposed to Merriam's emphasis on the intellectual achievements of the individual 'mind'.[61] While scientists were allegedly free to pursue their own research interests, Polanyi argued that they operated within an order guided by specific conceptions, traditions, and norms of behaviour. Thus, he described science as an idiosyncratic liberal order formed upon the free actions of individuals who shared faith in common traditions.

The liberty of the scientific community was a recurrent personal and theoretical concern for Polanyi. In 1938, a group of British left-wing scientists founded the Division for the Social and International Relations of Science as part of the British Association for the Advancement of Science. The following year, the X-ray crystallographer and convinced Marxist J. D. Bernal published *The Social Function of Science*, arguing that scientists had a social responsibility and should engage in politics.[62] Bernal and his associates argued that scientific research, like any other human activity, could not be detached from its social and political context. Scientists should undertake research to contribute to social progress by letting social values guide their work, at least in terms of problem choice and the technological applications of scientific theories.[63] The movement called scientists to intervene in public debate and consciously orient their research towards goals that they considered socially beneficial. Society could also employ various tools, including central planning and selective research funding, to encourage scientific research in line with political and social targets.

Polanyi became an important public speaker against the scientists' movement.[64] He considered Bernal's approach as an expression of a materialistic and deterministic philosophy that undermined the researcher's intellectual and professional freedom, and, fundamentally, delegitimised scientific quest for the truth for its own sake.[65] His liberal critique saw planning as the embodiment of a negative cultural tendency, extending from economics to social welfare, from science to culture. It reflected a holistic vision of society in which all parts had to align to a common vision

---

[61] Polanyi's biographer Mary Jo Nye suggests he anticipated many of Thomas Kuhn's ideas. See Nye, *Michael Polanyi and His Generation*, 235–250.

[62] J. D. Bernal, *The Social Function of Science* (London: Routledge, 1939); Andrew Brown, *J. D. Bernal: The Sage of Science* (Oxford: Oxford University Press, 2005); Brenda Swann and Francis Aprahamian, *J. D. Bernal: A Life in Science and Politics* (London: Verso, 1999).

[63] Nye, *Michael Polanyi and His Generation*, 195–196.

[64] Philip Mirowski, 'Economics, Science and Knowledge: Polanyi vs. Hayek', *Tradition and Discovery* 25 (1998): 29–42.

[65] Michael Polanyi, 'Social Message of Pure Science' (1945), in *Logic of Liberty*. The collection of essays was published with the active encouragement of Karl Mannheim, who was the editor of the series. For the correspondence of Mannheim and Polanyi, see Karl Mannheim, *Selected Correspondence (1911–1946) of Karl Mannheim, Scientist, Philosopher, and Sociologist*, edited by Éva Gábor (Lewiston, NY: Edwin Mellen Press, 2003), 309–320.

226 · CHAPTER 7

of rational progress. The scientific community, however, constituted for Polanyi a liberal order with particular social rules and values. Scientific research depended on the universal acceptance of practices of apprenticeship, on mutual respect between scientists, and on a shared belief in a common set of values. Subjecting scientific activities to political or social control, he feared, would compromise the idiosyncratic practices of the scientific community and by consequence its liberty.

The universality of scientific knowledge meant, for Polanyi, that science had a universal obligation to truth.[66] Therefore, social planning of scientific research, he warned, would subjugate the scientists' collective and individual liberty to particular interests, undermining the scientific commitment to universal truth.[67] Scientific progress depended on individual freedom to contribute spontaneously to the advancement of knowledge, without prior precise knowledge of the final goal of scientific research. From this idea, Polanyi derived the notion of 'atomised sovereignty'. Individuals were free to decide independently to give their support to the community in its quest for the common good (or, in scientific research, universal truth). These individual acts formed the collective consensus that legitimised public life, and set the basis for the 'spontaneous order of society', the conceptual foundation for Polanyi's global thought.[68]

After the New Deal and the Beveridge Report, public opinion in the United States and Britain had become more receptive of planning as a means for improving social and economic standards. Thus, both Polanyi and Hayek considered their opposition to planning as a topical and timely reminder to Americans and Britons alike of the fragility of individual freedom. In his review of Polanyi's 1940 book *The Contempt of Freedom*, Hayek agreed with Polanyi's idea that it would be wrong, superficial, and ignorant to seek a comprehensive understanding of the goals and practices of science. He added that without such knowledge, however, planning of science and society would result in an unjustified restriction of liberty.[69]

Evidently, as Philip Mirowski notes, Polanyi and Hayek shared a strong conviction that individual liberty was the supreme value of social life.[70] However, each offered a different outlook about the capacity of science to provide a model for world order. Polanyi thought that through free interaction and traditional values, the scientific community was able to discern universal truths about the world, which then served as the foundation for

[66] Michael Polanyi, *Science, Faith and Society* (1946; repr., Chicago: University of Chicago Press, 1964).
[67] Michael Polanyi, 'Planned Science' (1948), in *Logic of Liberty*, 86–90.
[68] It is not clear if Polanyi or Hayek used the term first, but the two influenced each other in developing the idea of spontaneous/dynamic order. Caldwell, *Hayek's Challenge*, 294.
[69] Friedrich A. Hayek, 'Review of *The Contempt of Freedom* by Michael Polanyi', *Economica* 8 (1941): 212. On Hayek's ideas on planning, see chapter 5.
[70] Mirowski, 'Economics, Science and Knowledge', 35–38.

a global dynamic order of discovery and invention. The discovery of universal truths in the context of the scientific community drove, for him, human progress. Hayek doubted the capacity of science to provide sufficient knowledge about human activities, and took Polanyi's critique of the limits of rational knowledge further towards the claim that human ignorance would obstruct *any* form of widespread collective planned action.

Doubtlessly, Polanyi and Hayek directed their criticism at people like Merriam, who thought they embodied the greatest menace to the hope for improving the human condition by scientific and rational planning on national and world scales. In 1939, Merriam criticised Hayek's misguided notion of planning, and in 1946, he dismissed Polanyi's opposition to political control of science as inconclusive, right-wing diffidence about social planning.[71] When Merriam and Hayek participated in a radio discussion at the University of Chicago about Hayek's new book *The Road to Serfdom*, Merriam's vitriol could hardly be contained.[72] Although Hayek took a lenient position asserting that some degree of governmental planning would be desirable to realise political and social aims, Merriam dismissed his views as a misconceived interpretation of American politics and suggested that Hayek's notion of central planning would exclude any kind of federal politics in the United States. Refusing to engage in real debate, Merriam feared that Hayek's critique would bring down his life project of creating a free and prosperous world order through rational and scientific planning, and mocked Polanyi and Hayek's opposition to planning as 'planning against planning'.[73]

Polanyi was critical of the idea that calculating reason should lay the groundwork for social and political order, but was keener than Hayek to find a positive and constructive foundation for liberalism. This foundation was rendered through 'tacit knowledge', a concept that Polanyi started to elaborate in the 1940s and developed in detail in the 1960s. 'Tacit knowledge' rested on the assumption that some of the information and skills that individuals accumulated could not be consciously formulated or accounted for, but nonetheless influenced their personal, political, and professional decisions.

In his 1946 Riddell Memorial Lectures on science, faith, and society, Polanyi argued that scientific conventions were based, in the final analysis, on a body of ideas, unverified beliefs, intuitions, and concepts held by

[71] Merriam, 'Physics and Politics', *Bulletin of the Atomic Scientists*, 10; Merriam, *New Democracy*, 149, 167.

[72] Hayek, Krueger, and Merriam, *Road to Serfdom*, 6–8.

[73] In 1947, Michael Oakeshott levelled at Hayek similar criticism: 'a plan to resist all planning may be better than its opposite, but it belongs to the same style of politics'. See Michael Oakeshott, 'Rationalism in Politics' (1947), in *Rationalism in Politics and Other Essays*, edited by Timothy Fuller (Indianapolis: Liberty Press, 1991), 26.

each individual consciously or not.[74] Tacit knowledge constituted the collective and mutable traditions on which the liberal society, according to Polanyi, depended. Individuals could share these traditional skills, ideas, and beliefs through interaction with other members of the community. Polanyi pointed to the scientific practice of apprenticeship as an example of the means to initiate individuals into the traditions of science: the master transmitted skills, axioms, beliefs, and ideas to the pupil, who was at liberty to change and improve them.

Polanyi's assertion that tacit knowledge is acquired through social interaction in the public sphere highlights the important distinction he drew between private and public individual freedom. For Polanyi, tacit knowledge of traditions set the foundation for the political and social dynamic order. Thus, the necessary condition for the accumulation and transmission of knowledge was *public* not private freedom. Individuals are privately free, for Polanyi, if they can decide their actions for themselves. Private freedom is, put simply, the opposite of slavery. However, this entailed not any responsibility to set the purposes of society as a whole, but only the responsibility to act within the limited sphere that society dedicated to individual action. Public freedom is, by contrast, the ability not only to act freely as an individual, but also to define and eventually implement the public good. For example, authoritarian regimes may allow their citizens private—but not public—freedom.[75] Polanyi's concept of public freedom is therefore distinct from Hayek's idea of freedom: for Polanyi, public freedom meant that, in the dynamic political order, each individual could freely and responsibly decide not only her own actions but also the public good.[76]

The human and natural world was made of various interacting dynamic orders, including the international economy, the system of common law, and the scientific community. Private freedom was of secondary importance in this framework. The dynamic order is a precondition of the liberal society, where individuals are free to pursue different forms and aspects of truth like religion, science, law, and art, and contribute in their own way to the progress of humanity. Once constituted, the operation of the dynamic orders depended on the individual's freedom to act consciously and without constraint and to take part in deciding the purpose of society as a whole.

In his essay 'The Growth of Thought in Society', Polanyi described society through the notion of 'dynamic order'. He proposed to 'analyse the part played in society by the ideals of science and the ideals of other aspects of truth'. His idea of order emerged from observations of the natural biophysical world and the scientific community. Both were characterised by

[74] Polanyi, *Science, Faith and Society*, 42–53.
[75] See general discussion in Struan Jacobs and Phil Mullins, 'Faith, Tradition, and Dynamic Order: Michael Polanyi's Liberal Thought from 1941 to 1951', *History of European Ideas* 34 (2008): 126–128.
[76] Polanyi, 'Introduction', in *Logic of Liberty*.

lack of fixed hierarchy or centralised governing authority.[77] In the natural world, he argued, particles, atoms, and organisms were subject to universal rules like gravity and electromagnetism, but acted spontaneously without specific directions or restrictions. Each organism or cell followed an individually determined life cycle and existed harmoniously with other specimens or species. This conception of dynamic and spontaneous order reflected the Gestalt psychological theory of Wolfgang Köhler, which suggested to Polanyi that the spontaneous mutual adjustment of all elements in society could attain a sort of order without compromising liberty.[78]

In the sphere of economics, the principles of dynamic order unfolded very clearly. Polanyi perceived the free market economy as a model of operation of human freedom, but not as its sole foundation. The market and free competition, he argued, should be indiscriminately accessible to all members of society, who retain the freedom to act spontaneously within the political space of public freedom. Polanyi's interpretation of the market as a facilitator of liberty led to his invitation, in 1938, to participate in the Colloque Walter Lippmann in Paris, a conference about Lippmann's book *The Good Society*, which had just been translated into French. The meeting brought together liberal intellectuals including Raymond Aron, Hayek, Wilhelm Röpke, Alexander Rüstow, Ludwig von Mises, Robert Marjolin, Louis Rougier, and Jacques Rueff, who aimed at promoting a new vision of international economic liberalism. This event encouraged him to develop more seriously his economic thought.[79]

A decade later, Hayek invited Polanyi to join his classic liberal think tank, the Mont Pèlerin Society, to reinforce the society's theoretical backbone.[80] Yet Polanyi, like Raymond Aron, felt out of place among liberal economists, because his own liberal political theory was not grounded in economic interactions alone. He was critical of laissez-faire economics and endorsed governmental interventionist distributive policies to mitigate socioeconomic contradictions.[81] His lack of interest in private liberty and his interest in Gestalt theory also reflected his view that society was not an atomistic multitude of individuals. Order could be implemented through the natural tendency of society towards free social interaction. But the cohesion

[77] Michael Polanyi, 'The Growth of Thought in Society', *Economica* 8 (1941): 421–456; Jacobs and Mullins, 'Faith, Tradition, and Dynamic Order': 120–131.

[78] Jacobs and Mullins, 'Faith, Tradition, and Dynamic Order', 125–126.

[79] Walter Lippmann, *An Inquiry into the Principles of the Good Society* (Boston: Little, Brown, 1937). On the Colloque Lippmann in Paris, see Audier, *Le Colloque Lippmann*; Burgin, *Great Persuasion*, 56–70. See also chapters 2 and 5.

[80] Francois Denord, 'French Neoliberalism and Its Divisions: From the Colloque Walter Lippmann to the Fifth Republic', in Mirowski and Plehwe, *Road from Mont Pèlerin*, 45–67; Scott and Moleski, *Michael Polanyi*, 168.

[81] Michael Polanyi, *Full Employment and Free Trade* (Cambridge: Cambridge University Press, 1945).

of this dynamic order depended on a shared belief in the emancipatory role of the traditions on which political consensus was based.[82]

The atomic bomb set a new threat to the idea of public freedom and encouraged Polanyi to think about the problem of order on a global scale. In the aftermath of the war, he turned to the question of world order, arguing that 'modern weapons, in particular the atomic bomb, rendered armed nations too dangerous to one another, and in consequence . . . the political organisation of the world threatens to collapse'.[83] The atomic bomb would not exclude warfare, as Merriam suggested, but required rethinking the foundations of world politics: the states system, the balance of powers, national sovereignty. The liberal principles of the scientific community could set a model for social and political interaction in the global political arena.

Polanyi developed his idea of liberty in the atomic age in an article on the 'Foundations of Freedom in Science', published in 1946 in the *Bulletin of the Atomic Scientists*.[84] Scientists, he opined, formed a spiritual and moral community based on their belief in the pursuit of universal truth and covenanted to the service of this goal. This could be the model for a political society based on the pursuit of universal truth with the assistance of traditions, conventions, and practices to ensure its primacy. Traditions were repositories of knowledge and methods transmitted across generations. They were not fixed or stable, but subject to continuous change and elaboration. Beside traditions, scientists also shared a commitment—which Polanyi defined as 'faith'—to certain ideals like truth, original research, and so on. Accordingly, in the political dynamic order, traditions and faith in common ideals were foundational to the collective consensus that formed the polity.[85]

Polanyi prioritised faith over doubt as the foundation of scientific knowledge. Human actions could be spontaneously coherent, even if stemming from different intellectual and spiritual traditions: 'the restrained interplay of [these traditions] forms the constitution and the essence of a free society'.[86] However, his theory implicitly suggests that there must be a general agreement about human nature. In 1948, he posited that international relations depended on 'some universal belief concerning the nature of man. [The interacting nations] must believe that all men, as well as all nations, are subject to certain moral obligations, and that people can be relied on to observe these obligations. The challenge of our time

[82] See more on Hayek's idea of planning and international order in chapter 5. Hayek's critique of reason and science went further than Polanyi's, since the latter still maintained a strong belief in the ability of science to attain the truth through scientific inquiry, whereas Hayek grounded his social theory on human ignorance and on a strong doubt of science's quest for the truth.

[83] Michael Polanyi, 'Memorandum on the Atomic Bomb', March 1947, MPP, box 31, folder 2.

[84] Michael Polanyi, 'The Foundations of Freedom in Science', *Bulletin of the Atomic Scientists* 2 (1 December 1946): 6–7.

[85] Michael Polanyi, 'Self-Government of Science' (1942), in *Logic of Liberty*, 53.

[86] Polanyi, 'Foundations of Freedom in Science', 6.

is to gain general acceptance for certain beliefs about the nature of man, and make these the basis of a new and free world-government'.[87]

Certain shared traditional values, like tolerance, fairness, and equality, were central to liberalism and could, in the atomic age, set the basis for democratic government on a global scale. However, Polanyi was inconsistent about the universality of values. Elsewhere he suggested that these traditional values were not universal but the outcome of contingent historical processes in England and the United States.[88] He saw Hayek as a fellow traveller in the crusade to restore the British traditional values of liberty, free trade, and commerce against the tide of socialist ideas from Continental Europe, where different intellectual and moral trajectories brought about totalitarianism not liberalism. Yet he did not specify if and how these values could extend beyond the British cultural sphere to form the foundation for his global liberal world order.

Polanyi discussed both science and politics in terms of faith and moral values, rather than using exclusively the vocabulary of rationality and objectivity. In that, he opposed the views of the philosopher Karl Popper (1902–1994), whose liberal critique was based on the idea that the scientific principle of critical rationalism and 'falsifiability' should set the terms for political order as well.[89] Popper and Polanyi were friends and frequent correspondents in the 1930s and early 1940s.[90] Both were Austro-Hungarian émigrés in London, scientists by training and profession who found inspiration in science to critique and defend liberal democracy in the era of totalitarianism. Like Polanyi, Popper also saw the community of science as based on certain agreed practices, but he suggested different ones: experiments, trial and error, and the principles of verification and falsification. Apprenticeship, faith in accepted traditions, and mutual trust were for Popper the characteristics of the tribal—not the scientific—society. Thus, Popper and Polanyi offered two irreconcilable interpretations of the advance of scientific knowledge, leading to their different ideas of liberalism. As opposed to Polanyi's idea that consensus in liberal democracies was based on fiduciary faith, Popper's *Open Society and Its Enemies* suggested that the foundation of society was faith in reason, empowered by the notion of critical doubt.[91]

The idea that the universality of science depended on faith in shared traditional values encouraged Polanyi to see the universality of faith as

---

[87] Polanyi, 'Can Science Bring Peace?', 43.

[88] Michael Polanyi, 'The Socialist Error. Review of *The Road to Serfdom* by F. A. v Hayek', *Spectator*, 30 March 1944, 293; Michael Polanyi, 'The English and the Continent', *Political Quarterly* 14 (1943): 372–381.

[89] Karl Popper, *The Open Society and Its Enemies* (1945; repr., Princeton, NJ: Princeton University Press, 2013).

[90] Struan Jacobs and Phil Mullins, 'Michael Polanyi and Karl Popper: The Fraying of a Long-Standing Acquaintance', *Tradition and Discovery* 38 (2011): 61–93.

[91] Ibid., 70–88.

the foundation of a new world order.[92] Patterns of thinking that originated in religious faith played, for him, a central role in building consensus in modern liberal societies.[93] Polanyi's own religious views were grounded in an eclectic, unorthodox form of Christianity.[94] Yet the centrality of religion to his conception of political consensus did not imply an attachment to ecclesiastic hierarchy; the power of modernity emerged from its 'rebellion against the medieval ecclesiastic authority', which cannot be restored without risking a collapse into reactionary dogmatism.[95] Thus, in the dynamic order of science, 'faith' had no necessary religious implications beyond a shared belief in the validity of universal truth. Scientific research, liberal political stance, and religious beliefs were in no contradiction for Polanyi, as long as they shared a commitment to freedom: 'freedom in society depends on a universal belief in truth, justice, charity and tolerance, accepted dedication to the service of those realities'.[96] Freedom depended on the recognition of the centrality of faith, not only reason, in science: 'if we were to become fully aware of the beliefs underlying science and of the facts that we do actually hold these beliefs; and if we were to recognize . . . that the denial of these beliefs must entail sooner or later the destruction of science—perhaps that we may then get used to it once more that the holding of certain beliefs on the grounds of our own ultimate responsibility is both necessary and possible. Perhaps this may help us even to restore once more the balance between our craving for ultimate certainty and our radical distaste for any definite creed or dogma'.[97]

Grounding political consensus in faith in common values implied that a new world order could emerge only from a preexisting common outlook, not as a revolutionary new approach introduced to social relations: 'it is by the recognition of man's moral nature that men may find that mutual confidence which is needed for the establishment of a free order of the

---

[92] The interplay of secular and religious faith in Polanyi's thought suggests some similarities with Raymond Aron's writings on 'secular religions' during the same period. Aron and Polanyi met at the Colloque Walter Lippmann in 1938 and corresponded frequently after the late 1950s. However, Aron feared that religions could also be used to reinforce totalitarian regimes, not only to set the intellectual foundation for liberal societies. On Aron's use of secular religions and political myth, see chapter 2.

[93] Polanyi, 'English and the Continent'.

[94] Polanyi was born to a secular Jewish family, but religion had played little part in his early life. He was baptised into the Catholic Church in 1919, but after moving to England in 1934 his belief moved closer to the Protestant Church. As Drusilla Scott, a family friend, writes in her biography of Polanyi, he did not discuss his personal beliefs with his family and friends. However, he joined the Moot, a Christian intellectual group led by Mannheim, Eliot, and Oldham. He opposed religious extremist dogmatism, yet argued that science and religion were in many ways similar, since both were 'dynamic orders'. See Drusilla Scott, *Everyman Revived: The Common Sense of Michael Polanyi* (Lewes: Book Guild, 1985), 184.

[95] Michael Polanyi, 'Modern Science and Modern Thought' (1947), MPP, box 31, folder 2, folio 9.

[96] Michael Polanyi, 'Foundation of Academic Freedom', *Lancet* 249 (1947): 583–586, reprint in *Logic of Liberty*, 32–48, 47.

[97] Polanyi, 'Modern Science and Modern Thought', 25.

world'.[98] Specifically, this recognition was an indispensable foundation for efficient international atomic control.[99] Yet, the order he had imagined was amorphous, abstract, held together by ideas rather than institutions. Furthermore, the possibility and means of implementing the traditions of liberty around the world remain unclear. These traditions could, perhaps, be slowly introduced to society through the master-to-pupil apprenticeship processes of political and intellectual initiation. However, the historical foundation of the political and fiduciary traditions that grounded the liberal order remained circumscribed to the geo-cultural sphere of the Anglo-American world.

The emphasis on traditions and faith in Polanyi's liberal world order embodied an attempt to restore the moral and cultural values of Western civilisation after the traumatic experience of totalitarianism. His quest for a new positive and constructive form of liberalism consisted of a return to an idealised past in which faith in a common cause would set the foundation of a society of free individuals. Despite its universal aspiration, the historical foundation of liberal traditional values like tolerance, equality, fairness, and individual liberty risked creating an exclusive Western-centred political space. As a political project, the universality of science and faith attained a more restricted political space than initially intended.

The link between scientific research and faith in shared values was elaborated in the writings of Polanyi's friend, the sociologist Edward Shils (1910–1995).[100] As a sociologist at the University of Chicago, he was closely involved with the Chicago scientists' movement, and acted as special advisor to the *Bulletin of the Atomic Scientists*. He spent the war years in London working at the Office of Strategic Services, and in 1946 became reader in sociology at the London School of Economics. In 1961, he was elected a fellow at King's College, Cambridge, and later at Peterhouse.[101] He shared a close friendship with Polanyi, and followed with interest his campaign against social planning of science.

Shils suggested that an international moral consensus was necessary to create a liberal world order. In 1948, he published a pamphlet on atomic weapons, arguing that most common 'doctrines' of international relations expired with the first atomic bomb: containment, federation of Western Europe, balance of power, declaration of neutrality.[102] For him, the atomic revolution meant that peace could not be maintained under the threat of

---

[98] Polanyi, 'Can Science Bring Peace?', 43.

[99] Michael Polanyi, 'The Policy of Atomic Science', *Time and Tide* 27 (1946): 749.

[100] Edward Shils, 'A Critique of Planning in Science: The Society for Freedom in Science', *Bulletin of the Atomic Scientists* 3 (1947): 80–82.

[101] Ann T. Keene, 'Shils, Edward Albert', in *American National Biography* (2005), www.anb.org/articles/14/14-01145.html.

[102] Edward Shils, *The Atomic Bomb in World Politics* (London: National Peace Council, 1948), 75.

arms and could be attained only through a moral revolution. The global moral consensus depended, for him, not on the mere sense of belonging to the community, but on the shared recognition of the importance of certain moral beliefs. He argued that 'only when human beings regard themselves as members of the same collectivity, will the dangers of war be held in check . . . this moral consensus cannot easily be manufactured, even where the will to do so exists'.[103] Lack of consensus failed the plans for international control of atomic weapons, and exacerbated global political disagreement.

Shils identified a gap between the universality of politics and science, arguing that the absence of universal morality hindered any possibility of cooperation. Yet, he did not despair of science's capacity for change. Sharing Polanyi's belief in the community of scientists as a model for liberal and flexible cooperation, he indicated intellectual exchange, free flow of ideas, and international cooperative institutions as the potential foundational values of a new global morality. Without this consensual morality, international control of atomic energy would be of 'no value' since the international sphere would be dominated by another form of universal mentality: the regime of fear. Alongside the crisis of moral values and the general indifference to the heavy human cost of the bomb, the growing fear of atomic war contributed to the mounting hostility that threatened the modern fragmented humanity.

LEWIS MUMFORD'S REMEDY TO GLOBAL MADNESS

The American reaction to the atomic bomb was characterised by an unprecedented rhetoric of urgency, anxious fear, and doomsday imagery.[104] Samuel Moyn noted that in the late 1940s, there was no widespread Holocaust consciousness in American public opinion, but there certainly was a strong awareness of the horrors of atomic destruction.[105] In 1948, however, Edward Shils suggested that 'the detonation of the first atomic bomb against the Japanese in August 1945 was greeted with great enthusiasm by most journalists and by the populace at large'.[106] The ambivalent accounts of the American public reception of the atomic bombs highlight the need to strip the political arguments of their stylistic attire to understand the degree to which 'the atomic revolution' changed common perceptions of politics.

I have discussed competing attempts to interpret the universality of science as the foundation for a new peaceful global order that would provide

---

[103] Ibid., 37.

[104] Boyer, *By the Bomb's Early Light*, 5.

[105] For the argument that the Holocaust was not a central part of post-war public opinion, see Moyn, *Last Utopia*, 7.

[106] Shils, *Atomic Bomb in World Politics*, 63.

substantial and effective defence of individual liberty. Robert Hutchins voiced a common concern when he argued that 'our greatest problems are how to exist at all in the world which science and technology have made, and how to direct the power they have placed in our hands'.[107] Although scientific knowledge had shaped the conditions for post-war global order, it was unclear whether science could also provide guidelines for living in the global world.

The American historian, philosopher, and commentator Lewis Mumford (1895–1990) set the problem in similar—yet more decisive—terms in his article 'Gentlemen: You Are Mad!'[108] He was concerned with the negative effects of the atomic arms race on the achievements of civilisation, and primarily on liberty. Unlike Merriam and Wells, Mumford was wary of experts, in particular politicians and scientists, whom he accused of narrowing down human knowledge into specific and well-delineated fields of expertise. The atomic bomb was, he wrote in 1949, 'a scientific form of genocide'.[109] In his dystopian vision, he identified the solution in the idea of a world government, as advanced by the world federalist Grenville Clark, by Albert Einstein and Arnold J. Toynbee, and by the Chicago Committee headed by his friend Giuseppe Antonio Borgese.[110] In the last part of this chapter, I discuss Mumford's mid-century quest for a humanist moral universalism as a reaction to the universal political space created by the atomic bomb.

Mumford was not unprepared for the 'devastating' invention of the atomic weapon. As a young reader of Jules Verne and H. G. Wells, he had already anticipated the day when terrifying weapons would put an end to the scientific and civilisational advance of humanity. As an influential cultural critic and author, his writings on the atomic dangers between 1945 and 1948 were widely read by the general public. However, his tone was significantly different from that of Merriam or Polanyi. Rather than attempting to explore the possible contribution of scientific knowledge and practices to the political field, or theorising a way to safeguard individual liberty from the peril of atomic destruction or military rule, Mumford wanted to discard both politics and science for failing to deliver on their promise of peace, order, and progress. Opposed to the 'near veneration' of atomic scientists, he warned against the dark side of scientific progress that could lead to moral nihilism.[111]

This idea resonates with the cultural critique of the Frankfurt School, most explicitly expressed in *Dialectic of Enlightenment* by Max Horkheimer

---

[107] Robert M. Hutchins, *The Atom Bomb and Education* (London: National Peace Council, 1947), 16.
[108] Mumford, 'Gentlemen'.
[109] Lewis Mumford, *Atomic War—The Way Out* (London: National Peace Council, 1949), 1.
[110] Ibid., 19.
[111] Mumford, 'Gentlemen'; Boyer, *By the Bomb's Early Light*, 60.

236 · CHAPTER 7

and Theodor Adorno.[112] The thematic congruence between Mumford and the California-based German émigrés revolves around the ambiguity of the Enlightenment notion of the intellectual supremacy of rationality and science. According to the conventional narrative, the Enlightenment project proposed to eliminate myth and replace it with rational science. However, according to Horkheimer and Adorno, mid-century collapse of reason into myth reversed this process, discarding the meaning of 'truth' and morality and resorting to calculating and technical reasoning instead. The result was the domination of man not only over nature but also over other human beings. They expanded their critique to a wider reconsideration of Western culture, capitalistic society, and political liberalism.

Similarly, for Mumford the scientific discovery of the atom was not the first step towards civilisational progress, economic revival, and global social equality, as Merriam suggested. Mumford despaired of scientific progress because it undermined morality. His critique resonates with Horkheimer and Adorno's 'myth of Enlightenment' as the reification of reason and science replacing a sincere quest for the truth. He shared the Frankfurt theorists' assessment of the subjugation of humanity to the concerns and interests of scientific progress. Yet Mumford was far more convinced than Adorno and Horkheimer that humanity could undo the negative impact of scientific modernity and return to 'sanity'. He also had an idea about how this positive revival could come about. On 8 August 1945, he wrote in his diary that 'nothing will be a proof against a suicide anxiety except an absolute submission to a universal standard of human conduct'.[113]

The atomic bomb could lead, according to Mumford, to one of four scenarios for the post-war world: American imperialism facilitated by preemptive atomic attacks; the emergence of a bipolar belligerent system in which the United States would confront the Soviet Union as a rival with atomic capabilities; a multilateral order in which many states attained nuclear capacities, eventually leading to a total war; and finally a century-long atomic arms race that would condemn humanity to an existence of fear and deprivation. All four scenarios represented humanity's political and moral ineptness in the age of promethean technology. Unlike Horkheimer and Adorno, Mumford did not proceed dialectically to find the philosophical antithesis of the negative form of reason. Rather, he turned to the millennial history of Western civilisation for the fundamental values of moral humanism to revive mankind.[114] For Mark Greif, the difference between Mumford and the Frankfurt theorists boiled down to the former's optimism about the pos-

---

[112] Theodor Adorno and Max Horkheimer, *Dialectic of Enlightenment* (1944; repr., London: Verso, 1986).

[113] Lewis Mumford, *My Works and Days: A Personal Chronicle* (New York: Harcourt Brace Jovanovich, 1979); Thomas Parke Hughes and Agatha C. Hughes, eds., *Lewis Mumford: Public Intellectual* (Oxford: Oxford University Press, 1990).

[114] Greif, *Age of the Crisis of Man,* 59.

sibility of 'a renewal of human character'. Yet the difference unfolded also in political terms: Mumford was an enthusiastic supporter of world government, convinced that public intellectuals could lead humanity towards a better world order by subjugating science to humanist moral control. Such ideas were foreign to the realm of thought of Adorno and Horkheimer, who espoused a more pessimistic view on the political conditions of modernity and the possibility of its transcendence.

Mumford discussed world order in terms of 'all-or-nothing': total destruction or global community. This binary also characterised the world of the Chicago constitutionalists, with whom Mumford exchanged frequent letters. The realisation that scientific progress threatened the annihilation of humanity was shared by Hutchins, Borgese, and McKeon and motivated their project for a world constitution. Among the Chicago constitutionalists, Mumford saw Borgese as his partner in the quest 'to bring order and wisdom back to the human race'.[115] In his memoir, Mumford recounts how in 1940 Borgese invited him along with Hans Kohn, Reinhold Niebuhr, Thomas Mann, and others to form the 'Council of Wisdom', a group of public intellectuals tasked with outlining a proposal for a new democratic world order. After two conferences, Mumford posited that the invasion of France had rendered their project irrelevant, but supported Borgese's declaration in favour of American intervention in the war as an act of faith.[116]

At the end of the war, when Borgese launched his new project for a world constitution, Mumford also reflected on the legal and institutional aspects of the post-atomic world. Before a world government could be established, a universal spiritual revival was needed to teach people that their highest allegiance should be to humanity as a whole. Like Shils, Mumford argued that the universal implications of atomic energy, rendering every spot on Earth a target for destruction, created a global regime of fear that could be countered only by the rise of universal humanism. The first step was a moral—rather than military, political, or diplomatic—reform. Eventually, he hoped, this moral humanistic universalism would (in an unspecified manner) lead to the foundation of a world government.[117]

Mumford's moral universalism differed from interwar ideas of liberal internationalism in his pessimistic diffidence about rationality and

[115] Mumford, *My Works and Days*, 389.
[116] Ibid. This project resulted in the publication of the declaration *City of Man*, which is discussed in detail in chapter 6.
[117] Mumford was a supporter of the Chicago constitution, and a member of the advisory board of United World Federalists. For the correspondence between Borgese and Mumford in the context of the Chicago Committee to Frame a World Constitution, see CFWC, box 21, folder 2. On Mumford's world federalism, see, for example, Mumford to Borgese, 14 June 1949, in CFWC, box 21, folder 2. Mumford's active support of the Chicago plan for world government shakes the ground under the argument that he was a 'prophet of doom', whose sole contribution was to reveal the dangers of atomic weapons without proposing any positive solution. See Everett Mendelsohn, 'Prophet of Our Discontent: Lewis Mumford Confronts the Bomb', in Hughes and Hughes, *Lewis Mumford: Public Intellectual*, 351.

scientific progress. He argued that the optimistic and rational universalism, which he associated with the writings of Wells, resulted in despair on a planetary scale. The blind belief in rationality as the solution to conflicts was no longer applicable in the atomic age, when the armament race promised not calculated victory but common decline. Thus, Mumford turned to the human spirit, not the human mind, as a source of hope in the nuclear era. Charity, unrequited generosity, brotherhood, and piety should be the fundamental values of the new global humanity.

Mumford considered the universal crisis of moral values as the source of international strife and conflict. Yet his lament concealed a more particular concern about the moral decline of Western civilisation, caused by the loss of its traditional moral values. The critique was targeted primarily at the liberal democracies. The advancement of technology and the discovery of the atomic weapons exacerbated the moral deprivation of human society as a whole, but its impact on liberal democracies was acute. If Shils and Polanyi argued that the community of scientists could offer a model for international cooperation and good will, Mumford thought the scientific practice of ignoring the social and political implications of scientific innovations for the sake of pure science intensified the moral degradation of post-war humanity. Mumford's earlier hopes for technology as a power of renewal of human society were shattered by the disastrous applications of science during the war. The only salvation of scientific knowledge was its reconnection with the moral aspects of human life. By harmonising all human activities, the social and natural sciences, technology and morality, a new liberal political global order could emerge and the freedom of humanity would be saved.

A TURN TO FAITH

In the 1940s, there were two influential proxies for 'science' in public discussion on the relations between scientific research and political order: the atomic bomb and planning. By perceiving 'science' through these symbolic lenses, political commentators touched upon the foundations of global order: the tension between political power and individual liberty. After the war, the diplomatic and political attempts to reach an agreement about international control of atomic weaponry led to lively public controversies in which the discovery of atomic energy was seen as an intellectual human achievement, but also as an imminent threat of global annihilation. While discussions about the bomb were accompanied by a degree of ambiguity about its potential benefits, the idea of social and economic planning was received with either great enthusiasm or overt dismissal. Planning was either an indispensable means to social and economic progress, or an illegitimate limit on individual liberty, but never both at the same time.

As I outlined in this chapter, what science could offer politics was no longer specific expertise but an example for successful intellectual collaboration, and perhaps a model for a moral community. The Wellsian idea that scientists, engineers, and technicians should provide specific expert knowledge on the world as the foundation of global governance had lost its appeal during the 1940s. Rather, the atomic bomb and the idea of planning were seen as instances of the new global dimension of political order that required a new perception of the role of science and politics in society. A key aspect of the debate was the best means to contain the negative and destructive implications of science. In the 1940s, this shape-giving boundary was often discussed in terms of faith in the common traditions of humanity.

The notion of a shared humanity provided a sense of limit to the expansive threat that science could pose. Merriam hoped to address the limits of the Wellsian ethos of scientifically informed world government by substituting political and social scientists for natural scientists as the holders of essential expert knowledge about the world. Furthermore, participatory democracy would invite every citizen to engage in politics and shape the common good. Yet, as Niebuhr argued in his review of Merriam's *Systematic Politics* in 1945, 'the talk of establishing a genuine community within the framework of a technical civilisation is more difficult . . . than the author assumes'.[118] Mumford had far more limited trust in the knowledge generated by scientists—including political scientists—about the political world and human nature. Instead, he resorted to the conception of harmony of interests between science, faith, and politics, which, he argued, could be attained if humanity would restore its faith in the value of human life.

The evident problem remained defining those values that rendered humanity 'human'. Humanity was depicted as global and inclusive, yet the practices and values it embodied reflected, often enough, the historical and sociological trajectory of a particular society. For instance, the notion of faith in shared values did not necessarily refer to a specific religious system of belief, but Polanyi, Mumford, and Merriam alluded to the historical importance of Christian (Protestant) values in defending individual liberty. Niebuhr argued in his review of Mumford's book that the liberal humanity that Mumford applauded was vaguely defined as 'the Roman conception of humanity, united in the pursuit of freedom and justice and embracing all races and conditions'.[119]

---

[118] Reinhold Niebuhr, 'Dr Merriam Sums Up', *Nation*, 13 October 1945, 380.
[119] Reinhold Niebuhr, 'Challenge to Liberals', *Nation*, 14 September 1940, 221–222.

Similarly, for Polanyi and Shils, the practices, methods, and intellectual achievements of the global scientific community set an example for collaborative and successful social order that could be replicated in the global political sphere. The scientific community provided a pattern of dynamic and free social interaction; they still had misgivings about integrating specific findings of the sciences into their visions of world order. Possibly, theirs was an idealised interpretation of scientific practice, yet they hoped that the political dimension of human interaction would imitate the behavioural patterns and the social rules that guided scientists and the scientific community in the pursuit of the common good, the truth.

The mid-century turn to a global political order based on moral universalism embodied an effort to reformulate the defence of liberty on a global scale. However, the focus on faith, fiduciary relations, and traditional values fashioned liberalism as the historical outcome of Western civilisation and the so-called Judeo-Christian-Roman culture. The cultural, historical, and geographic specificity of this liberal ethos undermined its universality. While these thinkers applauded, each in his own manner, the value of pluralism and diversity, their novel notions of global liberalism actually aimed at reviving Western civilisation after the tragic turn taken at the Second World War. Despite the apparent universality of science, politics, and morality, their real essence was a Western-centred humanism.

While integrating different cultural and political experiences into a new global liberal humanist order seemed like a desirable goal, the means for its realisation were not taken into serious consideration. Merriam, Polanyi, Mumford, and Shils looked at the world as a whole as they reinterpreted the relations of politics and science, but their contingent experience and political concerns restricted their view to their own portion of the globe. The preceding discussion revealed their struggle to come to terms with the globality of politics, which they diagnosed as an important condition of their age. Flexibility, dynamism, participation, and pragmatic policies were highlighted as means to preserve diversity and liberty in the global order. Yet in view of the rising American and British fear that the universality of science did not have the expected liberating function, the urgent need to defend liberty and 'civilisation' led political commentators to outline a global order that preserved rather than transcended the hierarchical, conservative traits of their own reality. It was faith, rather than the findings of science, that still held the potential power to refashion political order on a global scale.

CHAPTER 8

Catholicism, Pluralism, and Global Democracy

IN 1944, REINHOLD Niebuhr argued that the global war gave rise to two kinds of universalisms: material and spiritual.[1] Material universalism emerged from new communication and transport technologies that connected the world and shortened the distance between faraway places. Spiritual universalism created a sense of moral obligation between people from different states and cultures. He noted that many political thinkers hoped the post-war era would provide the opportunity to translate the material and spiritual universalisms into a new political structure. He thought, however, that they were bound for disappointment: the new universalisms did not necessarily announce the emergence of a global political order. Assessing the political implications of spiritual and material universalism, he argued that particular loyalties and national interests still presented an important challenge that prevented the realisation of a structured universal political order. The post-war era would be an age of global anarchy, in which new tendencies towards universalism could not find an adequate political expression. The universal community of mankind was still a distant ideal.

This chapter explores how mid-century intellectuals employed—and reinterpreted—Catholic theology to address the challenge of finding a global political expression for the emerging material and spiritual universalisms. By charting the conceptual components of the global order envisaged by Catholic intellectuals in the 1940s, I explore the interplay of moral universalism and political pluralism as the foundation of a new global democracy. Catholics considered themselves particularly equipped to contribute to the debate on the prospects of a democratic world order.

---

[1] Niebuhr, *Children of Light*, 162–166. On Niebuhr's political thought, see Andrew Preston, *Sword of the Spirit, Shield of Faith: Religion in American War and Diplomacy* (New York: Knopf, 2012); Mark T. Edwards, *The Right of the Protestant Left: God's Totalitarianism* (Basingstoke: Palgrave, 2012); David A. Hollinger, *After Cloven Tongues of Fire: Protestant Liberalism in Modern American History* (Princeton, NJ: Princeton University Press, 2013); Richard Wightman Fox, *Reinhold Niebuhr: A Biography* (New York: Pantheon Books, 1985).

They thought that theological conceptualisations of universalism and particularism lent themselves well to improve the public discussion on the tensions between local communities and the global sphere. The notion of the 'human person' could set, they argued, a solid foundation to a novel way of thinking about the place of the individual in the political world. The precepts of the Catholic faith created a moral code based on a shared notion of the 'common good' that had, for them, a universal relevance regardless of national, racial, or economic differences. In this context, Catholic thinkers saw their church as a well-ordered international community that provided not only spiritual guidance but potentially also a structural model of cooperation across borders.[2]

During and after the war, there was an 'unprecedented outburst of Catholic activity' in the public sphere.[3] It is well known that European Catholics became leaders of post-war national reconstruction, and Catholic politicians also had a significant part in shaping the European Union.[4] However, the contribution of Catholics to the evolution of mid-century international thought has been given little scholarly attention. One of the reasons may be the complicated historical relationship between Catholics and democratic politics. It is not my intention here to analyse the reaction of the Catholic Church to the rise of modern democracy. Instead, I argue that in the 1940s, the rise of totalitarian regimes in Europe challenged Catholics to rethink their attitude towards democracy on a global, not only national scale.

The ecclesiastic institutions, however, did not always provide clear guidelines on the matter. The year 1919 marked an important moment for Catholic politics when Pope Benedict XV partially reversed the Vatican's ban on participation in Italian political life. This permitted Italian Catholics to engage in elections and advance a distinct Catholic vision of democratic politics. The Catholic Church, however, did not take sides for or against

[2] On the history of Catholic internationalism in the twentieth century, see, for example, Americo Miranda, *Santa Sede e Società delle Nazioni: Benedetto XV, Pio XI e il nuovo internazionalismo cattolico* (Rome: Studium, 2013); Giuliana Chamedes, 'Cardinal Pizzardo and the Internationalization of Catholic Action', in *Gouvernement pontifical sous Pie XI*, ed. Laura Pettinaroli (Rome: École française de Rome, 2012); Carla Meneguzzi Rostagni, 'Il Vaticano e la costruzione europea (1948–1957)', in *L'Italia e la politica di potenza in Europa (1950–1960)*, ed. Ennio di Nolfo, Romain H. Rainero, and Brunello Vigezzi (Milan: Marzorati, 1992), 143–172.

[3] Udi Greenberg, *The Weimar Century: German Émigrés and the Ideological Foundations of the Cold War* (Princeton, NJ: Princeton University Press, 2015), 120.

[4] On Catholics in European politics, see Wolfram Kaiser and Helmut Wohnout, eds., *Political Catholicism in Europe 1918–45* (London: Routledge, 2004); on Catholics in Italian politics, see Guido Formigoni, *L'Italia dei cattolici: Dal Risorgimento a oggi* (Bologna: Il Mulino, 2010). More generally, on the influence of Catholic thought on European politics and Christian democracy, see Paolo Pombeni, *Il gruppo dossettiano e la fondazione della democrazia italiana (1938–1948)* (Bologna: Il Mulino, 1979); Paolo Acanfora, 'Myths and the Political Use of Religion in Christian Democratic Culture', *Journal of Modern Italian Studies* 12 (2007): 307–338; Tom Buchanan and Martin Conway, eds., *Political Catholicism in Europe, 1918–1965* (Oxford: Oxford University Press, 1996). On Catholics in European politics, see Wolfram Kaiser, *Christian Democracy and the Origins of European Union* (Cambridge: Cambridge University Press, 2007).

the European totalitarian regimes: in 1933, the Vatican condemned both Nazism and communism as hostile to Catholicism, but did not revoke its 1929 Lateran Treaty with the Italian Kingdom. Many Italian, German, and French Catholics similarly avoided criticising their governments' antidemocratic policies, and those who did voice their dissent were often forced to exile.

In the United States, these exiles shared a sentiment of frustration with Catholic leaders unwilling to oppose and resist the authoritarian regimes in Europe.[5] Catholic intellectuals like Waldemar Gurian, Jacques Maritain, Luigi Sturzo, Dietrich von Hildebrand, Yves Simon, and Paul Vignaux warned their fellow believers against allying with fascist and totalitarian regimes. Democracy, they reasoned, offered a better defence of the human person and the civil community than authoritarianism. The universal aspects of Catholic theology led some Catholic thinkers to embrace an internationalist stance and set as their political objective the replacement of the modern political system with an alternative world order. Through a critique of the state, which embodied a rejection of liberalism, communism, fascism, as well as nationalism, Catholic thinkers proposed a new scheme for democratic politics across national borders, based on a personalist communitarian order.[6]

Despite their critique of modern politics, not all Catholic internationalists proposed a conservative, reactionary alternative. Instead, some wanted to elaborate a pluralistic, democratic, and secular world order, in which Catholic theology would serve as a moral guideline for building a world community. My discussion focuses on the visions of universal community of two leading European Catholic thinkers: Luigi Sturzo and Jacques Maritain. Like other European Catholic dissidents who opposed totalitarianism and fascism in Europe, they spent the war in the United States. Before the war, both Sturzo and Maritain had already attained an important status as public intellectuals and political thinkers in Italy and France. During their sojourn in America, they dedicated their attention to the problem of democracy and world order. By comparing and contrasting their mid-century views on world order, I suggest that their common adherence to a 'pluralism of fear' did not undermine the substantial divergence between their interpretations of global democracy: while Maritain embraced a substantially conservative and subdued vision of democracy, Sturzo highlighted the social emancipatory potential of a dialectical democratic order.

---

[5] See John T. McGreevy, *Catholics and American Freedom: A History* (New York: Norton, 2003), 197.

[6] On antidemocratic Catholicism, see John Hellman, 'The Anti-Democratic Impulse in Catholicism: Jacques Maritain, Yves Simon and Charles de Gaulle during World War II', *Journal of Church and State* 33 (1991): 453–471.

Sturzo and Maritain offer two competing visions of the potential contribution of Catholicism to post-war world order. Maritain's idea of a universal pluralistic regime of human rights embodied a conservative, even reactionary position that assumed liberty could be defended only in the context of a regimented Catholic-inspired order. Sturzo, by contrast, advanced a Catholic-inspired order that grounded the political liberation of the human person in a strong commitment to parliamentary democracy in which the Catholic position would be one of many legitimate contenders for public support. If Maritain's position exemplified, to a certain extent, a 'reformulation of conservatism in the name of a vision of moral constraint',[7] Sturzo's writings embodied a sincere interest in strengthening democracy's capacity to defend liberty. Even though his attempts were not always successful, Sturzo's universalism reflected an agonistic position that accepted the constant presence of conflict and struggle in political life. For this reason, I suggest, Sturzo's writings presented an influential yet not widely accepted alternative to Maritain's viewpoint, challenging Catholics to engage in an authentic way in the pluralistic democratic order of the post-war world.

LUIGI STURZO, JACQUES MARITAIN, AND DEMOCRACY IN EXILE

Luigi Sturzo (1871–1959) was a Catholic priest, sociologist, and democratic thinker who shaped the conceptual basis of social Catholicism and Christian democracy in Italy. In 1919 he founded the Partito popolare italiano (PPI), the Italian People's Party, which he defined as 'a party for Catholics', encouraging believers to become actively involved in democratic pluralist politics.[8] During his long exile, first in London, then in New York and Florida, he shifted his interest to theoretical problems, first in international law, then in sociology.[9] His English publications, praised by G. P. Gooch, Gilbert Murray, Quincy Wright, and Miner Searle Bates, merged observations about international politics with theoretical reflections.[10] He was among the first to use the term 'totalitarian' to describe Italian fascism, and later also

[7] Samuel Moyn, *Christian Human Rights* (Philadelphia: University of Pennsylvania Press, 2015), 10.

[8] Orazio Bonaccorsi, *La laicità nel pensiero politico e giuridico di Don Luigi Sturzo* (Soveria Mannelli: Rubbettino, 2011).

[9] Gianni La Bella, *Luigi Sturzo e l'esilio negli Stati Uniti* (Brescia: Morcelliana, 1990), 14. On the English-language reception of Sturzo's sociology, see Filippo Barbano, 'Luigi Sturzo esiliato e la sociologia in America', in *Universalità e cultura nel pensiero di Luigi Sturzo: Atti del convegno internazionale di studio svoltosi presso l'Istituto Luigi Sturzo dal 28 al 30 ottobre 1999* (Soveria Mannelli: Rubbettino, 2001), 133–158.

[10] On the reception of Sturzo in London, see Giovanna Farrell-Vinay, 'The London Exile of Don Luigi Sturzo (1924–1940)', *Heythrop Journal* 45 (2004): 158–177. On his reception in the United States, see Alfred Di Lascia, 'Luigi Sturzo nella cultura degli Stati Uniti', in *Luigi Sturzo e la democrazia europea*, ed. Gabriele De Rosa (Rome: Laterza, 1990), 119–145.

bolshevism and national socialism. Totalitarian ideologies, for him, 'are and must be religions', and therefore inherently opposed to Christianity.[11] The theoretical and political battle against totalitarianism brought Sturzo and Maritain closer, as European exiles in the United States. In the interwar years, Maritain (1882–1973), a Catholic convert and neo-Thomist philosopher, was one of the world's leading Catholic intellectuals.[12] His works called for a Catholic renewal through a reappraisal of Aquinas, who, for him, provided an alternative to the enlightenment philosophical genealogy of modernity. During the 1930s, he became increasingly influential in Latin and North America, where he spent the war years lecturing in local universities. After the war, he famously participated in writing the Universal Declaration of Human Rights (1948), which incorporated his earlier ideas about the human person as the subject of inalienable rights.

Maritain and Sturzo shaped their ideas about a communitarian pluralistic order in conversation with émigré intellectuals from Italy and France, but they were also interested in taking part in American intellectual life.[13] They exchanged letters with other exponents of the transnational network of public intellectuals whom I have presented here: Borgese, Niebuhr, Aron, and Adler. Maritain became an influential interlocutor of leading public intellectuals including Robert Hutchins and Waldemar Gurian, and Sturzo's opinion on international politics was sought by the Office for Strategic Services, a US wartime intelligence agency.[14] They wrote letters, editorials, and articles for leading publications such as *Commonweal, Review of Politics, New York Times, Foreign Affairs*, and the *Catholic Worker*, commenting on world politics, the future of Europe, as well as the American involvement in the war.[15]

---

[11] Luigi Sturzo, *Italy and Fascism* (London: Faber and Gwyer, 1926); Sturzo, *Politics and Morality*, trans. Barbara Barkley Carter (London: Burns, Oates and Washbourne, 1938), later republished in Italian in *Opera Omnia* 1, 4 (Bologna: Zanichelli, 1972), 40. On Sturzo's original totalitarian theory, see Michael Schäfer, 'Luigi Sturzo as a Theorist of Totalitarianism', in *Totalitarianism and Political Religions: Concepts for the Comparison of Dictatorships*, ed. Hans Maier (London: Routledge, 2004), 22–31.

[12] McGreevy, *Catholics and American Freedom*, 189.

[13] For the correspondence of Sturzo and Maritain, see Émile Goichot, ed., *Luigi Sturzo e gli intellettuali cattolici francesi: carteggi (1925–1945)* (Soveria Mannelli: Rubbettino, 2003).

[14] Lawrence Gray, 'L'America di Roosevelt negli anni dell'esilio di Luigi Sturzo fra Jacksonville e New York: Quale America ha conosciuto?', in *Universalità e cultura nel pensiero di Luigi Sturzo*, 521–549.

[15] On Sturzo's American years, see Luigi Sturzo, *La mia battaglia da New York* (1949; repr., Rome: Edizioni di storia e letteratura, 2004); Gabriele De Rosa, *Luigi Sturzo* (Turin: UTET, 1977); Corrado Malandrino, ed., *Corrispondenza americana 1940–1944/Luigi Sturzo, Mario Einaudi* (Florence: Olschki, 1998); Corrado Malandrino, 'L'iniziativa sturziana del People and Freedom Group of America nell'esilio di Jacksonville (1940–1944)', in *Luigi Sturzo e la democrazia nella prospettiva del terzo millennio*, vol. 1, ed. Eugenio Guccione (Florence: Olschki, 2004), 193–214. On Maritain's American years, see Jean-Luc Barré, *Jacques et Raïssa Maritain: les mendiants du Ciel, biographies croisées* (Paris: Stock, 1995); Christopher Cullen and Joseph Allan Clair, eds., *Maritain and America* (Washington, DC: American Maritain Association, 2009); Gavin T. Colvert, ed., *The Renewal of Civilization: Essays in Honor of Jacques Maritain* (Washington, DC: American Maritain Association, 2010).

The exile in the United States enhanced the interaction between democracy and Catholicism in Sturzo and Maritain's thought. The admiring encounter with the American democratic culture inspired them to consider democracy as a political expression of Catholic values.[16] Sturzo had doubtlessly been a convinced democrat since the beginning of the century, but his sojourn in the United States led him to believe that the American leadership could help bring about a democratic world order that Europe had failed to realise. Like Borgese and Niebuhr, Maritain and Sturzo also assigned to the United States a role of leadership in the battle against totalitarianism and in the formation of the new democratic order. The Christian heritage of the American people guaranteed, according to the Catholic thinkers, the revival of Christian values as the foundation of a new universal community, in which every human person had the right—and duty—to participate in the realisation of the common good. Their writings highlighted the importance of the idea of the political community as a bridge between the universal and the particular aspects of political order.

During the 1940s, the Catholic thought of Sturzo and Maritain represented but a fraction of a wide range of religious ideas on world order. The focus on Maritain and Sturzo does not intend to exhaust the discussion on mid-century debates on religion and politics.[17] Rather, I shed light on two innovative and sophisticated approaches to Catholicism and world order that were embedded in larger political trends in interwar Europe and influenced democratic party politics after the war.[18] Sturzo and Maritain saw the war against totalitarianism as a window of opportunity that could allow a real transformation of the political order they had criticised so severely. Notwithstanding the clear conceptual continuity with their interwar political thought, the lived experience of European totalitarianism and world war endowed their writings with a sense of urgency, motivated by the idea that the time was ripe for the realisation of their visions.

Sturzo and Maritain saw themselves as proponents of new versions of Catholic thought, employing the intellectual sources of Catholic theology to formulate a global response to totalitarianism. They proposed, in essence, a communitarian global order based on the human person. For Maritain, personalism could provide the necessary theoretical tools to revise the Thomist dogma, which was confirmed as a fundamental part of Catholic theology

---

[16] La Bella, *Luigi Sturzo*; Florian Michel, 'L'expérience de la démocratie américaine chez Jacques Maritain', in *Penser la mondialisation avec Jacques Maritain. Enjeux et défis*, ed. Jean-Dominique Durand and René Mougel (Lyon: University of Lyon, 2013), 99–114.

[17] Many historical studies have explored the relations between Protestantism and internationalism. See, for example, Michael G. Thompson, *For God and Globe* (Ithaca, NY: Cornell University Press, 2015); Heather A. Warren, *Theologians of a New World Order: Reinhold Niebuhr and the Christian Realists, 1920–1948* (New York: Oxford University Press, 1997).

[18] For a concise overview of the ideology of Christian democracy in Europe, see Paolo Pombeni, 'The Ideology of Christian Democracy', *Journal of Political Ideologies* 5 (2000): 289–300.

since Leo XIII's encyclical *Aeterni Patris* in 1879. Maritain's personalism re-lied heavily on Thomist theology as a source of absolute knowledge of the divine and the world. Aquinas's doctrine of natural order, based for Ma-ritain on the 'unwritten law' of Ancient Greece, posited there is a pre-given divine order of things, on which human order depended.[19] By locating the individual within a complex net of social interactions, Maritain suggested that human beings were more than a 'bundle of matter', and had a unique and important—yet pre-given—function within the natural order of the universe.

The emphasis on the 'person' helped Maritain to adapt Thomism for the conceptual realm of modern democracies. The person was the sociopolitical subject of human life, an active moral agent who flourished in interaction with other members of society, but could not be subordinated to the re-quirements of the political system. Maritain, like Sturzo, distinguished—somewhat simplistically—between the atomised and independent individ-ual and the person, who was fully integrated in a web of social and political relations. They imagined the ideal global political community to allow each person to participate actively in politics and to pursue the common good.[20]

In France and Italy alike, personalism emerged as a reaction against political currents that Catholic thinkers identified as a social threat. Over the previous decade, as a student of theology and philosophy, Maritain found guidance in the writings of Henri Bergson and Aquinas on the re-lations between reason, faith, and politics. He started to write about the idea of the human person in the 1920s, when he became interested in political and social problems and associated briefly with Action Française, a French Catholic nationalist authoritarian movement. But in 1926, when Pope Pius XI condemned Action Française, Maritain officially broke off his relations with the group, rejecting the right-wing nationalistic and anti-democratic views of its charismatic leader Charles Maurras (1868–1952). Then, in 1927, after meeting the French personalist philosopher Emman-uel Mounier, Maritain found that neo-Thomist personalism provided a more politically legitimate means to criticise individualism and liberal-ism.[21] Following Maritain's involvement with Action Française, Sturzo remained ever suspicious of Maritain's commitment to democracy. Ma-ritain's personalism was, for Sturzo, a relic of his experience with the far right.[22] Only when both were in the United States did Sturzo accept that

[19] Jacques Maritain, *Distinguer pour unir: ou, les degrès du savoir* (Paris: Desclée de Brouwer, 1932), translated into English as *The Degrees of Knowledge* (London: Bles, 1937).

[20] Jacques Maritain, *The Rights of Man and Natural Law* (New York: Scribner, 1943), 5–7.

[21] On Maritain and Mounier, see Moyn, 'Personalism, Community, and the Origins of Human Rights', 85–106.

[22] Maritain discussed his personalist ideas in his book on the founding fathers of modernity, *Three Reformers: Luther, Descartes, Rousseau* (1925; repr., London: Sheed & Ward, 1929). Moyn also suggests

Maritain became more open to democratic interpretations of personalism, which brought him further away from right-wing nationalism towards the idea of pluralism and 'rights'.

In 1949, Maritain delivered the prestigious Walgreen Lecture series at the University of Chicago.[23] There, his personalist idea had acquired a distinct political function: checking the power of the totalitarian state.[24] Free social interaction was a fundamental part of human life, for Maritain, because through this process the atomised individual could develop into a person. He asserted that 'man is a political animal, which means that the human person craves political life, communal life, not only with regard to the family community but also with regard to the civil community. And the commonwealth, in so far as it deserves the name, is a society of human persons'.[25]

Maritain's lectures emphasised the person's embeddedness in different 'communities' on various sociopolitical scales, all aimed at pursuing the common good. His interpretation of the common good relied, arguably, on the Catholic assumption that there was a divine scheme, a good order of the universe, which humanity could—at least partially—both discover and aspire to.[26] While this universal scheme was external to human history, it remained, in his vision, the guiding light of a good universal human political order. The defence of personal liberty relied on accepting that each person had a role in the universal communal project, although its meaning remained external to the realm of human agency. This allowed Maritain to propose a postliberal alternative interpretation of liberty that conditioned individual self-realisation in the advancement of communal welfare. Freedom did not mean full individual autonomy, and its defence could not be grounded on a presumed right to do whatever one pleases.

As opposed to other contemporary French interpreters of Aquinas, such as Maurras and Bossuet, Maritain insisted on Aquinas's relevance to modern democratic political thought. Thomism offered, for him, an attractive alternative to the liberal rationalistic genealogy of modernity.[27] Into the ahistorical template constructed by eternal and divine natural laws Maritain poured the necessary ingredients to create a democratic world order.

---

that Maritain shaped his personalist thought before breaking with Action Française; see *Christian Human Rights*, 70–73.

[23] The lectures were later published as Jacques Maritain, *Man and the State* (Chicago: University of Chicago Press, 1951), 148.

[24] Ibid., 115.

[25] Ibid., 8.

[26] Jacques Maritain, *The Person and the Common Good* (London: Bles, 1948), 12–20. Maritain was aware of the 'misunderstandings' surrounding his position on personalism and the common good and sought in 1946 to elucidate his views on the matter.

[27] Émile Perreau-Saussine, *Catholicism and Democracy: An Essay in the History of Political Thought*, trans. Richard Rex (Princeton, NJ: Princeton University Press, 2012), 16, 110–111.

His praises for Aquinas's medieval idea of Christendom were not meant as a reactionary rejection of modernity, or a call to reestablish a bygone system (an argument he had made in some of his earlier writings).[28] Instead, when the totalitarian threat on the world's democracies became concrete, Maritain found in Aquinas's personalist and communitarian impulse the most efficient moral defence of democracy.[29]

Sturzo's trajectory towards personalism was more politically coherent than Maritain's: ever since the 1910s, he argued that the human person was the subject of democratic politics. For Sturzo, the foundation for the Catholic interpretation of democracy was shaped by practical experience, not philosophical contemplation. His practical political experience rendered Sturzo much more committed to democracy than Maritain. In 1905, after completing his seminary studies in Rome, he was elected mayor of his native Sicilian city of Caltagirone. He played a leading role in founding the Christian Democratic political movement and held significant political purchase in pre-fascist Italy, and in 1919 became the secretary of the movement's parliamentary expression, the Italian People's Party (PPI).[30] The rise of Italian extreme nationalism and fascism meant for Sturzo that the human person could flourish and thrive only in a democratic order.[31] When, in 1924, he was forced to escape fascist Italy and settle in London, Sturzo continued to propose closer interaction between Catholics and democratic politics, around the association of the People and Freedom Group.[32]

Sturzo never challenged the canonical position of Aquinas as an interpreter of Christian theology, but his own eclectic and inclusive thought could not be defined as 'Thomist'. For him, the Thomist tradition of thought was too rationalist and intellectually rigid. Despite Maritain's apparent rejection of the reactionary counterrevolutionary interpretation of Thomist political philosophy, Sturzo remained suspicious of Maritain's invocation of Aquinas as the foundation of a universal democratic order. It was only after their meeting in London in 1939 that Sturzo accepted the change in Maritain's political approach and counted him among the supporters of democracy.[33] Sturzo integrated the Thomist premises of natural law and human sociability as the theological core in a historicist approach to moral and

[28] See, for example, Jacques Maritain, *Antimoderne* (Paris: Éditions de la Revue des Jeunes, 1922).

[29] Jacques Maritain, *Christianity and Democracy* (1943; repr., London: Bles, 1945), 55–60.

[30] Formigoni, *L'Italia dei cattolici: Dal Risorgimento a oggi.*

[31] Sturzo penned an early critique in English of Italian Catholics who failed to recognise the danger of nationalism in 1941. It was later included in the volume *Nationalism and Internationalism* (New York: Roy, 1946), 1–46.

[32] On the London-based People and Freedom Group and its American followers, see Kaiser, *Christian Democracy and the Origins of European Union*, 140–144; Malandrino, 'L'iniziativa sturziana'. In London, Sturzo established a close relationship with Henry Wickham Steed. Giovanna Farrell-Vinay, ed., *Luigi Sturzo a Londra: Carteggi e documenti, 1925–1946* (Soveria Mannelli: Rubbettino, 2003).

[33] See Luigi Sturzo, 'Chiarimenti su Maritain', *Le mouvement des faits et des idées* 25 (1927); Piero Viotto, *Grandi Amicizie: i Maritain e i loro contemporanei* (Rome: Città nuova, 2008), 204–205.

political thought, which outlined dialectical relations of contrasting powers in society—such as church and state—as a powerful motor of social
change.[34] In *La Società. Sua natura e leggi*, Sturzo defined historicism as
'the systematic conception of history as a human process, which realises
itself through immanent forces united with rationality, but emerges from
and aims at an absolute transcendental goal'.[35] Divine law still grounded
Sturzo's conception of natural law and the political order of humanity
alike, but this ultimate good was not the main concern of his social and political thought. Rather, he was interested in the historical evolution of morality through the constant interaction between the person and the political society.

The historicist sociological approach allowed Sturzo to discern from the
past the lessons needed for improving the political order of the world that
could not be created by moral contemplation alone.[36] Attracted by practical
politics and not by abstract ideas, Sturzo emphasised the advantages of the
historicist method for understanding the lessons of the past and employing them to plan the future.[37] Careful students of history would know that
different, often opposing interpretations of the common good were competing for political power throughout the ages, while human social order
continued to change and evolve. As Francesco Traniello suggests, Sturzo's
interpretation of natural law and his sociological historicism were reconciled through the argument that history provided valuable lessons about
humanity because human nature was essentially unchanged.[38] However,
for Sturzo, human history also taught another lesson, about the endless
variety of human models for social and political order. None of the many
possible political models could be seen as an unchallenged, universally applicable system. Thus, democracy, like any other system of social order, was
in a permanent state of becoming.

Comparing the notion of the human person proposed by Maritain and
Sturzo reveals that Sturzo advanced a more eclectic interpretation that

[34] In the 1930s, philosophers like M. D. Chenu underlined the historical context of Aquinas's writings
as a key to understand his thought. See Marie-Dominique Chenu, *Une école de théologie: Le Saulchoir*
(Kain-les-Tournai: Étoilles, 1937).

[35] Luigi Sturzo, *La società. Sua natura e leggi* (1935), repr., *Opera Omnia* 3 (Bologna: Zanichelli, 1953),
19. Benedetto Croce, the Italian philosopher who developed the idea of 'absolute historicism', rejected
any similarities between his own ideas and the sociological historicism of Sturzo, whom he considered
a dilettante rather than a serious thinker. Sturzo accused Croce of avoiding value judgment of history,
but welcomed his—apparent—rapprochement with Christianity in his *Italy and the New World Order*,
210–211. See Marco Paolino, 'Benedetto Croce e Luigi Sturzo', in De Rosa, *Luigi Sturzo e la democrazia
europea*, 418.

[36] Sturzo, *La società. Sua natura e leggi*, 13–18.

[37] Giorgio Campanini, 'Luigi Sturzo e la laicità dello stato', in Guccione, *Luigi Sturzo e la democrazia
nella prospettiva del terzo millennio*, 709.

[38] Francesco Traniello, 'Sturzo e il problema storico della democrazia in Italia', in Guccione, *Luigi
Sturzo e la democrazia nella prospettiva del terzo millennio*, 55.

sought to mitigate the Thomist universal vision of human nature with a historicist approach to political diversity. Despite the immutability of human nature, the political, social, and economic reality of the world is in a continuing process of evolution. The personalist vision of Sturzo echoed Maritain's emphasis on the valorisation of the unique qualities of every human being, developed through social interaction. Yet, by highlighting social interaction Sturzo insisted on the need to lock any theoretical proposal into an attentive 'scientific' observation of reality and, eventually, into political action. Sociological analysis would lead to better understanding of the means to improve people's social and political reality and contribute to their development as 'persons'.

The human person was endowed by nature, for Sturzo and Maritain, with universal rights. In 1943, Maritain described human rights as the right to life, the right to personal freedom in responsibility to God and the community, the right to pursue 'the perfection of moral and rational human life', the right to private ownership of material goods, the right to marriage and family, and the right of association.[39] He proposed to tie the contemplative notion of the human person with a political idea of universal human rights grounded in the natural dignity of the human person that antedated the state and its political order.[40] In the 1940s, Maritain's notion of human rights was anchored in a specific political project: to undermine the political primacy of the modern state and thus limit the power of totalitarian regimes. The person and not the state was the subject and the source of law and rights. Thus, human rights were meant to guarantee a space for persons' social interaction and moral development, not to provide the foundation for individual emancipation or social reform.

Sturzo shared Maritain's conception of rights as a set of pre-political entitlements emerging from the person's natural dignity and uniqueness. Human rights had a social function as the building blocks of community: the complementarity of rights and duties meant that each right matched a duty that every person was obliged to comply with. The motivation to comply was not only rational, but also spiritual: fulfilling one's duties to others advanced the entire society towards the realisation of the common good. The Catholic social doctrine that Sturzo advocated throughout his political career aimed at safeguarding liberty but also at improving the social and economic living standards of the masses. This idea was evident

---

[39] Maritain, *Rights of Man and Natural Law*.

[40] Samuel Moyn has written on Maritain as one of the first proponents of the idea of human rights in 'Personalism, Community, and the Origins of Human Rights' and *Christian Human Rights*. Marco Duranti highlighted the debate between Catholics and liberals about the versatile meanings of 'human rights' in the context of the European Convention. Duranti, 'Conservatives and the European Convention on Human Rights', in *Toward a New Moral World Order. Menschenrechtspolitik und Volkerrecht seit 1945*, ed. Norbert Frei and Annette Weinke (Weimar: Wallstein Verlag, 2013), 82–93.

in his suggestion that human rights could lay the foundation for democracy if they could address the difficulties of the workers and thus provide an alternative to Marxism and socialism.[41]

Democracy based on human rights was, for Sturzo, about equality and not only about freedom. He was much more concerned than Maritain with extending human rights to the social and economic sphere, well beyond the defence of the moral and physical integrity of the person. Catholic political thought embodied a vision of social and economic rights that provided, for him, a viable alternative to socialism. The ideal realisation of Catholic thought in politics would be 'a popular government inspired by Christian principles, opposed to the Rousseauian and anticlerical ideas of the modern democracies, and a social Christian movement opposed to socialism'.[42] The Catholic 'popularist' social movement reflected for Sturzo the religious commitment for a better social, economic, and political order around the needs of the person.[43] Thus, human rights could do more than limit the power of the state and curb the rise of totalitarianism: human rights entailed a promise for social and economic reform, potentially on a global scale.

POLITICAL PLURALISM AND THE
CHALLENGE OF ORDER

In 1941, Sturzo wrote a letter to his friend Mario Einaudi about a new book on English political pluralism by Henry Meyer Magid, soon to be published in New York. Sturzo associated pluralism not only with Harold Laski's writings but also with Maritain's thought, which aimed at avoiding the theoretical premises of liberalism. He asked Einaudi if Magid's book advanced a similar thesis, and if it was interesting.[44] Sturzo's curiosity towards pluralism reflected his ambivalence about the normative value of empirical diversity. He appreciated Harold Laski's attempt to overcome the negative aspects of state sovereignty by establishing a pluralist order, but feared that as a political theory, 'pluralism' would merely be synonymous with anarchy, and avoided defining his own position as pluralist, despite a certain conceptual affinity.[45] As I show in this section, Sturzo and Maritain provided two alternative visions for political, institutional, and—to a certain extent—value

---

[41] Sturzo, *La società. Sua natura e leggi*, 3.

[42] Luigi Sturzo, 'Il Popularismo', *Politique*, 15 August 1928.

[43] For a collection of Sturzo's writings on popularism, see Luigi Sturzo, *Il Partito popolare italiano* (Rome: Istituto Luigi Sturzo, 2003). For the history of the PPI, see Gabriele De Rosa, *Il Partito Popolare Italiano* (Rome: Laterza, 1988).

[44] Sturzo to Mario Einaudi, 30 September 1941, in Malandrino, *Corrispondenza Americana*, 63; Henry Meyer Magid, *English Political Pluralism* (New York: Columbia University Press, 1941).

[45] Harold Laski, *Studies in the Problems of Sovereignty* (Oxford: Oxford University Press, 1917); Luigi Sturzo, *Politica e morale* (1938), in *Opera Omnia*, vol. 4 (Bologna: Zanichelli, 1972), 25–33. Sturzo, *La*

pluralism as the foundation of a new democratic Catholic-inspired order: while Maritain accepted political pluralism as part of a unified moral order, Sturzo embraced pluralism as the foundation for his dialectical agonism. Despite the evident divergences, both thinkers were united in their conceptions of 'pluralism of fear' as the foundation of the post-war order.

The pluralistic vision of Maritain and Sturzo emerged from their critique of the state, inherited from British pluralists like Laski and Lord Acton (a fellow Catholic).[46] Maritain was convinced that there could be a viable alternative world order to the existing system of sovereign states. Already in 1940, he argued that 'truly our times require a complete recasting of the modern idea of the State and of the relations between states'.[47] In tune with the discussions at the Chicago Committee, which I explored in chapter 6, he suggested that the concept of sovereignty, as developed by Charles Merriam and his German mentor Hugo Preuss, was philosophically and politically misconceived and should be banished from political vocabulary.[48] The world already comprised a variety of institutions and social organisations, which represented a diversity of ideas and creeds, and deserved autonomous political space.[49] Theoretical and political observations about the dangers of authoritarian regimes led him to conclude that political pluralism embodied a positive normative value in society, which the post-war world order should uphold.   *Maritain =*

The new philosophical foundation of a post-sovereign pluralist order would, for Maritain, recognise the distinction between the state—a set of institutions and organisations—and the body politic—the perfect political society. The state was contingent and functional, while the body politic embodied the moral ethos of a civil society oriented towards the common good, unbounded by national or geographical borders. The state could not enjoy absolute sovereignty, because it represented only a part of a larger and morally superior society, the body politic. The body politic provided Maritain with conceptual tools to fight the battle against totalitarian regimes that, he argued, wrongly assumed that the state could have the final word in all human affairs. In fact, he opined, the state could manage political affairs using the limited power given to it by the people who are part of the body politic. Nonetheless, he did not dwell upon the institutional

---

società. Sua natura e leggi, 224; Filippo Barbano, Pluralismo, un lessico per la democrazia (Turin: Bollati Boringhieri, 1999), 35–43.

[46] On British pluralists, see Jacob T. Levy, 'From Liberal Constitutionalism to Pluralism', in Bevir, Modern Pluralism, 21–40; Nicholls, Pluralist State.

[47] Jacques Maritain, 'Europe and the Federal Idea', Commonweal, 19 April 1940.

[48] Maritain, Man and the State.

[49] For Maritain's early pluralist position, see Humanisme integral (Paris: F. Aubier, 1936); for his account of his American experience, see Jacques Maritain, Réflexions sur l'Amérique (1958), repr. in Œuvres complètes, vol. 10 (Fribourg: Éditions universitaires, 1985); Florian Michel, 'Jacques Maritain en Amérique du Nord', Cahiers Jacques Maritain 45 (2002): 26–86.

dimension of the body politic, which emerged from his writings as a global formless civil society without any particular obligation to democracy.

Sturzo was similarly critical of the state's pretences to absolute sovereignty. He was, however, less interested in attacking the philosophical foundation of sovereignty than in outlining a new structure that could be politically acceptable in the world of his times. The solution would have to address moral and political deficiencies, as well as economic inequalities across national borders.[50] The establishment of a new and better universal order demanded, for Sturzo, that the states would give up part of their sovereignty in favour of a pluralist secular democratic global organisation inspired by Catholic values, allowing space for the positive dialectical confrontation of opposed elements.[51]

Pluralism was a useful political weapon not only against totalitarian states but also against liberal democracies that, for Maritain and Sturzo, had failed to deliver on their promise to safeguard the autonomy of persons and communities from the destructive power of the state. Sturzo identified in liberal democracies the same 'irrationality' that characterised the totalitarian approach towards the person in society. He challenged the idea that liberal democracies could mediate between the particular qualities of the person and the universal need for political order. While advocating individual liberty, the liberal democracies prioritised the centralised state over other communal associations in which individuals freely united. The crisis of democracy could not be resolved by individualistic rationalism or by a totalitarian centralised state. The only solution was to give political space to the plurality of communities and associations that human persons chose to create. Sturzo and Maritain's interpretations of liberalism might have been misguided, but they help explain why political pluralism became such a central part of their international thought. Pluralism was a framework for the encouragement of social associations, which were essential for the moral development of the human person and could form the foundation of a universal community. Thus, pluralism was a form of order, rather than a theoretical acceptance of international anarchy.

Deeply indebted to Thomist ideas, Maritain's commitment to pluralism remains limited to the political and social arenas, where he endorsed a range of institutions, political structures, and social associations as an expression of humanity's natural diversity. By reclaiming political authority from the state, the pluralist order had the important advantage of allowing all individuals to pursue their own idea of the truth. Pluralism could not, however, obfuscate the fact that for Maritain only one truth

---

[50] Luigi Sturzo, 'Economia del dopoguerra' (1940), in *Miscellanea londinese. Anni 1937–1940* (Soveria Mannelli: Rubbettino, 2008), 337–339.

[51] Sturzo, *Italy and the New World Order*, 247.

was valid. He acknowledged the multiplicity of religious creeds in the world, but argued that only one was ethically and philosophically correct: Catholicism.

The universal and absolute veracity of Christianity—and especially Catholicism—was an insuperable part of Maritain's political thought. Since religion represented a transcendental unity that could not be divided into a plurality of forms, his pluralism proposed to 'distinguish in order to unite'. He accepted diversity in human society only as a means to promote a greater unity of mankind around the idea of the common good. Therefore, his pluralism did not endow each position with an equal value, but tolerated diversity as a necessary evil without relinquishing Christianity's exclusively valid interpretation of the truth. The political and religious spheres were distinct, because 'like philosophy, the political order has its own proper specifications. But like philosophy, it can receive influence from Christianity and thus be under Christian existential conditions'.[52] Maritain's pluralism rested on the assumption that the political order is separated from—but subordinated to—the ethical order. The two spheres also operate according to different principles: the political order should be pluralistic, the moral one should express a high degree of unity.

Maritain diverged significantly from Richard McKeon's pluralism, which insisted that each philosophical position held a potential for attaining the truth.[53] McKeon would not deny the existence of the supreme truth, but he definitely did not identify it with Christianity, Catholicism, or any other particular position. His semantic philosophical apparatus aimed at discovering the various expressions of the truth, which were no less important for him than truth itself. McKeon, like Sturzo, must have found Maritain's neo-Thomism a significant limit for his commitment to democracy and political pluralism. Despite Maritain's emphasis on the ethical value of human diversity, expressed in the infinite variety of human personalities, his notion of political order was still anchored in a theologically dogmatic universalism.

This theoretical disagreement had practical implications for Maritain's personal life. In 1940, Hutchins tried to secure him a position as a visiting scholar at the philosophy department at the university, but the department turned down his application three times. The head of the department, Charner Perry, wrote to McKeon that 'Professor Maritain's reputation in this part of the world is largely that of an apologist or propagandist for Catholic doctrine'.[54] Thomism embodied, he explained, a support for

---

[52] Ibid., 296.

[53] See chapter 6.

[54] Charner Perry to Richard McKeon, 30 July 1940, quoted in John McGreevy, 'Catholics, Catholicism and the Humanities since World War II', in *The Humanities and the Dynamics of Inclusion since World War II*, ed. David A. Hollinger (Baltimore: Johns Hopkins University Press, 2006), 198, 212n70. The perceived

Catholic authoritarianism. He associated Maritain's neo-Thomism with Mortimer Adler's medieval philosophy and conservative agenda, which he, like other members of the department, resented on political and intellectual grounds.[55] Neo-Thomism was perceived as a conservative attack on liberty in society and academe alike. Despite his own interest in Aquinas, McKeon admitted that he shared the philosophers' view 'at least of questioning the propriety of the indefinite association of Maritain with the university'.[56]

On one point, however, McKeon, Maritain and Sturzo were in full agreement: people of different creeds and philosophical convictions could join forces and work together if they shared a common political aim. The practice of political interaction had, for them, the power to reinforce unity even on a world scale. The UNESCO bill of human rights was an exemplary case of a universal project based on shared political aims and not on common ideology or philosophy.[57] This position represents a certain continuity with McKeon's earlier pragmatism, and embodies another step away from Maritain's early Thomism. In their discussions at UNESCO, the political sphere emerges as an arena of debate in which potential agreement can overcome differences. Politics is a process of mediation of particular interests and the universal good. Yet the emphasis remains on the positive value of universality: both Maritain and McKeon argued that the possibility of collective action depended, ultimately, on recognising the political force of unity, rather than on valorising pluralism and diversity.

Sturzo similarly drew on his political experience to argue that practical politics could help bridge over theoretical and ideological divides. Yet he offered a different solution to the problem of political pluralism and universality: a dialectical mediation. He recognised that the world was characterised by a variety of worldviews, cultures, and philosophies, but feared that these might create an anarchic multitude. Wary of the term 'pluralism', he used 'plurality' to describe the existing multiplicity of social relations of each person in society, and 'plutarchy' to denote a disordered, anarchical

---

antipathy towards Catholics at the University of Chicago is confirmed in the correspondence of Jerome G. Kerwin, professor of political science, and Giuseppe Antonio Borgese in 1940. Interestingly, while Kerwin was in favour of inviting Luigi Sturzo to lecture at the university, Borgese thought that the 'orthodox Catholic' Sturzo should be juxtaposed with another, non-orthodox interpreter of Catholicism, like the historian Gaetano Salvemini. In 1941, Borgese explained his misgivings, referring to Adler's 'attempt to monopolise the University for a medievalistic [sic] attitude'. See Kerwin-Borgese correspondence in the archive of the Istituto Sturzo, Rome.

[55] On the tensions between Hutchins, Adler, and the faculty at Chicago, see Dzuback, *Robert M. Hutchins*, chap. 9.

[56] McKeon to Hutchins, 3 October 1940, quoted in Thomas, 'Enlightenment and Authority', 399.

[57] Maritain, *Man and the State*, 109; Maritain, *Human Rights, Comments and Interpretations. A Symposium Edited by UNESCO with an Introduction by Jacques Maritain* (New York: Columbia University Press, 1949).

society with multiple centres of power.[58] He accepted the descriptive power of 'plurality', but considered 'plutarchy' normatively undesirable.[59]

Without committing his thought to normative 'pluralism', Sturzo's political thought advanced a form of pluralism de facto, which attacked the idea of the absolute power of the state from moral and social perspectives. He agreed with Laski that the state was only one association among many, competing for support and legitimacy. Yet unlike Maritain he espoused his pluralist vision with a strong support for parliamentary democracy. Therefore, as Giorgio Campanini suggests, he advanced a pluralism of social forms aimed at undoing state monism through the division of its powers across organisations in civil society and a range of distinctly democratic institutions, including political parties.[60] Political parties had a major role in mediating conflict between different factions of society. The organisational capacity of civil society expressed its inherent autonomy and its ability to create alternative sites of political power untouched by the centralised state and legitimated by popular support.

The conception of the role of conflict in pluralist politics is an important point of disagreement between Sturzo and Maritain. I define Sturzo's approach to politics as 'agonistic' to suggest that for him political ideas and decisions emerged through a process of dialectic confrontation between different parts of society. Persons, parties, associations, and societies interacted in world-spanning dialectical dynamics that set the foundation for a durable order, that had no temporal solution in form of a Hegelian synthesis (the final resolution of Sturzo's dialectic would be divine, and for this reason beyond the reach of human understanding).[61] Each of the contending powers, such as the state and the church, maintained its autonomy through the conflict. The concrete reality of life was, for Sturzo, an ongoing encounter of differences. The existence of a plurality of power centres in society was not sufficient to generate political energy; only the encounter between opposites could bring about social progress.

Sturzo rejected therefore Maritain's soft form of pluralistic toleration that concealed a predetermined notion of natural order. Instead of a 'New Christendom' guised as a pluralist order, Sturzo suggested that the democratic distribution of political power between various associations, representing different cultural, geographical, and political interests, would provide a better foundation for a universal order.[62] His pluralism emerged from an agonistic position: even a peaceful order necessitated a degree of

---

[58] Sturzo, *La società. Sua natura e leggi*, 236.

[59] Barbano, 'Luigi Sturzo esiliato e la sociologia in America', 149.

[60] Giorgio Campanini, *Il pensiero politico di Luigi Sturzo* (Caltanissetta: Salvatore Sciascia Editore, 2001), 131.

[61] Sturzo, *La società. Sua natura e leggi*, 224–247.

[62] Sturzo, *Italy and the New World Order*, chap. 11.

conflict to maintain its dynamism and social energy. The challenge was to employ the democratic, pluralist institutions to mediate and channel the conflict towards positive outcomes.

MARITAIN, STURZO, AND ARON PROPOSE FEDERALISM AGAINST MACHIAVELLIANISM

Maritain's vision for the political future of Europe was embedded in his notion of morality in politics. In his 1940 essay on European federalism, he asserted that 'first of all and above all else, the peoples of Europe, all the peoples of Europe, must understand that if a federal Europe is to be born, and if it is to be viable, politics must be intrinsically bound to ethics, and that a good politics is a just and humane politics, and that without political justice there can be neither peace nor liberty nor honor among nations. This is to say that the nations must definitely renounce the principles of Machiavelli and the dogmas of that realpolitik which have poisoned modern history'.[63] Serge Audier argues that thinking with Machiavelli allowed many mid-century thinkers, including Maritain, Sturzo, and others, to do more than merely attack the immorality of the totalitarian regimes: the reference to Machiavelli as an archetypal approach to politics stimulated a discussion on the role of morality in building a new political order.[64] Their reception of Machiavelli's ideas was not particularly original or insightful: they used the Florentine writer, and especially *The Prince*, as a stalking horse for their own moralising arguments about international politics.[65] Maritain's idea of a federation emerged from his concern about the moral qualities of political life. The rise of immoral Machiavellian politics could be contained by a distinctly moral political form, a federation of states united for the common good.

Federal proposals featured in Maritain's writings throughout the decade, although he was aware of the practical and political difficulties facing the federalist project. In 1940, he advocated for a federal solution in Europe, but doubted that federalism would be a viable political structure on a larger geopolitical scale, and criticised those who thought that after the war 'the entire planet could enter into a federal regime which would forever guarantee universal peace'.[66] Like Raymond Aron and Lionel Robbins, Maritain

[63] Jacques Maritain, 'Europe and the Federal Idea II', *Commonweal*, 26 April 1940, 11.

[64] René Avord (Raymond Aron), 'Jacques Maritain et la querelle de Machiavel', *La France libre*, July 1943, reprint in *Chroniques de guerre*; Raymond Aron, 'Sur le machiavélisme, dialogue avec Jacques Maritain', *Commentaire* 8 (1985); Serge Audier, *Machiavel: Conflit et liberté* (Paris: Vrin-EHESS, 2005), 72.

[65] In his 1950s lectures at the LSE, Martin Wight famously emphasised the paradigmatic role of Machiavelli in international relations theory. See Martin Wight, *Four Seminal Thinkers in International Theory: Machiavelli, Grotius, Kant, and Mazzini* (Oxford: Oxford University Press, 2005).

[66] Maritain, 'Europe and the Federal Idea', 545.

thought that federalism demanded a high degree of cultural homogene-ity, as well as a collective political awareness.[67] Economic interdependence was, as Robbins suggested, a necessary but insufficient condition for federa-tion. Common history and a shared idea of the common good were required in order to uphold the political unity of states. Maritain argued that Europe was the only world region with a concrete potential for federation: its com-plex history of wars united the continent in a common past, albeit not a peaceful one, and provided a common idea of the good as a stable, long-lasting peace.

The major unifying factor in European history was, for Maritain, its Chris-tian heritage.[68] Despite the long history of wars of religion that marked Eu-rope's past, and the privileged position endowed to one confessional strand—Catholicism—Maritain still considered religion a shared patrimony of the European civilisation.[69] Christianity could become an important unifying element for the construction of a new democratic and pluralistic order in Europe, guaranteeing freedom of transnational cultural associations across state borders. The European integration project was outlined in messianic terms, as 'a new Christendom'.[70] The central place that religion occupied in the European collective identity raised, however, a serious doubt about the possibility of extending the federal order beyond the continent. While Maritain thought that people of different religions and 'civilisations' could agree on practical issues and unite in a pluralist world order, he doubted that there was a sufficient political, cultural, and historical similarity to support the realisation of a world federation.

Nevertheless, after the war, Maritain opened up to the potential benefits of visions of a new universal—not only European—order. In March 1947, he travelled to Mexico City to participate at the second session of the gen-eral conference of UNESCO. As the head of the French delegation, he gave a speech before the assembly, referring to the Chicago World Constitution Draft as 'the best among many plans of international organisation which are being elaborated today, and the most comprehensive and well-balanced ideal pattern that outstanding political scientists could work out in order to exasperate the self-styled realists, and to prod the thought and meditation of men of good will'.[71] He was personally acquainted with the constitution's

[67] For discussions of the ideas of Raymond Aron and Lionel Robbins, see chapters 2 and 5, respectively.

[68] For a parallel discussion on the benefits of federalism to the establishment of Christendom, see Philip M. Coupland, *Britannia, Europa and Christendom: British Christians and European Integration* (Basing-stoke: Palgrave Macmillan, 2006).

[69] Judaism belonged, in this context, to the same civilisational tradition as Christianity. See John Connelly, *From Enemy to Brother: The Revolution in Catholic Teaching on the Jews, 1933–1965* (Cambridge, MA: Harvard University Press, 2012).

[70] Maritain, 'Europe and the Federal Idea II', 11.

[71] Jacques Maritain, *La Voie de la paix* (1947), reprint in Jacques Maritain, *Œuvres complètes*, vol. 9 (Fribourg: Editions Universitaires, 1991), 143–164. Albert Guérard reported from the UNESCO conference

drafters Borgese, McKeon, Hutchins, and Adler, but was not involved in the committee's deliberations. He found that the constitution reflected many of the ideas he had advocated since the outbreak of the war: the dignity of the human person, the juxtaposition of reason with faith as the foundation of political order, and the distribution of power across a range of institutions based on but not limited to the state. Most importantly, the document included a commitment to the rights and duties of man, in line with his interpretation of Catholic thought. Maritain was not fully confident in the feasibility of the world federation project, but still saw it as an important road map for an improved future order.

The reference to Machiavelli in Maritain's writings about federal Europe emphasises the close intellectual link between his communitarian pluralist vision of world order and his argument about the need to infuse politics with moral values inspired by Catholicism. On 26 September 1941, a few months before the attack on Pearl Harbor and the US entry into the war, he delivered a lecture at the symposium on 'The Place of Ethics in Social Science' to celebrate the fiftieth anniversary of the University of Chicago. The other speakers were Hutchins, R. H. Tawney, and Charles McIlwain. The lecture, 'The End of Machiavellianism', was later published in Waldemar Gurian's *The Review of Politics*.[72] In his lecture, Maritain discussed the historical experience of totalitarianism as a modern form of Machiavellian politics. To win over the totalitarian regimes, democracies should engage in a different kind of politics, rather than adopt a benign, weaker form of Machiavellianism. 'If for the time being absolute Machiavellianism is to be crushed, and I hope so, it will only be because what remains of Christian civilization will have been able to oppose it with the principle of political justice integrally recognized, and to proclaim to the world the very end of Machiavellianism'.[73]

Justice clearly stands in the centre of Maritain's conception of good politics. His idea of political justice relies heavily on his communitarian interpretation of the Thomist notion of the 'common good'. He explained that 'common good is at once material, intellectual and moral, and principally moral, as man himself is; it is a common good of human persons. Therefore, it is not only something useful, an ensemble of advantages and profits, it is essentially something good in itself,—what the Ancients termed *bonum honestum*. Justice and civic friendship are its cement'.[74] Federation embodied an inherently moral decision: the preference for the common good over particular national interests.

---

to the Chicago Committee members in a letter dated 7 November 1947, providing an English translation of Maritain's speech. See CFWC, box 36. For Maritain's comments on the constitution, see chapter 6.
[72] Jacques Maritain, 'The End of Machiavellianism', *Review of Politics* 4 (1942): 1–33.
[73] Ibid., 31.
[74] Ibid., 10.

The common good served as an important motivation for Sturzo's support of federalism as well. Yet he approached this concept from a political, not just moral, angle. His agonistic reflection on the nature of political conflict led him to support federalism as the optimal political solution for preserving the freedom of small states. In a wartime article on geopolitics, he criticised the political logic of geopolitical visions of world order, which focused on the interests of large states in disregard for the rights of small states.[75] But he did not propose to uphold the pre-war status quo, which created a world system of small states and large empires tied together by treaties. Instead, he joined those who considered regional federations a more solid basis for a new world order.[76] When discussing the prospects of European federation, he considered Great Britain and Russia as indispensable parts of the new polity, for historical and geopolitical reasons alike.[77] The motivations to federate included war prevention, but also, and more importantly, the construction of an adequate political framework for safeguarding justice and freedom. By uniting in federations, smaller states could uphold their common interests without capitulating to stronger states or compromising their cultural and political particularity.

Maritain and Sturzo proposed two different visions of the 'post-Machiavellian' age. Despite apparent similarities—the emphasis on the human person, pluralistic federalism, and communitarian solidarity—their views diverged on the role of conflict in the universal order. Maritain's call for 'the end of Machiavellianism' reflected his assumption that the post-war era should bring about a new moral attitude to politics based on universal accord. He hoped that the Western democracies would embrace the idea of the 'common good' as their guiding ethos for creating, after their victory on totalitarianism, a peaceful, federal universal order. Maritain's predictions about the post-war order embodied a sense of finality. The democratic victory could potentially end the practices of immoral politics, but for Maritain the real achievement would be to overcome the antinomies of politics and establish a universal moral order where agreement could be reached across different political philosophies and opinions.

The idea of a federation could not be understood in separation from the concept of the 'common good', which was, for Sturzo and Maritain, the end of political order and an indispensable part of their communitarian ethos of solidarity and pluralism. They evidently rejected the pursuit of power or glory as legitimate ends of political rule. Sturzo argued that 'we should give the word "politics" its highest significance: participating in governing a country towards the common good. As such, the end of all political

---

[75] Luigi Sturzo, '"Geopolitik" e "realipolitik" contro i piccoli stati', *Il Mondo*, June 1942, reprint in *La mia battaglia da New York*, 64–68.

[76] For a discussion of regional federalism, see chapter 5.

[77] Sturzo, *Italy and the New World Order*, 240–245.

activity is the advantage of the state, considered as the common good. In this sense, politics should be part of the moral order, because looking for the common good with the appropriate means is surely a moral goal'.[78] The common good had a deeper meaning then mere utilitarian benefit: it became, for him, the appropriate aim for a moral person. The pursuit of the moral good of the political community is a crucial part of the process of so-cialisation that makes an individual a person. Negating the moral aspects of politics necessarily means robbing the individual of the opportunity to become a person, an active part of a universal community.

Sturzo, like Maritain, denounced Machiavelli as a precursor of totali-tarian politics. Nonetheless, he suggested that Machiavellianism had one theoretical merit: highlighting the place of conflict in politics. Politics was about temporal, human, and historical relations, characterised by diver-sity and disagreement. The antinomies of politics—democracy and oligar-chy, church and state, universalism and particularism, liberty and order—represented the insuperable and eternal tension between two different political powers.[79] Sturzo acknowledged the effectiveness of Machiavel-lian politics in preserving the political energies of conflict in society, but hoped that by leading a moral and Christian life, each individual could help channel these energies towards a temporary equilibrium. Federal and communitarian democracy played, for him, an important part in forming the institutions and the practices that could mediate and transform politi-cal conflict into a constructive element in the universal world order.

Sturzo's views on political conflict resemble the ideas proposed by an-other mid-century European intellectual, Raymond Aron. I return to Aron's thought, which I explored in more detail in chapter 2, because in the early 1940s he engaged in debate with Maritain on the theme of Machiavellian-ism. Interestingly, Aron's interpretation of politics as a sphere of perpetual conflict resonated with Sturzo's agonism. But, more importantly, Aron's critique of politics in morality sheds light on the limitations of the Catho-lic approach to world order advanced by Sturzo and Maritain.

In 1942, Maritain's essay on Machiavelli attracted the attention of Aron, who had already explored Machiavellianism in a series of four essays written between 1938 and 1940 and in an article in the very first issue of *La France libre*.[80] He agreed with Maritain that 'modern Machiavellianism' reconfigured the state according to the 'doctrine of the modern tyranny', a system of government by terror and trickery based on a set of ideas and acts associated with the original author but transcending his historical

---

[78] Sturzo, *Politica e morale*, 61 (my translation).

[79] Ibid.; Luigi Barbieri, *Persona, Chiesa e Stato nel pensiero di Luigi Sturzo* (Soveria Mannelli: Rubbet-tino, 2002), 72.

[80] On Aron and his political philosophy in the 1940s, see chapter 2. The four essays were later pub-lished in a collection of essays on Machiavellianism, in Raymond Aron, *Machiavel et les tyrannies modernes*, ed. Rémy Freymond (Paris: Éditions de Fallois, 1993).

heritage.[81] While accepting many of the basic premises of Maritain's article—the need for moral politics, the importance of just leadership, and the possibility of shared human interests—Aron opined that morality could not exclude conflict from the realm of politics. But unlike Sturzo, he refused to accept that any idea of the common good—including pluralistic democracy or Catholic morality—could become a stable foundation for a peaceful world order.[82]

As I argued in chapter 2, for Aron no pre-political moral principle, like natural law, could unify humanity and transcend all political differences. Rather, he suggested that a new myth of Europe should be *invented* to create the foundation of a unified European identity. If a European myth was possible—Aron remained sceptical—it was because concrete historical relations between the European states created some contingent cultural affinities between their individual citizens. But a world order that demanded all states and peoples to align with a universal morality of the common good was dangerously naïve. Ultimately, he reasoned, politics should not be subjugated to morality, but should remain a distinct and independent sphere of human activity, in which religion played a secular, non-transcendental part.[83]

In a non-ideal world, Aron argued, the essence of good politics was *legitimacy* and not morality. Often, legitimacy depended on the mutual compatibility of the moral and religious standards of the leaders, the state, and the people. But the debate around legitimacy remained fundamentally political not moral. Aron's arguments underlined the historical, contingent, and temporal foundation of politics, in which religious and moral concerns were but one part of a more complex picture. Politics was a quest for effective and legitimate political power to establish stable government within the polity and overcome political and military conflicts beyond the state. If a global community could be realised, it would be based on a political decision, not on Christian morality.

GLOBAL DEMOCRACY AND CATHOLIC MORALITY

The universality of human nature implied, for Sturzo and Maritain, that the precepts of morality should also be universal. The natural and voluntary character of social interaction was not restricted to any particular

---

[81] Aron and Maritain's attention to Machiavellianism resembles the well-known thesis advanced in Friedrich Meinecke's study of Machiavellianism and reason of state, *Die Idee der Staatsräson in der Neueren Geschichte* (Munich: Oldenbourg, 1924); Raymond Aron, 'Le Machiavélisme, doctrine des tyrannies modernes', in *L'homme contre les tyrans*, republished in *Chroniques de guerre*, 417–426; Maritain, 'End of Machiavellianism', 327n1.

[82] Audier, *Machiavel*, 114.

[83] On Aron's concept of secular religions, see Stewart, 'Raymond Aron', 89–96.

community; it was certainly not limited to Christians. But Christians, and especially Catholics, were particularly skilful at social interaction across borders, and therefore could lead the construction of a global community with distinct political institutions.[84]

The main challenge remained defining the desired political nature of social interaction. Surely, not any kind of societal relations would lead to the creation of a new—and better—world order. In this context, 'democracy' became a fundamentally important idea. Sturzo sought to convince his English-speaking readers that Catholicism and democracy were not only compatible but mutually empowering. Only a democratic political order could guarantee to Catholics—and to any other religious or cultural minorities—the liberty to live according to their creed. Maritain argued that people of all philosophical positions and religions could join a democratic polity if they agreed on the importance of truth, intelligence, human dignity, freedom, brotherly love, and the absolute value of moral good.[85] Yet it is around the idea of democracy that the differences between the world visions of Maritain and Sturzo receive the clearest expression: Sturzo insisted that democracy should be understood as a popular government based on parliamentary institutions, while Maritain remained attached to an abstract, moral view of democracy that had no immediate or necessary institutional expression.

Democracy became a weapon in the battle against totalitarianism for the salvation of Western civilisation. By insisting that the foundational values of democracy should be Catholic—and more specifically Thomist—Maritain effectively emptied the democratic polity of substance.[86] In 1941, he participated in writing the *Manifesto on the War*, an initiative of forty-three European Catholics in the United States aimed at castigating the totalitarian European regimes and developing a personalist vision of a post-war world democracy.[87] The manifesto expressed the Catholic commitment to fight totalitarian regimes—Nazism, fascism, and importantly also communism—in the name of Western values of democracy and human rights. When Maritain asked Sturzo to add his signature to the document, the Italian priest was less than keen. The manifesto, he argued, was too critical of the individualist liberal democracies, while remaining silent about the fascist connections of the Catholic Church.[88] The Catholic commitment to social democracy,

---

[84] Alessandro Fruci, *La comunità internazionale nel pensiero politico di Luigi Sturzo* (Rome: Aracne, 2009), 140.

[85] Jacques Maritain, 'The Pluralist Principle in Democracy', *Nation*, 21 April 1945.

[86] James Chappel, 'Slaying the Leviathan: Catholicism and the Rebirth of European Conservatism, 1920–1950' (PhD dissertation, Columbia University, 2012), 342.

[87] 'In the Face of the World's Crisis: A Manifesto by European Catholics Sojourning in America', *Commonweal*, 12 August 1942, 415–421. See also Greenberg, *Weimar Century*, 148–149.

[88] Sturzo to Maritain, 6 March 1942, in Goichot, *Luigi Sturzo e gli intellettuali cattolici francesi*, 426–427.

which he sought to advance throughout his career, was never mentioned. Democracy was, for the authors of the manifesto, not a valuable political goal but a rhetorical tool in the Catholic battle against formidable enemies.

From a personal perspective, Sturzo thought that leading a Catholic life was the only path to salvation. He followed the Catholic rites with scrupulous dedication because he thought they embodied an eternal truth. Yet leading a Catholic *political* life was another matter. In politics, there was no universal moral dogma, but a wide spectrum of legitimate opinions. Parliamentary democracy was the only political system suitable for Catholics, and for everyone else, because it channelled political conflict towards constructive policy making. In 1946, Sturzo insisted that it was wrong to believe that 'there was a dogmatic (?) impossibility for Catholics to be democratic', because in fact democracy offered the only defence for minority rights, personal dignity, and pluralism, three fundamental elements of Catholic doctrine.[89] This idea was a central part of Sturzo's contribution to popularism, an Italian Catholic social movement that underlined the political and moral values of improving the social and economic conditions of the masses. At the court of Pope Pius XII, where Maritain served as an appreciated and inspirational ambassador, Sturzo was almost a persona non grata. The emphasis on parliamentary democracy and on social economic reforms excluded him from the sphere of political influence. While Sturzo respected the ecclesiastic hierarchy in confessional and moral matters, he rejected its primacy in political issues and opposed the unmediated intervention of the Church in political debate.

It was easier for Maritain to reconcile his views about the human person with a conservative stance on democracy because the moralisation of politics implied that papal direct intervention in politics was possible and even desirable. While insisting that the nascent world order would be pluralistic and secular, he was less persuaded than Sturzo about the importance of democracy, and about the people's right to participate as active political agents. Democracy was a spiritual ideal, not a political system. Democracy was about the political and social life of a community of free people, not about a particular government, or a particular political form. For Maritain, a monarchic regime could also be democratic, if it followed the spiritual democratic ethos.[90] Democracy meant evangelic inspiration, not institutions or popular participation.

In the 1942 manifesto, the rejection of the institutional interpretation of democracy was explained as a pluralistic stance that accepted the right of each society to define its own political regime, without following any existing democratic model. Yet Sturzo remained unconvinced. Taking a

---

[89] Sturzo, *Nationalism and Internationalism*, 71.
[90] 'In the Face of the World's Crisis'; Maritain, *Christianity and Democracy*.

historicist approach, he agreed that no existing democratic model could claim absolute superiority over other alternative proposals.[91] Each democratic state had its advantages and flaws. His solution was not to undermine the importance of parliamentary democracy, as the manifesto suggested, but to sketch an open-ended vision of democratic order based on agonistic interaction and pluralist institutional decentralisation. He defined democracy as the inalienable right of people to govern themselves in full autonomy and listed a set of rights that constituted the foundation of a democratic regime: equality before the law, right to life, right to property, and habeas corpus. The positive value of democracy was liberty, safeguarded by active popular participation in politics. The absence of privilege and the equality of rights for all citizens were also distinct qualities of a democratic regime. His longtime vision of a political—and economic—democracy became in the 1940s a universal notion of world order.[92]

The integrity of the democratic state demanded a strong popular commitment. Here, the Catholic moral ethos entered into play as the motivational element grounding the popular legitimacy for democratic constitutions.[93] Unlike Maritain, Sturzo thought that the contribution of Catholicism to democracy extended beyond the spiritual realm to the practical sphere. In 1946, he wrote that the French theory of personalism was important because it inspired Christians to embed their social thought in democratic theory.[94] But he did not think that abstract ideas about personalism and pluralism should exhaust the Catholic role in the post-war democratic order. The concrete role of Catholicism was exemplified by the Social Catholic and Christian Democratic movements in Europe and the United States that paved the way for the Catholic masses to take an active stance on politics and embrace the principles of democracy in practice. It is through concrete action in political parties, religious associations, and social organisations that Catholic democracy could shape the form of the post-war world. The historicist understanding of the changing dynamics between the church and the state complicated the simple 'recipe' for a global Catholic democratic order that assumes both concepts were fixed and unchanging.[95] Sturzo's democratic vision was separate from, and at times opposed to, the

---

[91] Nonetheless, in the Italian constitutional referendum of 1946, Sturzo favoured republicanism over the preservation of the monarchy. This position was largely in opposition to the Vatican's preference, as emerged from Sturzo's correspondence with Alcide De Gasperi, leader of the Christian Democratic Party. See Luigi Sturzo and Alcide De Gasperi, *Luigi Sturzo e Alcide De Gasperi, Carteggio (1920–1953)* (Soveria Mannelli: Rubbettino, 2006), 112–120.

[92] Sturzo, *Nationalism and Internationalism*, 300–327.

[93] Traniello, 'Sturzo e il problema storico della democrazia in Italia', 61.

[94] Sturzo, *Nationalism and Internationalism*, 320.

[95] Ibid., 306–328. For a critique of the 'essentialist' interpretation of the interplay between democracy and Christianity, see James Chappel, 'Beyond Tocqueville: A Plea to Stop "Taking Religion Seriously"', *Modern Intellectual History* 10 (2013): 697–708.

ecclesiastic hierarchy that accepted only its own social movements as legitimate contributors to human emancipation and political change.

The theoretical contribution of Catholic faith was for Sturzo its worldmaking power to connect the particular and the universal. He discussed the 'international community' as a global hub of social interaction with potential for political change. Its slow-paced formation depended not on a single authoritative decision of specific states, but on the spontaneous and continuous interaction of millions of persons around the world. Thus, Sturzo's future world community would be global, not international. It would not be a mere reflection of its member states, but have its own moral-political personality, shaped through the actions and thoughts of the persons who compose it. If, as Sturzo diagnosed, the crisis of democracy was caused by atomising and alienating individualism that broke the social cohesion between people, then the solution could be to build an international community through global democratic interaction.[96]

The 'international community' that Sturzo envisaged resembled Maritain's 'body politic' as a sphere of faith in universal values, but operated through a dialectic that did not seek to transform political contradictions into unity. The multiple sources of democratic social interaction between, across, and above states led Sturzo to favour a plurality of locations of political power, each with its own limited autonomy and authority. In one of his most famous publications, an interwar treatise on international law, he argued that private international relations could create collective organisations that would serve as the foundation of international institutions.[97] In the 1940s, this idea, he suggested, acquired a concrete possibility of realisation. Despite his perceptive observations of power politics, Sturzo did not construct a clear blueprint for translating the moral and emotional sense of global interdependence into an institutional democratic scheme: he contended with suggesting that the shedding off of national prejudices would take education, time, and practice.[98] Unlike Maritain he doubted that the will to resolve disputes through political practice could suffice to overcome conflicts. Faithful to his dialectic worldview, he envisaged the foundation

[96] Sturzo, *Nationalism and Internationalism*, 236.

[97] Luigi Sturzo, *The International Community and the Right of War*, trans. Barbara Barclay Carter (London: Unwin, 1929), 20–41; Fruci, *La comunità internazionale*. For the reception of this work, see Mario D'Addio, 'Democrazia e comunità internazionale in Luigi Sturzo', in *Luigi Sturzo e la democrazia nella prospettiva del terzo millennio: Atti del seminario internazionale, Erice, 7–11 ottobre 2000* (Florence: L.S. Olschki, 2004), 1–25.

[98] Sturzo, *Nationalism and Internationalism*, 226. Fruci, *La comunità internazionale*, 192; Francesco Malgeri, 'L'opera di Sturzo per la comunità internazionale dalla società delle nazioni all'ONU', in *Luigi Sturzo e la comunità internazionale. Atti del Quinto Corso della Cattedra Sturzo* (Catania: Istituto di sociologia Luigi Sturzo, 1988), 20.

268 · CHAPTER 8

of a global democratic order through a dual motion of grassroots activities
and a centralised political act of leadership.[99]

The democratic order that Maritain proposed was anchored in his commitment to humanism, 'a political philosophy much broader and deeper
than a particular form of government'.[100] The universal civil society, the
'body politic', had for Maritain the capacity to bring together persons
from different places and cultures in a common pursuit of the good. Rejecting the 'false' philosophy of democracy, which sets as its goal the
freedom of the power-holding multitude that obeys no one, he argued
that his vision would bring about 'an advance towards justice and law and
towards the liberation of the human being'. The new democracy should
be based on republican freedom and on aristocratic leadership that would
have the moral responsibility to establish a 'brotherly city' of all citizens,
and to foster an 'organic link between civil society and religion' without
nonetheless subjugating politics to clerical interests. Since human nature
embodied the capacity for rational behaviour, but also the potential for
irrational—and therefore immoral—action, the democratic leaders should
provide moral direction, especially to the undefined masses of people who
'still behave like minors'.[101]

GLOBAL 'PLURALISM(S) OF FEAR'

The reflection of Maritain and Sturzo on the political order of the post-
war world emerged from their lived experience of exile. In their adop-
tive homeland they engaged in public debate to convince the public of
the importance of a certain type of democracy as the foundation of world
order: a democracy inspired by personalism and pluralism.[102] Like Niebuhr and Aron, they endeavoured to reinforce the democratic regimes
against totalitarianism. For them, this entailed providing the supporters
of democracy with the necessary—Catholic—moral values for its survival.
The collapse of Western civilisation was caused by the modern turn away
from the solid moral values of religion, and could be averted if the global
community of persons would evolve into an order based on pluralism,
federalism, and democracy.

The idea that democracy should be reconceptualised on a global scale
to defend the human persons from the threat of totalitarianism situates the

[99] Sturzo, *Nationalism and Internationalism*, 229.
[100] Maritain, *Christianity and Democracy*, 30.
[101] Maritain, *Rights of Man and Natural Law*, 35.
[102] Thomas A. Howard suggested that Maritain's sojourn in the United States led him to reinforce
the democratic aspect of his political thought, yet did not discuss in detail the content of democracy for
Maritain. See *God and the Atlantic* (Oxford: Oxford University Press, 2001), chap. 5.

writings of Maritain and Sturzo at the Cold War intellectual horizon. Despite the differences between their visions, both advanced a position that could be defined as a 'pluralism of fear'. They employed a moralised notion of diversity as weapon in an ongoing ideological battle against materialism, in both its communist and capitalistic renditions. In this last section of the chapter, I explore how their pluralistic visions of global order were, in fact, oriented toward the preservation of the best of Western civilisation, as they defined it, from the menacing powers of bourgeois liberalism, dictatorial totalitarianism, and communism. The growing attention dedicated to identifying and attacking the common enemy undermined their pluralistic, democratic political ethos, resulting in a loose 'pluralism of fear' that aimed at arming the persons and their communities with sufficient rights and political autonomy to resist abuse and oppression.

In the 1940s, Sturzo's prime concern was still fascism rather than communism. Indeed, Mussolini accused him of 'black bolshevism' for introducing to the Catholic world the devious idea of combatting communism by adopting the same organisational and political techniques of socialism.[103] For Sturzo the negative aspects of communism remained its atheistic materialism and authoritarianism, which threatened the Catholic way of life. By endorsing democratic pluralism, Sturzo hoped to provide alternative responses to the concrete social problems that communism addressed, without sacrificing Catholic morality.

The fear that Catholicism was under attack had accompanied Sturzo since the Spanish Civil War. The Vatican was not without fault: in 1936, he suggested that the Spanish people were 'spiritually abandoned and socially left prey to socialism and syndicalism and today to communism'.[104] The rise of communism in Europe, and the massacres during the Spanish War, were the unwanted legacy of the Catholic failure to respond to popular social needs. Yet Catholic social and political thought still merited, for Sturzo, a second chance at directing the world's peoples towards political well-being and moral salvation. Sturzo's endorsement of democratic pluralism was not always convincing. In 1940, Giuseppe Antonio Borgese reviewed Sturzo's book *State and Church* in the *Nation*. While in theory he supported the vision of the liberating power of Catholic moral and social doctrine, he doubted that it would be possible to separate the moral ethos from the Church's reactionary politics and fundamental fear of dissent. Arguing that 'all the Church has done or tried to do as a "directive power" in the nearly seventy years during which it could have acted from the experimental vacuum of its wholly

---

[103] Gaspare Ambrosini, 'Il saluto dell'Istituto Luigi Sturzo', in *Luigi Sturzo nella storia d'Italia*, ed. Francesco Malgeri (Rome: Edizioni di storia e Letteratura, 1973), 84.

[104] Francesco Malgeri, 'Sturzo e il Vaticano negli anni del fascismo', in Malgeri, *Luigi Sturzo nella Storia d'Italia*, 369. Compare to Giuliana Chamedes, 'The Vatican and the Reshaping of the European International Order after World War I', *Historical Journal* 56 (2013): 955–976.

spiritualized independence has consistently been along the line of absolutism and reaction'.[105] Borgese's argument highlighted the underlying anxiety that motivated Sturzo's democratic pluralism, a profound fear about the effect of totalitarianism on humanity's moral convictions, as well as a deep concern for the Catholic Church's marginalisation in the post-war order.

Maritain, by contrast, identified in communism a particular threat to the Church: its universalist, militant revolutionary atheism 'fights its own battle on the very ground upon which Christianity has its foundations'.[106] The response to this challenge must, for him, be spiritual, through persons' submission to the common good, 'after an irreducibly human and specifically ethico-social pattern, that is, personalist and communist at the same time'.[107] The personalist approach gained momentum by the Catholic attack on communism in the late 1930s, fuelled by Pius XI's encyclical *Divinis redemptoris*, which condemned the communists' failure to respect the dignity of the human person.[108] The pontifical words inspired, as Moyn suggests, Maritain's political and theoretical stance on personalism and human dignity as the source for humanity's salvation. Yet for Sturzo, excluding communism would not set stable foundations for a new post-war order. While bolshevism was authoritarian and therefore politically illegitimate, communism should not be barred from political debate in a democratic context. Communist and labour parties had, for Sturzo, full political legitimacy as long as they played along the rules of parliamentary democracy. The Catholic battle against communism should be conducted on the ideological and discursive plane.[109] To convince the public that the communist emancipatory promise is false, Catholics must offer a viable and persuasive alternative social policy. The communists knew how to respond in a swaying— yet wrong—manner to the great popular demand for social rights, political emancipation, and better living conditions. These should also be the concerns of the Catholic political leaders in a pluralist, democratic order.

Building a pluralist democratic order would help, Sturzo opined, distinguish more clearly between democratic Western labour parties and the authoritarian politics of Stalinist Russia. While he supported the rights to private property as part of the human rights of the person, he also recognised that trade unions and workers associations had an important role in transforming modern society towards a more democratic order. He opposed conservative Catholics who sought to defend the existing social and economic order at any cost and suggested that the Catholic Church

---

[105] G. A. Borgese, 'Don Sturzo's Liberal Catholicism', *Nation*, 27 April 1940, 543–545.
[106] Maritain, *Person and the Common Good*, 69.
[107] Ibid., 71.
[108] Moyn, *Christian Human Rights*, 38–39.
[109] Luigi Sturzo, 'La lutte contre le communisme', *La Terre Wallonne* 35 (1936): 75–84.

CATHOLICISM AND GLOBAL DEMOCRACY · 271

should become an active agent in the emancipation of the subaltern populations, a goal that he tried to promote through the Italian People's Party.

It becomes clear that the two versions of 'pluralism of fear' that Sturzo and Maritain advanced emerged from different conceptions of the role of Catholicism in shaping post-war order. For Maritain, the pluralist democratic global order was based on a conservative interpretation of universalism bounded by morality. Sturzo, by contrast, advanced a version of pluralist democracy based on an agonistic conception of moral universalism. Rather than fighting a common battle, the visions of Maritain and Sturzo embodied irreconcilable attitudes about the role of democracy in the global order.

Maritain's reliance on Catholic morality as the foundation for a new ethos of democracy was a means to restore a conservative, traditional morality that had lost—temporarily, he hoped—its power to generate universal political order. By granting Catholics a privileged position in this vision, he undermined the pluralist and democratic values he tried to uphold. Sturzo offered a different view. His idea of the Catholic contribution centred on the value of participation in democratic politics, where party representation and political debates could give voice—or rather a plurality of voices—to the popular masses, who were the real subjects of politics. Pluralism meant accepting a variety of positions that, through a democratic dialectic, could lead to common action against a dangerous enemy. This did not imply that Catholicism had lost its moral primacy, but rather that in the post-war universal democratic order its *political* primacy could not be taken as given, but should rather be earned.

CHAPTER 9

Conclusion

The Genealogy of Globalism

IN THE 1940s, the 'global' emerged as a new, all-encompassing space. The global was imagined as a point of reference for all other political units, embodying the tension between the oneness of planet Earth and the diverse communities that inhabit it. Transnational conversations assembled a vocabulary of globalist ideas deployed to characterise the normative and institutional shape of the new dimension of politics.[1] These languages of globalism thus formed the conceptual basis for a loose, transnational, multifaceted, and dynamic ideology that emphasised the need for new forms of political associations beyond the state: regional and world federations, religious networks, transnational liberal communities, functional agencies, and constitutional unions. In response to the devastating total war, these global conceptions of politics entailed a promise of a new world order.

'Practical men in positions of power', Barbara Wootton wrote in her memoir, 'can always demonstrate the impracticability of idealistic proposals by the simple device of making sure that these are never tried'.[2] Although many of the globalist plans I have dissected in this book remained, as Wootton feared, on the theoretical plane, some of the seeds sown in the mid-century debates about globalism developed eventually into institutions, organisations, and political movements. One of the most important outcomes of the wartime efforts to design a new world order was the new international organisation, the United Nations.[3] At first sight, one may be

---

[1] The question of order remains a fundamental aspect of the study of international relations today. For a general discussion, see Andrew Hurrell, *On Global Order: Power, Values, and the Constitution of International Society* (Oxford: Oxford University Press, 2007).

[2] Barbara Wootton, *In a World I Never Made* (London: Allen & Unwin, 1967), 98.

[3] There is a vast scholarship on the US involvement in the creation of the UN. See, for example, Borgwardt, *New Deal for the World*; Townsend Hoopes and Douglas Brinkley, *FDR and the Creation of the U.N.* (New Haven, CT: Yale University Press, 1997); Stephen Schlesinger, *Act of Creation: The Founding of the United Nations* (Boulder, CO: Westview, 2003). For revisionist accounts, see Mazower, *No Enchanted Palace*; Wertheim, 'Tomorrow, the World'.

tempted to associate the foundation of the United Nations with the globalist agenda I have discussed here. The UN Charter and the Chicago constitution seem to share a commitment to upholding the values of justice, tolerance, and freedom, in a world framed by the precepts of international law. The 1948 Universal Declaration of Human Rights similarly benefited from the active contributions of Richard McKeon and Jacques Maritain, who built upon the Chicago constitution to theorise human rights in the twentieth century.

However, most of the thinkers examined here identified more differences than similarities between their visions and the conception of world order in which the United Nations is embedded. For them, the United Nations did not reflect the global change they envisaged. Instead, it embodied important and undesirable continuities with earlier imperial and state-centric conceptions of world order, which would, they feared, set limits to the effectiveness and success of the post-war political arrangements.

The most significant substantial limit of the United Nations was its structural and conceptual support for state sovereignty. Those who opposed the centrality of state sovereignty to politics, like the Chicago constitutionalists, H. G. Wells, Michael Polanyi, Friedrich Hayek, and Barbara Wootton, had misgivings about the establishment of an international organisation that depended upon and reinforced the sovereignty of its member states. 'The League of Nations and now the United Nations, as their names imply, rest upon national separateness', wrote David Mitrany in 1948. Due to its state-centric structure, the United Nations lacked the authority to initiate or prescribe political, economic, or social action.[4] For Mitrany, as for many others, the United Nations was a reproduction of the failed League of Nations, with no greater promise of success.

The organisation's autonomy and power were further limited by its restricted possibility to intervene in the domestic affairs of member states. Thus, in 1954 Raymond Aron argued that the United Nations could not provide efficacious tools for conflict resolution. Without challenging the principle of state sovereignty, he reasoned, the United Nations could reflect only the interests of its member states, not those of the world as a whole. The excessive emphasis on translating political conflicts into legal language undermined the political force of the organisation, precluding its evolution into an arena for political debate that could generate a truly novel global order. Without such autonomy and legitimacy, the United Nations could never overcome the dominating influence of the great powers, and growing tendency towards a bipolar division of the world.

[4] Mitrany, 'Functional Approach to World Organization', 351.

Without resisting these tensions, there could be no authentic global sense of unity.[5]

What seemed most alarming to many mid-century globalists about the new structural design of the United Nations was, however, the unequal distribution of power between its members. The new international ethos of the UN was not based on equality. The privileged position of a few select states, namely the permanent members of the Security Council, could render it a vehicle to implement power politics in the post-war world. Thus, as Spykman hoped and the Chicago constitutionalists feared, the United Nations would permit the United States to occupy a position of world leadership and become a new imperial power de facto. The UN could perpetuate rather than challenge the extant hierarchical and unequal structure of world politics, drawing a conceptual link between the obsolete imperial order and the post-war world.

Owen Lattimore, by contrast, was optimistic about the reformist potential of the United Nations, especially when China was granted a permanent seat and a veto right on the Security Council. The confirmation of China's global status as a great power was in tune with Lattimore's vision of a pluralist order in which Asia emerged as an innovative democratic region. A meeting with Nehru convinced Lattimore that India could also play a leading role in forming a democratic alternative within the bipolar post-war order. The establishment in 1961 of the Non-Aliened Movement of states that refused to support or oppose any major power bloc also reflected his conviction that Asia could become a 'Third World', an alternative to both Soviet Russia and the United States. However, after undertaking diplomatic missions for the United Nations in the 1950s, by the late 1970s Lattimore came to regret his 'overoptimism' about the effectiveness of the organisation and its capacity to overturn the power relations in the world in favour of new Asian democracies.[6]

Europe provides another interesting case in point, where some of the plans I have charted in this study attained a regional—albeit not global—expression. The 1951 Treaty of Paris, which established the European Coal and Steel Community, reflected Mitrany's conviction that common economic interests could enhance political cooperation between the European countries. On a more theoretical level, Mitrany's functionalism set the foundation for the influential neo-functionalist approach to European integration.[7] The writings of Federal Union about democratic federalism inspired the Italian federalists Altiero Spinelli, Ernesto Rossi, and Luigi Ein-

[5] Raymond Aron, 'Limits to the Powers of the United Nations', *Annals of the American Academy of Political and Social Science* 296 (1954): 20–26.

[6] Lattimore, *Situation in Asia*; Newman, *Owen Lattimore*, 125n7.

[7] See, for example, Arne Niemann and Demosthenes Ioannou, 'European Economic Integration in Times of Crisis: A Case of Neofunctionalism?', *Journal of European Public Policy* 22 (2015): 196–218.

audi to promote federation as a form of political organisation based not on the imperial experience but on a transnational vision of economic and social welfare.[8] These ideas set the intellectual grounding for the post-war development of the European Union's cultural, legal, and economic institutions. Nonetheless, the European Union stopped short of embracing the political federalism that Robbins and Wootton proposed.

Despite significant transformations of the structure and institutions of world order after the Second World War, by the beginning of the 1950s, the globalist agenda had lost its vitality. Many proponents of globalism had turned their interest to other aspects of political and public debate. One of the reasons for the demise of globalism may be the establishment of the United Nations as a hub for an alternative state-centred internationalist agenda. A second reason is the rise of the Cold War mentality. For the protagonists of this book, at least three different decisive episodes changed the settings of world politics, rendering their visions impractical: the Chicago Committee suggested the rejection of the Baruch Plan at the UN (1946), Aron pointed to the dividing up of Europe in the spring of 1947, and Lattimore emphasised the impact of the Communist victory in the Chinese Civil War (1949). The 1948 coup d'état in Czechoslovakia, and the outbreak of the Korean War in 1950 were also perceived as generators of profound political change.[9] Many public intellectuals in Britain and the United States were struck by the acceleration of East-West hostilities, although only a few explicitly predicted bipolarity (Raymond Aron was a notable exception). By the end of the decade, however, it was widely accepted that the Cold War rendered the globalist proposals for a new world order politically outmoded.

The marginalisation of the globalist discourse after 1950 was not, however, wholly dependent on external factors. The particular conceptual formulations of globalism in the 1940s also contributed to its limited efficacy. As I argued in chapter 3, despite their popularity, mid-century arguments about the shrinkage of space and time were hardly new, and invariably naïve. As many ideologues of globalism were to discover, there was no direct path from world-spanning technological advances to a global political order that transcended existing geopolitical and economic frontiers.

Furthermore, the 'global' sphere was less inclusive than its proponents suggested. While the global space has often been outlined as an all-encompassing, democratic sphere of political action, in which different

---

[8] On Federal Union's influence on the Italian federalist movement and on European federalism, see Daniela Preda, 'Le débat fédéraliste dans le Royaume-Uni entre les deux guerres', in Bosco, *Federal Idea*, vol. 1, 271–290. For Wootton's influence on Einaudi and Spinelli, see Castelli, *Una pace da costruire*, chap. 11.

[9] Many other time frames for the Cold War are, of course, possible. See Isaac and Bell, *Uncertain Empire*.

political communities—states, regions, and federal unions—could freely interact, many groups were in fact excluded from the global order. Lattimore stands out in his decision to refer to the 'Third World' as a bearer of political agency. The Chicago Committee presented the recasting of political space as an emancipatory move but struggled to take into account the political desires of the non-Western peoples, who often sought self-rule rather than inclusion in a new order designed by others. The imperial mind-set had largely lost its appeal at Federal Union, but the colonial populations did not become equal participants in shaping these proposals for federation.[10] In Asia and Africa, ex-colonies explored federal models on their paths to statehood, yet their debates and struggles remained largely separate from the globalist conversation in Britain and the United States.[11] Since the problem of race relations was never a major concern for these globalist ideologues, the 'global' did not necessarily include a substantial promise of political, economic, and social liberation, while the notion of the 'nation' did.

The discourse on globalism was further constrained by its political commitment to assist the liberal cause in the fight against totalitarianism. The global battle against totalitarianism and the decline of the European powers emphasised, for some mid-century commentators, the need for a powerful theoretical and structural defence of individual liberty and political independence.[12] Totalitarianism was the ideological 'other' of these visions of world order, the constant menace they hoped to avert by employing a variety of new political and institutional arrangements. Yet by orienting the idea of the global against a particular enemy, the globalist ideologues downplayed disagreements in their own camp, assuming that the claims of all political, religious, ethnic, and social minorities could be easily accommodated in the democratic, pluralistic world order they envisaged. This was a colossal enterprise, and its failure is hardly surprising.

THE PUBLIC ROLE OF INTELLECTUALS

The Emergence of Globalism invites a reflection on the role of public intellectuals in political debate. The public responsibilities of intellectuals had different meanings for different people. If Aron considered himself a *spectateur engagé*, a political observer well aware of the necessary limits and

[10] On mid-century African proposals for regional federations, see, for example, Michael Collins, 'Decolonisation and the "Federal Moment"', *Diplomacy & Statecraft* 24 (2013): 21–40.

[11] On African federalism, see Cooper, *Citizenship between Empire and Nation*; on Asian debates on federal orders, see Baogang He, Brian Galligan, and Takashi Inoguchi, eds., *Federalism in Asia* (Cheltenham: Edward Elgar, 2009).

[12] For Robert Latham, the Western quest for a new liberal world order contributed more than Soviet politics to the rise of the Cold War. See *The Liberal Moment: Modernity, Security and the Making of Postwar International Order* (New York: Columbia University Press, 1997).

subjectivity of his own perspective on human knowledge, others were more ambitious. Borgese was confident that the Chicago Committee of scholars could deliver a truthful and clear-cut analysis of the world's political problems, and elaborate these into a coherent working constitution, which would then be scrutinised by global public opinion. Curtis shared with Maritain and Sturzo the sense that public engagement was an almost religious vocation, a sacred duty aimed at restoring a long-lost order. For Wootton and Robbins, the war furnished an opportunity to give a practical expression to their passion for public affairs that motivated their scholarly research about society and economics.

The intellectuals I have examined here did not define their public role merely in terms of providing expert knowledge on their specific field of study. They often suggested that their position outside the realm of political power, in the civil space yet distinct from the rest of society by their erudition and prestige, enabled them to look beyond social and political conventions. They felt better positioned to challenge national politics that others appeared to take for granted and to outline plans that others deemed idealistic or utopian. The role of public intellectuals supposedly meant a self-invested responsibility towards the common good, but at the same time also freedom from the constraints of professional and institutional politics.

The public engagement of these intellectuals led them often to consider private organisations, think tanks, and their publications as transcending the boundaries of academic disciplines and their epistemological paradigms.[13] In the 1940s, these organisations provided institutional frameworks for sustained discussions that reflected a commitment to engage with concerns shared by the public. Federal Union, the Chicago Committee, Chatham House, and the *Bulletin of the Atomic Scientists* were meeting points for a range of disciplines and political opinions, creating the dynamic environment that characterised the development of mid-century globalist ideas. The organised setting magnified the ideas proposed by these individuals, and connected them with a wider enthusiastic audience. Through these forums, the dividing line between academic scholarship and public debates was crossed and to some degree blurred.

The focus on public intellectuals rather than on politicians or official bureaucrats as the proponents of a globalist agenda seeks to question the centrality of the state to history writing. The narrative that I outline challenges

---

[13] For a similar use of private institutional context—the Mont Pèlerin Society—as a hub for intellectual exchange, see recent studies including Mirowski and Plehwe, *Road from Mont Pèlerin*; Burgin, *Great Persuasion*. Other studies explored private foundations as the backdrop of international thought, for example, Inderjeet Parmar, *Foundations of the American Century: The Ford, Carnegie, and Rockefeller Foundations in the Rise of American Power* (New York: Columbia University Press, 2012); Katharina Rietzler, 'Before the Cultural Cold Wars: American Philanthropy and Cultural Diplomacy in the Inter-war Years', *Historical Research* 84 (2011): 148–164.

the idea that the history of political thought beyond the state should be explored through the concept of the state, as 'international' history. This study examines aspects of the development of the languages of globalism, deconstructing the complex and nonlinear genealogy of political thought beyond both statism and internationalism. This mode of thinking about world politics could not be understood by a 'present-oriented' study aimed at discovering the wartime 'origins' of the current world order.[14] Such an approach would obscure the multiple controversies and debates on world order that took place at the time, and would give historical narrative a misleading sense of teleological progress. One of my objectives has been, therefore, to complicate the conventional history of the 1940s, and thereby to reveal the wide range of global plans advanced by a group of public intellectuals in Britain and the United States in order to provide a more sophisticated history of twentieth-century political thought.

The intellectual history of globalism reveals the shortcomings of the common paradigmatic disciplinary history of International Relations, one that is based on a rigid binary of realism and idealism/utopianism, or liberalism and imperialism.[15] Historical paradigms may be useful to highlight major controversies, but they can also anachronistically project present interests onto past debates. I suggest that the conventional paradigms of International Relations are particularly unhelpful for understanding mid-century global visions because many of the period's intellectual protagonists appropriated the languages and concerns of more than one 'paradigm'. Moreover, these visions had often evolved through interdisciplinary debates between experts in different fields of knowledge who shared a common interest in global politics and order.

THE GLOBALIST IDEOLOGY AND THE GLOBALISED FUTURE

The main normative claim of the discourse of 'globalism' was that the existing political system should be revised and reorganised with reference to the world as a whole, and not only to national, regional, or imperial interests.

---

[14] There are various historical accounts of the 1940s and the origin of American power, but it is not possible to discuss this literature in detail here. For some examples of this approach, see Daniel Deudney and G. John Ikenberry, 'The Nature and Sources of Liberal International Order', *Review of International Studies* 25 (1999): 179–196; G. John Ikenberry, *Liberal Leviathan: The Origins, Crisis and Transformation of the American World Order* (Princeton, NJ: Princeton University Press, 2011); Tony Smith, *America's Mission: The United States and the Worldwide Struggle for Democracy* (Princeton, NJ: Princeton University Press, 2012).

[15] On the disciplinary history of IR, see, for example, Brian C. Schmidt, ed., *International Relations and the First Great Debate* (London: Routledge 2012); David Long and Brian C. Schmidt, eds., *Imperialism and Internationalism in the Discipline of International Relations* (Albany: State University of New York Press, 2005).

This argument was based on the perception of the world as an increasingly interconnected space, laced with technological and economic bonds. The global space of politics did not supersede or undermine all existing political structures, but these had to be scrutinised against the novel conditions of world politics. Mid-century globalism did not necessarily entail a perception of the world as a homogeneous, uniform political space (although it sometimes did imply this). Wells's suggestion of a world state was not greeted with enthusiasm, while the Chicago Committee posited that their world federation would be a pluralistic order, not an extended all-encompassing state. Within the complex global space, most mid-century globalists envisaged constructing a new order around the extant states, limiting their power without abolishing them. As Moyn suggests, for many the state remained 'the aspirational forum for humanity'.[16]

If states could retain their political relevance in the global age, empires could not. The global political system was to be multilayered, complex, and intertwined, rather than hierarchical and discriminatory. The advocates of globalism envisaged the transformation of perceptions of political space towards a new order that would overcome the legacy of empire, which entailed a formalised hierarchical political order based on force and exploitative economic relations.[17] Some, like Wells, Curtis, and Spykman, still deployed elements pertaining to the language of empire—such as the idea of Western political, economic, and moral supremacy—to discuss the new world order. But their views encountered growing opposition from those who believed in establishing a more egalitarian and liberal global system that could overcome economic discrepancies and political inequalities.

Proponents of globalism increasingly perceived liberty as a universal entitlement. For Hayek, Robbins, and Polanyi, all human beings had the right to free decision making; Wootton and Merriam added the right to a universal standard of living, and Lattimore added the right to political agency. Borgese and Maritain favoured the formulation of universal bills of human rights to outline the contents of liberty in the post-war order. The fundamental imperial division of the world's peoples into civilised and uncivilised seemed ever less justified. This does not mean that the principle of equality guided all theories of world order. Yet it reveals that some mid-century global thinkers sought—not always successfully—to distance themselves from previous conceptions of world order based on an essentially discriminatory conception of humanity grounded in racial, civilisational, or national differences.

[16] Moyn, *Last Utopia*, 212.
[17] For a similar definition of the imperial system in the 1940s, see Baker, *Constructing a Post-war Order*, 21–22.

Without necessarily reflecting directly on imperialism, Wootton, Lattimore, Borgese, McKeon, and others attempted to formulate a new attitude to global politics inspired by social and economic justice and the ubiquitous universal rights of man. They did not ignore the question of power in world politics, but implied that power should be negotiated in view of other principles like independence, justice, and liberty. In this sense, they mirrored ongoing concerns about racial equality at the time. As Marilyn Lake and Henry Reynolds affirm, there was in 1945 a '"rising wind" of protest against white domination. The trend of "such awakening and revolution" was clearly seen in China's demand at Dumbarton Oakes that the allied nations "unequivocally declare themselves for complete racial equality"'.[18] Nonetheless, as Lattimore suggested, the emancipatory efficacy of the global visions of equality depended on a concrete understanding of the conditions of discrimination and exploitation around the world, which only a few globalist thinkers had acquired.

Mid-century thinkers were hardly original in claiming that technological innovations were incentives for global political interconnectedness. Yet they added moral claims about the normative value of both universalism and pluralism. Globalism embodied a universalist approach in positing that all individuals were entitled to some rights (and duties) regardless of their territorial location and national association. At the same time, globalism was embedded in a conception of pluralism that referred to both values and political structures. Value pluralism gave legitimacy to a range of political, cultural, and social forms. Structural pluralism meant that some political, economic, and cultural processes operated across—rather than above—the space of national politics. Therefore, a pluralistic global system would integrate a range of national and non-national associations, agencies, and communities. The idea of structural pluralism emerged clearly in the functionalist writings of Mitrany, and in a very different form, in the Catholic-inspired proposals of Maritain and Sturzo. But others, including Wootton and the Chicago federalists, also envisaged a complex and multilayered pluralistic political structure in which the state remained a central political unit but would no longer be the exclusive space of political agency.

The emphasis on the universal validity of a particular rendition of human rights could not be easily reconciled with the growing willingness to recognise the value of a plurality of political ideas and structures in the global order. Mid-century public intellectuals had shown a greater awareness of non-Western political traditions than interwar internationalists. Many, like Lattimore, Aron, Maritain, Mitrany, McKeon, and Wootton, explicitly underlined the need to formulate an inclusive world order to

---

[18] Marilyn Lake and Henry Reynolds, *Drawing the Global Colour Line: White Men's Countries and the International Challenge of Racial Equality* (Cambridge: Cambridge University Press, 2008), 342.

accommodate all sorts of conceptions of politics. Yet their interpretation of politics remained constrained by their own historical experiences; they did not engage in active dialogue with non-Western or colonial populations, relying on the assumption that their (eventual) inclusion in the global, pluralistic, rights-based democratic order would suffice to redress the consequences of imperial or racial inequality.

Alongside this sensitivity to political and value pluralism emerged a new sense of urgency about the need to defend Western civilisation from political and cultural attacks. The decline of the imperial order and the threat posed by totalitarianism encouraged visions of world order oriented towards preserving Western values. Borgese, Polanyi, Mumford, and Aron idealised the West as the birthplace of individual liberty, cultural tolerance, and social equality, which was now facing mortal threats by two of its own homicidal creations, totalitarianism and the atomic bomb. The challenge was, therefore, to extract from Western political and intellectual traditions the conceptual means for their own defence. Thus, for some mid-century thinkers, the turn to pluralism and inclusiveness remained an exercise of drawing the borders of civilisation. The global aspirations of their divergent visions of world order were undermined by the evident intellectual—if not geopolitical—focus on a restricted and allegedly exceptional political space.

In a similar move, democracy was deemed the appropriate political system for the new global world order. The pervasive rhetoric of the 'democracy' discourse was accompanied by a degree of ambiguity about its meaning. Multiple interpretations of democracy emerged, each highlighting a different aspect: parliamentary structures, political representation, local participation, economic welfare, individual liberty and rights. The only clear attributes of democracy all thinkers agreed upon were its global potential and desirability.

In the 1940s commentators added to their democratic proposals the qualifier 'liberty' as democracy's main value and political goal. Aron employed the term 'liberal-democracy' to distinguish between the desirable form of democracy that defends individual liberty and rights and the undesirable populist democracy, which might lead to totalitarianism. Linking liberalism to democracy entailed economic consequences as well. Robbins, Hayek, Wootton, McKeon, and Lattimore all argued that the global democratic order should advance economic liberty, but there was no consensus around its meaning or policy implications. For supporters of capitalistic laissez-faire, economic liberty entailed freedom from domination and exploitation, while for advocates of planning it meant freedom of opportunities and access to resources.

The difficulty of formulating a consensual position on the content of the globalist discourse is exemplified by the debate about the foundations of democracy. As I have shown in chapters 7 and 8, public intellectuals in the

1940s had strong misgivings about the idea that science could guarantee progress towards greater individual liberty. The confidence in the power of reason to advance the shared causes of humanity diminished. The disillusionment with the power of reason to bring about global progress through scientific and technological innovation led some globalist thinkers to turn to other common denominators as the foundation of world order. Commentators of diverse political worldviews such as Aron, Sturzo, Maritain, Polanyi, and Mumford perceived faith, belief, and myth as alternative foundations for democracy, which could foster the necessary cohesion to sustain global politics despite social and political pluralism.[19] Faith in universal values and emotional attachment to traditional communities were accepted as foundations for a global order. Belief in the myth of Europe would set the stage for an eventual political integration, according to Aron.[20] Yet the emphasis on faith embodied a support for a form of cultural monism, suggesting that the benefits carried in the idea of the global—such as individual freedom and democratic participation—depended on adherence to shared values. Such a position risked limiting the space for dissent and protest, thus undermining the democratic ethos that the globalist ideology was supposed to propose.

Historical renditions of the globalist discourse acquire a particular importance against the rise of the idea of 'globalisation' as a defining aspect of the post-1989 world.[21] Today, there are constant references to globalisation in public debates, academic scholarship, and political deliberations. Economic and technological transformations have generated a perception of a new global space, a unified and interconnected world that has a concrete impact on the everyday life of intellectuals, politicians, and citizens around the world. New communication technologies, most importantly the Internet, have contributed to the return of the perception of the shrinkage of space, a common trope of 1940s globalism. However, the contours of the *political* global space remain imprecise. Without a clear political meaning, the 'global' could be a space of exchanges and interconnections, or of disempowerment and alienation.

The 1940s debates about global order constitute a key element in the history of the idea of globalisation. Looking back at interpretations of the global by mid-century public intellectuals reveals the multiple ways in which the world was imagined as an interconnected and 'globalised' political space. Visions of the global as a new area of political—rather than

---

[19] A similar interpretation of the role of faith in pluralist democracy in the American context, rather than on the global scale, was advanced in the classic study by Purcell, *Crisis of Democratic Theory*.

[20] 'Faith' was generally discussed in terms of belief, not of a religious creed. For an analysis of the role of religion in American foreign politics, see Preston, *Sword of the Spirit*.

[21] On the history of globalisation, see A. G. Hopkins, ed., *Globalization in World History* (London: Pimlico, 2002); C. A. Bayly, *The Making of the Modern World, 1780–1914* (Oxford: Oxford University Press, 2003).

merely technological, geographical, or economic—relations mark a foundational moment in the process of shaping global political consciousness.
The 1940s discourse on globalism highlights the wide-ranging political implications of global interconnectedness, reaching far beyond the dynamics
of economic capitalism with which this phenomenon has often been associated. In this study, I have suggested that the mid-century globalist discourse was distinctly *political*: visions of global order sought to adapt political ideas like democracy, liberty, pluralism, and empire to the changing
perceptions of the spatial conditions of the world. As the political and ethical implications of globalisation continue to attract the attention of philosophers, public intellectuals, politicians, and the general public, a historical
understanding of the basic terms of debate will furnish a more sophisticated
and nuanced foundation for reflection about the global space of politics.

Acknowledgments

IT IS WITH great pleasure that I thank the people and organisations that helped make this research possible. I would like to thank my colleagues at Queens' College, Cambridge who provided a supportive environment for the completion of this research. I owe an especially large debt of gratitude to Duncan Bell, whose advice, support, and criticism helped shape this project from its inception. I would like to thank Peter Mandler for the inspiring conversations, and for asking the tough questions at key moments.

I am very grateful to Luke Ashworth, Duncan Kelly, Samuel Moyn, Andrew Preston, and Andrew Williams who commented on my work and gave me valuable ideas and encouragement. Special thanks are also due to Giuliana Chamedes, Giulio De Ligio, Marco Duranti, Lior Erez, Daniel Steinmetz Jenkins, Andrew Jewett, Udi Greenberg, Nicolas Guilhot, Ian Hall, Sue Howson, Jeanne Morefield, Joël Mouric, Katharina Rietzler, Iain Stewart, John A. Thompson, Michael T. Thompson, Stephen Wertheim, and Gene Zubovich, who read parts of the manuscript and helped me improve it. I am thankful to John Darwin, Carlo Galli, David Hollinger, Joel Isaac, Chandran Kukathas, Stefano Recchia, Glenda Sluga, and Casper Sylvest who have all listened to my ideas and arguments and offered their thoughts. I am grateful to my friends in Cambridge, Tomohito Baji, Tom Barker, Marc Mierowsky, Lucy Thirkell Storm, Agnes Upshall, and Samuel Garrett Zeitlin, who read my work and provided helpful comments. Special thanks to Matthew Fright, who provided much needed assistance for the completion of this project.

My research benefited from the assistance of library staff and archivists at the University Library, Cambridge, Bibliothèque nationale de France, LSE, the Library of Congress, the Bodleian Library, Girton College, Cambridge, Johns Hopkins University, the University of Chicago, the Institute for Advanced Study in Princeton, Istituto Luigi Sturzo, and the Royal Institute of International Affairs. Special thanks go to the UL Italian librarian Bettina Rex, and to Dominique Schnapper for giving me her permission to consult the papers of her father, Raymond Aron.

Chapter 3 is a revised version of my article 'Geopolitics and Empire: Visions of Regional World Order in the 1940s' published in *Modern Intellectual History*, Cambridge University Press in 2014. Chapter 5 is derived in part from an article published in *The International History Review*, Taylor &

Francis Online, on 13 Feb 2014. Also available at http://www.tandfonline .com/ http://dx.doi.org/10.1080/07075332.2013.871320. I thank Cambridge University Press and Taylor & Francis for their permission to reproduce this material.

This project benefited from many conversations with friends whose companionship rendered the completion of this research very enjoyable. I would like to thank my friends in Cambridge: Víctor Acedo Matellán, Elisabetta Brighi, Alison Bumke, Hugo Drochon, Nicole Janz, Hannah Malone, Nivi Manchanda, Dana Mills, David Neave (and Agnes, again), Burcu Ozcelik, Diana Siclovan, and Waseem Yaqoob. In Bologna (and beyond), Valentina Montalto, Andrea Garnero, Annalisa Loviglio, Paolo Bailo, Gianandrea Lanzara, Luca Marcolin, Michele Filippone, Dimitrii Tanese, Daniele Pinna, Elisa Pievani, and Gilad Mayshar have never failed to show their comradeship and enthusiasm. In Paris, Clothilde Morgan De Rivery and François-Xavier Colin provided hospitality and friendship. In Washington DC, Colleen Glair and Tommy Hanavan kindly hosted me in their lovely home. In London, I enjoyed the stimulating company and insightful advice of Shiri Mosenzon-Erez and Lior Erez. Daniela Sherer, Daphne Hart, Yaelie Borochov, and Asaf Abir have been a source of indispensable support from near and far.

I would like to extend very special thanks to Umberto Marengo for sharing my global adventure and making it so much more fun.

Finally, I could not thank enough my parents, Ilana Efrati and Shlomi Rosenboim, for their infinite love, care, and encouragement, which made this project possible. This book is dedicated to them, and to my grandmothers Shulamit and Tova, who were active witnesses to many of the world-changing events that I discuss in the book.

Bibliography

PRIMARY SOURCES

Archives

BIBLIOTHÈQUE NATIONALE DE FRANCE, PARIS
Raymond Aron Papers

LONDON SCHOOL OF ECONOMICS, LONDON
William Beveridge Papers
David Mitrany Papers
Records of Federal Union and Federal Trust for Education and Research
Records of League of Nations Union
Lionel Robbins Papers

GIRTON COLLEGE ARCHIVE, CAMBRIDGE
Barbara Wootton Personal Papers

FERDINAND HAMBURGER JR. ARCHIVES, JOHNS HOPKINS
UNIVERSITY, BALTIMORE
Records of the Walter Hines Page School of International Relations

ISTITUTO LUIGI STURZO, ROME
Luigi Sturzo Papers

MANUSCRIPT DIVISION, LIBRARY OF CONGRESS, WASHINGTON, DC
Owen Lattimore Papers

ROYAL INSTITUTE OF INTERNATIONAL AFFAIRS, LONDON
Records of Royal Institute of International Affairs

SPECIAL COLLECTIONS, BODLEIAN LIBRARY, OXFORD
Lionel George Curtis Papers

SPECIAL COLLECTIONS RESEARCH CENTER, UNIVERSITY OF CHICAGO
LIBRARY, CHICAGO
Charles E. Merriam Papers
Michael Polanyi Papers
Records of the Atomic Scientists of Chicago
Records of the Committee to Frame a World Constitution
Records of *Common Cause*

SHELBY WHITE AND LEON LEVY ARCHIVES CENTER, INSTITUTE FOR
ADVANCED STUDY, PRINCETON, NJ
Records of the Office of the Director

Newspapers and Magazines

Bulletin of the Atomic Scientists
Commonweal
Federal Union News
Le Figaro
La France libre
Life
Manchester Guardian
Nation
Point de Vue
Saturday Review of Literature
Spectator
Time
Times

Published Documents

Adler, Mortimer. *How to Think about the Great Ideas: From the Great Books of Western Civilization.* Chicago: Open Court, 2007.

Agar, Herbert, Frank Aydelotte, Giuseppe Antonio Borgese, William Allen Neilson, Hermann Broch, and Van Wyck Brooks. *The City of Man: A Declaration on World Democracy.* New York: Viking, 1941.

Anesaki, Masaharu. 'Review of *Civitas Dei* by Lionel Curtis'. *Pacific Affairs* 8 (1935): 92–95.

Aron, Raymond. *Chroniques de guerre: La France libre: 1940–1945.* Edited by Christian Bachelier. Paris: Gallimard, 1990.

———. *Dimensions de la conscience historique.* Paris: Les Belles Lettres, 2011.

———. 'Discours à des étudiants allemands sur l'avenir de l'Europe'. *Table Ronde* 1 (1948): 63–86.

———. 'États démocratiques et états totalitaires'. 1939. Reprint in Aron, *Penser la liberté, penser la démocratie.* Paris: Gallimard, 2005.

———. 'Europe avenir d'un mythe'. *Cahiers Européens* 3 (1975): 8–10.

———. 'Fin de l'âge idéologique?' In *Max Horkheimer zum 60. Geburststag gewidmet, Sociologica Aufsätze,* edited by Theodor Adorno and Walter Dirks, 219–233. Frankfurt: Europäische Verlagsanstalt, 1955.

———. 'Foreign News: The French Presence in North Africa'. *Time*, 4 July 1955.

———. *France and Europe*. Hinsdale, IL: Henry Regnery, 1949.

———. *Il destino delle nazioni, l'avvenire dell'Europa*. Translated by Giulio De Ligio. Soveria Mannelli: Rubbettino, 2013.

———. *Introduction to the Philosophy of History: An Essay on the Limits of Historical Objectivity*. Translated by George J. Irwin. 1938. Reprint, London: Weidenfeld and Nicolson, 1961.

———. *La sociologie allemande contemporaine*. Paris: Alcan, 1935. Translated into English as *German Sociology*. Glencoe, IL: Free Press, 1964.

———. *Le grand schisme*. Paris: Gallimard, 1948.

———. 'Le partage de l'Europe'. *Point de Vue*, 26 July 1945.

———. *Les articles du Figaro. La guerre froide*. Vol. 1. Paris: Editions de Fallois, 1990.

———. 'Les limites de la théorie économique classique'. *Critique* 6 (1946): 510–519.

———. 'L'Europe peut-elle devenir une unité politique?' *Terre d'Europe* 33 (1947): 12–21.

———. *L'homme contre les tyrans*. Paris: Gallimard, 1946.

———. 'Limits to the Powers of the United Nations'. *Annals of the American Academy of Political and Social Science* 296 (1954): 20–26.

——— [René Avord]. 'L'universalisme de Wells, Tribute to H. G. Wells on His 75th Birthday'. *Adam: International Review* 153 (1941): 6–7.

———. *Machiavel et les tyrannies modernes*. Edited by Rémy Freymond. Paris: Éditions de Fallois, 1993.

———. *Memoirs: Fifty Years of Political Reflection*. 1983. Reprint, New York: Holmes and Meier, 1990.

———. 'Nouvelle carte du monde'. *Point de Vue*, 7 May 1945.

———. *The Opium of the Intellectuals*. Translated by Terence Kilmartin. 1955. Reprint, New Brunswick, NJ: Transaction, 2001.

———. *Paix et guerre entre les nations*. Paris: Calmann-Lévy, 1962.

———. *Penser la liberté, penser la démocratie*. Paris: Gallimard, 2005.

———. 'Social Structure and the Ruling Class: Part 1'. *British Journal of Sociology* 1 (1950): 1–16.

———. 'Sur le machiavélisme, dialogue avec Jacques Maritain' (1982). *Commentaire* 8 (1985): 511–516.

———. *Thinking Politically: A Liberal in the Age of Ideology*. New Brunswick, NJ: Transaction, 1997.

———. 'Transformations du monde de 1900 à 1950: Déplacement du centre de gravité international'. *Réalités* 47 (1949): 70–111.

Avord, René [Raymond Aron]. 'Jacques Maritain et la querelle de Machiavel'. *La France libre*, July 1943.

Bentwich, Norman. 'The Colonial Problem and the Federal Solution'. Federal Tracts, no. 3. London: Macmillan, 1941. Reprint in *Studies in Federal Planning*, edited by Patrick Ransome, 108–137. London: Macmillan, 1943.

Berdahl, Clarence A. 'Review of *Civitas Dei* by Lionel Curtis'. *American Political Science Review* 33 (1939): 894–896.

Bernal, J. D. *The Social Function of Science*. London: Routledge, 1939.

Beveridge, William H. *Full Employment in a Free Society: A Report*. London: Allen & Unwin, 1944.

——. *Peace by Federation?* London: Federal Union, 1940.

——. *Social Insurance and Allied Services*. London: HMSO, 1942.

Bodin, Jean. *On Sovereignty: Four Chapters from the Six Books of the Commonwealth*. Edited by Julian H. Franklin. Cambridge: Cambridge University Press, 1992.

Borchard, Edwin M., ed. *Proceedings of the Fourth Conference of Teachers of International Law and Related Subjects, Held at Briarcliff Lodge, New York, 16–17 October 1929*. New York: Carnegie Endowment for International Peace, 1930.

Borgese, Giuseppe Antonio. *Common Cause*. London: V. Gollancz, 1943.

——. 'Don Sturzo's Liberal Catholicism'. *Nation*, 27 April 1940, 543–545.

——. *Goliath: The March of Fascism*. New York: Viking, 1937.

——. *Imbarco per l'America e altre corrispondenze al* Corriere della Sera. Cuneo: Nerosubianco, 2012.

——. *L'Italia e la nuova alleanza*. Milan: Treves, 1917.

Bowman, Isaiah. 'Geography vs. Geopolitics'. In *Compass of the World: A Symposium on Political Geography*, edited by Hans W. Weigert and Vilhjalmur Stefansson, 40–52. London: Harrap, 1946.

——. *The New World: Problems in Political Geography*. 1921. 4th ed. Yonkers-on-Hudson, NY: World Book Company, 1928.

——. 'Review: Political Geography of Power'. *Geographical Review* 32 (1942): 349–352.

Brailsford, Henry N. *The Federal Idea*. London: Federal Union, 1940.

——. *Olives of Endless Age: Being a Study of This Distracted World and Its Need of Unity*. New York: Harper, 1928.

Carr, Edward H. 'The Moral Foundations of World Order'. In *Foundations for World Order*, edited by E. L. Woodward et al., 70–75. Denver, CO: University of Denver Press, 1949.

——. *Nationalism and After*. 1945. Reprint, London: Macmillan, 1968.

——. *The Twenty Years' Crisis, 1919–1939: An Introduction to the Study of International Relations*. 1939. Reprint, Basingstoke: Palgrave, 2001.

Catlin, George. 'Anglo-American Union as a Nucleus of World Federation'. In *Studies in Federal Planning*, edited by Patrick Ransome, 299–336. London: Macmillan, 1943.

Chaning-Pearce, Melville, ed. *Federal Union: A Symposium*. London: J. Cape, 1940.

Chenu, Marie-Dominique. *Une école de théologie: Le Saulchoir*. Kain-les-Tournai: Étoilles, 1937.

Clark, Grenville, and Louis B. Sohn. *World Peace through World Law*. Cambridge, MA: Harvard University Press, 1958.

Clokie, H. McD. 'Systematic Politics'. *Canadian Journal of Economics and Political Science* 13 (1947): 123.

Coudenhove-Kalergi, Richard. *Paneuropa*. Vienna: Paneuropa Verlag, 1923, 1926.

Cousins, Norman. *Modern Man Is Obsolete*. New York: Viking, 1945.

Creighton, D. G. 'Review of *Civitas Dei* by Lionel Curtis'. *University of Toronto Law Journal* 3 (1939): 249–251.

Culbertson, Ely. *Summary of the World Federation Plan: An Outline of a Practical and Detailed Plan for World Settlement*. London: Faber and Faber, 1944.

Curry, William B. *The Case for Federal Union*. London: Penguin, 1939.

Curtis, Lionel. *Action*. London: Oxford University Press, 1942.

———. *Civitas Dei*. 1934–1937. 2nd rev. ed., London: Allen & Unwin, 1950.

———. *The Commonwealth of Nations: An Inquiry into the Nature of Citizenship in the British Empire, and into the Mutual Relations of the Several Communities Thereof*. London: Macmillan, 1916.

———. *Decision*. London: Oxford University Press, 1941.

———. *Decision and Action*. London: Oxford University Press, 1942.

———. *Faith & Works*. London: Oxford University Press, 1943.

———. *Freedom and International Peace*. Glasgow: Royal Philosophical Society, 1946.

———. *Letters to the People of India on Responsible Government*. London: Macmillan, 1918.

———. *The Master-Key to Peace*. Oxford: Oxford University Press, 1947.

———. *An Open Letter to Lords, Commons and Press*. Oxford: Oxford University Press, 1943.

———. *Papers Relating to the Application of the Principle of Dyarchy to the Government of India, to Which Are Appended the Report of the Joint Select Committee and the Government of India Act, 1919*. Oxford: Clarendon, 1920.

———. *The Political Future of the British Commonwealth and Empire*. Oxford: Oxford University Press, 1945.

———. *The Political Repercussions of Atomic Power*. London: Allen & Unwin, 1949.

———. *The Problem of the Commonwealth*. London: Macmillan, 1916.

———. *A Reply to 'British Commonwealth and Western Union'*. London: Oxford University Press, 1948.

———. *Towards a World Order*. London: National Peace Council, 1943.

———. *War or Peace?* London: Oxford University Press, 1946.

———. *The Way to Peace*. London: Oxford University Press, 1944.

———. 'World Order'. *International Affairs* 18 (1939): 301–320.

———. *World Revolution in the Cause of Peace*. Oxford: Blackwell, 1949.

———. *World War: Its Cause and Cure*. Oxford: Oxford University Press, 1945.

Curtis, Lionel, and Richard Crossman. 'United Europe Yes, but How?' *Oxford Mail*, 6 February 1948.

Farrell-Vinay, Giovanna, ed. *Luigi Sturzo a Londra: Carteggi e documenti, 1925–1946*. Soveria Mannelli: Rubbettino, 2003.

Febvre, Lucien. *L'Europe: Genèse d'une civilisation: Cours professé au collège de France en 1944–1945*. Edited by Thérèse Charmasson. Paris: Perrin, 1999.

Federal Union. *Federal Union Official Policy*. London: Federal Union, July 1942.

———. *How We Shall Win*. London: Federal Union, 1940.

Fosdick, Raymond B. *The Old Savage and the New Civilization*. Garden City, NY: Doubleday and Doran, 1928.

Fyfe, W. Hamilton. 'Review of *Civitas Dei* by Lionel Curtis'. *International Affairs* 28 (1952): 70–71.

Goichot, Émile, ed. *Luigi Sturzo e gli intellettuali cattolici francesi: carteggi (1925–1945)*. Soveria Mannelli: Rubbettino, 2003.

Hagan, Charles B. 'Geopolitics'. *Journal of Politics* 4 (1942): 478.

Halévy, Élie. *Histoire du socialisme Européen; rédigée d'après des notes de cours par un groupe d'amis et d'élèves*. Paris: Gallimard, 1948.
———. *L'ère des tyrannies*. Paris: Gallimard, 1938.
Hallowell, John H. 'Review Article'. *Journal of Politics* 5 (1943): 187–189.
Harrison, R. E., and H. W. Weigert. 'World View and Strategy'. In *Compass of the World: A Symposium on Political Geography*, edited by Hans W. Weigert and Vilhjalmur Stefansson, 74–88. London: Harrap, 1946.
Haushofer, Karl. *Geopolitik der Pan-Ideen*. Berlin: Zentral-Verlag, 1931.
———. *Wehr-Geopolitik: Geographische Grundlagen Einer Wehrkunde*. Berlin: Junker und Dünnhaupt, 1932.
Hayek, Friedrich A. 'Economic Conditions of Inter-state Federalism'. *New Commonwealth Quarterly* 5 (1939): 131–149.
———. *Freedom and the Economic System*. Chicago: University of Chicago Press, 1939.
———. *Hayek on Hayek: An Autobiographical Dialogue*. Edited by Stephen Kresge and Lief Wenar. Indianapolis: Liberty Fund, 2008.
———. 'Review of *The Contempt of Freedom* by Michael Polanyi'. *Economica* 8 (1941): 212.
———. *The Road to Serfdom*. 1944. Reprint, London: Routledge, 2001.
———. *The Sensory Order*. London: Routledge & Kegan Paul, 1952.
Hayek, Friedrich A., Maynard C. Krueger, and Charles E. Merriam. *The Road to Serfdom: A Radio Discussion*. University of Chicago Roundtable 370. Chicago: University of Chicago Press, 1945.
Herz, John. 'Review of World Constitution Draft'. *Western Political Quarterly* 3 (1950): 267–268.
Hobson, John A. *Democracy after the War*. London: Allen & Unwin, 1917.
———. *Democracy and a Changing Civilisation*. London: John Lane, 1934.
———. *Selected Writing of John A. Hobson, 1932–1938: The Struggle for the International Mind*. Edited by John M. Hobson and Colin Tyler. London: Routledge, 2011.
———. *Towards International Government*. London: Allen & Unwin, 1915.
Hutchins, Robert M. *The Atom Bomb and Education*. London: National Peace Council, 1947.
Hutchins, Robert M., Giuseppe Antonio Borgese, Mortimer J. Adler, Stringfellow Barr, Albert Guérard, Harold A. Innis, Erich Kahler, and Wilber G. Katz. *Preliminary Draft of a World Constitution*. Chicago: University of Chicago Press, 1948.
'In the Face of the World's Crisis: A Manifesto by European Catholics Sojourning in America'. *Commonweal*, 12 August 1942, 415–421.
Kelsen, Hans. *Pure Theory of Law*. 1934. Reprint, Clark: Lawbook Exchange, 2008.
Kohn, Hans. 'Review of *Systematic Politics* by Charles E. Merriam'. *American Journal of Sociology* 51 (1946): 575–576.
———. *World Order in Historical Perspective*. Cambridge, MA: Harvard University Press, 1942.
Laski, Harold J. *Democracy in Crisis*. London: Allen & Unwin, 1933.
———. *Liberty in the Modern State*. Harmondsworth: Penguin, 1937.
———. *Studies in the Problems of Sovereignty*. Oxford: Oxford University Press, 1917.
Lattimore, Owen. 'After Four Years'. *Pacific Affairs* 14 (1941): 142.

———. *America and Asia: Problems of Today's War and the Peace*. Claremont, CA: Claremont College, 1943.

———. 'America and the Future of China'. *Amerasia* 5 (1941): 296–297.

———. 'America Has No Time to Lose'. *Asia* 41 (1941): 159–162.

———. 'American Responsibilities in the Far East'. *Virginia Quarterly Review* 16 (1940): 161–174.

———. 'Asia in a New World Order'. *Foreign Policy Reports* 28 (1942): 150–163.

———. 'The Chessboard of Power and Politics'. *Virginia Quarterly Review* 24 (1948): 185.

———. *China Memoirs: Chiang Kai-shek and the War Against Japan*. Edited by Fujiko Isono. Tokyo: University of Tokyo Press, 1990.

———. 'The Czech Exception Disproves the Rules'. *New Republic*, 22 September 1947.

———. 'The Fight for Democracy in Asia'. *Foreign Affairs* 20 (1942): 694–704.

———. 'The Inland Crossroads of Asia'. In *Compass of the World: A Symposium on Political Geography*, edited by Hans W. Weigert and Vilhjalmur Stefansson, 374–394. London: Harrap, 1946.

———. *Inner Asian Frontiers of China*. New York: American Geographic Society, 1940.

———. 'International Chess Game'. *New Republic* 112 (28 May 1945): 731–733.

———. 'The Issue in Asia'. *Annals of the American Academy of Political and Social Science* 243 (1946): 51.

———. *Ordeal by Slander*. Boston: Little, Brown, 1950.

———. *The Situation in Asia*. Boston: Little, Brown, 1949.

———. *Solution in Asia*. London: Cresset Press, 1945.

———. 'Spengler and Toynbee'. *Atlantic Monthly* 181 (1948): 104–105.

———. *Studies in Frontier History: Collected Papers, 1928–1958*. London: Oxford University Press, 1962.

Lattimore, Owen, and Eleanor Holgate Lattimore. *The Making of Modern China: A Short History*. New York: F. Watts, 1944.

Laves, Walter H. C. *The Foundations of a More Stable World Order*. Chicago: University of Chicago Press, 1941.

Lippmann, Walter. *An Inquiry into the Principles of the Good Society*. Boston: Little, Brown, 1937.

Loyseau, Charles. *A Treatise of Orders and Plain Dignities*. Edited by Howell A. Lloyd. Cambridge: Cambridge University Press, 1994.

Luce, Henry R. 'The American Century'. *Life*, 17 February 1941.

Lugard, Frederick. *The Dual Mandate*. 1922. Reprint, London: William Blackwood, 1926.

———. 'Federal Union and the Colonies'. In *Studies in Federal Planning*, edited by Patrick Ransome, 137–166. London: Macmillan, 1943.

Mackinder, Halford J. *Democratic Ideals and Reality*. Harmondsworth: Penguin, 1944.

———. 'The Geographical Pivot of History'. *Geographical Journal* 23 (1904): 421–437.

———. 'The Round World and the Winning of Peace'. In *Compass of the World: A Symposium on Political Geography*, edited by Hans Werner Weigert and Vilhjalmur Stefansson, 161–173. London: Harrap, 1946.

Mahan, Alfred T. *The Influence of Sea Power upon History, 1660–1783*. London: Sampson Low, Marston, 1889.

Malandrino, Corrado, ed. *Corrispondenza americana 1940–1944/Luigi Sturzo, Mario Einaudi*. Florence: Olschki, 1998.

Mann Borgese, Elisabeth. 'Why a Maximalist Constitution'. *Bulletin of the Atomic Scientists* 4 (July 1948): 199–203.

Mannheim, Karl. *Essays on the Sociology of Knowledge*. 1952. Reprint, London: Routledge, 1997.

———. *Ideology and Utopia: An Introduction to the Sociology of Knowledge*. London: Trench, Trubner, 1936.

———. *Man and Society in an Age of Reconstruction: Studies in Modern Social Structure*. 1935. Translated by Edward Shils. London: Routledge, 1940.

———. *Selected Correspondence (1911–1946) of Karl Mannheim, Scientist, Philosopher, and Sociologist*. Edited by Éva Gábor. Lewiston, NY: Edwin Mellen Press, 2003.

Maritain, Jacques. *Antimoderne*. Paris: Éditions de la Revue des Jeunes, 1922.

———. *Christianity and Democracy*. 1943. Reprint, London: Bles, 1945.

———. *Distinguer pour unir: ou, les degrés du savoir*. Paris: Desclée de Brouwer, 1932. Translated into English as *The Degrees of Knowledge*. London: Bles, 1937.

———. 'The End of Machiavellianism'. *Review of Politics* 4 (1942): 1–33.

———. 'Europe and the Federal Idea'. *Commonweal*, 19 April 1940.

———. 'Europe and the Federal Idea II'. *Commonweal*, 26 April 1940.

———. *Humanisme integral*. Paris: F. Aubier, 1936.

———. *Human Rights, Comments and Interpretations. A Symposium Edited by UNESCO with an Introduction by Jacques Maritain*. New York: Columbia University Press, 1949.

———. *La Voie de la paix*. 1947. Reprint in *Œuvres complètes*, vol. 9, 143–164. Fribourg: Editions Universitaires, 1991.

———. *Man and the State*. Chicago: University of Chicago Press, 1951.

———. *Oeuvres Complètes de Jacques Maritain 1939–1943*. Vol. 7. Fribourg: Editions Universitaires, 1988.

———. *The Person and the Common Good*. London: Bles, 1948.

———. 'The Pluralist Principle in Democracy'. *Nation*, 21 April 1945.

———. *Réflexions sur l'Amérique*. 1958. Reprint in *Œuvres complètes*, vol. 10. Fribourg: Editions Universitaires, 1985.

———. *The Rights of Man and Natural Law*. New York: Scribner, 1943.

———. *Three Reformers: Luther, Descartes, Rousseau*. 1925. Reprint, London: Sheed & Ward, 1929.

Mattusch, Kurt R. 'Geopolitics—"Science" of Power Politics'. *Amerasia* 6 (1942): 236–243.

McKeon, Richard. *Freedom and History*. Edited by Zahava Karl McKeon. Chicago: University of Chicago Press, 1990.

———. 'A Philosopher Meditates on Discovery'. In *Moments of Personal Discovery*, edited by R. M. MacIver, 105–132. New York: Institute for Religious and Social Studies, 1952.

———. 'The Philosophic Bases and Material Circumstances of the Rights of Man'. *Ethics* 58 (1948): 180–187.

———. 'A Philosophy for UNESCO'. *Philosophy and Phenomenological Research* 8 (1948): 573.

———. 'Richard McKeon'. In *Thirteen Americans: Their Spiritual Autobiographies*, edited by Louis Finkelstein, 77–114. New York: Institute for Religious and Social Studies, 1953.

———. *Selected Writings of Richard McK... n*. Edited by Zahava Karl McKeon and William G. Swenson. Chicago: Univer. ... of Chicago Press, 1998.

Meinecke, Friedrich. *Die Idee der Staatsräs. in der Neueren Geschichte*. Munich: Oldenbourg, 1924.

Merriam, Charles E. 'The Ends of Government'. *American Political Science Review* 38 (1944): 21–40.

———. 'The Meaning of Democracy'. *Journal of Negro Education* 10 (1941): 309–317.

———. 'The National Resources Planning Board'. *Public Administration Review* 1, no. 2 (1941): 116–121.

———. *New Aspects of Politics*. Chicago: University of Chicago Press, 1925.

———. *The New Democracy and the New Despotism*. New York: McGraw-Hill, 1939.

———. *On the Agenda of Democracy*. Cambridge, MA: Harvard University Press, 1941.

———. 'Physics and Politics'. *American Political Science Review* 40 (1946): 445–457.

———. 'Physics and Politics'. *Bulletin of the Atomic Scientists* 1 (1 May 1946): 9–11.

———. *Political Power: Its Composition and Incidence*. New York: McGraw-Hill, 1934.

———. 'Review of *The New World Order* by H. G. Wells'. *American Journal of Sociology* 46 (1940): 402–403.

———. *Systematic Politics*. Chicago: University of Chicago Press, 1945.

Meston, James. 'Review of *Civitas Dei* by Lionel Curtis'. *International Affairs* 13 (1934): 561–562.

Meyer Magid, Henry. *English Political Pluralism*. New York: Columbia University Press, 1941.

Mitrany, David. *American Interpretations: Four Political Essays*. London: Contact, 1946.

———. 'The Functional Approach to World Organization'. *International Affairs* 24 (1948): 350–363.

———. *The Functional Theory of Politics*. London: London School of Economics, 1975.

———. *Marx against the Peasant: A Study in Social Dogmatism*. London: Weidenfeld and Nicolson, 1951.

———. *A Working Peace System*. London: Royal Institute of International Affairs, 1943.

Mumford, Lewis. *Atomic War—The Way Out*. London: National Peace Council, 1949.

———. 'Gentlemen: You Are Mad!' *Saturday Review of Literature*, 2 March 1946, 5–6.

———. *My Works and Days: A Personal Chronicle*. New York: Harcourt Brace Jovanovich, 1979.

———. *Technics and Civilization.* New York: Harcourt, Brace, 1934.

National Peace Council. *On the New World Order.* London: National Peace Council, 1940.

Niebuhr, Reinhold. 'Authority and Liberty'. *Nation*, 21 March 1942, 347.

———. 'Challenge to Liberals'. *Nation*, 14 September 1940, 221–222.

———. *The Children of Light and the Children of Darkness: A Vindication of Democracy and a Critique of Its Traditional Defenders.* New York: Charles Scribner's Sons, 1944.

———. 'Dr Merriam Sums Up'. *Nation*, 13 October 1945, 380.

———. *Moral Man and Immoral Society: A Study in Ethics and Politics.* New York: Charles Scribner, 1932.

Oakeshott, Michael J. 'Rationalism in Politics'. 1947. In *Rationalism in Politics and Other Essays*, edited by Timothy Fuller, 6–42. Indianapolis: Liberty Press, 1991.

Orwell, George. *Nineteen Eighty-Four.* 1948. Reprint, Harlow: Longman, 1983.

———. 'Not Counting Niggers'. In *The Collected Letters, Essays, and Journalism of George Orwell*, vol. 1, edited by Sonia Orwell and Ian Angus, 360–361. London: Secker and Warburg, 1968.

Pareto, Vilfredo. *Trattato di sociologia generale.* Florence: G. Barbèra, 1916.

Polanyi, Karl. *The Great Transformation: The Political and Economic Origins of Our Time.* New York: Amereon House, 1944.

Polanyi, Michael. 'Can Science Bring Peace?' In *The Challenge of Our Time*, 40–65. London: P. Marshall, 1948.

———. *The Contempt of Freedom: The Russian Experiment and After.* London: Watts, 1940.

———. 'The English and the Continent'. *Political Quarterly* 14 (1943): 372–381.

———. 'Foundation of Academic Freedom'. *Lancet* 249 (1947): 583–586. Reprint in *Logic of Liberty*, 32–48.

———. 'The Foundations of Freedom in Science'. *Bulletin of the Atomic Scientists* 2 (1 December 1946): 6–7.

———. *Full Employment and Free Trade.* Cambridge: Cambridge University Press, 1945.

———. 'The Growth of Thought in Society'. *Economica* 8 (1941): 421–456.

———. *The Logic of Liberty: Reflections and Rejoinders.* London: Routledge, 1951.

———. 'The Policy of Atomic Science'. *Time and Tide* 27 (1946): 749.

———. *Science, Faith and Society.* 1946. 2nd ed., Chicago: University of Chicago Press, 1964.

———. 'The Socialist Error. Review of *The Road to Serfdom* by F. A. v Hayek'. *Spectator*, 30 March 1944, 293.

Popper, Karl R. *The Open Society and Its Enemies.* 1945. Reprint, Princeton, NJ: Princeton University Press, 2013.

Ransome, Patrick, ed. *Studies in Federal Planning.* London: Macmillan, 1943.

———. *Towards the United States of Europe: Studies on the Making of the European Constitution.* London: Lothian Foundation Press, 1991.

Ratzel, Friedrich. *Anthropo-geographie.* Stuttgart: J. Englehorn, 1882–1912.

———. *Politische Geographie.* 1897. Reprint, Berlin: Oldenbourg, 1923.

A Report on the International Control of Atomic Energy. Washington, DC: Government Printing Office, 1946. Prepared for the Secretary of State's Committee on Atomic Energy by a Board of Consultants: Chester I. Bernard, J. R. Oppenheimer, Charles A. Thomas, Harry A. Winne, David E. Lilienthal, Chairman.

Robbins, Lionel. 'An Anglo-French Federation?' *Spectator*, 24 November 1939, 11–12.

———. *Economic Aspects of Federation*. London: Macmillan, 1941.

———. *The Economic Causes of War*. London: Jonathan Cape, 1939.

———. *Economic Planning and International Order*. London: Macmillan, 1937.

———. *An Essay on the Nature and Significance of Economic Science*. London: Macmillan, 1932.

———. 'Interim Report on Economic Aspects of the Federal Constitution'. In *Towards the United States of Europe: Studies on the Making of the European Constitution*, edited by Patrick Ransome, 91–97. London: Lothian Foundation Press, 1991.

———. 'The Optimum Theory of Population'. In *Essays in Economics: In Honour of Edwin Cannan*, edited by T. E. Gregory and Hugh Dalton, 103–133. London: Routledge, 1927.

Schmitt, Carl. *Land and Sea: A World-Historical Meditation.* 1942. Translated by Samuel Garrett Zeitlin. Reprint, Candor, NY: Telos, 2015.

———. *The Nomos of the Earth in the International Law of the Jus Publicum Europaeum.* 1951. Translated by G. L. Ulmen. Reprint, New York: Telos Press, 2003.

———. *Völkerrechtliche Großraumordnung mit Interventionsverbot für raumfremde Mächte: Ein Beitrag zum Reichsbegriff im Völkerrecht.* 1939. Reprint, Berlin: Duncker Humblot, 1991.

Shils, Edward. *The Atomic Bomb in World Politics*. London: National Peace Council, 1948.

———. 'The Society for Freedom in Science'. *Bulletin of the Atomic Scientists* 3 (March 1947): 80–82.

Spengler, Oswald. *The Decline of the West.* 1922. Reprint, New York: Knopf, 1939.

Sprout, Harold, and Margaret Sprout. *Toward a New Order of Sea Power: American Naval Policy and the World Scene, 1918–1922.* 1940. 2nd ed., Princeton, NJ: Princeton University Press, 1943.

Spykman, Nicholas J. *America's Strategy in World Politics: The United States and the Balance of Power*. New York: Harcourt, Brace, 1942.

———. 'Frontiers, Security, and International Organization'. *Geographical Review* 32 (1942): 436–447.

———. *The Geography of the Peace.* New York: Harcourt Brace and Co., 1944.

———. *The Social Theory of Georg Simmel.* 1923. Reprint, New York: Transaction, 2007.

Stefansson, Vilhjalmur. 'The North American Arctic'. In *Compass of the World: A Symposium on Political Geography*, edited by Hans W. Weigert and Vilhjalmur Stefansson, 215–265. London: Harrap, 1946.

Strausz-Hupé, Robert. *Geopolitics: The Struggle for Space and Power.* 1942. Reprint, New York: Arno Press, 1972.

Streit, Clarence K. 'Lionel Curtis—The Federalist'. *Freedom and Union* 9 (1949): 8–9.

———. 'Lionel Curtis—Prophet of Federal Union'. *Freedom & Union* 11 (1956): 11–12.

———. *Union Now: A Proposal for a Federal Union of the Democracies of the North Atlantic*. New York: Harper, 1939.

———. *Union Now with Britain*. London: Right Book Club, 1941.

Sturzo, Luigi. 'Chiarimenti su Maritain'. *Le mouvement des faits et des idées* 25 (1927).

———. *Il Partito popolare italiano*. Rome: Istituto Luigi Sturzo, 2003.

———. 'Il Popularismo'. *Politique*, 15 August 1928.

———. *The International Community and the Right of War*. Translated by Barbara Barclay Carter. London: Unwin, 1929.

———. *Italy and Fascism*. London: Faber and Gwyer, 1926.

———. *Italy and the New World Order*. New York: Macdonald, 1944.

———. 'La lutte contre le communisme'. *La Terre Wallonne* 35 (1936): 75–84.

———. *La mia battaglia da New York*. 1949. Reprint, Rome: Edizioni di storia e letteratura, 2004.

———. *La società. Sua natura e leggi*. 1935. Reprint in *Opera Omnia* 3, Bologna: Zanichelli, 1953.

———. *Miscellanea londinese. Anni 1937–1940*. Soveria Mannelli: Rubbettino, 2008.

———. *Nationalism and Internationalism*. New York: Roy, 1946.

———. *Politica e morale*. 1938. Reprint in *Opera Omnia*, vol. 4. Bologna: Zanichelli, 1972.

Sturzo, Luigi, and Alcide De Gasperi. *Luigi Sturzo e Alcide De Gasperi, Carteggio (1920–1953)*. Soveria Mannelli: Rubbettino, 2006.

Toynbee, Arnold J. *A Study of History*. Edited by Edward D. Myers. London: Oxford University Press, 1934.

Turner, Frederick Jackson. *The Frontier in American History*. 1893. Reprint, New York: Henry Holt, 1947.

Voegelin, Eric. 'The Origins of Scientism'. *Social Research* 15 (1948): 462–494.

Wallace, Henry A. *New Frontiers*. New York: Reynal and Hitchcock, 1934.

Wallace, Henry A., Francis J. McConnell, Willis J. King, Edgar S. Brightman, Umphrey Lee, G. Baez-Embrago, et al. *Christian Bases of World Order*. New York: Abingdon-Cokesbury Press, 1943.

Weigert, Hans W. *Generals and Geographers: The Twilight of Geopolitics*. New York: Oxford University Press, 1942.

———. 'Oswald Spengler, Twenty-Five Years After'. *Foreign Affairs* 21 (1942): 120.

———. 'Review of *The Geography of the Peace* by N. J. Spykman'. *Saturday Review*, 22 April 1944, 10.

Weigert, Hans W., and Vilhjalmur Stefansson, eds. *Compass of the World: A Symposium on Political Geography*. London: Harrap, 1946.

Weigert, Hans W., Vilhjalmur Stefansson, and Richard Edes Harrison, eds. *New Compass of the World: A Symposium on Political Geography*. London: Harrap, 1949.

Wells, H. G. *After Democracy: Addresses and Papers on the Present World Situation*. London: Watts, 1932.

————. *Anticipations of the Reaction of Mechanical and Scientific Progress upon Human Life and Thought.* London: Chapman and Hall, 1902.

————. *Guide to the New World: A Handbook of Constructive World Revolution.* London: V. Gollancz, 1941.

————. *A Modern Utopia.* London: Chapman and Hall, 1905.

————. *The New World Order. Whether It Is Attainable, How It Can Be Attained and What Sort of World a World at Peace Will Have to Be.* London: Secker and Warburg, 1940.

————. *New Worlds for Old: A Plain Account of Modern Socialism.* London: Archibald Constable, 1909.

————. *The Open Conspiracy: Blueprints for a World Revolution.* London: V. Gollancz, 1928.

————. *Phœnix: A Summary of the Inescapable Conditions of World Reorganisation.* London: Secker and Warburg, 1942.

————. *The Rights of Man: An Essay in Collective Definition.* Brighton: Poynings Press, 1943.

————. *The War in the Air.* London: George Bell & Sons, 1908.

————. *What Is Coming? A Forecast of Things after the War.* London: Cassell, 1916.

————. *The World Set Free.* 1914. Reprint, London: Hogarth, 1988.

Wight, Martin. *Four Seminal Thinkers in International Theory: Machiavelli, Grotius, Kant, and Mazzini.* Oxford: Oxford University Press, 2005.

Willkie, Wendell L. *One World.* New York: Simon & Schuster, 1943.

Wilson, Harold. 'Economic Aspects of Federation'. In *Towards the United States of Europe: Studies on the Making of the European Constitution,* edited by Patrick Ransome, 205–212. London: Lothian Foundation Press, 1991.

Wohl, Paul. 'An American "Geopolitical Masterhand"'. *Asia* 41 (1941): 601.

Woodward, Ernest L., ed. *Foundations of World Order.* Denver: University of Denver, 1949.

Wootton, Barbara. 'Economic Problems of Federal Union'. *New Commonwealth Quarterly* 5 (1939): 150–156.

————. *End Social Inequality: A Programme for Ordinary People.* London: Kegan Paul, Trench, Trubner, 1941.

————. *Freedom under Planning.* London: Allen & Unwin, 1945.

————. *In a World I Never Made.* London: Allen & Unwin, 1967.

————. *Lament for Economics.* London: Allen & Unwin, 1938.

————. *Plan or No Plan.* London: V. Gollancz, 1934.

————. 'Review of *Essays on the Sociology of Knowledge* by Karl Mannheim. Edited by Paul Kecskemeti'. *Philosophy* 28 (1953): 278–279.

————. *Socialism and Federation.* Federal Tracts 6. London: Macmillan, 1941. Reprint in *Studies in Federal Planning,* edited by Patrick Ransome, 269–298. London: Macmillan, 1943.

Wootton, Barbara, and Friedrich Hayek. 'Economic Planning: Road to Serfdom or Freedom?' *Left* 121 (1946): 255–261.

Wright, Quincy. 'Constitution Making as Process'. *Common Cause* 2 (1948): 284–285.

————. *Human Rights and the World Order.* New York: Commission to Study the Organization of Peace, 1943.

Zimmern, Alfred E. *Nationality and Government, with Other Wartime Essays*. London: Chatto and Windus, 1918.

———. *The Third British Empire*. London: Oxford University Press, 1926.

SECONDARY SOURCES

Acanfora, Paolo. 'Myths and the Political Use of Religion in Christian Democratic Culture'. *Journal of Modern Italian Studies* 12 (2007): 307–338.

Adcock, Robert. 'Interpreting Behavioralism'. In *Modern Political Science: Anglo-American Exchanges since 1880*, edited by Robert Adcock, Mark Bevir, and Shannon C. Stimson, 180–208. Princeton, NJ: Princeton University Press, 2007.

Adcock, Robert, Mark Bevir, and Shannon C. Stimson, eds. *Modern Political Science: Anglo-American Exchanges since 1880*. Princeton, NJ: Princeton University Press, 2007.

Addison, Paul. *The Road to 1945: British Politics and the Second World War*. 1975. Reprint, London: Pimlico, 1994.

Adorno, Theodor, and Max Horkheimer. *Dialectic of Enlightenment*. 1944. Reprint, London: Verso, 1986.

Ageron, Charles-Robert. 'L'idée d'Eurafrique et le débat colonial Franco-allemand dans l'entre-deux-guerres'. *Revue d'histoire moderne et contemporaine* 22 (1975): 446–475.

Agnew, John A. *Globalization & Sovereignty*. Lanham, MD: Rowman & Littlefield, 2009.

Ambrosini, Gaspare. 'Il saluto dell'Istituto Luigi Sturzo'. In *Luigi Sturzo nella Storia d'Italia*, ed. Francesco Malgeri, 84. Rome: Edizioni di Storia e Letteratura, 1973.

Amrith, Sunil, and Glenda Sluga. 'New Histories of the United Nations'. *Journal of World History* 19 (2008): 251–274.

Anderson, Brian C. *Raymond Aron: The Recovery of the Political*. Lanham, MD: Rowman & Littlefield, 1997.

Anderson, Dorothy. 'David Mitrany (1888–1975): An Appreciation of His Life and Work'. *Review of International Studies* 24 (1998): 577–592.

Anderson, Perry. 'Imperium'. *New Left Review* 83 (2013): 6–111.

Archibugi, Daniele, and David Held. *Cosmopolitan Democracy: An Agenda for a New World Order*. Cambridge: Polity, 1995.

Archibugi, Daniele, Mathias Koenig-Archibugi, and Raffaele Marchetti, eds. *Global Democracy: Normative and Empirical Perspectives*. Cambridge: Cambridge University Press, 2012.

Armitage, David. 'The Fifty Years Rift: Intellectual History and International Relations'. *Modern Intellectual History* 1 (2004): 97–109.

———. *Foundations of Modern International Thought*. Cambridge: Cambridge University Press, 2013.

———. 'Globalizing Jeremy Bentham'. *History of Political Thought* 32 (2011): 63–82.

Ashworth, Lucian M. *Creating International Studies: Angell, Mitrany and the Liberal Tradition*. Aldershot: Ashgate, 1999.

———. *International Relations and the Labour Party: Intellectuals and Policy Making from 1918–1945*. London: Tauris, 2007.

————. 'Mapping a New World: Geography and the Interwar Study of International Relations'. *International Studies Quarterly* 57 (2013): 138–149.

————. 'A New Politics for a Global Age: David Mitrany's *A Working Peace System*'. In *Classics of International Relations: Essays in Criticism and Appreciation*, edited by Henrik Bliddal, Casper Sylvest, and Peter Wilson, 59–68. Abingdon: Routledge, 2013.

————. 'Where Are the Idealists in Interwar International Relations?' *Review of International Studies* 32 (2006): 291–308.

Ashworth, Lucian M., and David Long, eds. *New Perspectives on International Functionalism*. London: Macmillan, 1999.

Audier, Serge. *Le Colloque Lippmann: Aux origines du néo-libéralisme*. Lomont: Le Bord de l'Eau, 2008.

————. *Machiavel: Conflit et liberté*. Paris: Vrin-EHESS, 2005.

Baker, Andrew. *Constructing a Post-war Order: The Rise of US Hegemony and the Origins of the Cold War*. London: I.B. Tauris, 2011.

Banerjee, Sukanya. *Becoming Imperial Citizens: Indians in the Late-Victorian Empire*. Durham, NC: Duke University Press, 2010.

Baratta, Joseph P. 'The Internationalist History of the World Federalist Movement'. *Peace & Change* 14 (1989): 372–403.

————. *The Politics of World Federation: From World Federalism to Global Governance*. New York: Greenwood, 2004.

————. *Strengthening the United Nations: A Bibliography on U.N. Reform and World Federalism*. New York: Greenwood, 1987.

Barbano, Filippo. 'Luigi Sturzo esiliato e la sociologia in America'. In *Universalità e cultura nel pensiero di Luigi Sturzo: Atti del convegno internazionale di studio svoltosi presso l'Istituto Luigi Sturzo dal 28 al 30 ottobre 1999*, 133–158. Soveria Mannelli: Rubbettino, 2001.

————. *Pluralismo, un lessico per la democrazia*. Turin: Bollati Boringhieri, 1999.

Barbieri, Luigi. *Persona, Chiesa e Stato nel pensiero di Luigi Sturzo*. Soveria Mannelli: Rubbettino, 2002.

Barnes, Dayna. 'Think Tanks and a New Order in East Asia: The Council of Foreign Relations and the Institute of Pacific Relations during World War II'. *Journal of American-East Asian Relations* 22 (2015): 89–119.

Barraclough, Geoffrey. *European Unity in Thought and Action*. Oxford: Blackwell, 1963.

Barré, Jean-Luc. *Jacques et Raïssa Maritain: les mendiants du Ciel, biographies croisées*. Paris: Stock, 1995.

Bauernfeind, Neil D. 'Lord Davies and the New Commonwealth Society 1932–1944'. MPhil dissertation, University of Wales at Aberystwyth, 1990.

Baverez, Nicolas. *Raymond Aron: Un moraliste au temps des idéologies*. Paris: Flammarion, 1993.

Bayly, C. A. *The Making of the Modern World, 1780–1914*. Oxford: Oxford University Press, 2003.

Bayly, C. A., Sven Beckert, Matthew Connelly, Isabel Hofmeyr, Wendy Kozol, and Patricia Seed. 'AHR Conversation: On Transnational History'. *American Historical Review* 111 (2006): 1441–1464.

Bell, Daniel. *The End of Ideology: On Exhaustion of Political Ideas in the Fifties.* London: Glencoe, 1960.

Bell, Duncan. 'Before the Democratic Peace: Racial Utopianism, Empire, and the Abolition of War'. *European Journal of International Relations* 20 (2014): 647–670.

———. 'Beware of False Prophets: Biology, Human Nature and the Future of International Relations Theory'. *International Affairs* 82 (2006) 493–494.

———. *The Idea of Greater Britain: Empire and the Future of World Order, 1860–1900.* Princeton, NJ: Princeton University Press, 2007.

———. 'Language, Legitimacy, and the Project of Critique'. *Alternatives* 27 (2002): 327–350.

———. 'The Project for a New Anglo Century: Race, Space, and Global Order'. In *Anglo-America and Its Discontents: Civilizational Identities beyond West and East,* edited by Peter Katzenstein, 33–56. London: Routledge, 2012.

———. 'The Victorian Idea of a Global State'. In *Victorian Visions of Global Order: Empire and International Relations in Nineteenth-Century Political Thought,* edited by Duncan Bell, 159–185. Cambridge: Cambridge University Press, 2007.

———, ed. *Victorian Visions of Global Order: Empire and International Relations in Nineteenth-Century Political Thought.* Cambridge: Cambridge University Press, 2007.

———. 'Writing the World: Disciplinary History and Beyond'. *International Affairs* 85 (2009): 3–22.

Betz, Joseph. 'Review of *Pluralism in Theory and Practice: Richard McKeon and American Philosophy* by Eugene Garver and Richard Buchanan'. *Transactions of the Charles S. Peirce Society* 37 (2001): 436–441.

Bevir, Mark. *The Making of British Socialism.* Princeton, NJ: Princeton University Press, 2011.

———, ed. *Modern Pluralism: Anglo-American Debates since 1880.* Cambridge: Cambridge University Press, 2012.

Billington, David P. *Lothian: Philip Kerr and the Quest for World Order.* Westport, CT: Praeger, 2006.

Bisceglia, Louis. *Norman Angell and Liberal Internationalism in Britain, 1931–1935.* New York: Garland, 1982.

Bitsch, Marie-Thérèse, and Gérard Bossuat, eds. *L'Europe unie et l'Afrique: de l'idée d'Eurafrique à la convention de Lomé.* Brussels: Bruylant, 2005.

Bliddal, Henrik, Casper Sylvest, and Peter Wilson, eds. *Classics of International Relations: Essays in Criticism and Appreciation.* Abingdon: Routledge, 2013.

Blouet, Brian W. *Geopolitics and Globalization in the Twentieth Century.* London: Reaktion Books, 2001.

Blower, Brooke. "From Isolationism to Neutrality: A New Framework for Understanding American Political Culture, 1919–1941." *Diplomatic History* 38 (2014): 345–376.

Boer, Pim den, Peter Bugge, and Ole Wæver. *The History of the Idea of Europe.* London: Routledge, 1995.

Bohman, James. *Democracy across Borders: From Dêmos to Dêmoi.* Cambridge, MA: MIT Press, 2007.

Bonaccorsi, Orazio. *La laicità nel pensiero politico e giuridico di Don Luigi Sturzo.* Soveria Mannelli: Rubbettino, 2011.

Bonfreschi, Lucia. *Raymond Aron e il Gollismo, 1940–1969*. Soveria Mannelli: Rubbettino, 2013.

Borgwardt, Elizabeth. *A New Deal for the World: America's Vision for Human Rights*. Cambridge, MA: Harvard University Press, 2005.

Bosco, Andrea, ed. *The Federal Idea vol. 1: The History of Federalism from the Enlightenment to 1945*. London: Lothian Foundation Press, 1991.

———, ed. *The Federal Idea vol. 2: The History of Federalism since 1945*. London: Lothian Foundation Press, 1992.

———. 'Federal Union, Chatham House, the Foreign Office and Anglo-French Union in Spring 1940'. In *The Federal Idea vol. 1: The History of Federalism from the Enlightenment to 1945*, edited by Andrea Bosco, 291–325. London: Lothian Foundation Press, 1991.

———. *Federal Union and the Origins of the 'Churchill Proposal': The Federalist Debate in the UK from Munich to the Fall of France, 1938–1940*. London: Lothian Foundation Press, 1992.

———. 'Lothian, Curtis, Kimber and the Federal Union Movement (1938–40)'. *Journal of Contemporary History* 23 (1988): 465–502.

Bosco, Andrea, and Alex May. *The Round Table: The Empire/Commonwealth and British Foreign Policy*. London: Lothian Foundation Press, 1997.

Bottici, Chiara. *A Philosophy of Political Myth*. Cambridge: Cambridge University Press, 2010.

Bowden, Brett. *The Empire of Civilization: The Evolution of an Imperial Idea*. Chicago: University of Chicago Press, 2009.

Boyer, Paul S. *By the Bomb's Early Light: American Thought and Culture at the Dawn of the Atomic Age*. New York: Pantheon, 1985.

Braumoeller, Bear F. "The Myth of American Isolationism." *Foreign Policy Analysis* 6 (2010): 349–371.

Brendon, Piers. *The Decline and Fall of the British Empire, 1781–1997*. London: Vintage, 2008.

Briggs, Laura, Gladys McCormick, and J. T. Way. 'Transnationalism: A Category of Analysis'. *American Quarterly* 60 (2008): 625–648.

Brittan, Samuel. 'Hayek, Friedrich August (1899–1992)'. In *Oxford Dictionary of National Biography*. 2004. www.oxforddnb.com.

Brome, Vincent. *H. G. Wells*. London: House of Stratus, 2001.

Brown, Andrew. *J. D. Bernal: The Sage of Science*. Oxford: Oxford University Press, 2005.

Buchanan, Tom, and Martin Conway, eds. *Political Catholicism in Europe, 1918–1965*. Oxford: Oxford University Press, 1996.

Buck, David D. 'Lattimore, Owen'. In *American National Biography*. 2000. www.anb.org/articles/14/14-00355.html.

Burgess, Michael. *The British Tradition of Federalism*. Madison: Fairleigh Dickinson University Press, 1995.

———. *Federalism and the European Union: The Building of Europe, 1950–2000*. London: Routledge, 2013.

Burgin, Angus. *The Great Persuasion: Reinventing Free Markets since the Depression*. Cambridge, MA: Harvard University Press, 2012.

Butler, James. *Lord Lothian (Philip Kerr), 1882–1940*. London: Macmillan, 1960.

Caldwell, Bruce. *Hayek's Challenge: An Intellectual Biography of F. A. Hayek.* Chicago: University of Chicago Press, 2004.

Callahan, Michael D. *Mandates and Empire: The League of Nations and Africa, 1914–1931.* Brighton: Sussex Academic Press, 1999.

Campanini, Giorgio. *Il pensiero politico di Luigi Sturzo.* Caltanissetta: Salvatore Sciascia Editore, 2001.

———. 'Luigi Sturzo e la laicità dello stato'. In *Luigi Sturzo e la democrazia nella prospettiva del terzo millennio*, vol. 1, edited by Eugenio Guccione, 705–712. Florence: Olschki, 2004.

Campbell, Stuart L. 'The Four Paretos of Raymond Aron'. *Journal of the History of Ideas* 47 (1986): 287–298.

———. 'Raymond Aron: The Making of a Cold Warrior'. *Historian* 51 (1989): 551–573.

Carter, April, and Geoff Stokes, eds. *Democratic Theory Today: Challenges for the 21st Century.* Cambridge: Polity, 2002.

Case, Shirley Jackson. 'Review of *Civitas Dei* by Lionel Curtis'. *Journal of Religion* 18 (1938): 311–313.

Castelli, Alberto. 'Pianificazione e libertà'. *Il Politico* 3 (2001): 399–431.

———. *Una pace da costruire: i socialisti britannici e il federalismo.* Milan: Franco Angeli, 2002.

Castellin, Luca G. 'Lo "Sguardo" Di Arnold J. Toynbee sulla politica internazionale del XX Secolo'. *Filosofia Politica* 25 (2011): 57–70.

Cataldo, Salvatore. *Giuseppe Antonio Borgese.* Messina: Sicania, 1990.

Ceadel, Martin. *Living the Great Illusion: Sir Norman Angell, 1872–1967.* Oxford: Oxford University Press, 2009.

———. *Semi-detached Idealists: The British Peace Movement and International Relations, 1854–1945.* Oxford: Oxford University Press, 2000.

Chang, Ha-Joon. *Economics: A User's Guide.* London: Penguin, 2014.

Chappel, James. 'Beyond Tocqueville: A Plea to Stop "Taking Religion Seriously"'. *Modern Intellectual History* 10 (2013): 697–708.

———. 'Slaying the Leviathan: Catholicism and the Rebirth of European Conservatism, 1920–1950'. PhD dissertation, Columbia University, 2012.

Chamedes, Giuliana. 'Cardinal Pizzardo and the Internationalization of Catholic Action'. In *Gouvernement pontifical sous Pie XI*, edited by Laura Pettinaroli, 359–378. Rome: École française de Rome, 2012.

———. 'The Vatican and the Reshaping of the European International Order after World War I'. *Historical Journal* 56 (2013): 955–976.

Clavin, Patricia. 'Defining Transnationalism'. *Contemporary European History* 14 (2005): 421–439.

———. *Securing the World Economy: The Reinvention of the League of Nations, 1920–1946.* Oxford: Oxford University Press, 2013.

Cohen, Jean. *Globalization and Sovereignty.* Cambridge: Cambridge University Press, 2012.

Collini, Stefan. *Absent Minds: Intellectuals in Britain.* Oxford: Oxford University Press, 2007.

———. *Public Moralists: Political Thought and Intellectual Life in Britain 1850–1930.* Oxford: Clarendon, 1991.

Collins, Michael. 'Decolonisation and the "Federal Moment"'. *Diplomacy & State-craft* 24 (2013): 21–40.

Colombo, Alessandro. 'L'Europa e la società internazionale: Gli aspetti culturali e istitutuzionali della convivenza internazionale in Raymond Aron, Martin Wight e Carl Schmitt'. *Quaderni di Scienza Politica* 6 (1999): 251–301.

Colvert, Gavin T., ed. *The Renewal of Civilization: Essays in Honor of Jacques Maritain.* Washington, DC: American Maritain Association, 2010.

Connelly, John. *From Enemy to Brother: The Revolution in Catholic Teaching on the Jews, 1933–1965.* Cambridge, MA: Harvard University Press, 2012.

Conrad, Sebastian, and Dominic Sachsenmaier. *Competing Visions of World Order: Global Moments and Movements, 1880s–1930s.* New York: Palgrave Macmillan, 2007.

Cooper, Frederick. *Citizenship between Empire and Nation: Remaking France and French Africa, 1945–1960.* Princeton, NJ: Princeton University Press, 2014.

Cosgrove, Denis E. *Apollo's Eye: A Cartographic Genealogy of the Earth in the Western Imagination.* Baltimore: Johns Hopkins University Press, 2001.

Cotton, James. *Asian Frontier Nationalism: Owen Lattimore and the American Policy Debate.* Manchester: Manchester University Press, 1989.

Coupland, Philip M. *Britannia, Europa and Christendom: British Christians and European Integration.* Basingstoke: Palgrave Macmillan, 2006.

Craig, Campbell. *Glimmer of a New Leviathan: Total War in the Realism of Niebuhr, Morgenthau, and Waltz.* New York: Columbia University Press, 2003.

———. 'The Resurgent Idea of World Government'. *Ethics & International Affairs* 22 (2008): 133–142.

Craig, Campbell, and Sergey Radchenko. *The Atomic Bomb and the Origins of the Cold War.* New Haven, CT: Yale University Press, 2008.

Cramer, Gisela, and Ursula Prutsch. 'Nelson A. Rockefeller's Office of Inter-American Affairs and the Quest for Pan-American Unity: An Introductory Essay'. In *¡Américas Unidas! Nelson A. Rockefeller's Office of Inter-American Affairs (1940–46)*, edited by Gisela Cramer and Ursula Prutch, 15–51. Madrid: Iberoamericana Vervuert, 2012.

Crampton, Andrew, and Gearóid Ó Tuathail. 'Intellectuals, Institutions and Ideology: The Case of Robert Strausz-Hupé and "American Geopolitics"'. *Political Geography* 15 (1996): 533–555.

Cullen, Christopher, and Joseph Allan Clair, eds. *Maritain and America.* Washington, DC: American Maritain Association, 2009.

D'Addio, Mario. 'Democrazia e comunità internazionale in Luigi Sturzo'. In *Luigi Sturzo e la democrazia nella prospettiva del terzo millennio: Atti del Seminario internazionale, Erice, 7–11 ottobre 2000*, 1–25. Florence: L.S. Olschki, 2004.

Darwin, John. *After Tamerlane: The Global History of Empire since 1405.* London: Allen Lane, 2007.

———. *The Empire Project.* Cambridge: Cambridge University Press, 2009.

———. *The End of the British Empire: The Historical Debate.* Oxford: Blackwell, 1991.

Daunton, Martin. 'Britain and Globalization since 1850: The Rise of Insular Capitalism 1914–1939'. *Transactions of the Royal Historical Society* 17 (2007): 1–33.

Deák, István, Jan Tomasz Gross, and Tony Judt, eds. *The Politics of Retribution in Europe: World War II and Its Aftermath*. Princeton, NJ: Princeton University Press, 2000.

Dedman, Martin J. *The Origins and Development of the European Union, 1945–95: A History of European Integration*. London: Routledge, 1996.

Deighton, Anne. 'Entente Neo-Coloniale? Ernest Bevin and the Proposals for an Anglo–French Third World Power, 1945–1949'. *Diplomacy & Statecraft* 17 (2006): 835–852.

De Ligio, Giulio, ed. *Raymond Aron, penseur de l'Europe et de la nation*. Brussels: P. Lang, 2012.

Delzell, Charles F. 'The European Federalist Movement in Italy: First Phase, 1918–1947'. *Journal of Modern History* 32 (1960): 241–250.

Denord, Francois. 'French Neoliberalism and Its Divisions: From the Colloque Walter Lippmann to the Fifth Republic'. In *The Road from Mont Pèlerin: The Making of the Neoliberal Thought Collective*, edited by Philip Mirowski and Dieter Plehwe, 45–67. Cambridge, MA: Harvard University Press, 2009.

Depew, David J. 'Between Pragmatism and Realism: Richard McKeon's Philosophic Semantics'. In *Pluralism in Theory and Practice*, edited by Eugene Garver and Richard Buchanan, 30–39. Nashville: Vanderbilt University Press, 2000.

De Rosa, Gabriele. *Il Partito Popolare Italiano*. Rome: Laterza, 1988.

———. *Luigi Sturzo*. Turin: UTET, 1977.

Deudney, Daniel H. *Bounding Power: Republican Security Theory from the Polis to the Global Village*. Princeton, NJ: Princeton University Press, 2007.

Deudney, Daniel H., and G. John Ikenberry. 'The Nature and Sources of Liberal International Order'. *Review of International Studies* 25 (1999): 179–196.

Dickès-Lafargue, Godeleine, and Claude Rousseau. *Le dilemme de Jacques Maritain: L'évolution d'une pensée en philosophie politique*. Versailles: Editions de Paris, 2005.

Di Lascia, Alfred. 'Luigi Sturzo nella cultura degli Stati Uniti'. In *Luigi Sturzo e la democrazia europea*, edited by Gabriele De Rosa, 119–145. Rome: Laterza, 1990.

Drake, David. *Intellectuals and Politics in Post-war France*. Basingstoke: Palgrave, 2002.

———. 'Raymond Aron and *La France libre* (June 1940–September 1944)'. In *A History of the French in London: Liberty, Equality, Opportunity*, edited by Debra Kelly and Martyn Cornick, 373–391. London: University of London Institute of Historical Research, 2013.

Dramé, Papa, and Samir Saul. 'Le projet d'Eurafrique en France (1946–1960): Quête de puissance ou atavisme colonial?' *Guerres mondiales et conflits contemporains* 216 (2004): 95–114.

Dryzek, John S. 'Transnational Democracy in an Insecure World'. *International Political Science Review* 27 (2006): 101–119.

Dubow, Saul. 'Colonial Nationalism, the Milner Kindergarten and the Rise of "South Africanism", 1902–10'. *History Workshop Journal* 43 (1997): 53–85.

Duranti, Marco. 'Conservatives and the European Convention on Human Rights'. In *Toward a New Moral World Order. Menschenrechtspolitik und Volkerrecht seit*

1945, edited by Norbert Frei and Annette Weinke, 82–93. Weimar: Wallstein Verlag, 2013.

Durbin, Elizabeth. *New Jerusalems: The Labour Party and the Economics of Democratic Socialism*. London: Routledge & Kegan Paul, 1985.

Dzuback, Mary Ann. *Robert M. Hutchins: Portrait of an Educator*. Chicago: University of Chicago Press, 1991.

Ebenstein, Alan. *Friedrich Hayek: A Biography*. Chicago: University of Chicago Press, 2003.

Edgerton, David. *England and the Aeroplane: An Essay on a Militant and Technological Nation*. Basingstoke: Macmillan, 1980.

Edwards, Mark T. *The Right of the Protestant Left: God's Totalitarianism*. Basingstoke: Palgrave, 2012.

Eisenberg, Avigail I. *Reconstructing Political Pluralism*. New York: State University of New York Press, 1995.

Erdmann, Martin. *Building the Kingdom of God on Earth: The Churches' Contribution to Marshal Public Support for World Order and Peace, 1919–1945*. Eugene, OR: Wipf and Stock, 2005.

Esposito, Roberto, and Carlo Galli, eds. *Enciclopedia del pensiero politico. Autori, concetti, dottrine*. Rome: Laterza, 2005.

Farish, Matthew. *The Contours of America's Cold War*. Minneapolis: University of Minnesota Press, 2010.

Farrell-Vinay, Giovanna. 'The London Exile of Don Luigi Sturzo (1924–1940)'. *Heythrop Journal* 45 (2004): 158–177.

Ferguson, Yale H., and R. J. Barry Jones, eds. *Political Space: Frontiers of Change and Governance in a Globalizing World*. Albany: State University of New York Press, 2002.

Fioravanti, Maurizio. *Costituzione*. Bologna: Il Mulino, 1999.

Flood, Christopher. 'André Labarthe and Raymond Aron: Political Myth and Ideology in La France Libre'. *Journal of European Studies* 23 (1993): 139–158.

Formigoni, Guido. *L'Italia dei cattolici: Dal Risorgimento a oggi*. Bologna: Il Mulino, 2010.

Fox, Richard Wightman. *Reinhold Niebuhr: A Biography*. New York: Pantheon Books, 1985.

Freeden, Michael. *Ideologies and Political Theory: A Conceptual Approach*. Oxford: Clarendon, 1998.

———. 'Ideology, Political Theory and Political Philosophy'. In *Handbook of Political Theory*, edited by Gerald Gaus and Chandran Kukathas, 3–17. London: Sage, 2004.

Frei, Christoph. *Hans J. Morgenthau: An Intellectual Biography*. Baton Rouge: Louisiana State University Press, 2001.

Frémeaux, Jacques. *Les empires coloniaux dans le processus de mondialisation*. Paris: Maisonneuve et Larose, 2002.

Frost, Bryan-Paul, and Daniel J. Mahoney, eds. *Political Reason in the Age of Ideology: Essays in Honor of Raymond Aron*. New Brunswick, NJ: Transaction, 2011.

Fruci, Alessandro. *La comunità internazionale nel pensiero politico di Luigi Sturzo*. Rome: Aracne, 2009.

Gagliardi, Alessio. *Il corporativismo fascista.* Rome: Laterza, 2010.
Galli, Carlo. *Political Spaces and Global War.* Translated by Elisabeth Fay. Edited by Adam Sitze. Minneapolis: University of Minnesota Press, 2010.
Galston, William A. *Liberal Pluralism: The Implications of Value Pluralism for Political Theory and Practice.* Cambridge: Cambridge University Press, 2002.
Gamble, Andrew. *Hayek: The Iron Cage of Liberty.* Cambridge: Polity, 1996.
Gerace, Michael P. 'Between Mackinder and Spykman: Geopolitics, Containment and After'. *Comparative Strategy* 10 (1991): 347–364.
Gerber, Larry G. 'The Baruch Plan and the Origins of the Cold War'. *Diplomatic History* 6 (1982): 69–96.
Gervasoni, Marco. *Georges Sorel: una biografia intellettuale.* Milan: Unicopli, 1997.
Gianinazzi, Willy. *Naissance du mythe moderne: Georges Sorel et la crise de la pensée savante, 1889–1914.* Paris: Les Editions de la Maison des sciences de l'homme, 2006.
Gildea, Robert. *France since 1945.* Oxford: Oxford University Press, 1997.
Glendon, Mary Ann. *A World Made New: Eleanor Roosevelt and the Universal Declaration of Human Rights.* New York: Random House, 2002.
Glossop, Ronald J. *World Federation? A Critical Analysis of Federal World Government.* Jefferson, NC: McFarland, 1993.
Goldman, Harvey. 'From Social Theory to Sociology of Knowledge and Back: Karl Mannheim and the Sociology of Intellectual Knowledge Production'. *Sociological Theory* 12 (1994): 266–278.
Gong, Gerrit W. *The Standard of 'Civilization' in International Society.* Oxford: Clarendon, 1984.
Gordon, Adi, and Udi Greenberg. 'The City of Man, European Émigrés, and the Genesis of Post-war Conservative Thought'. *Religions* 3 (2012): 681–698.
Gorman, Daniel. *The Emergence of International Society in the 1920s.* Cambridge: Cambridge University Press, 2012.
———. *Imperial Citizenship: Empire and the Question of Belonging.* Manchester: Manchester University Press, 2007.
Gowan, Peter, and Perry Anderson, eds. *The Question of Europe.* London: Verso, 1997.
Gowan, Richard. 'Raymond Aron, the History of Ideas and the Idea of France'. *European Journal of Political Theory* 2 (2003): 383–399.
———. 'Raymond Aron and the Problems of Sovereignty and Order in International Relations, 1940–1966'. MPhil thesis, University of Cambridge, 2002.
Graebner, William. *The Age of Doubt: American Thought and Culture in the 1940s.* Boston: Twayne, 1993.
Gray, Lawrence. 'L'America di Roosevelt negli anni dell'esilio di Luigi Sturzo fra Jacksonville e New York: Quale America ha conosciuto?' In *Universalità e cultura nel pensiero di Luigi Sturzo: Atti del convegno internazionale di studio svoltosi presso l'Istituto Luigi Sturzo dal 28 al 30 ottobre 1999,* 521–549. Soveria Mannelli: Rubbettino, 2001.
Greenberg, Udi. *The Weimar Century: German Émigrés and the Ideological Foundations of the Cold War.* Princeton, NJ: Princeton University Press, 2015.
Gregory, Derek. *Geographical Imaginations.* Oxford: Blackwell, 1994.

Greif, Mark. *The Age of the Crisis of Man: Thought and Fiction in America, 1933–1973*. Princeton, NJ: Princeton University Press, 2015.

Grimley, Matthew. *Citizenship, Community and the Church of England: Liberal Anglican Theories of the State between the Wars*. Oxford: Clarendon, 2004.

Groom, A. J. R., and Paul Taylor, eds. *Functionalism: Theory and Practice in International Relations*. London: University of London Press, 1975.

Gross, Neil. *Richard Rorty: The Making of an American Philosopher*. Chicago: University of Chicago Press, 2008.

Guilhot, Nicolas. 'Imperial Realism: Post-War Theory and Decolonisation'. *International History Review* 36 (2014): 698–.

———, ed. *The Invention of International Relations Theory: Realism, the Rockefeller Foundation, and the 1954 Conference on Theory*. Columbia University Press, 2011.

Gunnell, John G. 'Continuity and Innovation in the History of Political Science: The Case of Charles Merriam'. *Journal of the History of the Behavioral Sciences* 28 (1992): 133–142.

———. *The Descent of Political Theory: The Genealogy of an American Vocation*. Chicago: University of Chicago Press, 1993.

———. *Imagining the American Polity: Political Science and the Discourse of Democracy*. University Park: Penn State University Press, 2004.

Haar, Edwin René van de. *Classical Liberalism and International Relations Theory: Hume, Smith, Mises, Hayek and International Society*. Basingstoke: Palgrave, 2009.

Hall, Ian. *Dilemmas of Decline: British Intellectuals and World Politics, 1945–1975*. Berkeley: University of California Press, 2012.

———. *The International Thought of Martin Wight*. Basingstoke: Palgrave, 2006.

Hall, Ian, and Lisa Hill, eds. *British International Thinkers from Hobbes to Namier*. Basingstoke: Palgrave, 2010.

Halsey, A. H. 'Wootton, Barbara Frances, Baroness Wootton of Abinger (1897–1988)'. In *Oxford Dictionary of National Biography*. 2004. www.oxforddnb.com.

Hansen, Peo, and Stefan Jonsson. *Eurafrica: The Untold History of European Integration and Colonialism*. London: Bloomsbury, 2014.

Harris, Jose. *William Beveridge: A Biography*. Oxford: Clarendon, 1997.

Harvey, David. 'Owen Lattimore: A Memoire'. *Antipode* 15 (1983): 3–11.

Haslam, Jonathan. *No Virtue Like Necessity: Realist Thought in International Relations since Machiavelli*. New Haven, CT: Yale University Press, 2002.

———. *The Vices of Integrity: E. H. Carr, 1892–1982*. London: Verso, 2000.

He, Baogang, Brian Galligan, and Takashi Inoguchi, eds. *Federalism in Asia*. Cheltenham: Edward Elgar, 2009.

Hearden, Patrick J. *Architects of Globalism: Building a New World Order during World War II*. Fayetteville: University of Arkansas Press, 2002.

Heffernan, Michael J. *The European Geographical Imagination*. Stuttgart: Steiner, 2007.

Hellman, John. 'The Anti-Democratic Impulse in Catholicism: Jacques Maritain, Yves Simon and Charles de Gaulle during World War II'. *Journal of Church and State* 33 (1991): 453–471.

Henrikson, Alan K. 'The Map as an "Idea": The Role of Cartographic Imagery during the Second World War'. *American Cartographer* 2 (1975): 19–53.

Hewlett, Richard G., and Oscar E. Anderson, Jr. *The New World, 1939–1946: A History of the United States Atomic Energy Commission.* Vol. 1. University Park: Pennsylvania State University Press, 1962.

Hobson, John M. *The Eurocentric Conception of World Politics: Western International Theory, 1760–2010.* Cambridge: Cambridge University Press, 2012.

Hodgkin, R. A. 'Polanyi, Michael (1891–1976)'. In *Oxford Dictionary of National Biography.* 2004. www.oxforddnb.com.

Holeindre, Jean-Vincent, and Jean-Baptiste Jeangène Vilmer, eds. 'Raymond Aron et les relations internationales: 50 ans après Paix et guerre entre les nations'. *Études internationales* 43 (2012): 319–492.

Holland, William Lancelot. *Remembering the Institute of Pacific Relations: The Memoirs of William L. Holland.* Tokyo: Ryukei Shyosha, 1995.

Hollinger, David A. *After Cloven Tongues of Fire: Protestant Liberalism in Modern American History.* Princeton, NJ: Princeton University Press, 2013.

Hoopes, Townsend, and Douglas Brinkley, *FDR and the Creation of the U.N.* New Haven, CT: Yale University Press, 1997.

Hopkins, A. G., ed. *Globalization in World History.* London: Pimlico, 2002.

Horn, Gerd-Rainer, and Emmanuel Gerard. *Left Catholicism, 1943–1955: Catholics and Society in Western Europe at the Point of Liberation.* Leuven: Leuven University Press, 2001.

Housden, Martyn. *The League of Nations and the Organisation of Peace.* Harlow: Longman, 2012.

Howard, Thomas A. *God and the Atlantic.* Oxford: Oxford University Press, 2001.

Howson, Susan. *Lionel Robbins.* Cambridge: Cambridge University Press, 2011.

Hughes, Thomas Parke, and Agatha C. Hughes, eds. *Lewis Mumford: Public Intellectual.* Oxford: Oxford University Press, 1990.

Hurrell, Andrew. *On Global Order: Power, Values, and the Constitution of International Society.* Oxford: Oxford University Press, 2007.

Ikenberry, G. John. *After Victory: Institutions, Strategic Restraint, and the Rebuilding of Order after Major Wars.* Princeton, NJ: Princeton University Press, 2001.

———. *Liberal Leviathan: The Origins, Crisis and Transformation of the American World Order.* Princeton, NJ: Princeton University Press, 2011.

Imber, Mark F. 'Re-reading Mitrany: A Pragmatic Assessment of Sovereignty'. *Review of International Studies* 10 (1984): 103–123.

Iriye, Akira. *Global Community: The Role of International Organizations in the Making of the Contemporary World.* Berkeley: University of California Press, 2002.

———. *Global and Transnational History: The Past, Present, and Future.* Basingstoke: Palgrave, 2013.

Isaac, Joel. *Working Knowledge: Making the Human Sciences from Parsons to Kuhn.* Cambridge, MA: Harvard University Press, 2012.

Isaac, Joel, and Duncan Bell, eds. *Uncertain Empire: American History and the Idea of the Cold War.* Oxford: Oxford University Press, 2012.

Jackson, Ben. *Equality and the British Left.* Manchester: Manchester University Press, 2007.

———. 'Freedom, the Common Good, and the Rule of Law: Lippmann and Hayek on Economic Planning'. *Journal of the History of Ideas* 73 (2012): 47–68.

Jacobs, Struan, and Phil Mullins. 'Faith, Tradition, and Dynamic Order: Michael Polanyi's Liberal Thought from 1941 to 1951'. *History of European Ideas* 34 (2008): 120–131.

———. 'Michael Polanyi and Karl Popper: The Fraying of a Long-Standing Acquaintance'. *Tradition and Discovery* 38 (2011): 61–93.

Jerram, Leif. 'Space: A Useless Category for Historical Analysis?' *History and Theory* 52 (2013): 400–419.

Jewett, Andrew. *Science, Democracy, and the American University: From the Civil War to the Cold War*. Cambridge: Cambridge University Press, 2012.

Jones, Charles. *E. H. Carr and International Relations: A Duty to Lie*. Cambridge: Cambridge University Press, 1998.

Jones, Daniel Stedman. *Masters of the Universe: Hayek, Friedman, and the Birth of Neoliberal Politics*. Princeton, NJ: Princeton University Press, 2012.

Judt, Tony. *The Burden of Responsibility: Blum, Camus, Aron, and the French Twentieth Century*. Chicago: University of Chicago Press, 1998.

———. *Past Imperfect French Intellectuals, 1944–1956*. New York: New York University Press, 2011.

Kaiser, Wolfram. *Christian Democracy and the Origins of European Union*. Cambridge: Cambridge University Press, 2007.

Kaiser, Wolfram, and Helmut Wohnout, eds. *Political Catholicism in Europe 1918–45*. London: Routledge, 2004.

Karl, Barry Dean. *Charles E. Merriam and the Study of Politics*. Chicago: University of Chicago Press, 1974.

Katzenstein, Peter J., ed. *Anglo-America and Its Discontents: Civilizational Identities beyond West and East*. London: Routledge, 2012.

———. 'The West as Anglo-America'. In *Anglo-America and Its Discontents: Civilizational Identities beyond West and East*, edited by Peter J. Katzenstein, 1–30. London: Routledge, 2012.

Katznelson, Ira. *Desolation and Enlightenment: Political Knowledge after Total War, Totalitarianism, and the Holocaust*. New York: Columbia University Press, 2003.

———. *Fear Itself: The New Deal and the Origins of Our Time*. New York: Liveright, 2013.

Kearns, Gerry. *Geopolitics and Empire: The Legacy of Halford Mackinder*. New York: Oxford University Press, 2009.

———. 'Imperial Geopolitics: Geopolitical Visions at the Dawn of the American Century'. In *A Companion to Political Geography*, edited by John Agnew, Katharyne Mitchell, and Gerard Toal, 173–186. Oxford: Blackwell, 2007.

———. 'The Political Pivot of Geography'. *Geographical Journal* 170 (2004): 337–346.

Keene, Ann T. 'Shils, Edward Albert'. In *American National Biography*. 2005. www.anb.org/articles/14/14-01145.html.

Kendle, John E. *Federal Britain: A History*. London: Routledge, 1997.

———. *The Round Table Movement and Imperial Union*. Toronto: University of Toronto Press, 1975.

Kennedy, Paul M. *The Parliament of Man: The United Nations and the Quest for World Government.* London: Allen Lane, 2006.

Kent, John. *The Internationalization of Colonialism: Britain, France and Black Africa, 1939–1956.* Oxford: Clarendon, 1992.

Kettler, David, and Volker Meja. *Karl Mannheim and the Crisis of Liberalism: The Secret of These New Times.* New Brunswick, NJ: Transaction, 1995.

Keynes, John Maynard. *The General Theory of Employment, Interest and Money.* London: Macmillan, 1936.

Kincaid, John, ed. *Federalism.* London: Sage, 2011.

Kirk-Greene, A. H. M. 'Lugard, Frederick John Dealtry, Baron Lugard (1858–1945)'. In *Oxford Dictionary of National Biography.* 2004. www.oxforddnb.com.

Klein, Kerwin Lee. *Frontiers of Historical Imagination: Narrating the European Conquest of Native America, 1890–1990.* Berkeley: University of California Press, 1999.

Kleingeld, Pauline. *Kant and Cosmopolitanism: The Philosophical Ideal of World Citizenship.* Cambridge: Cambridge University Press, 2011.

Koskenniemi, Martti. *From Apology to Utopia: The Structure of International Legal Argument.* Helsinki: Lakimiesliiton Kustannus, 1989.

———. *The Gentle Civilizer of Nations: The Rise and Fall of International Law 1870–1960.* Cambridge: Cambridge University Press, 2002.

La Bella, Gianni. *Luigi Sturzo e l'esilio negli Stati Uniti.* Brescia: Morcelliana, 1990.

Lacroix, Justine. '"Borderline Europe". French Visions of the European Union'. In *European Stories: Intellectual Debates on Europe in National Contexts*, edited by Justine Lacroix and Kalypso Nicolaïdis, 107–109. Oxford: Oxford University Press, 2010.

Lacroix, Justine, and Kalypso Nicolaïdis, eds. *European Stories: Intellectual Debates on Europe in National Contexts.* Oxford: Oxford University Press, 2010.

Lake, Marilyn, and Henry Reynolds. *Drawing the Global Colour Line: White Men's Countries and the International Challenge of Racial Equality.* Cambridge: Cambridge University Press, 2008.

Lamb, Peter. *Laski on Egalitarian Democracy and Freedom.* Manchester: Manchester Centre for Political Thought, 1997.

Lapparent, Olivier de. *Raymond Aron et l'Europe: Itinéraire d'un européen dans le siècle.* Bern: P. Lang, 2010.

Laqua, Daniel, ed. *Internationalism Reconfigured: Transnational Ideas and Movements between the World Wars.* London: I.B. Tauris, 2011.

Latham, Robert. *The Liberal Moment: Modernity, Security and the Making of Postwar International Order.* New York: Columbia University Press, 1997.

Lavin, Deborah. *From Empire to International Commonwealth: A Biography of Lionel Curtis.* Oxford: Clarendon, 1995.

Legg, Stephen, ed. *Spatiality, Sovereignty and Carl Schmitt: Geographies of the Nomos.* London: Routledge, 2011.

Le Melle, Tilden J. 'Race in International Relations'. *International Studies Perspectives* 10 (2009): 77–83.

Lerer, Ron F. *Avoiding the French Tragedy: Raymond Aron and the Franco-Algerian War.* Jerusalem: Hebrew University of Jerusalem Press, 2003.

Levy, Jacob T. 'From Liberal Constitutionalism to Pluralism'. In *Modern Pluralism: Anglo-American Debates since 1880*, edited by Mark Bevir, 21–40. Cambridge: Cambridge University Press, 2012.

———. *Rationalism, Pluralism, and Freedom*. Oxford: Oxford University Press, 2014.

Lewis, Martin W. *The Myth of Continents: A Critique of Metageography*. Berkeley: University of California Press, 1997.

Librizzi, Gandolfo. *'No, Io Non Giuro': Il rifiuto di G. A. Borgese, una storia antifascista*. Marsala: Navarra Editore, 2013.

Lloyd, Howell A. 'The Political Thought of Charles Loyseau (1564–1627)'. *European Studies Review* 11 (1981): 53–82.

Loader, Colin. *The Intellectual Development of Karl Mannheim: Culture, Politics, and Planning*. Cambridge: Cambridge University Press, 1985.

Long, David. *Towards a New Liberal Internationalism: The International Theory of J. A. Hobson*. Cambridge: Cambridge University Press, 1996.

Long, David, and Brian C. Schmidt, eds. *Imperialism and Internationalism in the Discipline of International Relations*. Albany: State University of New York Press, 2005.

Louis, Wm. Roger. *Imperialism at Bay, 1941–1945: The United States and the Decolonization of the British Empire*. Oxford: Clarendon, 1977.

Luard, Evan. *A History of the United Nations*. London: Macmillan, 1982.

Lyon, Stina. 'Karl Mannheim and Viola Klein: Refugee Sociologists in Search of Social Democratic Practice'. In *In Defence of Learning: The Plight, Persecution, and Placement of Academic Refugees, 1933–1980s*, edited by Shula Marks, Paul Weindling, and Laura Wintour, 177–190. Oxford: Oxford University Press, 2011.

MacQueen, Norrie. *The United Nations since 1945: Peacekeeping and the Cold War*. London: Longman, 1999.

Mahoney, Daniel J. *The Liberal Political Science of Raymond Aron: A Critical Introduction*. Lanham, MD: Rowman & Littlefield, 1992.

Malandrino, Corrado. 'L'iniziativa sturziana del People and Freedom Group of America nell'esilio di Jacksonville (1940–1944)'. In *Luigi Sturzo e la democrazia nella prospettiva del terzo millennio*, vol. 1, edited by Eugenio Guccione, 193–214. Florence: Olschki, 2004.

Malgeri, Francesco. 'L'opera di Sturzo per la comunità internazionale dalla società delle nazioni all'ONU'. In *Luigi Sturzo e la comunità internazionale. Atti del Quinto Corso della Cattedra Sturzo*, 5–21. Catania: Istituto di sociologia Luigi Sturzo, 1988.

———. *Luigi Sturzo nella storia d'Italia*. Rome: Edizioni di Storia e Letteratura, 1973.

Manela, Erez. *The Wilsonian Moment: Self-Determination and the International Origins of Anticolonial Nationalism*. Oxford: Oxford University Press, 2007.

Mantena, Karuna. *Alibis of Empire: Henry Maine and the Ends of Liberal Imperialism*. Princeton, NJ: Princeton University Press, 2010.

Martore, Antonio. 'Mito'. In *Enciclopedia del pensiero politico. Autori, concetti, dottrine*, edited by Roberto Esposito and Carlo Galli, 545. Rome: Laterza, 2005.

May, Alexander. 'Curtis, Lionel George (1872–1955)'. In *Oxford Dictionary of National Biography*. 2004. www.oxforddnb.com.

———. 'The Round Table, 1910–66'. DPhil thesis, University of Oxford, 1995.

Mayne, Richard, John Pinder, and John C. Roberts. *Federal Union, the Pioneers: A History of Federal Union*. Basingstoke: Macmillan, 1990.

Mazower, Mark. *Governing the World: The History of an Idea*. London: Allen Lane, 2012.

———. *No Enchanted Palace: The End of Empire and the Ideological Origins of the United Nations*. Princeton, NJ: Princeton University Press, 2009.

Mazower, Mark, Jessica Reinisch, and David Feldman, eds. *Post-war Reconstruction in Europe: International Perspectives, 1945–1949*. Oxford: Oxford University Press, 2011.

McGreevy, John T. *Catholics and American Freedom: A History*. New York: Norton, 2003.

———. 'Catholics, Catholicism and the Humanities since World War II'. In *The Humanities and the Dynamics of Inclusion since World War II*, edited by David A. Hollinger, 189–216. Baltimore: Johns Hopkins University Press, 2006.

McGrew, Anthony. 'Transnational Democracy'. In *Democratic Theory Today: Challenges for the 21st Century*, edited by April Carter and Geoff Stokes, 269–294. Cambridge: Polity, 2002.

McGucken, William. 'On Freedom and Planning in Science: The Society for Freedom in Science 1940–1946'. *Minerva* 16 (1978): 42–72.

McLuhan, Marshall. *The Classical Trivium: The Place of Thomas Nashe in the Learning of His Time*. Corte Madera, CA: Gingko Press, 2006.

McNeill, William H. *Hutchins' University: A Memoir of the University of Chicago, 1929–1950*. Chicago: University of Chicago Press, 1991.

Mearsheimer, John. 'E. H. Carr vs. Idealism: The Battle Rages On'. *International Relations* 19 (2005): 139–152.

Mehta, Uday Singh. *Liberalism and Empire: A Study in Nineteenth-Century British Liberal Thought*. Chicago: University of Chicago Press, 1999.

Mendelsohn, Everett. 'Prophet of Our Discontent: Lewis Mumford Confronts the Bomb'. In *Lewis Mumford: Public Intellectual*, edited by Thomas Parke Hughes and Agatha C. Hughes, 343–360. Oxford: Oxford University Press, 1990.

Meneguzzi Rostagni, Carla. 'Il Vaticano e la costruzione europea (1948–1957)'. In *L'Italia e la politica di potenza in Europa (1950–1960)*, edited by Ennio di Nolfo, Romain H. Rainero, and Brunello Vigezzi, 143–172. Milan: Marzorati, 1992.

Michel, Florian. 'Jacques Maritain en Amérique du Nord'. *Cahiers Jacques Maritain* 45 (2002): 26–86.

———. 'L'expérience de la démocratie américaine chez Jacques Maritain'. In *Penser la mondialisation avec Jacques Maritain. Enjeux et défis*, edited by Jean-Dominique Durand and René Mougel, 99–114. Lyon: University of Lyon, 2013.

Milward, Alan S. *The European Rescue of the Nation-State*. London: Routledge, 1994.

———. *The Reconstruction of Western Europe 1945–51*. London: Methuen, 1984.

Miranda, Americo. *Santa Sede e Società delle Nazioni: Benedetto XV, Pio XI e il nuovo internazionalismo cattolico*. Rome: Studium, 2013.

Mirowski, Philip. 'Economics, Science and Knowledge: Polanyi vs. Hayek'. *Tradition and Discovery* 25 (1998): 29–42.

Mirowski, Philip, and Dieter Plehwe, eds. *The Road from Mont Pèlerin: The Making of the Neoliberal Thought Collective*. Cambridge, MA: Harvard University Press, 2009.

Monarsolo, Yves. *L'Eurafrique—contrepoint de l'idée d'Europe: Le cas français de la fin de la deuxième guerre mondiale aux négociations de Traites de Rome*. Aix-en-Provence: Publications de l'Université de Provence, 2010.

Monbiot, George. *The Age of Consent: A Manifesto for a New World Order*. London: Flamingo, 2003.

Monmonier, Mark. *Rhumb Lines and Map Wars: A Social History of the Mercator Projection*. Chicago: University of Chicago Press, 2004.

Morefield, Jeanne. *Covenants without Swords: Idealist Liberalism and the Spirit of Empire*. Princeton, NJ: Princeton University Press, 2005.

———. 'An Education to Greece: The Round Table, Imperial Theory and the Uses of History'. *History of Political Thought* 28 (2007): 328–361.

———. *Empires without Imperialism: Anglo-American Decline and the Politics of Deflection*. New York: Oxford University Press, 2014.

Morelli, Umberto, ed. *Altiero Spinelli: il pensiero e l'azione per la federazione europea*. Milan: Giuffrè, 2010.

Mouric, Joël. *Raymond Aron et l'Europe*. Rennes: Rennes University Press, 2013.

Moyn, Samuel. *Christian Human Rights*. Philadelphia: University of Pennsylvania Press, 2015.

———. *The Last Utopia: Human Rights in History*. Cambridge, MA: Belknap, 2010.

———. 'Personalism, Community, and the Origins of Human Rights'. In *Human Rights in the Twentieth Century*, edited by Stefan-Ludwig Hoffmann, 85–106. Cambridge: Cambridge University Press, 2010.

Muhtu, Sankar. 'Adam Smith's Critique of International Trading Companies: Theorizing "Globalization" in the Age of Enlightenment'. *Political Theory* 36 (2008): 185–212.

Müller, Jan-Werner. *Contesting Democracy: Political Ideas in Twentieth-Century Europe*. New Haven, CT: Yale University Press, 2011.

———. *A Dangerous Mind: Carl Schmitt in Post-war European Thought*. New Haven, CT: Yale University Press, 2003.

———. 'Fear and Freedom: On "Cold War Liberalism"'. *European Journal of Political Theory* 7 (2008): 45–64.

———. 'Vision of Global Order in a "Posteuropean Age". Carl Schmitt, Raymond Aron and the Civil Servant of the World Spirit'. *Ricerche di storia politica* 2 (2004): 205–226.

Muñiz-Fraticelli, Victor. *The Structure of Pluralism*. Oxford: Oxford University Press, 2014.

Navari, Cornelia. 'David Mitrany and International Functionalism'. In *Thinkers of the Twenty Years' Crisis: Inter-war Idealism Reassessed*, edited by Peter Wilson and David Long, 214–246. Oxford: Clarendon, 1995.

———. *Internationalism and the State in the Twentieth Century*. London: Routledge, 2000.

———. *Public Intellectuals and International Affairs: Essays on Public Thinkers and Political Projects*. Dordrecht: Republic of Letters, 2012.

Nelsen, Brent F., and Alexander C.-G. Stubb. *The European Union: Readings on the Theory and Practice of European Integration*. London: Palgrave, 2003.

Newman, Robert P. *Owen Lattimore and the 'Loss' of China*. Berkeley: University of California Press, 1992.

Nicholls, David. *The Pluralist State: The Political Ideas of J. N. Figgis and His Contemporaries*. New York: St. Martin's Press, 1975.

Niemann, Arne, and Demosthenes Ioannou. 'European Economic Integration in Times of Crisis: A Case of Neofunctionalism?' *Journal of European Public Policy* 22 (2015): 196–218.

Nogee, Joseph L., and John W. Spanier. 'The Politics of Tripolarity'. *World Affairs* 139 (1977): 319–333.

Nord, Philip. *France's New Deal from the Thirties to the Postwar Era*. Princeton, NJ: Princeton University Press, 2010.

Nye, Mary Jo. *Michael Polanyi and His Generation: Origins of the Social Construction of Science*. Chicago: University of Chicago Press, 2011.

———. 'Michael Polanyi and the Social Construction of Science'. *Tradition and Discovery* 39 (2012): 7–17.

Oakley, Ann. *A Critical Woman: Barbara Wootton, Social Science and Public Policy in the Twentieth Century*. London: Bloomsbury Academic, 2011.

Oppermann, Matthias. *Raymond Aron und Deutschland: Die Verteidigung der Freiheit und das Problem des Totalitarismus*. Ostfildern: Thorbecke Verlag, 2008.

Osterhammel, Jürgen. *The Transformation of the World: A Global History of the Nineteenth Century*. Princeton, NJ: Princeton University Press, 2014.

O'Sullivan, Christopher D. *Sumner Welles, Post-war Planning, and the Quest for a New World Order, 1937–1943*. New York: Columbia University Press, 2008.

Owen, Nicholas. *The British Left and India: Metropolitan Anti-imperialism, 1885–1947*. Oxford: Oxford University Press, 2007.

Pagden, Anthony, 'Human Rights, Natural Rights, and Europe's Imperial Legacy'. *Political Theory* 31 (2003): 171–199.

Paolino, Marco. 'Benedetto Croce e Luigi Sturzo'. In *Luigi Sturzo e la democrazia europea*, edited by Gabriele De Rosa, 411–423. Rome: Laterza, 1990.

Papaioannou, Theo. *Reading Hayek in the 21st Century: A Critical Inquiry into His Political Thought*. Basingstoke: Palgrave, 2012.

Parisella, Antonio. *Cattolici e Democrazia cristiana nell'Italia repubblicana: Analisi di un consenso politico*. Rome: Gangemi, 2000.

Parisi, Luciano. *Borgese*. Turin: Tirrenia, 2000.

Parmar, Inderjeet. 'American Hegemony, the Rockefeller Foundation'. In *The Invention of International Relations Theory: Realism, the Rockefeller Foundation, and the 1954 Conference on Theory*, edited by Nicolas Guilhot, 182–209. New York: Columbia University Press, 2011.

———. 'Anglo-American Elites in the Interwar Years: Idealism and Power in the Intellectual Roots of Chatham House and the Council on Foreign Relations'. *International Relations* 16 (2002): 53–75.

———. *Foundations of the American Century: The Ford, Carnegie, and Rockefeller Foundations in the Rise of American Power*. New York: Columbia University Press, 2012.

Partington, John S. *Building Cosmopolis: The Political Thought of H. G. Wells.* Aldershot: Ashgate, 2003.

Passerini, Luisa. *Europe in Love, Love in Europe: Imagination and Politics in Britain between the Wars.* London: I.B. Tauris, 1999.

Patterson, Ian. *Guernica and Total War.* London: Profile Books, 2007.

Pedersen, Susan. *The Guardians: The League of Nations and the Crisis of Empire.* Oxford: Oxford University Press, 2015.

———. 'The Meaning of the Mandates System: An Argument'. *Geschichte und Gesellschaft* 32 (2006): 560–582.

Pemberton, Jo-Anne. *Global Metaphors: Modernity and the Quest for One World.* London: Pluto Press, 2001.

Perkins, Dexter. *A History of the Monroe Doctrine.* London: Little, Brown, 1941.

Perreau-Saussine, Emile. *Catholicism and Democracy: An Essay in the History of Political Thought.* Translated by Richard Rex. Princeton, NJ: Princeton University Press, 2012.

Pinder, John, ed. *Altiero Spinelli and the British Federalists: Writings by Beveridge, Robbins and Spinelli, 1937–1943.* London: Federal Trust, 1998.

Pitts, Jennifer. *A Turn to Empire: The Rise of Imperial Liberalism in Britain and France.* Princeton, NJ: Princeton University Press, 2005.

Plochmann, George Kimball. *Richard McKeon: A Study.* Chicago: University of Chicago Press, 1990.

Polsi, Alessandro. *Storia dell'ONU.* Rome: Laterza, 2006.

Pombeni, Paolo. 'The Ideology of Christian Democracy'. *Journal of Political Ideologies* 5 (2000): 289–300.

———. *Il gruppo dossettiano e la fondazione della democrazia italiana (1938–1948).* Bologna: Il Mulino, 1979.

Porter, Bernard. *Critics of Empire.* London: Macmillan, 1968.

Posner, Richard A. *Public Intellectuals: A Study of Decline.* Cambridge, MA: Harvard University Press, 2001.

Preda, Daniela, ed. *Altiero Spinelli e i movimenti per l'unità europea.* Padua: CEDAM, 2010.

Preston, Andrew. *Sword of the Spirit, Shield of Faith: Religion in American War and Diplomacy.* New York: Knopf, 2012.

Pugh, Michael C. *Liberal Internationalism: The Interwar Movement for Peace in Britain.* Basingstoke: Palgrave, 2012.

Purcell, Edward A., Jr. *The Crisis of Democratic Theory: Scientific Naturalism and the Problem of Value.* Lexington: University Press of Kentucky, 1973.

Ramos, Paulo Jorge Batista. 'The Role of the Yale Institute of International Studies in the Construction of the United States Security Ideology, 1935–1951'. PhD thesis, University of Manchester, 2003.

Raynaud, Philippe. 'Raymond Aron et Max Weber'. *Raymond Aron 1905–1983, Histoire et politique, Commentaire* 28–29 (1985): 213–221.

Reich, Cary. *The Life of Nelson A. Rockefeller: Worlds to Conquer, 1908–1958.* Vol. 1. New York: Doubleday, 1996.

Reynolds, David. *From World War to Cold War: Churchill, Roosevelt, and the International History of the 1940s.* Oxford: Oxford University Press, 2006.

———. *One World Divisible: A Global History since 1945*. London: Allen Lane, 2000.

Rice, Daniel F. *Reinhold Niebuhr and His Circle of Influence*. Cambridge: Cambridge University Press, 2013.

Rietzler, Katharina. 'Before the Cultural Cold Wars: American Philanthropy and Cultural Diplomacy in the Inter-war Years'. *Historical Research* 84 (2011): 148–164.

Ritschel, Daniel. *The Politics of Planning: The Debate on Economic Planning in Britain in the 1930s*. Oxford: Clarendon, 1997.

Rosenboim, Or. 'L'impero della libertà: imperialismo e internazionalismo nel pensiero liberale inglese, 1914–1936'. *Contemporanea* 17 (2014): 31–58.

Ross, Dorothy. *The Origins of American Social Science*. Cambridge: Cambridge University Press, 1991.

Rossini, Daniela, ed. *From Theodore Roosevelt to FDR: Internationalism and Isolationism in American Foreign Policy*. Keele: Ryburn, 1995.

Roth, Jack J. 'The Roots of Italian Fascism: Sorel and Sorelismo'. *Journal of Modern History* 38 (1967): 30–45.

Rothschild, Emma. 'The Archives of Universal History'. *Journal of World History* 19 (2008): 375–401.

Rowe, William T. 'Owen Lattimore, Asia, and Comparative History'. *Journal of Asian Studies* 66 (2007): 759–786.

Runciman, David. *The Confidence Trap*. Princeton, NJ: Princeton University Press, 2013.

———. *Pluralism and the Personality of the State*. Cambridge: Cambridge University Press, 1997.

Sagarin, Edward, and Robert J. Kelly. 'Karl Mannheim and the Sociology of Knowledge'. *Salmagundi* 10/11 (1969): 292–302.

Santomassimo, Gianpasquale. *La terza via fascista: Il mito del corporativismo*. Bologna: Carocci, 2006.

Sartori, Andrew. 'Robert Redfield's Comparative Civilizations Project and the Political Imagination of Post-war America'. *Positions: East Asia Cultures Critique* 6 (1998): 33–64.

Schäfer, Michael. 'Luigi Sturzo as a Theorist of Totalitarianism'. In *Totalitarianism and Political Religions: Concepts for the Comparison of Dictatorships*, edited by Hans Maier, 22–31. London: Routledge, 2004.

Scheuerman, William E. *Hans Morgenthau: Realism and Beyond*. Cambridge: Polity, 2009.

Schlesinger, Stephen. *Act of Creation: The Founding of the United Nations*. Boulder, CO: Westview, 2003.

Schmeller, Mark G. 'Charles E. Merriam'. In *American National Biography Online*. 2000. www.anb.org/articles/14/14-00408.html.

Schmidt, Brian C., ed. *International Relations and the First Great Debate*. London: Routledge, 2012.

———. *The Political Discourse of Anarchy: A Disciplinary History of International Relations*. Albany: State University of New York Press, 1998.

Schulten, Susan. *The Geographical Imagination in America, 1880–1950*. Chicago: University of Chicago Press, 2002.

———. 'Richard Edes Harrison and the Challenge to American Cartography'. *Imago Mundi* 50 (1998): 174–188.

Sciacca, Fabrizio, ed. *La dimensione istituzionale europea: teoria, storia e filosofia Politica*. Florence: Le Lettere, 2009.

Scott, Drusilla. *Everyman Revived: The Common Sense of Michael Polanyi*. Lewes: Book Guild, 1985.

Scott, James C. *The Art of Not Being Governed: An Anarchist History of Upland Southeast Asia*. New Haven, CT: Yale University Press, 2009.

Scott, William T., and Martin X. Moleski. *Michael Polanyi: Scientist and Philosopher*. Oxford: Oxford University Press, 2005.

Scuccimarra, Luca. *I confini del mondo: Storia del cosmopolitismo dall'antichità al settecento*. Bologna: Il Mulino, 2006.

Seidelman, Raymond. *Disenchanted Realists: Political Science and the American Crisis, 1884–1984*. Albany: State University of New York Press, 1986.

Sexton, Jay. *The Monroe Doctrine: Empire and Nation in Nineteenth-Century America*. New York: Hill & Wang, 2011.

Shahrani, M. Nazif Mohib. *The Kirghiz and Wakhi of Afghanistan: Adaptation to Closed Frontiers and War*. Seattle: University of Washington Press, 2002.

Shlaim, Avi. 'Prelude to Downfall: The British Offer of Union to France, June 1940'. *Journal of Contemporary History* 9 (1974): 27–63.

Simpson, A. W. Brian. *Human Rights and the End of Empire: Britain and the Genesis of the European Convention*. Oxford: Oxford University Press, 2001.

Skinner, Quentin. 'Meaning and Understanding in the History of Ideas'. *History and Theory* 8 (1969): 3–53.

———. *Visions of Politics*. Vol. 1. Cambridge: Cambridge University Press, 2002.

Slaney, Patrick David. 'Eugene Rabinowitch, the *Bulletin of the Atomic Scientists*, and the Nature of Scientific Internationalism in the Early Cold War'. *Historical Studies in the Natural Sciences* 42 (2012): 114–142.

Sluga, Glenda. *Internationalism in the Age of Nationalism*. Philadelphia: University of Pennsylvania Press, 2013.

———. 'UNESCO and the (One) World of Julian Huxley'. *Journal of World History* 21 (2010): 393–418.

Small, Helen, ed. *The Public Intellectual*. Oxford: Blackwell, 2002.

Smith, Alice K. *A Peril and a Hope: The Scientists' Movement in America, 1945–47*. Chicago: University of Chicago Press, 1965.

Smith, Mark C. *Social Science in the Crucible: The American Debate over Objectivity and Purpose, 1918–1941*. Durham, NC: Duke University Press, 1994.

———. 'A Tale of Two Charlies: Political Science, History and Civic Reform, 1890–1940'. In *Modern Political Science: Anglo-American Exchanges since 1880*, edited by Robert Adcock, Mark Bevir, and Shannon C. Stimson, 118–136. Princeton, NJ: Princeton University Press, 2007.

Smith, Neil. *American Empire: Roosevelt's Geographer and the Prelude to Globalization*. Berkeley: University of California Press, 2003.

———. 'Bowman's New World and the Council on Foreign Relations'. *Geographical Review* 76 (1986): 438–460.

————. *The Endgame of Globalization*. New York: Routledge, 2005.

Smith, Tony. *America's Mission: The United States and the Worldwide Struggle for Democracy*. Princeton, NJ: Princeton University Press, 2012.

Soutou, Georges-Henri. 'Was There a European Order in the Twentieth Century? From the Concert of Europe to the End of the Cold War'. *Contemporary European History* 9 (2000): 329–353.

Stapleton, Julia. *Political Intellectuals and Public Identities in Britain since 1850*. Manchester: Manchester University Press, 2001.

Starr, Harvey. 'On Geopolitics: Spaces and Places'. *International Studies Quarterly* 57 (2013): 433–439.

Stears, Marc. *Progressives, Pluralists, and the Problems of the State: Ideologies of Reform in the United States and Britain, 1909–1926*. Oxford: Oxford University Press, 2002.

Steil, Benn. *The Battle of Bretton Woods: John Maynard Keynes, Harry Dexter White, and the Making of a New World Order*. Princeton, NJ: Princeton University Press, 2013.

Steiner, George. *George Steiner at the New Yorker*. Edited by Robert Boyers. New York: New Directions, 2009.

Steinmetz-Jenkins, Daniel. 'Why Did Raymond Aron Write That Carl Schmitt Was Not a Nazi? An Alternative Genealogy of French Liberalism'. *Modern Intellectual History* 11 (2014): 549–574.

Stewart, Iain. 'Raymond Aron and the Roots of the French Liberal Renaissance'. PhD thesis, University of Manchester, 2011.

Stirk, Peter. 'John H. Herz: Realism and the Fragility of the International Order'. *Review of International Studies* 31 (2005): 285–306.

Studdert-Kennedy, Gerald. 'Christianity, Statecraft and Chatham House: Lionel Curtis and World Order'. *Diplomacy & Statecraft* 6 (1995): 470–489.

————. 'Political Science and Political Theology: Lionel Curtis, Federalism and India'. *Journal of Imperial and Commonwealth History* 24 (1996): 197–217.

Swann, Brenda, and Francis Aprahamian. *J. D. Bernal: A Life in Science and Politics*. London: Verso, 1999.

Sylvest, Casper. *British Liberal Internationalism, 1880–1930: Making Progress?* Manchester: Manchester University Press, 2009.

————. 'The Conditions and Consequences of Globality: John H. Herz's *International Politics in the Atomic Age*'. In *Classics of International Relations: Essays in Criticism and Appreciation*, edited by Henrik Bliddal, Casper Sylvest, and Peter Wilson, 89–98. Abingdon: Routledge, 2013.

————. 'Continuity and Change in British Liberal Internationalism, c. 1900–1930'. *Review of International Studies* 31 (2005): 263–283.

————. 'Interwar Internationalism, the British Labour Party, and the Historiography of International Relations'. *International Studies Quarterly* 48 (2004): 409–432.

Tanner, Duncan. 'The Politics of the Labour Movement, 1900–1939'. In *A Companion to Early Twentieth-Century Britain*, edited by C. Wrigley, 38–55. Oxford: Blackwell, 2003.

Thomas, John N. *The Institute of Pacific Relations: Asian Scholars and American Politics*. Seattle: University of Washington Press, 1974.

Thomas, Robert S. 'Enlightenment and Authority: The Committee on Social Thought and the Ideology of Postwar Conservatism (1927–1950)'. PhD dissertation, Columbia University, 2010.

Thompson, Andrew S. 'The Language of Imperialism and the Meanings of Empire: Imperial Discourse in British Politics, 1895–1914'. *Journal of British Studies* 36 (1997): 147–177.

Thompson, J. Lee. *A Wider Patriotism: Alfred Milner and the British Empire*. London: Pickering & Chatto, 2007.

Thompson, John A. 'The Geopolitical Vision: The Myth of an Outmatched USA'. In *Uncertain Empire: American History and the Idea of the Cold War*, edited by Joel Isaac and Duncan Bell, 91–114. Oxford: Oxford University Press, 2012.

———. *A Sense of Power*. Ithaca, NY: Cornell University Press, 2015.

Thompson, Kenneth W. *Masters of International Thought: Major Twentieth-Century Theorists and the World Crisis*. Baton Rouge: Louisiana State University Press, 1980.

Thompson, Michael G. *For God and Globe*. Ithaca, NY: Cornell University Press, 2015.

Tomlinson, B. R. 'What Was the Third World?' *Journal of Contemporary History* 38 (2003): 307–321.

Traniello, Francesco. 'Sturzo e il problema storico della democrazia in Italia'. In *Luigi Sturzo e la democrazia nella prospettiva del terzo millennio*, vol. 1, edited by Eugenio Guccione, 55–62. Florence: Olschki, 2004.

Tuathail, Gearóid Ó. *Critical Geopolitics: The Politics of Writing Global Space*. London: Routledge, 1996.

Tuck, Richard. *Natural Rights Theories: Their Origin and Development*. Cambridge: Cambridge University Press, 1979.

Turner, John, ed. *The Larger Idea: Lord Lothian and the Problem of National Sovereignty*. London: Historians' Press, 1988.

Van Vleck, Jenifer L. *Empire of the Air: Aviation and the American Ascendancy*. Cambridge, MA: Harvard University Press, 2013.

———. 'The "Logic of the Air": Aviation and the Globalism of the "American Century"'. *New Global Studies* 1 (2007).

Varouxakis, Georgios. '"Great" versus "Small" Nations: Size and "National Greatness" in Victorian Political Thought'. In *Victorian Visions of Global Order: Empire and International Relations in Nineteenth-Century Political Thought*, edited by Duncan Bell, 136–158. Cambridge: Cambridge University Press, 2007.

Verga, Marcello. *Storie d'Europa. Secoli XVIII–XXI*. Bologna: Carocci, 2004.

Viotto, Piero. *Grandi Amicizie: i Maritain e i loro contemporanei*. Rome: Città nuova, 2008.

Vitalis, Robert. 'The Graceful and Generous Liberal Gesture: Making Racism Invisible in American International Relations'. *Millennium* 29 (2000): 331–356.

———. 'Review of David Ekbladh, "Present at the Creation: Edward Mead Earle and the Depression-Era Origins of Security Studies". *International Security* 36 (2012)'. *H-Diplo*, 15 June 2012.

———. *White World Order, Black Power Politics: The Birth of American International Relations*. Ithaca, NY: Cornell University Press, 2015.

Völkel, Evelyn. *Der totalitäre Staat—das Produkt einer säkularen Religion? Die frühen Schriften von Frederick A. Voigt, Eric Voegelin sowie Raymond Aron und die totalitäre Wirklichkeit im Dritten Reich*. Baden-Baden: Nomos, 2009.

Von Bernstorff, Jochen. *The Public International Law Theory of Hans Kelsen*. Cambridge: Cambridge University Press, 2010.

Voparil, Christopher J., and Richard J. Bernstein, eds. *The Rorty Reader*. Oxford: Blackwell, 2010.

Wagar, W. Warren. *H. G. Wells and the World State*. New Haven, CT: Yale University Press, 1961.

Warren, Heather A. *Theologians of a New World Order: Reinhold Niebuhr and the Christian Realists, 1920–1948*. Oxford: Oxford University Press, 1997.

Watson, Walter. 'McKeon's Semantic Schema'. *Philosophy & Rhetoric* 27 (1994): 85–103.

Weiss, Thomas G. 'What Happened to the Idea of World Government'. *International Studies Quarterly* 53 (2009): 253–271.

Wertheim, Stephen A. 'The League of Nations: A Retreat from International Law?' *Journal of Global History* 7 (2012): 210–232.

———. 'The League That Wasn't: American Designs for a Legalist-Sanctionist League of Nations and the Intellectual Origins of International Organization, 1914–1920'. *Diplomatic History* 35 (2011): 797–836.

———. 'Tomorrow, the World: The Birth of U.S. Global Supremacy in World War II'. PhD dissertation, Columbia University, 2015.

White, Donald W. 'The "American Century" in World History'. *Journal of World History* 3 (1992): 105–127.

Whittaker, C. R. *Rome and Its Frontiers: The Dynamics of Empire*. London: Routledge, 2004.

Whitty, Geoff. 'Mannheim, Karl (1893–1947)'. In *Oxford Dictionary of National Biography*. 2004. www.oxforddnb.com.

Wight, Martin. *Four Seminal Thinkers in International Theory: Machiavelli, Grotius, Kant, and Mazzini*. Oxford: Oxford University Press, 2005.

Wilford, R. A. 'The Federal Union Campaign'. *European History Quarterly* 10 (1980): 101–114.

Wilkinson, David. 'Spykman and Geopolitics'. In *On Geopolitics*, edited by Ciro E. Zoppo and Charles Zorgbibe, 77–117. Dordrecht: Martinus Nijhoff, 1985.

Williams, Andrew J. *Failed Imagination? New World Orders of the Twentieth Century*. Manchester: Manchester University Press, 1998.

Williams, Francis. *Ernest Bevin: Portrait of a Great Englishman*. London: Hutchinson, 1952.

Wilson, Peter. 'The Myth of the "First Great Debate"'. *Review of International Studies* 24 (1998): 1–16.

———. 'The New Europe Debate in Wartime Britain'. In *Visions of European Unity*, edited by Philomena Murray and Paul Rich, 39–59. Oxford: Westview, 1996.

Wilson, Peter, and David Long, eds. *Thinkers of the Twenty Years' Crisis: Inter-war Idealism Reassessed*. Oxford: Clarendon, 1995.

Withers, Charles W. J. 'Place and the "Spatial Turn" in Geography and in History'. *Journal of the History of Ideas* 70 (2009): 637–658.

Wittner, Lawrence S. *One World or None: The Struggle Against the Bomb*. Stanford, CA: Stanford University Press, 1993.

Wolf, Eric R. *Europe and the People without History*. Berkeley: University of California Press, 1982.

Wolff, Kurt. *From Karl Mannheim*. New Brunswick, NJ: Transaction, 1993.

Wooley, Wesley T. *Alternatives to Anarchy: American Supranationalism since World War II*. Bloomington: Indiana University Press, 1988.

———. 'Finding a Usable Past: The Success of American World Federalism in the 1940s'. *Peace & Change* 24 (1999): 329–339.

Wrigley, C., ed. *A Companion to Early Twentieth-Century Britain*. Oxford: Blackwell, 2003.

Zagrebelsky, Gustavo. *Il diritto mite*. Turin: Einaudi, 1992.

Zaidi, Waqar H. '"Aviation Will Either Destroy or Save Our Civilization": Proposals for the International Control of Aviation, 1920–45'. *Journal of Contemporary History* 46 (2011): 150–178.

———. 'Liberal Internationalist Approaches to Science and Technology in Interwar Britain and the United States'. In *Internationalism Reconfigured: Transnational Ideas and Movements between the World Wars*, edited by Daniel Laqua, 17–44. London: I.B. Tauris, 2011.

Index

Page numbers in *italics* refer to figures.

Mayer, Cord, 201

McCarthy, Joseph, 59, 98

McIlwain, Charles Howard, 260; at Chicago Committee, 169, 173–174; on sovereignty, 178–179

McKeon, Richard, 17, 18, 22, 34, 171–172, 281; and anti-Catholicism, 255–256; at Chicago Committee, 168–170, 237, 260; contribution to 'renaissance of rhetoric', 171; on human rights, 191–192, 194, 205, 273, 280; and minimalist constitution, 175, 177, 178, 183–185, 188–189, 194; and pluralism, 172, 187, 189–191, 205–208, 255; rejection of Chicago constitution, 200, 205–208; at UNESCO, 222n52, 273. *See also* Chicago Committee to Frame a World Constitution Draft

Meinecke, Friedrich, 31, 174, 263n81

Mercator projection, 72, *87*, 87–88

Merriam, Charles E., 17, 18, 23, 210–211; on atomic bomb, 222, 230; on behaviouralism, 218–219; on Christian values, 239; Hayek and, 227; interest in science, 217–219, 235, 240; meaning of democracy for, 219–220; Mitrany and, 221–222; New Deal and, 147n61; Niebuhr on, 223, 239; on planning, 221, 227; on sovereignty, 253; and universal democratic world order, 211–212, 220–223, 224, 236, 239, 279; on world bill of rights, 222. See also *Bulletin of the Atomic Scientists*; New Deal; planning

migration, 137–141, 142, 146, 159, 165, 196

Miller projection, 72, 87–88, *88*

Milner, Alfred, 108, 110

Mises, Ludwig von, 38n60, 133, 158

Mitrany, David, 17, 18, 20, 24, 25, 27; admiration for Britain, 28; critique of federalism, 41, 46–49; dismissal of politics, 51–55; distinction between nationalism and nationality, 29–35, 41–42, 44; on elites, 51; and functionalism, 37, 43–46; on international planning, 36; on Marxism, 34; on mental health and international unity, 50; New Deal and, 28; *A Working Peace System*, 28. *See also* federalism; functionalism; Institute for Advanced

Study; nationalism; Royal Institute of International Affairs

Monroe Doctrine, 73, 85, 116

Mont Pèlerin Society, 38, 229, 277n13

Moot, the, 30n22, 232n94

morality: Aron on, 37; and conflict, 263; democracy and Catholic morality, 195, 250, 258, 262–263, 269–271; as foundation of world order, 9, 15, 23, 78, 108, 111, 135, 160, 193, 204, 238, 258; natural law and, 203; of unequal representation, 181; universality of, 113, 174, 177, 210, 234, 263, 271; Western-centrism and, 236, 240

Morgenthau, Hans, 28, 168

Mounier, Emmanuel, 247

Mumford, Lewis, 17, 210, 211; on atomic bomb, 209, 235–237; Borgese and, 18, 207, 237; on Chicago constitution, 169, 174, 201, 237; City of Man and, 175, 207; on experts, 235, 239; Frankfurt School and, 236; on universal moral reform, 238–240, 281–282

Murray, Gilbert, 244

Mussolini, Benito, 174, 269

Napoleon Bonaparte, 4

National Resources Planning Board, 219

National Socialism. *See* Nazism

nationalism, 24–25, 50, 141; Asian, 83n110; Carr on, 53–54; Catholic interpretation of, 248–249; competition and, 35; as ideology, 28–32, 37, 40–41, 43–44, 46, 53, 221, 243, 83; as mental illness, 50; nationality and, 35–36. *See also* ideology; nation-state

nation-state: distinctiveness of, 47; economy of, 35, 41, 137–140, 158–161, 219; foreign policy of, 63, 67; in global order, 44, 105, 131, 145, 149, 165, 178, 182, 188, 197, 221, 242, 280; interests of, 241, 260, 278; self-determination, 79, 108; sovereignty, 41, 43, 115, 134–136, 177–178, 230. *See also* nationalism

natural law. *See* law of nature

Nazism, 27, 130, 152; and geopolitics, 42, 63; ideology of, 35, 26, 96; opposition

state, 20, 38, 145, 180; uniformity of, 206, 235, 279; of Western democracies, 107, 128, 233. *See also* cartography; geography; geopolitics

Popper, Karl, 158, 211, 224, 231

pragmatism: McKeon and, 172, 256; sovereignty and, 44, 55

Preuss, Hugo, 218, 253

protectionism, 34, 41, 43, 136–138, 140

public intellectuals: on Cold War, 275; critique of, 202; definition of, 15–16; on federalism, 103, 116; role of, 168–169, 202, 211, 237, 243, 276–277; transnational network of, 17, 19, 245, 282; on world order, 2, 3, 5, 10, 14, 19, 24, 100, 210, 245, 278, 280, 283. *See also* elites; experts

race: in Asia, 76; as discriminatory political criterion, 94, 96–97, 113, 124, 126, 128, 142, 185–186, 279–280; marginality in globalism, 276, 281; in Streit's federalist vision, 120–121, 123; trusteeship of native race, 119n82; universality of human race, 187, 195, 203, 210, 215, 237, 239, 242

Ransome, Patrick, 103, 117, 123, 154, 156

rationality: as basis of planning, 37–38, 135–136, 139, 141, 150–151, 160–161, 163, 192, 214, 227; critical doubt of, 227; critique of, 236–237, 248–250; as guarantee of cooperation, 145; irrationality and, 9, 37, 48–55, 112, 145, 152, 201–202, 224, 231, 250–251, 254, 268; as means to identify common good, 220; political myth and, 49; world order based on, 29, 51–53, 153, 164, 212, 223, 225–226, 238

Ratzel, Friedrich, 62

Rawnsley, Derek, 103, 117

Raynaud, Paul, 130

Redfield, Robert, 169, 174, 183–184, 187

Reform Club, 36, 47, 158

regionalism: as defining principle of global order, 12, 73, 79–80, 85, 97–98, 134–135, 145, 181, 261, 272; democracy and, 69, 92–97, 167, 274; electoral,

181–184, 188, 193, 197, 200; and functionalism, 28; geopolitical, 43, 58, 98–99; in globalist discourse, 7, 8, 9, 20, 21, 22, 25, 29, 53–54 ,276, 278; and nationalism, 46, 50; pan-regionalism, 64, 276; and tripolarity, 39, 61–62, 86–91; universalism and, 97, 216

relativism. *See* perspectivism

religion, 9, 15, 23, 95, 108, 110, 195, 199, 232, 239, 264; as aspect of truth, 228, 255; and collapse of Western civilisation, 268; as defining aspect of politics, 95, 193, 232, 246, 252, 263, 268; in European history, 259; multiplicity of, 190, 255, 264, 276; secular, 37, 232n92; and totalitarianism, 244–245

Report on the International Control of Atomic Energy, 184, 198–199

representation: of colonies at Federal Union, 123; democratic, 112–13, 281; exogenous, 183–184; fiscal capacity as criterion for, 114; and legitimacy, 51, 106; party, 271; spatial, 5, 14, 22, 56, 57, 69, 71, 75, 88, 89; weighted, 181, 188, 202; in world parliament, 179–184, 188, 197

rights of man. *See* human rights

Rimland, 67, 69–70, *70*, 77–78, 85

Robbins, Lionel, 17, 18, 21, 26, 34, 36, 47, 101, 133, 177, 258–259, 279, 281; Anglo-French federation and, 130, 154; Curtis and, 132–133, 141; on economic aspects of federation, 128, 131, 132, 135–141; *The Economic Causes of War*, 134; *Economic Planning and International Order*, 134; on empire, 127; on European federation, 135, 275; at Federal Union, 103, 104, 114, 153, 154, 165–167; on free trade, 138; Hayek and, 158–162, 165; on inequality, 138; meaning of federation for, 134; on migration, 138–139; on money, 140–141; on national sentiment, 141; Wootton and, 142, 144, 145, 146, 157, 166, 277. *See also* Federal Union; federalism

Rockefeller, Nelson, 80

Roosevelt, Eleanor, 13